LOW-WAGE
AMERICA

LOW-WAGE AMERICA

How Employers Are Reshaping Opportunity in the Workplace

Eileen Appelbaum,
Annette Bernhardt, and
Richard J. Murnane,
Editors

Russell Sage Foundation / New York

The Russell Sage Foundation

The Russell Sage Foundation, one of the oldest of America's general purpose foundations, was established in 1907 by Mrs. Margaret Olivia Sage for "the improvement of social and living conditions in the United States." The Foundation seeks to fulfill this mandate by fostering the development and dissemination of knowledge about the country's political, social, and economic problems. While the Foundation endeavors to assure the accuracy and objectivity of each book it publishes, the conclusions and interpretations in Russell Sage Foundation publications are those of the authors and not of the Foundation, its Trustees, or its staff. Publication by Russell Sage, therefore, does not imply Foundation endorsement.

Library of Congress Cataloging-in-Publication Data

Low-wage America : how employers are reshaping opportunity in the workplace / Eileen Appelbaum, Annette Bernhardt, Richard Murnane, editors.
p. cm.
Includes bibliographical references and index.
ISBN 0-87154-025-8
1. Labor market—United States. 2. Unskilled labor—United States.
3. Semi-skilled labor—United States. 4. Manpower planning—United States.
5. Work environment—United States. 6. Industrial management—United States. 7. Employment forecasting—United States. I. Title: Low-wage jobs are changing. II. Appelbaum, Eileen, 1940– III. Bernhardt, Annette D., 1964– IV. Murnane, Richard J.

HD5724.L44 2003
331.7'98'0973—dc21

2003046584

Text design by Suzanne Nichols

RUSSELL SAGE FOUNDATION
112 East 64th Street, New York, New York 10021
10 9 8 7 6 5 4 3 2 1

Contents

Contributors

EILEEN APPELBAUM is professor and director of the Center for Women and Work at Rutgers University.

ANNETTE BERNHARDT is a sociologist and senior policy analyst at the Brennan Center for Justice at the New York University School of Law.

RICHARD J. MURNANE is the Thompson Professor of Education and Society at the Harvard Graduate School of Education and research associate at the National Bureau of Economic Research.

DAVID H. AUTOR is the Pentti J.K. Kouri Assistant Professor of Economics at the Massachusetts Institute of Technology and research fellow at the National Bureau of Economic Research.

JOHN W. BALLANTINE JR. is an associate of the Malcolm Weiner Center for Social Policy at the John F. Kennedy School of Government, Harvard University. He is also director of the Masters in Finance Program at the Brandeis International School of Business.

ANN P. BARTEL is the A. Barton Professor of Economics at Columbia Business School and research associate at the National Bureau of Economic Research.

ROSEMARY BATT is associate professor of human resource studies and the Alice H. Cook Professor of Women and Work at the Industrial and Labor Relations School, Cornell University.

PETER BERG is associate professor at the School of Labor and Industrial Relations, Michigan State University.

RACHEL CONNELLY is professor of economics at Bowdoin College.

DEBORAH S. DEGRAFF is associate professor of economics at Bowdoin College.

LAURA DRESSER is a labor economist and research director at the Center on Wisconsin Strategy at the University of Wisconsin, Madison.

GEORGE A. ERICKCEK is senior regional analyst at the W. E. Upjohn Institute for Employment Research.

RONALD F. FERGUSON is lecturer in public policy at the John F. Kennedy School of Government and senior research associate at the Malcolm Weiner Center for Social Policy, Harvard University.

DAVID FINEGOLD is associate professor at the Keck Graduate Institute of Applied Life Sciences.

ANN FROST is assistant professor at the Richard Ivey School of Business, the University of Western Ontario.

ERIN HATTON is a doctoral candidate in the Sociology Department at the University of Wisconsin, Madison, and research associate at the Center on Wisconsin Strategy.

SUSAN HELPER is professor of economics at the Weatherhead School of Management, Case Western Reserve University. She is also research associate of the National Bureau of Economic Research.

SUSAN N. HOUSEMAN is senior economist at the W. E. Upjohn Institute for Employment Research.

LARRY W. HUNTER is assistant professor of management and human resources at the School of Business at the University of Wisconsin, Madison.

CASEY ICHNIOWSKI is professor of management at Columbia Business School and research associate at the National Bureau of Economic Research.

DEREK C. JONES is the Irma M. and Robert D. Morris Professor of Economics at Hamilton College and research associate of the David Institute at the University of Michigan.

ARNE L. KALLEBERG is the Kenan Professor of Sociology at the University of North Carolina, Chapel Hill.

TAKAO KATO is professor of economics and presidential scholar at Colgate University. He is also research associate at the Center on Japanese Economy and Business at Columbia University and at the Tokyo Center for Economic Research.

MORRIS M. KLEINER is professor of labor policy at the Humphrey Institute and Industrial Relations Center at the University of Minnesota. He is also research associate of the National Bureau of Economic Research.

JULIA LANE is principal research associate at the Urban Institute and senior research fellow at the U.S. Census Bureau.

ALEC LEVENSON is assistant professor at the Center for Effective Organizations at the Marshall School of Business, the University of Southern California.

FRANK LEVY is the Daniel Rose Professor of Urban Education at the Massachusetts Institute of Technology.

PHILIP MOSS is professor of regional economic and social development at the University of Massachusetts, Lowell.

GIL PREUSS is assistant professor at the Weatherhead School of Management, Case Western Reserve University.

HAROLD SALZMAN is a sociologist and research professor at the Center for Industrial Competitiveness and director of the Center for Security, Safety, and Society.

KATHRYN SHAW is professor of economics at Carnegie Mellon University and research associate at the National Bureau of Economic Research.

CHRIS TILLY is the University Professor of Regional Economic and Social Development at the University of Massachusetts, Lowell.

MARK VAN BUREN is a strategic research consultant who heads the Learning and Development Roundtable for the Corporate Executive Board.

ADAM WEINBERG is associate professor of sociology and Dean of the College at Colgate University.

STEFFANIE WILK is assistant professor of management at the Wharton School of Business at the University of Pennsylvania.

RACHEL A. WILLIS is professor of American studies and economics at the University of North Carolina, Chapel Hill, where she is a Chapman Faculty Fellow at the Institute for the Arts and Humanities.

Acknowledgments

The unique research presented in this volume would not have been possible without the vision, guidance, and financial support of the Russell Sage and Rockefeller Foundations. The authors of the papers in this volume, and the academic and policy community in general, are deeply indebted to Katherine McFate, Eric Wanner, and Nancy Weinberg for their leadership and for their concern about the future of work for people without college degrees. The authors also thank the discussants of early drafts, who provided comments that were important in improving the chapters.

Above all, we thank the hundreds of workers, managers, union representatives, and industry experts who gave their time, energy and commitment to answering the many questions posed by the research teams.

Eileen Appelbaum
Annette Bernhardt
Richard J. Murnane

EDITORS

CHAPTER 1

Low-Wage America: An Overview

*Eileen Appelbaum, Annette Bernhardt,
and Richard J. Murnane*

This volume describes changes in the workplace for Americans who do not earn enough to support themselves and their families. The number of such workers is substantial. In 2001 about 27.5 million Americans, 23.9 percent of the labor force, earned less than $8.70 an hour (Mishel, Bernstein, and Boushey 2003, table 2.9). Working full-time for the entire year at this wage produces annual earnings of just $17,400—about equal to the poverty line for a family of four, and not nearly enough to sustain most working families. For example, a family with two parents and two children requires between $27,000 and $52,000 annually in order to maintain a basic standard of living, depending on the community; the national median is about $33,500. For a single working parent with two children, a basic family budget ranges from $22,000 to $48,600. Overall, in the late 1990s, fully 29 percent of working families with children under twelve had incomes lower than the basic family budget for their communities.[1]

As the chapters in this volume document, firms in all parts of the economy—in manufacturing, in retail sales, in telecommunications, in the hospitality industry, and in the health care industry—employ workers at wages below those needed to meet the basic family budget threshold. Low-wage workers are employed in a wide variety of occupations. They work as nursing assistants, food preparers and servers, customer service representatives, assembly-line workers, and housekeepers, and they include men and women from every racial and ethnic group.

The majority of low-wage workers in the United States have no educational credentials beyond a high school diploma. Many, including a large number of immigrants, lack even this credential. For this reason, we often refer to the frontline workers who are the

1

focus of this volume as "high school educated workers." It is important to keep in mind, however, that college enrollment has not allowed all workers to escape low-wage work. Several chapters in this
volume cite evidence that the low-wage workforce in particular industries includes a significant number of workers who have completed at least some college courses.[2]

High school educated workers have not always fared as badly in
the U.S. economy as they have over the last twenty years. As illustrated in the top panel of figure 1.1, male high school graduates
earned an average hourly wage (in 2001 dollars) of $16.16 in 1973.
Over the next twenty-two years the average real wage of male high
school graduates fell by 17 percent, with the most rapid decline
taking place during the 1980s. The strong economy of the last half
of the 1990s allowed male high school graduates to recover about
one-third of their lost ground, but they are still left with real wages
markedly lower than those earned by their counterparts twenty
years earlier (Mishel, Bernstein, and Boushey 2003, 158, table
2.18).

The wage trend for female high school graduates is somewhat
different. As illustrated in the bottom panel of figure 1.1, the average real hourly wage of female high school graduates has been consistently lower than the wage of their male counterparts. However,
the average real wage of female high school graduates was remarkably stable over the period 1973 to 1989 and rose by 9 percent
during the 1990s (Mishel, Bernstein, and Boushey 2003, 159, table
2.18).

The real wage trends of high school graduates illustrate two important themes of the volume. The first is the importance of economic growth. The rapid growth of the economy during the 1990s
created the tight labor markets that enabled high school educated
workers to increase their hourly earnings. The second theme is that
structural changes in the U.S. economy have increased the pressures faced by employers, and their responses have worsened labor
market outcomes for high school educated workers. These changes
are so profound that even the extremely tight 1990s labor markets,
which resulted in the lowest unemployment rates in thirty years,
did not allow the real earnings of male high school graduates to
return to their 1970s level.

Many factors contributed to the economic pressures that American employers have faced over the last twenty years. One is the

Figure 1.1 Average Hourly Wages by Education, 1973 to 2001

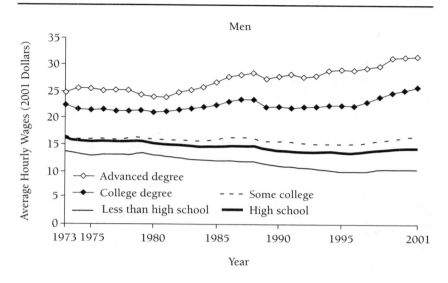

Men

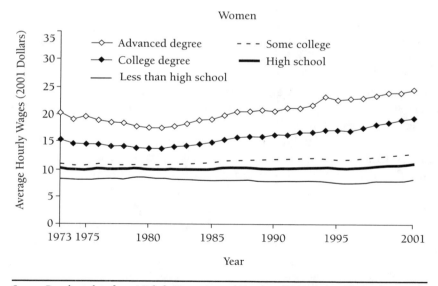

Women

Source: Based on data from Mishel, Bernstein, and Boushey (2003, 159, table 2.18).

globalization of markets. The internationalization of capital markets has increased the competition that American firms face in attracting capital. The growing potential to produce goods for the American market anywhere in the world has increased pressures on firms producing goods and services in the United States.

Advances in information technology (IT) have also increased economic pressures. Technological changes have led to the automation of many routine tasks (such as filing and bookkeeping and product assembly) that were previously carried out by high school educated American workers. Advances in IT have made it possible to locate data entry tasks and the work of customer service representatives anywhere in the world, not only in low-wage areas in the United States but also in countries with wages far below even the most modest U.S. wages. Technological changes have affected not only the jobs of workers who either use technology or whose work has been automated but also, indirectly, the jobs of many other workers as well. For example, new technologies have allowed large retail chains such as Wal-Mart to reduce costs dramatically, thus driving out of business smaller retailers that provided relatively better jobs for high school educated workers.

The deregulation of industries such as telecommunications, financial services, airlines, and trucking has increased price competition, intensifying pressures on firms to reduce costs. The introduction of health maintenance organizations (HMOs) in health care has altered the revenue stream for health care providers by breaking the link between service provision and revenue. This too has increased pressures to reduce costs.

Changes in financial markets have increased pressures on managers to achieve short-run results, making it increasingly difficult for them to embrace long-term investments, including investments in the skills of their workforces. One of these changes is the growth of mutual funds, which increases the power of institutional investors seeking steady increases in share prices. A second is the trend toward basing CEO compensation on the short-run performance of a company's stock (Appelbaum and Berg 1996).

Many studies have attempted to assess the relative importance of these factors—globalization, changes in technology, deregulation, and changes in financial markets—in explaining the increase in inequality that has characterized the U.S. income distribution in recent years.[3] In fact, these sources are deeply interrelated. For example, advances in information technology have made possible many aspects of globalization, including the development of worldwide markets in the delivery of services such as data entry and customer support. At the same time technological changes would not have had such large influences on the finance and air travel industries if deregulation had not taken place.

Institutional changes in the environment in which American firms operate have influenced their responses to competitive pressures. One such change is the decline in labor unions. In 1973, 24 percent of American workers were union members. That figure had declined to 14 percent by 2002, and among private-sector workers it was 9 percent. The decline in union representation has reduced the ability of workers to negotiate with managers about responses to increased competition and to bargain over the distribution of gains from improved productivity. The explanation for the decline in union representation lies partly in the market forces that are changing the economy. For example, historically, the manufacturing sector has been more heavily unionized than the service sector, and the percentage of the American nonfarm workforce employed in manufacturing fell from 28 percent in 1970 to 13 percent in 2001 (U.S. Department of Labor, various years). Some aspects of globalization, including the internationalization of production and a dramatic increase in the immigration of workers with relatively little formal education, have made traditional union organizing more difficult. A change in government attitudes toward unions has also contributed to their decline. From President Ronald Reagan's handling of the air traffic controllers' strike in 1981 to President George W. Bush's demand in 2002 that employees of the Department of Homeland Security be forbidden to belong to a union, all three branches of the national government in the last twenty years have exhibited greater hostility to unions than in earlier periods.

A second change in the institutional environment is the decline in the real value of the minimum wage. In 1974 the minimum wage in the United States, expressed in 2001 dollars, was $7.18 an hour.[4] In 2001 it was $5.15. This 28 percent decline in the real minimum wage has allowed firms to respond to economic pressures by cutting the real wages of their lowest-paid workers. Had this not been possible, at least some employers would have chosen the alternative response of investing in workers' skills or capital equipment so as to improve productivity.

Thus, today there are powerful forces that are reshaping the workplace. This book provides the most extensive study to date of how the world of work is changing for the 42 percent of U.S. workers who have never attended college.[5] The chapters investigate sectors that provide large numbers of jobs for these workers, sectors that are underresearched but vitally important in post-industrial economies. What is distinctive about the studies in this book is that they are based on interviews and data gathered from a wide range of managers and employees across a number of work sites in each industry. These empirical case studies examine the choices that managers make as they address the economic challenges confronting companies, and how these decisions affect outcomes for firms and workers.

THE CASE STUDIES

The case studies described in this book were designed to fill a large gap in knowledge about the consequences of economic restructuring for workers without a college degree. Data from national surveys such as the Current Population Survey have taught us a lot about changes in the aggregate wage structure over the past three decades. But they can only indirectly get at the complex reasons why those changes have occurred, and in particular, why there is significant variation in the wages of workers with similar education levels and in similar industries. Nor do these data provide any information on changes in the tasks done by frontline workers, the skills required for particular jobs, or the conditions of work. Finally, national survey data are the weakest when it comes to developing a deep, qualitative understanding of firm decisionmaking; such an understanding is critical to developing coherent policy responses.

To fill this gap, the Russell Sage and Rockefeller Foundations instituted the Future of Work Program and provided financial support for empirical case studies of firms in industries employing large numbers of relatively low-wage workers. This volume provides the results of twelve of these case studies, carried out by teams that included thirty-eight researchers and a great many graduate student assistants. Each chapter is guided by a specific set of research questions, but all of them try to come to an understanding of how firms have responded to increased economic pressures and how frontline workers have been affected by these responses. In particular, the case studies document how firms' responses to economic pressures have affected working conditions, work rules, productivity pressures, skill requirements, and opportunities for training and advancement for workers with less than a four-year college education.

The case studies funded by the Future of Work Program are industry-based. Some of the case studies focus on industries in which technological change has been rapid, such as telecommunications. Others focus on industries, such as hosiery production, in which international competition has been a force for change. Still others focus on industries, such as hospitals and hotels, in which technological change and international competition have had little effect on the jobs of high school educated workers, although increases in the number of immigrant workers have had important impacts.

A key feature of many of these studies is their use of research designs that compare firms facing similar economic pressures and competing in the same or similar industries. Such controlled comparisons allow the authors to ask whether firms have responded differently to these pressures and whether these different responses have led to different outcomes for their frontline workers.

Although the methodologies vary, all of the case studies make use of interviews, typically with both managers and workers in several firms within a particular industry. The interviews provide a great deal of information about changes in the competitive conditions that employers face, their responses to increased competition, and the impact of their responses on workers. A total of 464 establishments in 25 industries were studied. More than 1,700 managers and workers were interviewed, and more than 10,000 workers and managers completed surveys. Together these studies paint a vivid picture of how changes in the American economy have affected the work lives of tens of millions of workers at the bottom of the wage distribution.

The case studies in this volume are organized into five parts. The first part, "Services: Where the Jobs Are," includes two studies. In chapter 2, Annette Bernhardt, Laura Dresser, and Erin Hatton explore the impact of changes in the hotel industry, including widespread consolidation of ownership, on the large number of workers who clean rooms and prepare food. Chapter 3, by Eileen Appelbaum, Peter Berg, Ann Frost, and Gil Preuss, is an examination of how increasing cost pressures on hospitals have led to changes in the jobs, work conditions, and wages of housekeeping and food service workers. Chapters 2 and 3 show that employers in these industries have been subject to significant pressures to reduce costs and improve productivity, and that their extremely different responses have had different effects on labor market outcomes for the great many high school educated workers they employ.

The second part, "Technology: Fewer Better Jobs?," contains three chapters that focus on the impact of technological changes on labor market outcomes for high school educated workers. In chapter 4, David H. Autor, Frank Levy, and Richard J. Murnane lay out a model of what computers do and use this model to explain the very different impacts of a specific set of computer-based technological changes on the design of jobs in two departments of a large bank. Chapter 5, by Ann P. Bartel, Casey Ichniowski, and Kathryn Shaw, describes how new technologies altered production processes in three manufacturing industries and affected skill demands and worker outcomes for production workers in these industries. In chapter 6, John W. Ballantine Jr. and Ronald F. Ferguson examine the consequences for workers of the introduction of new technologies by relatively small firms that manufacture plastics products. Chapters 4, 5, and 6 document that the demand for skills is highly dependent on the market niche firms seek to embrace. They show both that technological changes have important impacts on outcomes for high school educated workers and that these outcomes are often not obvious.

The third part, "Career Ladders: The Past or the Future?," contains two chapters that examine changes in career ladders in two sets of industries employing a great many high school educated workers. Chapter 7, by Julia Lane, Philip Moss, Harold Salzman, and Chris Tilly, describes how changes in food service industries have disrupted traditional internal labor markets in food service organizations, such as restaurants and cafeterias, but have led to the introduction of new internal labor markets with job ladders in food manufacturing firms. In chapter 8, Rosemary Batt, Larry W. Hunter, and Steffanie Wilk describe how changes in the organization of call center work have affected job ladders for operators, customer service representatives, and telemarketers. These chapters demonstrate that outcomes for workers are heavily influenced by managerial choices in the design of call centers.

The two chapters in the fourth part, "Temps: Part of the Solution or Part of the Problem?," examine how the growth of the temporary staffing industry has affected labor market outcomes for high school educated workers. In chapter 9, David Finegold, Alec Levenson,

and Mark Van Buren examine employers' reasons for using temporary staffing firms to find workers, as well as workers' reasons for
using temporary staffing agencies to find jobs. Chapter 10, by George
Erickcek, Susan Houseman, and Arne Kalleberg, examines why auto
supply manufacturers, hospitals, and public school districts make
use of temporary staffing services and outsourcing, and how these
practices impact on labor market outcomes for workers. Chapters 9
and 10 show that the consequences of nontraditional staffing arrangements for high school educated workers vary: new opportunities are created for some workers, but others are left in dead-end,
low-paying jobs.

Part V, "Globalization: Always a Job Killer?," explores how the
increase in competition from abroad has affected the decisions of
domestic producers and labor market outcomes for production
workers. Chapter 11, by Rachel A. Willis, Rachel Connelly, and
Deborah S. DeGraff, describes workforce and technology trends in
the hosiery manufacturing industry and the impact of changes in
the purchasing requirements of large hosiery customers, such as
Wal-Mart. In chapter 12, Susan Helper and Morris Kleiner look at
what happened to production workers' pay and work conditions
when new human resource policies were introduced by a large auto
parts manufacturer in the face of growing foreign competition.
Chapter 13 is an examination by Derek C. Jones, Takao Kato, and
Adam Weinberg of the responses of ten manufacturing firms in central New York State to increases in competitive pressures. They
show that responses varied markedly, and that the different responses had very different consequences for worker outcomes. A
theme in part V is that access to information about technology, organization of work, and human resource practices varies across
firms; remote rural factories, for example, are often at a severe disadvantage. This has an important impact on how firms decide to
respond to increasing competition and on outcomes for workers.

A SYNTHESIS OF FINDINGS

The national discussion about changes in the American workplace
over the past three decades remains at a very rudimentary level.
"Globalization" is invoked to explain the actions of employers with
no recognition that the term has very different meanings in different contexts. "High-tech" is a term used to describe everything having to do with jobs, skill requirements, and why some workers have

succeeded in the new economy and others haven't. These catchall terms obfuscate the many and varied factors that contribute to increased economic pressures in different industries and divert attention from the careful analyses required for intelligent policy responses.

The chapters in this volume show that firms have come under greater economic pressure for a number of different reasons, only some of which are related to increases in international competition. The degree of that pressure has varied as well; many industries find that they still have room to maneuver. Technology has had quite different effects on the tasks that workers perform and the skills required; in a surprising number of cases, there is little effect at all. And as in the past, the determinants of whether or not workers succeeded are quite complex, not a simple function of years of education or computer acumen.

At the same time, some clear and important patterns emerge across the host of industries and workplaces studied. In the rest of this chapter, we provide a broad summary of how our case studies answer the following two questions: In what ways have firms responded to growing economic pressures? And what has been the impact of these responses on frontline workers who do not have college degrees?

In organizing the rich array of answers to this question, we focus on perhaps the most important insight from the research presented in this volume. Although employers' responses to growing economic pressures have had a generally negative effect on frontline workers, especially those with only a high school degree, there are significant exceptions to this pattern. These variations offer important clues about what public policy can do to support the job prospects of workers without a college degree, and we attempt to draw out several such implications at the end of the chapter. To start, we offer a summary of the dominant strategies.

DOMINANT STRATEGIES WITH RESPECT TO FRONTLINE WORKERS

Most employers have responded to increased economic pressure by reducing costs. For a great many of them, cost-cutting has focused on the wage bill, especially the bill for frontline workers, most of whom typically have little or no education beyond high school. As summarized in table 1.1, this focus on cutting labor costs has played out in a number of different ways.

One set of strategies has focused on continuing to use the same workers but freezing their wages, cutting their benefits, and increasing their workloads. These actions have unequivocally negative impacts on workers. For example, in several of the high-priced hotels studied in chapter 2, housekeepers have not received pay increases for six years, in several others yearly increases have been ten to twenty cents at most, yet the number of rooms each housekeeper has to clean each day has increased steadily over the past two decades. A similar story obtains in the hospitals studied in chapter 3: rising medical costs and declining reimbursements have squeezed the wages of nursing assistants, food service workers, and housekeepers even as staffing levels have declined. Nor is this only a service-sector story. In one of the auto parts supplier plants studied in chapter 12, management had changed compensation systems, and 45 percent of workers reported that they had suffered a pay cut as a result.

Another set of strategies focuses on reducing labor costs at the front line by using temporary workers, by subcontracting or outsourcing, or by relocating jobs to lower-wage areas, either in this country or abroad. Evidence of these cost-cutting responses is present in almost every industry studied in this volume, and lowering labor costs is a central motivation. As shown in chapter 10, workers are especially vulnerable to being replaced with temps when they are well-paid but less-skilled. If the work is also self-contained, it may be a good candidate for being contracted out altogether. In 1999, for example, 32 percent of hospitals reported that they outsourced their food services, 27 percent outsourced housekeeping, and 62 percent outsourced laundry. The subcontracting of hotel restaurants both to avoid unions and to gain access to cheaper labor has become virtually complete in the industry. A related strategy is to keep frontline jobs in-house but to centralize and relocate them to another part of the country. As discussed in chapter 8, the rapid growth of large call centers illustrates this response, its impact on productivity, and its typically negative impacts on frontline workers. Finally, moving frontline jobs overseas is, of course, a practice that has fundamentally transformed U.S. manufacturing industries and the job opportunities available to high school graduates.

One consequence of relocating work is the disruption of the in-

Table 1.1 Employer Responses to Increased Competition and the Impact on Frontline Workers

	Dominant Strategies (Effects on Frontline Workers Largely Negative)	Variations (Effects on Frontline Workers Both Negative and Positive)	Sources of Variation
Firms that focus on compensation and the organization of work	Freeze wages and increase workloads	Use work reorganization to increase productivity and reduce turnover	Unions
	Use contingent workers to cut labor costs	Innovate with respect to products	Regional labor market institutions
	Subcontract and outsource to cut costs and wages	Outsource to capture economies of scale; outsource only partially to gain better management	Quality of information available to managers about high-productivity strategies
	Relocate and consolidate functions	Use temps to screen risky workers for permanent jobs	Regulation (minimum wage, industry regulation)
			Tight labor markets
Firms that focus on new technology	Introduce new technology to automate routine tasks and reduce reliance on low-skilled workers	Train entry-level workers without college degrees for new technology	
	Technology deskills entry-level jobs	Link entry-level jobs to career ladders	

Source: Authors' compilation.

ternal labor markets that historically provided many frontline workers with promotion opportunities. For example, when telecommunications firms handled customer service locally, representatives could increase their earnings by being promoted from servicing residential customers to servicing small-business customers and, eventually, to serving larger business clients. This type of movement is now rarely possible and entails substantial geographic relocation when it does occur, since one call center handles all residential customer service work for several states and another call center located in a different state handles small-business services for a large geographical area.

We should note that there is suggestive evidence that immigration has played an important role in some of these trends. Especially in labor-intensive industries, recent immigrants have replaced native workers in a variety of entry-level jobs. While the chain of causality here is difficult to untangle, the new supply of immigrant workers has clearly facilitated the drive by employers to reduce costs, cut benefits, increase workloads, and shift jobs to subcontractors. The lobbying for pro-immigration legislation by several industry trade groups, including the National Restaurant Association, illustrates the operation of this mechanism.

Up to this point, our discussion has focused on workplaces where the dominant competitive focus has been on reducing the cost of labor. These strategies are most prevalent in labor-intensive activities that consist of providing in-person services rather than transactions that can be handled remotely. In these settings, using technology to make significant changes in the use of frontline labor is either not feasible (for example, nursing assistants and housekeepers) or not desirable (such as when there is a need to have a human face at the sales counter).

When jobs consist of routine, repetitive, and predictable tasks, whether processing information or handling materials, the opportunities for using technology to replace frontline workers are great. Our case studies describe a number of diverse settings where technology has been at the core of employers' competitive strategies. The prototypical case is banking, where the arrival of ATMs took over many of the high-volume, routine tasks previously done by tellers. But as chapter 4 illustrates, information technologies have penetrated deeper into banking. Check imaging and optical character recognition technology have effectively automated several key tasks in check-processing departments, reducing the demand for high school educated labor. Once again, the impact of technology is not confined to the service sector. In the valve manufacturing industries described in chapter 5, new computer-controlled metal working machines have automated key tasks, enabling a greater range of products to be produced faster, with fewer operators.

What happens to the jobs that remain? In the simplest scenario, the infusion of new technology into the workplace raises skill requirements for the workers whose jobs have not been automated. For example, skilled operators in the valve industry spend more of their time problem-solving. Yet other scenarios also obtain. The new information systems that support the call centers described in chapter 8 have facilitated a fragmentation of jobs that in the past combined a variety of activities. As a result, a typical telephone operator today handles one thousand calls a day and has a call completion cycle that is many times shorter than it was for operators thirty years ago. Similarly, in the banking example in chapter 4, one department responded to the new check-processing technology by creating several narrow jobs from what used to be a single job involving many tasks, with one of the new positions involving lower skills and lower pay than the original many-faceted job. To summarize, case-study evidence suggests that in the main, employers' competitive strategies over the past several decades have hurt the job prospects and job quality of workers without college degrees. In some workplaces the story has been one of squeezing labor costs—by freezing compensation, increasing workloads, and shifting frontline jobs to cheaper locations or cheaper contractors. In other workplaces it has been a technology story: firms have used computer-driven machinery to automate repetitive tasks previously carried out by high school educated workers.

The evidence gained from the case studies illustrates the dominant actions of employers that led to the aggregate trends in the wage and job structures that have been so well documented: stagnant wages, rapid growth in contingent or subcontracted jobs, and declining upward mobility. But luckily, the story does not stop there. Among the case studies are important examples in which employers adopted quite different strategies, sometimes with very different consequences for their workforces. After describing these variations and their impacts on workers, we explore the reasons why some employers have responded to increased economic pressures in atypical ways.

ALTERNATIVE COMPETITIVE STRATEGIES

Although the pressure to reduce labor costs is strong in all of the industries studied, wide variations in firms' competitive strategies can nevertheless be observed. Rather than freeze wages, reduce benefits, use temporary workers, or relocate jobs to another part of the country, some employers have developed other ways to improve their financial performance.

One alternative strategy has been to focus on reducing turnover and increasing productivity. High turnover at the front line is often costly to firms: the new workers who must be recruited are likely to require some period of on-the-job experience before they are fully up to speed.[6] The cost to firms may be even higher in periods of low unemployment, when jobs are difficult to fill; it is more likely that positions will remain vacant and customer satisfaction will suffer. One way to reduce turnover is to reorganize the work process so that jobs are more interesting and rewarding for workers. For example, several of the hospitals studied in chapter 3 have introduced enhanced jobs for nursing assistants and food service workers to increase worker retention. This strategy is evident as well in some of the small and medium-sized manufacturing firms in central New York State examined in chapter 13. In response to pressures from large retailers for rapid turnaround and/or improved quality control, some manufacturers have integrated tasks into more complex jobs and given workers greater responsibility for many aspects of the production process. Such changes in work organization—and the greater employee commitment that often results—can reduce costs by making it easier for employers to recruit and retain good employees.

Reorganizing the work process can also increase productivity. In the study of Cabot Bank in chapter 4, workflow was reorganized in anticipation of the introduction of new technology, and productivity shot up even before the new technology was put on line.[7] Key reasons for the workers' embrace of the reorganization were that management promised not only more interesting (and demanding) jobs but also extensive training, opportunities for wage increases, *and* no layoffs. Management was able to make and keep this last promise because the firm's purchases of other banks increased the volume of checks that Cabot Bank processed, offsetting the reduced need for workers that initially resulted from the productivity increase. Of course, only firms that are growing can both make investments to increase labor productivity and guarantee no layoffs.

Another way in which firms have avoided myopic cost-cutting is by emphasizing product innovation and adopting human resource practices that support this strategy. For example, the plastics manufacturers discussed in chapter 6 are firms that compete on the basis of their ability to innovate, and they have promised to deliver products with zero defects on time to their customers. Team-based, quality-oriented work processes play an important role in these firms' ability to meet customer expectations. The auto parts firm described in chapter 12 makes innovative products with a moderately skilled workforce. It has developed expertise in the design and manufacture of electronic and electromechanical systems and developed a compensation system as well as workplace practices (such as just-in-time inventory reduction techniques) that support rapid innovation. These changes in work processes and human resource practices have resulted in interesting jobs at moderately good wages—jobs that workers want to keep.

Alternative strategies are evident even when firms do things that are usually seen as detrimental to workers—for example, when subcontracting out functions that were previously performed in-house. A case in point is schools and hospitals, which often have difficulty hiring experienced and capable managers for their food service or environmental service operations. As chapters 7 and 10 show, it has become quite common for schools and hospitals to contract out these management functions, since contract companies can hire more skilled managers and provide them with better career paths, leading to productivity gains. But control over the hiring and pay of frontline employees remains in-house, which matters in these organizations because their workers come in contact with vulnerable populations—schoolchildren or the sick and elderly. A similar "mixed" model has been pursued by one of the unionized hotels discussed in chapter 2: the management of a hotel restaurant was subcontracted for brand-name recognition, but the workers remained on payroll, covered by the union contract. In general, the net impact on frontline workers varies, but in many cases jobs have been retained that would otherwise have been lost.

Even in the case of complete subcontracting, the ultimate impact on workers is not necessarily negative. Food contractors, for example, can achieve economies of scale in buying food and can afford to purchase machinery to automate food preparation. As a result, restaurants, hospitals, and other food servers are increasingly contracting out salad preparation, purchasing precut vegetables and serving more foods prepared off-site in factory settings. As described in chapter 7, the net effect has been to transfer jobs from small food service sites to large food manufacturers. This has reduced opportunities for promotion in the food service sites, which tend to be concentrated in urban areas. However, a surprising consequence of this shift has been increased job ladder opportunities in the manufacturing sites, which tend to be located in more suburban and rural areas where land is less expensive. Thus, subcontracting in this industry appears to have diminished opportunities for central-city workers but increased opportunities for workers in selected outlying areas.

A similar story can be found in the temporary help industry. As discussed earlier, the use of temporary workers often reduces compensation (including fringe benefits) and job security for high school educated workers. However, in the tight labor markets of the 1996 to 2001 period, employers encountered difficulties as they tried to fill vacant positions for frontline workers through their usual hiring channels. Some employers lacked the capacity to recruit and screen potential new hires from a broader population, including workers with criminal records and those with poor work histories. Temporary help agencies specialize in recruiting workers and matching worker skills and job requirements. The case studies of temporary help services reported in chapters 9 and 10 found that some employers are contracting with temporary agencies to screen applicants with unfavorable characteristics. In addition, hiring such job applicants through a temporary firm makes it easier for managers to terminate and replace workers whom they view as weak contributors. As a result, in some situations the use of temporary help firms has resulted in improved job opportunities for the least attractive workers.

So far we have discussed a range of alternative competitive strategies focused on the organization of work in settings in which technological change has played at most a secondary role. But as discussed earlier, in industries such as financial services, call centers, complex plastic products, medical devices, and steel, technology has had a significant impact on workers without a college degree. Usually, though not always, skill requirements for frontline jobs have increased. In these industries outcomes for workers depend critically on whether the firm provides training for both incumbent and new workers.

Some of the case-study firms have embraced training as the way to fill these more skilled jobs. This is especially evident in the study of the hosiery industry in chapter 11. A central strategy that has enabled the hosiery industry to survive in North Carolina has been the creation of the Hosiery Technology Center (HTC) at Catawba Valley Community College, in partnership with individual firms, industry suppliers, and the regional industry trade association. The HTC has been critical to the transfer of technological knowledge to new, largely immigrant labor force entrants and to the training of experienced and apprentice machine technicians in the repair and maintenance of more highly computerized knitting machines. Knitting operators have to be able to interface with computer functions, and all employees have to work with the new computerized tracking system. Training by the HTC is specialized both to the needs of the industry and to the low levels of formal education in the workforce. Materials are designed to be easily read by workers who are more comfortable with a diagram of machine schematics than a paragraph of instructions. This and other specific features of the HTC training programs make it possible for firms to use the new technology without requiring that workers have higher levels of formal education.

Yet U.S. employers typically provide little training for workers with a high school degree or less, and this is indeed the preference of many of the case-study employers as well. For example, in manufacturing firms where technology has increased skill requirements, managers expressed a preference for hiring relatively more able high school graduates. In particular, they seek new hires who are literate, have good basic math skills, have good interpersonal and communication skills, are good problem-solvers, and have good mechanical skills. But this ambition has largely been thwarted to date, either by the tight labor markets that prevailed in the late

1990s or by a lack of new hiring due to increases in worker productivity or declines in consumer demand. In the interim, firms that have adopted sophisticated computer-based technologies are addressing the rising skill requirements in production jobs through training of incumbent workers and new hires. A medical devices plant that makes products such as biopsy needles (see chapter 5) relies on a combination of training and compensation policies based on pay-for-skill to develop the desired skills in employees. The innovative plastics manufacturer described in chapter 6 opened its own training institute to upgrade worker skills by providing training in English as a second language as well as preparation for earning the general equivalency diploma (GED). The training institute also retrained some former operators for jobs as skilled plastics technicians.

In fact, one common theme that runs across several case studies is that lack of computer skills per se has not been a skills bottleneck. All of the case studies that examined greater use of computers by workers found that modest amounts of training were sufficient to impart the requisite computer skills. For example, in the case study describing the consequences of introducing new computer-based technology at Cabot Bank (chapter 4), the reorganization of one department led to greater skill demands. Training went a long way toward providing incumbent high school graduates with the necessary skills, especially computer skills.

At the same time, however, it was more difficult to teach abstract problem-solving skills to many incumbent workers. Accordingly, Cabot Bank introduced a new recruiting process that favors applicants who have completed at least some years of college. Similarly, chapter 8 reports that the call centers that offer high-quality service and compete on the basis of customer loyalty prefer to hire workers with a college degree. Half of the employees in the call center that services large companies have college degrees.

Nevertheless, the prospects for call center workers who lack a college degree are not always bleak. The presence of a union can make a difference. The unionized telecommunications firm has invested more than twice as much in initial training, pay, and benefits for workers with a high school education compared with the nonunion financial services firm, and the union has helped maintain internal job ladders by limiting the outsourcing of work and the relocation of call centers to other states. More generally, mobility opportunities for workers with less than a college degree depend on managerial decisions such as whether to locate call centers near other services provided by the firm or near other company offices.

The simple lesson, then, is that training can play a key role in enabling firms to pursue alternative competitive strategies that do not displace or deskill workers without college degrees. But training is a path not often taken, and even when this strategy is tried, it is not always implemented well.

WHAT EXPLAINS VARIATION IN FIRM STRATEGIES AND WORKER OUTCOMES?

The findings in this book inexorably lead to two questions. Why have most firms responded to increased economic pressures by adopting policies that have negative effects on their frontline workers, even when alternative responses seem possible? And why have some firms, when faced with the same pressures, adopted policies that have not only improved their competitive position but also led to desirable outcomes for workers? In this section, we explore the answers to these related questions.

UNIONS

At a time when many speak of the triumph of the free market, it may seem an anachronism to speak of wage-setting institutions. Yet one of the more surprising findings from this volume is the continuing relevance of unions in determining the quality of frontline jobs. To varying degrees, unions have been able to prevent the squeezing of labor costs that is the first competitive option chosen by many employers. Collective bargaining has been important in maintaining real wage levels and benefits and in preventing increases in workloads. Nor has this effect been limited to the traditional stronghold of unions, the goods-producing sector. In fact, the most interesting union effects were documented in hospitality, health care, and telecommunications—service-sector industries with a high proportion of workers without college degrees.

This is not to downplay the marked decline in union representation over the past three decades and the exceedingly difficult hurdles that the American labor movement faces today. The decline in union representation in the American workforce over the last thirty years has been quite pervasive. It will take significant changes in the application of labor law and in organizing strategies to reverse this trend.

At the same time, it is striking that in a number of the industries examined in this volume, unions have played an important role in influencing employers' responses to competitive pressures. The impact of worker representation is greatest where unions have significant density in a specific region and industry, creating conditions in which all employers are competing on a level field. In these settings, several service-industry unions have been able to move beyond the bread-and-butter issues of wages and benefits to mediate the reorganization of work in ways that do not hamper competitiveness or profitability.

Again, these examples are few and far between. Only a few unions have embraced the challenge of organizing low-skilled immigrant workers. However, the examples do suggest that unions could play a key role in reversing three decades of growing inequality. A hopeful sign is that the successful union examples described in this volume occur in growing service industries, where innovative organizing campaigns are embracing a new generation of immigrant workers.

REGIONAL LABOR MARKET INSTITUTIONS

Equally surprising was the appearance, across a number of case studies, of new labor market institutions that have shaped employers' responses to growing competition. These institutions come in a variety of forms. In the hosiery manufacturing industry of North Carolina, a regional training consortium of major employers and community colleges helped to save the industry from overseas competition and integrate a new generation of immigrant workers into the production process (see chapter 11). In San Francisco a labor-management hotel partnership has engaged the major employers and union in the city in a joint effort to solve training and productivity issues while at the same time sustaining entry-level wages that are significantly higher than in other comparable cities (see chapter 2). And in New York City a large, multi-employer training fund supports the skills upgrading and promotion of frontline workers who have historically been stuck in dead-end jobs (see chapter 3).

In each of these cases, firms under intense pressure have been able to avoid the short-term cost-cutting (and even flight overseas) that would have severely hurt the job prospects of entry-level workers. Our understanding of these and other examples around the country is still evolving. It is clear that regional, multi-employer structures can deliver resources to individual firms that allow firms to pursue alternative competitive strategies. In the examples described in this volume, such resources include pooled training funds and recruiting and placement through hiring halls, joint benchmarking and dissemination of best practices, and a stronger industry voice in the policy arena. Moreover, the incentive structures for individual firms change in such partnerships. For example, firms are more likely to make investments in their employees when they do not fear the poaching of their trained workers.

THE QUALITY OF THE INFORMATION AVAILABLE TO MANAGERS

Alternatives to cutting the wage bill, such as reorganizing work to increase productivity, requires knowledge that many employers do not have. Access to knowledge about innovative management and production techniques appears to be important in explaining why some firms have adopted atypical strategies. For example, in central New York State a number of manufacturing firms have gone against the local grain and adopted "high-performance" work practices and made significant investments in their less-skilled workers. Although similar to their competitors in most respects, these firms are different in that they tend to be located close to metropolitan areas. This location results in better access to colleges, well-trained managers, and other vehicles for exposure to best practices in the industry, such as local trade groups. This is not a minor point. In daily practice, employers must make numerous decisions about how to organize work and production, and in every industry there are clearly better and worse ways to do so. Since firms typically need considerable knowledge and technical assistance to succeed in restructuring their workplaces—especially when the restructuring makes use of high-performance practices—there is a clear role here for intermediary organizations such as community colleges. Although having good information about high-performance work practices does not guarantee that firms will adopt them, a lack of information poses a significant barrier to adoption.

REGULATION

The declining real value of the minimum wage over the last thirty years means that there has effectively been a deregulation of the wage-setting process. The falling wage floor has had direct effects on how firms restructure jobs at the front line. Besides making it relatively easy for firms to cut wages, a declining real minimum wage has indirect effects as well. As the wage floor falls, it creates room for temp agencies and subcontractors to offer their services at lower costs than were possible in-house, where incumbent workers may have acquired seniority and could be earning more than the minimum wage.

In a number of industries other forms of deregulation have also resulted in significant changes to employers' competitive options. For example, deregulation in the banking industry allowed the consolidation and relocation of call centers to remote locations in the Midwest, causing dramatic changes in customer service jobs. Similarly, the highly publicized breakup of AT&T in 1984 and the deregulation of telecommunications played no small role in that industry's deunionization and the erosion of the quality of non-managerial jobs. Changes in methods of regulating health care costs—in particular, the practice of basing hospital reimbursements on patients' diagnoses rather than on the cost of the care they receive—make it difficult for hospitals to increase wages.

The important point is that both the presence and absence of government regulation play important roles in shaping how the labor market operates. The withdrawal of various forms of regulation in the 1980s and 1990s clearly had an impact on firm behavior and worker outcomes. As such, deregulation should be understood as an active policy intervention.

TIGHT LABOR MARKETS

In several of the industries studied in this volume, tight labor markets clearly have had an effect on employer practices. This is not just a story of the extraordinarily low unemployment of the late 1990s. A number of industries have long had to deal with a tight labor supply, especially when trying to fill frontline jobs with low wages and difficult working conditions. It is not surprising that the problems of recruitment and retention in tight labor markets have increased employers' willingness to explore innovative approaches to the organization and compensation of entry-level jobs. However, it would be a mistake to draw the conclusion that good things happen only in tight labor markets. In principle, a high-productivity–high-wage model can work in normal times as well. The challenge for policymakers is to identify the supports necessary to nurture such a model.

POLICY RESPONSES

The studies in this volume analyze the competitive conditions facing industries that employ large numbers of workers without college degrees and the choices that employers make in meeting these challenges. A primary goal throughout has been to understand how firm-level decisions shape a variety of worker outcomes, including wages, fringe benefits, training and promotion opportunities, job quality, and employment security.

The chapters offer analysis, not policy prescriptives. Nevertheless, we believe that they offer several important lessons to policymakers. First, there is a clear role for government in supporting managerial choices and competitive strategies that are beneficial for workers. Second, there is a clear role for government in making work pay for the many Americans who work full-time in the mentally and physically demanding jobs that are the backbone of much economic activity.

What, then, are the points of intervention? Most obvious and direct is the minimum wage, which in real terms has fallen over the last twenty-five years and has enabled firms to reduce the wages of their most vulnerable employees. Raising the real wage back to its 1979 level or higher would create a level playing field for those employers who want to invest in workers' skills and compete on the basis of service or product quality. A higher minimum wage would not only reduce the possibility that these firms will be undermined by competitors engaged in a race to the bottom but also reduce the incentives for subcontracting and outsourcing to low-wage suppliers. It is important to keep in mind that the most recent economic research shows that the negative effects on employment stemming from an increase in the minimum wage are quite small.[8]

In the longer term, one of the striking findings to emerge from this volume is the importance of regional labor market institutions for workers without college degrees. The hosiery, hospital, and hotel industries provide powerful lessons in how interfirm cooperation can set industry standards and disseminate best practices; how training consortia can reduce training costs for individual employers and encourage cross-firm mobility; and how multi-employer bargaining and high local union density can establish strong job quality and productivity norms. Government is in a unique position to nurture these types of structures, which require a great deal of technical assistance, intermediary organizations, public leadership, coordination of public training monies, and a vital and flexible community college system. Of course, there needs to be deep and sustained engagement of the stakeholders themselves. But ultimately the growth of these new labor market institutions cannot happen without a conscious decision by government to create the conditions that nurture high-performance work organizations.

The enforcement of U.S. labor law is also essential if workers with limited leverage in the labor market are to have the ability to earn wages that will sustain them and their families. High union density, as several chapters in this book show, is quite effective in raising wages for such employees, especially in labor-intensive service industries. Yet in a recent study of workers' freedom to organize and bargain collectively in the United States, Human Rights Watch found that illegal reprisals against employees attempting to form unions have risen from fewer than one thousand a year in the 1950s to more than twenty-three thousand in 1998 (Human Rights Watch 2000). The simple act of reining in this illegal activity by employers would go a long way toward reestablishing unionization as a viable choice for workers in this country.[9]

It is important to stress that these types of policies are especially critical for immigrant workers. Changes in immigration laws have opened America's doors to less-educated workers from around the world. These workers increasingly fill the low-wage jobs studied in this volume but often do not have the economic power to better their lives on their own. More than half of employers with high proportions of undocumented workers threaten, during union representation election campaigns, to call the Immigration and Naturalization Service (INS) if workers vote for the union (Bronfenbrenner 2000).

Even with a dramatic change in political will, it will obviously take time to make any significant change in the prevalence of low-wage jobs. Immediate relief is needed, and a simple improvement to the Earned Income Tax Credit (EITC) could help to deliver it. The EITC provides workers with a refundable credit against federal income taxes. While not sufficient to bring most working families with children up to basic budget levels, it does raise the incomes of many families above the poverty line. But the credit currently phases out quite rapidly as income increases, with several unintended consequences.[10] Slowing the phaseout rate for the EITC would provide more help to families with incomes above $12,500, allow workers to earn higher incomes before losing the credit entirely, and reduce the marriage penalty for large numbers of low-wage workers (Cherry and Sawicky 2000). Given bipartisan support for the EITC, this is a front where progress could be made, and quickly.

The United States may be the richest of the industrialized countries, but a distressingly large number of Americans employed across a wide range of industries work at jobs that do not pay enough to live decently. The findings in this book call for a national self-examination. They challenge us to ask ourselves: What kind of country do we want to live in? Do we accept that large numbers of low-wage workers are necessary for U.S. prosperity and job creation? Are we willing to countenance the profound economic, social, and political effects of the growing gap between rich and poor?

Rising inequality is not required for economic growth. As the Princeton economist Paul Krugman (2002, 76) pointed out in the *New York Times Magazine*, "The most impressive economic growth in U.S. history coincided with the middle-class interregnum, the post–World War II generation, when incomes were most evenly distributed." It is necessary to go back to the 1920s to find a period of such great disparities in income among Americans. Government has an important role to play in reversing the slide from the middle-class society of the 1950s and 1960s to the stark inequality of today.

It is important to keep in mind that the economic consequences of having more than one-fifth of the workforce earning poverty-level wages are not straightforward. Americans do pay less for some goods and services than they would if they were produced by workers earning a living wage. However, the research described in this volume shows that low wages elicit responses from both workers and their employers that increase costs. For example, low wages increase the likelihood that workers will quit their jobs, imposing turnover costs on employers. They increase the likelihood that firms will fail to seek out the most efficient technologies and work organization practices and will underinvest in workers' skills and capital equipment. These responses can result in higher prices and lower quality than would have been the case if a decent minimum wage had compelled all employers to make the best use of their workforces.

Moreover, a national commitment to a living wage could help the country deal with the recurring problem of creating demand for the enormous amount of goods and services that the economy is capable of producing. In periods of recession, such as 2002 to 2003, paying a living wage is a powerful way to stimulate demand and spur employment.

While the economic consequences of low wages are complicated, the social consequences are less so. In one of the world's wealthiest countries, fully 29 percent of working families with children earn less than the amount needed to maintain a basic standard of living, and that is a national disgrace. Such income inequality threatens the social fabric of our society and the stability of our democracy. It's past time for Americans to speak out about the kind of country we want to live in.

NOTES

1. These statistics take into account benefits received under the Earned Income Tax Credit (EITC). A "basic family budget" is adjusted for the cost of living in local communities and for family size and offers a realistic measure of how much income a family needs to have a safe and decent standard of living. For more details on the measure and the above estimates, see Boushey et al. (2001).
2. Changes in the questions about educational attainment included in the U.S. Census of Population and the Current Population Survey (CPS) make it impossible to estimate with current data how many years of college were completed by sample respondents.
3. For a review of the wage inequality literature, see Katz and Autor (1999).
4. In 1974 the minimum wage was increased from $1.00 to $2.00 an hour.
5. An additional 30 percent of the U.S. workforce attended college but did not earn a four-year degree. The changes in work opportunities described in this volume pertain to many of these workers as well (Mishel, Bernstein, and Boushey 2003, 161, table 2.20).
6. For example, Marriott Hotels estimates that it costs $3,000 in re-

cruiting expenses and lost production to replace a housekeeper who leaves (Eileen Appelbaum, interview with Donna Klein of Marriott, Washington, D.C., July 25, 2001).

7. The Cabot Bank case also illustrates an important but often neglected pattern: namely, the interconnectedness of technological changes, organizational changes, and human resource policies (Brynjolfsson and Hitt 2000). It took the prospect of new technology for Cabot Bank to reorganize exceptions processing tasks into more complex, multidimensional jobs.

8. For a recent review of the evidence on the employment effects of changes in the minimum wage, see Brown (1999).

9. For recent evidence on changing attitudes toward unions, see Greenhouse (2002).

10. In 1999 the EITC provided a family with two children earning between $9,500 and $12,500 with a maximum credit of $3,618 a year. The credit phases out rapidly as family income increases, and it disappears entirely when family income reaches $30,850—equivalent to a steep marginal tax rate of 21 percent on earnings above $12,500. In addition, the rapid phaseout of the EITC creates a severe "marriage penalty" for low-wage workers. A man with two children earning $20,000 is eligible for some credit under the EITC, as is a woman in the same situation. But if they marry each other, they and their four children would lose the credit.

REFERENCES

Appelbaum, Eileen, and Peter Berg. 1996. "Financial Market Constraints and Business Strategy in the USA." In *Creating Industrial Capacity: Towards Full Employment,* edited by Jonathan Michie and John Grieve Smith. New York: Oxford University Press.

Boushey, Heather, Chauna Brocht, Bethney Gundersen, and Jared Bernstein. 2001. *Hardships in America: The Real Story of Working Families.* Washington, D.C.: Economic Policy Institute.

Bronfenbrenner, K. 2000. *Uneasy Terrain: The Impact of Capital Mobility on Workers, Wages, and Union Organizing.* Washington: U.S. Trade Deficit Review Commission.

Brown, Charles. 1999. "Minimum Wages, Employment, and the Distribution of Income." In *Handbook of Labor Economics,* vol. 3, edited by Orley Ashenfelter and David Card. Amsterdam: Elsevier.

Brynjolfsson, Erik, and Lorin M. Hitt. 2000. "Beyond Computation: Information Technology, Organizational Transformation, and Business Performance." *Journal of Economic Perspectives* 14(4): 23–48.

Cherry, Robert, and Max Sawicky. 2000. *Giving Tax Credit Where Credit Is Due*. Washington, D.C.: Economic Policy Institute.

Greenhouse, Steven. 2002. "The Mood at Work: Anger and Anxiety." *New York Times*, October 29, section C, p.1.

Human Rights Watch. 2000. *Unfair Advantage: Workers' Freedom of Association in the United States under International Human Rights Standards*. New York: Human Rights Watch.

Katz, Lawrence F., and David H. Autor. 1999. "Changes in the Wage Structure and Earnings Inequality." In *Handbook of Labor Economics*, vol. 3, edited by O. Ashenfelter and D. Card. Amsterdam: Elsevier.

Krugman, Paul. 2002. "For Richer: How the Permissive Capitalism of the Boom Destroyed American Equality." *New York Times*, October 20, p. 76.

Mishel, Lawrence, Jared Bernstein, and Heather Boushey. 2003. *The State of Working America 2002–2003*. Ithaca, N.Y.: ILR Press.

U.S. Department of Labor, Bureau of Labor Statistics. Various years. "Employment, Hours, and Earnings from the Current Employment Statistics Survey—National." Available at: *data.bls.gov/cgi-bin/surveymost?ee*.

PART I

Services: Where the Jobs Are

CHAPTER 2

The Coffee Pot Wars: Unions and Firm Restructuring in the Hotel Industry

Annette Bernhardt, Laura Dresser,
and Erin Hatton

After considerable debate about recent labor market trends in the United States, something of a consensus may finally be emerging on the major forces at work. Debate will undoubtedly continue over the relative weight of different factors, but it is clear that changes in markets, technologies, and institutions have all contributed to the sharp rise in inequality and the stagnation of real wages for many workers.[1]

Because less-educated workers have been hurt the most, policymakers have largely focused on education and training as remedies. But the translation of changes in trade and technology into greater inequality has been driven in part by the disintegration of postwar labor market institutions. Reconstructing institutional arrangements for "the new economy" thus seems like the most promising point of intervention, beyond the needed improvements in human capital formation. Firm restructuring continues to redefine the nature of work and opportunity in virtually every sector of the economy and in ways that a supply-side policy alone cannot harness. "Perhaps the most important implications of the new employment relationship concern increased inequality in the workplace and, ultimately, in society as a whole" (Cappelli et al. 1997, 11). Put another way, while globalization and technological change are largely beyond our control, the distribution of their burdens and benefits is not. Firm choices about the setting of wages and the allocation of labor are made within a set of constraints and opportunities, which derive not just from product markets but also from surrounding institutional arrangements.

The problem is that we know much less about these institutional effects than, say, the effects of new technologies. Our focus on the hospitality industry provides an ideal case study for rectifying this gap. The hospitality industry is a classic low-wage, labor-intensive service industry that employs large numbers of low-income people, especially workers of color and immigrants. Firm restructuring is prevalent and shares many characteristics (including consolidation, subcontracting, and flexible staffing) with other service industries. Most important, although unions represent only a small share of the workforce nationwide, union density remains high in key urban areas, particularly among larger hotels at the higher end of the market.

Hospitality thus affords us a window on a key labor market institution—unions—in the context of a rapidly changing industry. Specifically, our goal in this study is to isolate the impact of union density and worker voice on how firm restructuring occurs and how it affects jobs and workers. Drawing on a series of in-depth case studies and background industry research on the hotel industry, we ask the following questions: How have hotels reorganized their operations over the past two decades, and why? How has firm restructuring affected workers, especially those in entry-level jobs who have no college education? How have unions been able to mediate those effects, and does the answer depend on union density in the region?

Our hope is that a close reading of why employers choose different competitive strategies (which have different effects on workers) will help develop a viable policy response to growing inequality, and in particular to the growing number of workers trapped in low-wage service careers. From anecdotal evidence, we anticipate that unions have indeed had an impact on restructuring in the hotel industry. The question is, how much of an impact? How have unions achieved that effect, and under what conditions? And to what extent have workers without a college education benefited as a result?

RESEARCH DESIGN AND METHODS

This study consists of two parts: background research on trends in the hotel industry, and in-depth case studies of eight hotels in four U.S. cities. The background research allowed us to chart the history of the hospitality industry and identify the competitive challenges that it faces; here we relied on industry trade magazines, the business press, academic publications, and government data.[2] We also present descriptive data on wages, unionization levels, and demographics for hotel workers in metropolitan areas (as defined by the U.S. Bureau of the Census). We use the Current Population Survey Outgoing Rotation Group (CPS-ORG) file; results are weighted to adjust for oversampling of certain groups within the CPS-ORG.

We then chose four cities from one broad region of the country to serve as our research sites. All four cities are major business, convention, and urban tourist markets and rank in the top thirty hospitality markets nationwide.[3] They are all also characterized by strong competition, an expanding hotel sector, a rapidly changing labor pool, and wage trends that mirror national changes over the past several decades. They vary, however, in degree of immigration and type of immigrants; this variation will become important in our analysis.

Finally, two of the cities have high union density in the hotel industry, and two have low density. This is an integral part of our research design. As shown in table 2.1, in each city we selected two hotels—one unionized, one not unionized—yielding a total of eight case-study hotels. In each of the four unionized hotels we studied the vast majority of workers are represented by the Hotel Employees and Restaurant Employees International (the dominant union in the industry). The resulting research design compares unionized to non-unionized hotels, in both high-density and low-density markets.[4] To wit, we are isolating differences in institutional arrangements so that we can examine variation in how unions mediate employers' restructuring decisions and the effects of those decisions on worker outcomes.

Another important feature of this design is that we control for industry segment. Our choice of hotels was restricted to high-end, full-service "Class A" hotels that cater to the business, convention, and tourist markets—we would not want to compare a highway Motel 8 to a Hyatt, for example. But the choice of the high-end segment is strategic for another reason. Class A hotels typically have high profit margins, averaging between 20 and 40 percent in our case studies. If there is any potential for employers to take the "high road" in this decidedly low-wage industry, it will be found here. Moreover, this segment of the industry has considerable influence over other segments in terms of practices and strategies. Thus, if we identify, for example, important institutional effects on re-

Table 2.1 Distribution and Location of Eight Union
and Non-Union Case-Study Hotels,
by Union Density

	Union Density	
Unionized	Low	High
No	City A, Hotel 1	City C, Hotel 3
	City B, Hotel 2	City D, Hotel 4
Yes	City A, Hotel 5	City C, Hotel 7
	City B, Hotel 6	City D, Hotel 8

Source: Authors' compilation.

structuring and worker outcomes in our study, then there is the
potential for diffusion and dissemination to other, perhaps less innovative, parts in the industry.

We focused our fieldwork on those departments where the majority of low-wage and less-educated workers are employed: the
housekeeping department (responsible for the cleaning of rooms
and public areas) and food and beverage services (restaurants, ban-
quets, and room service). These jobs embody the archetype of low-
wage, dead-end service jobs—room cleaners, dishwashers, bussers,
cooks—with the exception that they are more backbreaking than
many other jobs.

In 2001 we conducted intensive research at each of the eight
hotels. First, we interviewed managers, ranging from decisionmakers high in the organization to immediate supervisors in the
housekeeping and food and beverage departments. Second, we conducted interviews and focus groups with workers in both of these
areas, and in unionized hotels with the appropriate union representatives. Third, as much as possible we collected primary data on the
hotel's performance, occupancy rates, distribution of job classifications, wages, benefits, work hours, and so forth. The one-on-one
interviews typically lasted 1 hour, and the focus groups 2 hours.
Both were guided by semistructured protocols that focused on
changes in business strategy, the organization of work, wages and
compensation, training and promotion practices, worker characteristics, and labor management relations. The results of all interviews were summarized in standardized write-ups and data invento-

ries. Each hotel visit lasted between 3 and 5 days, often with follow-up calls to verify information and obtain hotel data. Across the 8 hotels we interviewed a total of 128 individuals.[5]

Last, we note several limitations to our research design. While subcontracting has become quite prevalent in the hotel industry, we were not able to gain access to any contractor firms in order to assess directly the effect of the practice on job quality. We did consistently ask both managers and workers to compare subcontracted to in-house jobs, and while their answers provided only indirect evidence, we gathered a pretty consistent picture of the effects of subcontracting. Another limitation is that most of our research was conducted during the spring and summer of 2001, a time of strong economic performance and extraordinarily tight labor markets in the hotel industry. Such conditions have historically been a boon for less-educated workers; we take up this point in detail in our conclusion.

RESTRUCTURING IN THE HOTEL INDUSTRY

Hospitality is an $86.5 billion a year industry that employs roughly 1.9 million workers in more than 40,000 establishments nationwide.[6] It is a highly urban industry (metropolitan areas account for about two-thirds of the rooms) and, until recently, a fast-growing one. (Employment almost tripled between 1970 and 2000.) Like almost every sector of the economy, the industry has undergone pronounced changes over the past several decades in terms of competition, industry concentration, market segments, the organization of production, and corporate governance. And as is the case with a number of other service industries, these changes have been largely domestic, for the obvious reason that much of what hotels do is firmly rooted in time and place—rooms and casinos are not movable, and neither are the workers who make the beds and dice the vegetables. To the extent that globalization has had a direct impact, it has been through the large influx of less-educated immigrant workers in recent years, a development that has clearly enabled some of the low-wage business strategies that we document in this chapter (see Cranford 1998).

THE CHANGING COMPETITIVE ENVIRONMENT

On balance, what we see in hospitality is a set of shifts that are firmly rooted in domestic dynamics. Most dramatic have been changes around ownership in the form of widespread consolidation and the growth of publicly held corporations. Both trends signal a much more intense competitive environment and have complex roots in the overbuilding that occurred during the 1980s, as well as in the vagaries of the real estate market and shifts in financing practices. The consequence is that a few very large corporate chains, each owning a range of brand-name hotels that serve a variety of markets, now dominate an industry once populated by a myriad of small, family-owned hotels.

The merger trend has been so pronounced in the last decade that analysts predict that "eventually five mega-hotel companies will control the worldwide hotel business" (Watkins 2000, 2). In fact, in 1997 the four largest firms in the hotel industry (excluding casino hotels) accounted for a full one-fifth of total sales in the entire industry, and the largest fifty firms account for just under half of all sales in the industry (U.S. Bureau of the Census 1997).

The motivations here are straightforward. Hotels consolidated to increase market share, diversify their markets and spread their risk, acquire high-quality brand names, and achieve economies of scale (Webb 2000). By the late 1990s industry practices were effectively being dictated by a handful of hotel companies, such as Accor, Bass, Marriott, Hilton, and Starwood. And with only a few exceptions, these emergent entities were publicly held. From 1991 to 1994 an average of sixteen hotel companies went public per year, compared to an average of just under seven in the previous decade (Canina 1996). Going public has given companies better access to capital, but with the price tag of significantly increased external pressure for short-term performance. "You're only as good as your last quarter" was the mantra of our management interviews. It is telling that the president of one of the few remaining private hotel chains (Hyatt) explicitly cited the freedom from Wall Street analysts and their pressure for short-term performance as the main advantage of not going public (McCann 2000). Similarly, a recent survey of hospitality managers yielded "public ownership" as one of their top ten concerns, particularly in terms of its effect on managerial decision-making (Yetzer 2000).

THE RESTRUCTURING OF WORK AND PRODUCTION

On the ground, intensifying competition and performance pressures have resulted in organizational restructuring to cut costs and increase revenue flows. Industry analysts explain this effort to "trim the fat" as a response to the overbuilding and overindulgence of the 1980s, when hotels were built without regard to demand and amenities were offered without regard to price (Bernstein 1999). The prevailing dictum in the industry today is "do more with less" (Gillette 1995). Yet at the same time, there has also been a push to provide more and better quality service (Marinko 1991). This obvious tension is rarely resolved successfully. At present most hotels seem to be focusing on cutting costs first and improving service quality second.

The range of cost-cutting strategies is long and diverse. Some hotels focus solely on reducing labor costs by cutting staff, freezing wages, eliminating or combining job categories, and reducing work hours. Other strategies are aimed at increasing revenue flow: raising menu and banquet prices, extending local telephone call charges, and increasing early departure charges (McCarthy and Simmons 1995). Other, more complex strategies include streamlining operations across departments, redesigning rooms to make cleaning easier, and taking food offerings "back to the basics" (Nozar 1995). The push to make each hotel department a profit center has led to a significant increase in subcontracting, the most visible of all the restructuring strategies.[7] Functions that are being subcontracted include payroll and benefits processing, central purchasing, tax compliance and systems maintenance, as well as valet, public area cleaning, nighttime cleaning, and laundry (Francis 1998; Lattin 1993). The benefits of subcontracting usually include lower labor costs (since subcontracting often means shifting to non-union labor), reduced workers' compensation claims, lower utility and water costs, and freedom from scrutiny over environmental issues.

Most prevalent, however, is the subcontracting of restaurants (Andorka 1999; Lomanno 1998). In-house full-service restaurants, once the standard in this industry, were increasingly subcontracted during the 1990s. Historically, hotel restaurants have been seen as "necessary evils"—money-losing amenities that hoteliers had to provide to guests. With increased pressure to cut costs, hotel operators have most often turned to subcontracting rather than revamp the quality of their food offerings. They have largely contracted out to big-name brand restaurants and even fast-food chains such as Pizza Hut, so much so that three companies—ARAMARK, Compass Group, and Sodexo Alliance—have gained a quasi-monopoly in providing on-site food service to hotels (Reynolds 1990). The growing pressure from Wall Street plays an important role here. The fact is that not all food and beverage outlets lose money. In the late 1980s, when subcontracting started gaining hold, hotel food and beverage profit margins averaged around 15 percent. But under the new pressure of quarterly performance reviews, these relatively low margins effectively became a loss—a drag on the hotel's performance that had to be redressed.[8]

Not all hotels have succumbed to endless cost-cutting. Especially in the early 1990s, there was something of a total quality management (TQM) movement in the industry, during which hotels proclaimed that they were developing innovative organizational structures to enhance employee involvement and satisfaction and, as a result, reduce turnover (Kaestle 1990; Barbee and Bott 1991). It is difficult, however, to judge the prevalence of such practices. The industry press frequently heralds such innovative strategies, but it is telling that the same example is cited over and over again—the TQM program at the Ritz-Carlton, which apparently boosted worker satisfaction, reduced turnover from 100 to 30 percent, and increased productivity and profits. At the end of this chapter, we describe several other examples of innovative practices, but these are the exception, and skepticism over such experiments remains prevalent in the industry.

The Role of Technology

The impact of new technology is a common explanation for changes in the organization of work and production and parallel changes in the wage structure. But in the hotel industry and other similarly labor-intensive service industries, there is actually little evidence of a profound impact of skill-biased technical change. To date, hotels have used technology largely to streamline administrative functions and boost customer service. For example, new management information systems have automated the process of labor planning, scheduling, budgeting, payroll process, and forecasting. Point-of-sale terminals are increasingly integrated across the hotel so that all charges accrue to the hotel bill. Online reservations are becoming the norm. And in business-oriented hotels, rooms are increasingly sporting high-speed Internet connections, fax machines, printers, scanners, voice mail, and room sensors to turn lights on and off (Null 2000).

But the bread-and-butter work of hotels—cleaning rooms, preparing and serving foods and beverages—remains at heart a labor-intensive process. In both the industry literature and our case-study hotels, we have not found significant effects of either technology substitution or technology-induced skill upgrading. True, room cleaners now use an automated system to track their progress through their daily quota, and integrated information systems are enabling better monitoring of workers' payroll abuses. But these are, at best, effects at the margins. The only place where technology appears to have had a substantial labor effect is in recent advances in the packaging, refrigeration, and delivery of precut foods (Baumann 1997). These new systems have enabled a rather pronounced shift in the hotel industry to buying prepared foods (such as diced onions, soup stock, and sliced meats) rather than making them from scratch in-house. This shift has clearly moved frontline jobs to subcontractors; in the next section, we explore in detail the effect of this and other practices on jobs and workers.

CHANGES IN JOB QUALITY

The majority of hotel work—housing and feeding guests—is performed by a mass of frontline workers in just a few occupations.[9] In examining the impact of firm restructuring on job quality in this industry, our focus is on housekeepers and cleaners, who in 2000 constituted 24.8 percent of industry employment, and food preparers and servers, who accounted for another 25.5 percent (U.S. Department of Labor 2002a). The picture that emerges is one of difficult jobs that, in a number of important respects, have become even more difficult in recent years because of the push toward leaner staffing and the drive to contain labor costs.

JOB CONTENT

Despite the significant reorganization of work that hotels have instituted in recent years, entry-level jobs have changed very little in terms of content (Cappelli 1993). Housekeepers continue to be responsible for cleaning rooms from top to bottom: scrubbing bathtubs and toilets, mopping and vacuuming floors, changing sheets, towels, and shower curtains, making beds, and dusting lightbulbs and lampshades. They are also responsible for maintaining their service area and supply carts, coordinating and adjusting throughout the day which rooms get cleaned when, as well as responding immediately to guests' requests. In fact, while housekeeping is generally considered an "unskilled job," it requires a fair number of abilities, including attention to detail, agility, customer interaction, organizing ability, and considerable strength. "There's so much stress in this job, I believe they should be the highest paid in the entire hotel," said the director of housekeeping at one hotel we visited. Over and over again, managers, supervisors, and the workers themselves identified housekeeping as the hardest job in the hotel—"the backbone of the industry."

Similarly, jobs in food and beverage (F&B) departments have experienced little change in content over time. Working in the "front of the house" are bussers, servers, hosts, cocktail waitresses, and bartenders. With the exception of bussers, these jobs tend to be better-quality (especially the tipped and banquet positions) than those in the "back of the house" (the kitchen). At the bottom of the kitchen hierarchy are dishwashers, and above them lies a range of job classifications, including food prep or cook's helper, pantry (cold food preparation), and several different levels of cook. Across the board, F&B jobs tend to be demanding, hectic, and fluid and involve a fair amount of informal teamwork and on-the-fly decisionmaking.

LEAN STAFFING

Although the *content* of frontline hotel jobs has changed little, the *amount* of work has increased substantially as hotels have adopted lean staffing strategies in an effort to cut costs and raise revenue. For housekeepers, "doing more work with fewer people" has raised the number of rooms each worker must clean in a day.[10] The room quota typically ranges between fifteen and seventeen rooms, and in all of our case-study hotels the figure is significantly higher than in the past.[11] Meeting the room quota can be very difficult, and housekeepers routinely report having to skip breaks and lunch in order to do so. At the same time that hotels have raised quotas to cut labor costs, they have also added more amenities so as to simultaneously increase service quality. Such amenities include coffeepots, hair dryers, irons and ironing boards, bathrobes, extra sheets and pillows, and even printers and fax machines—all of which the housekeepers are responsible for cleaning and maintaining. The added time and effort is significant; one hotel requires that hair dryers be cleaned on the *inside*. Even casino hotels—which are known for keeping their rooms spare and easy to clean in order to keep labor costs low—are feeling the pressure to increase guest room amenities. According to a casino hotel manager, "Guests expect to have the same amenities in a $60 hotel as they do in a $150 hotel."

Staffing has become even leaner in restaurants and kitchens because food and beverage departments have come under particularly intense pressure to cut costs and increase profit margins. Some hotels have reduced F&B staff gradually through attrition, but others have aggressively eliminated job categories, and some have even done away with entire departments. As one restaurant manager observed: "We always run lean. Always." One hotel, for example, has eliminated nighttime dishwashers: dishes pile up overnight until the arrival of the morning dishwashers, whose work has thus been doubled. A sous-chef at another hotel observed that cutbacks have made the workers in her kitchen resentful, since the hotel expects them to do more work with fewer people and without annual cost-of-living pay raises.

Hotels have been able to "do more with less" through a near-universal reliance on cross-training—moving an employee from one job category to another on an as-needed basis. As one low-level cook observed: "There's not really a choice whether or not to work other stations. Everybody cross-trains, not as much for advancement—which is the reason they give us—but mostly in order to fill in for other employees." The wage savings of this strategy are obvious: if all low-level cooks are able to do every job in the kitchen, the hotel need not hire as many high-level cooks.

Increasing workload is one of the top issues in worker-management relations in this industry; in several of our worker focus groups, in fact, this issue topped compensation as the main complaint. At one hotel, for example, housekeepers fought "tooth and nail" against the addition of extra pillows, irons, ironing boards, and hair dryers in the rooms, since management expected them to maintain the same quota of sixteen rooms a day. But after lengthy meetings, the quota remained unchanged. The executive housekeeper said, "If a housekeeper feels she can't handle the job, she can go elsewhere. They should be able to clean sixteen rooms, no problem. But there will always be the 'crybabies' that complain about the room quota."

HOURS AND SCHEDULING

Closely related to lean staffing is lean scheduling. In an industry that has seasonal fluctuations in demand, cutting staff also creates more part-time staff. This has been a contentious issue for hotel workers and managers. Industry data show that weekly hours worked have dropped slowly over time, from an average of 39.9 in 1960 down to 31.0 in 2000 (U.S. Department of Labor 2002b). At the same time hotels are increasing the number of "on-call" workers—employees who are not regularly scheduled but are available on an as-needed basis. As a result, most hotels have a small core of high-seniority workers who are guaranteed forty hours of work each week, with fixed schedules and specific days off. The remainder of the workforce—and most often the majority—has unpredictable hours and schedules that change from week to week, with no set days off. Some of these employees work regularly—albeit part-time and without guarantee—while others are truly contingent. Predictably, with this kind of lean scheduling, hotels regularly do not have enough employees when business surges. The solution for many hotels is overtime work; although working overtime is usually optional, in at least two of the hotels that we profiled it was mandatory. Housekeepers at one hotel often complained about forced overtime, telling the supervisor, "I'm so tired, I just can't clean another room." These complaints have been to no avail, however, and overtime remains a de facto requirement of the job.[12]

COMPENSATION

Even as the hospitality industry has experienced rapid expansion and considerable success, especially in the late 1990s, the bulk of frontline hotel jobs continue to garner very low wages. For example, housekeepers nationally earned a median wage of $7.09 an hour in 2000; the median for food preparation workers was $7.91, and the median for dishwashers was $7.45 (U.S. Department of Labor 2002a).[13] Such low pay levels are the result of several decades of stagnation and growing inequality in the industry's wage struc-

Table 2.2 The Changing Wage Structure of the
          Hotel Industry in U.S. Metropolitan Areas,
          1979 to 2000

	1979	1983	1989	1995	2000
Median hotel hourly wage	$8.56	$7.79	$8.34	$7.91	$9.20
90/10 ratio	2.37	2.61	3.06	3.45	3.29
College/high school ratio	1.39	1.24	1.35	1.56	1.88
Private-sector median wage	$13.04	$12.11	$12.41	$11.58	$12.50

Source: Authors' analysis of CPS-ORG files.
Note: All hourly wages in 2000 dollars.

ture, as shown in table 2.2. Even in metropolitan areas, median
hourly wages in the hotel industry are still in the single digits and
remain well below the private-sector medians.

Our eight case-study hotels are no exception. As shown in table
2.3, housekeepers and entry-level food and beverage workers earn
between $6 and $10 an hour. Wages for cooks, the second rung in
the kitchen hierarchy, are higher, ranging between $8 and $12 an
hour, but even these earnings are low in an industry where yearly
raises are not at all guaranteed and in cities where $15 per hour
barely approaches the median income.[14]

Like Jeffrey Waddoups (2001), we find that between low wages
and lack of guaranteed work hours, a large number of entry-level
hotel workers have to hold two jobs—often doing the same job in
another hotel—in order to make ends meet. The manager of one
hotel kitchen estimated that at least 60 percent of his staff worked
at two jobs, and at every hotel workers and managers alike reported
that "almost everyone" had to work multiple jobs. One kitchen
worker recounted his complicated work history of balancing multiple hotel and fast-food jobs (working sixteen-hour days, making $5
an hour, and having to share an apartment with several people)
since moving to the United States. Only after ten years, getting at
most a $0.25 raise each year, was he able to live alone with his wife
and work one job. Many hotel managers we interviewed—particularly line supervisors, who work closely with entry-level workers—recognized that the wages for many hotel workers were too
low and caused a myriad of problems for both hotels and their
workers. "All of our wages are too low basically," said the director
of human resources at one hotel we visited.

Table 2.3 Typical Hotel Job Hierarchy, 2000

	Housekeeping-Rooms	Food and Beverage	Front Desk
Entry-level I	• Housekeepers • Housemen $6 to $9 per hr. 93 to 96% of rooms division	• Dishwashers and bussers • Cook's helpers $6 to $10 per hr. 40 to 50% of food division	• Phones • Valet and bell desk $7 to $10 per hr. 30 to 50% of front desk
Entry-level II		• Cooks • Servers, bartenders, hosts $9 to $13 per hr. 30 to 40% of food division	• Front-desk clerks • Accounting clerks $9 to $15 per hr. 30 to 50% of front desk
Frontline supervisors and mid-level managers	• Inspectresses • Trainer • Assistant managers $25 to $35k a year 1 to 5% of rooms division	• Sous chefs, lead cooks • Room service manager • Assistant executive chef $35 to $45k 1 to 5% of food division	• Line managers • Assistant director of hotel operations $25 to $45k a year 1 to 5% of front desk
"Craft" occupations		• Banquet catering servers • High-end restaurant servers and bartenders • Cocktail waitresses $25k to $70k 20% of food division	

Table 2.3 *Continued*

	Housekeeping-Rooms	Food and Beverage	Front Desk
Senior managers	• Director of housekeeping	• Director of food and beverage • Executive chef • Restaurant managers	• Director of hotel operations
	$$$	$$$	$$$
	1 to 3% of rooms division	1 to 3% of food division	1 to 3% of front desk

Source: Authors' analysis of eight case-study hotels.
Note: Dollar amounts are entry-level wages or salaries, and vary depending on the local cost of living and whether they are negotiated by a union contract. $$$: Precise figures for senior managers are unavailable, but salaries are generally high.

It is important to reiterate that our case-study hotels were drawn from the upper segment of the industry. They are not, in the main, struggling to make profits, and so the very low wages of their housekeeping and F&B workers are striking. In fact, these two departments are the primary generators of revenue (in the sense that it is the rooms and the food and beverages that the guests pay for). In the hotels that we studied, the profit margins in housekeeping were extremely high, ranging between 70 and 80 percent. The profit margins in food and beverage varied a bit more, ranging between 20 and 45 percent. Although both of these departments subsidize the rest of the hotel operation (for example, sales and administration), overall profit margins still tend to net between 25 and 40 percent. Yet entry-level wages in these hotels are about the same as those paid by budget highway hotels (which have tiny profit margins).

What, then, is driving the low wages, and why have they stagnated over time? We examine this question in detail later when we examine the impact of unions, but in general increasing pressure from corporate holding companies to boost profits is undoubtedly playing an important role. In our case studies, managers in both the housekeeping and F&B departments repeatedly talked about the intense pressure to stay within shrinking budgets, even as they recognized that their entry-level wages were below market rates for the type of work required and that this was a leading cause of their labor shortage. As one hotel executive noted: "Anytime you're a publicly held company, there is always a quarter-to-quarter comparison." Another hotel executive observed: "Under private owners, in the eighties, numbers weren't even an issue. Now we wouldn't even dare *not* making our numbers. Now it's paramount." This mounting pressure has clearly affected the hotels' organization of work, including increasing wages for long-term gain; according to at least one hotel executive we interviewed, this pressure "hampers our ability to have a long-term strategy."

Since very little fat remains to be cut in-house, the growing trend is to subcontract functions and extract savings from the contracting companies. Industry analysts argue that subcontracting should be done for reasons of efficiency, but most of our respondents saw the strategy as simply a cost-saving device. Contracting companies almost always have low labor costs, in part because they tend to be non-unionized and in part because they invest in better technologies. In the case of big corporate chains, subcontracting often takes the form of one hotel performing a function for all the other hotels, thus gaining economies of scale. One hotel, for example, will make over eight hundred gallons of sauce for each of its local sister hotels, saving labor and equipment costs for the corporation as a whole as well as for each of the other hotels.

How has subcontracting affected workers? Although our evidence is purely secondhand (we were not able to gain access to the contracting companies), the story seems pretty clear. Subcontracting shifts jobs outside the hotel to contracting companies, which—according to both managers and workers—pay less, sometimes significantly less, for the same work. For example, when one of our hotels began to subcontract nighttime cleaning, the displaced workers refused to work for the contractor because the jobs paid much less; some of these employees moved to other nighttime jobs at the hotel, and others simply lost their jobs. In another hotel, door attendants filed a grievance because they believed that the subcontracted valet workers were "taking over" the door attendants' jobs and they were losing hours of work.

TRAINING

For the most part, hotel kitchens and restaurants have no formal training systems. Workers learn on the job by teaming up with experienced workers and gradually taking on more responsibilities.

Thus, while the kitchen cross-training strategy described above is often exploitative in nature, it can also benefit workers, since it is effectively the only chance for entry-level workers to learn a new skill that could lead to a promotion. Training for housekeepers, on the other hand, is more formalized, though it varies in length (one to three weeks) and content (the degree to which speed and efficiency are stressed over safety). However, even though managers tended to describe housekeeping training as a well-structured, gradual training program, workers often recounted cursory "sink or swim" initiation.[15]

Beyond new-worker training, we found that hotel employers provide little advanced training that would enable frontline workers to bid for managerial positions, and that even where such training existed in the past it is increasingly being trimmed or cut altogether. Such training includes not only new-worker training but English as a second language (ESL) classes, injury prevention classes, and management training. One hotel, for example, had offered safety training twice a year and ESL classes on a regular basis. All training programs at this hotel have recently been eliminated altogether, however, because of "budgetary constraints." Several managers were quite frank in admitting that these "constraints" were actually mandates handed down by corporate headquarters. (This hotel had recently been acquired by one of the mega-chains.)

INJURIES

In 2000, according to official statistics, 6.9 of every 100 employees in the hotel industry suffered an on-the-job injury—well above the 4.9 rate for service industries, higher than the 4.7 rate for mining, and not far away from the 7.8 rate for manufacturing (U.S. Department of Labor 2001). Although the data show declining injury rates over the 1990s, our fieldwork clearly suggests a tie between injuries and lean staffing practices. Injuries are concentrated among housekeepers—not a surprising finding given that their daily tasks include repetitive motions and heavy lifting, often in awkward positions, day after day. With the pressure from rising room quotas, safety regulations, by all accounts, are routinely ignored. For example, many workers reported that they did not follow safety-bending rules when changing beds because of the time squeeze. There was also a clear (and alarming) preference among housekeepers for the more toxic cleaning agents of the old days, since these were more powerful and the new, weaker cleaning fluids required more cleaning time.

Although injuries figured routinely in our worker interviews, the majority of our case-study hotels did not actively address the issue—some did not even recognize the problem—except to try out incentive programs to reduce the reporting (rather than the occurrence) of injuries.[16]

CAREER LADDERS

In theory, the dismal working conditions and wages described so far could be tempered by a strong system of internal promotion, so that entry-level workers quickly move out of these bad jobs into good ones. But upward mobility in the hotel industry has always been, and remains today, severely circumscribed. As the regional vice president of human resources at a large hotel corporation observed: "This industry doesn't focus on mobility. We've done a really poor job of recognizing talent and building our own." Figure 2.1 shows the typical mobility paths of entry-level workers. As the flow of arrows makes clear, the only viable route to higher-level jobs from the bottom is through the front-desk division, commonly called the "launching pad." Workers gain experience as front-desk clerks, usually for a year or two, and then begin their move up the managerial ladder, often moving into management positions in different departments and even at other hotels.

For workers who enter in the housekeeping or F&B departments, however, mobility opportunities are quite slim. Housekeepers effectively have only one option—becoming a line supervisor. A large number of workers, however, are usually vying for a very small number of supervisory slots. Furthermore, housekeeping supervisors almost never move up higher in the managerial hierarchy, nor do they move laterally into other positions in the hotel. Likewise, upward mobility for kitchen workers is limited. Dishwashers, cook's helpers, and bussers often move up to become low-level cooks and, on occasion, higher-level cooks, servers, or bartenders; almost never do they move any further up. Managerial positions and the high-wage craft occupations in F&B (banquet servers, sous-chefs, executive chefs) are usually filled from the outside.[17]

Underlying this static job and mobility structure has been a

Figure 2.1 Typical Mobility Paths in Eight Case-Study Hotels

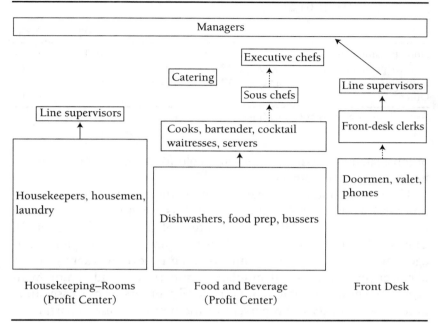

Source: Authors' configuration.

marked shift toward hiring immigrant workers to occupy the bottom of that structure (see table 2.4). African Americans were once the largest minority group in the industry, dominating "back of the house" jobs and housekeeping in particular. Now, in contrast, the vast majority of housekeepers are Hispanic or Asian immigrants—or, increasingly, Eastern Europeans (see Bates 1999; Consortium for Retention and Advancement 2001; Waldinger 1996). Likewise, while kitchen and restaurant departments are generally more diverse than housekeeping departments (because cooks still tend to be white), entry-level workers are now almost exclusively Hispanic and Asian immigrants. In contrast, the gender mix of entry-level hotel workers has changed much more slowly. Housekeepers continue to be exclusively female, and while women have recently made inroads into the traditionally male-dominated kitchen and restaurant jobs, they remain a distinct minority and tend to occupy a narrow range

Table 2.4   Racial and Ethnic Composition of the Hotel Industry in U.S. Metropolitan Areas, 1979 to 2000

	1979	1983	1989	1995	2000
Non-Hispanic white	70.0%	61.1%	56.1%	51.9%	47.5%
Non-Hispanic black	20.0	18.5	17.2	17.9	16.8
Hispanic	12.1	13.7	20.4	23.1	25.2
Other	5.9	6.7	6.2	7.1	10.4

Source: Authors' analysis of CPS-ORG files.

of jobs, such as making pastries and cold foods, rather than work as hot line cooks or sous-chefs.

The critical question remains: Why is there so little upward mobility in this industry? A number of factors are at work. Perhaps the biggest barrier to mobility is the nature of the job structure itself. The two biggest departments—housekeeping and food and beverage—are made up of large numbers of entry-level workers who are overseen by a very small number of supervisors and senior managers. As shown in table 2.3, entry-level workers in our case-study hotels are a full 93 to 96 percent of the housekeeping department's staff. Food and beverage departments are not quite as heavily weighted toward the bottom but are also quite flat. In both divisions, frontline supervisors are only 1 to 5 percent of the staff, and senior managers only 1 to 3 percent. As a result, an impossibly disproportionate number of workers are vying for very few promotion opportunities. Moreover, while the job structure in the hotel industry has always been flat, in recent years there has been a trend toward eliminating many supervisory positions. For example, in seven of our eight hotels, the position of inspectress—a supervisory position—had been eliminated, and in most cases the work was simply distributed among the remaining workers.

In our interviews, however, hotel managers repeatedly cited lack of skills—in particular, lack of English-language fluency—as the primary reason housekeepers and kitchen workers were stuck in their jobs. English was in fact the second language for the vast majority of the housekeepers and F&B workers we interviewed, but there was a considerable range of fluency; for many of them the language barrier simply was not as dire a problem as managers depicted it.[18] During the labor crunch of the late 1990s, some hotels began to experiment with ESL classes, but judging from our case studies, these classes have generally had little success. They are rarely offered during work hours and often scheduled only intermittently, allowing little real opportunity to advance. For a workforce trying to hold down two jobs and raise a family, the result is low participation rates. Moreover, all but two of our hotels had eliminated their ESL classes in the past year, owing to the slowdown in the hospitality industry.

Besides language skills, managers cited the lack of "people skills" and managerial ability as other barriers to advancement. In this area, it was quite difficult to get specific explanations: "Some people just have managerial potential, others don't." "Some managers are trained, but they still don't get it." "Managing takes special skills and common sense." As a result, the hiring and promotion process for supervisory positions can be vague and has very few "hard" requirements—college degrees are still not generally required in this industry (except at the highest level of hotel manager). This leaves a lot of room for "gut instinct" that someone has "that special it."[19] Housekeepers and kitchen workers in our focus groups argued strongly that they do in fact, have good customer service and "people skills"—that they go out of their way to help guests, as a matter of pride—but managers across the board did not consider entry-level hotel workers to have these necessary, yet nebulous, skills. It is not surprising, then, that the majority of our case-study hotels have never offered formal or consistent managerial training to their frontline workers.[20]

This discrepancy between management's view of frontline workers' skills and workers' own perceptions raises the question of discrimination. In our interviews we found clear evidence that discrimination continues to pervade the hiring and promotion practices of hotels, on two fronts.[21] First, hotel managers widely expressed a preference for hiring immigrants for "back of the house" jobs.[22] In fact, there appears to be a ranking of color and ethnicity, with Asians first in line ("they're quiet and do the work"), Hispanics next (Mexicans especially), and African Americans last.[23] Second, with immigrant workers providing such a ready (and often captive) labor supply for the worst jobs, there is little incentive for managers to view them as promotion material. For example, one hotel manager explained that dishwashers have "a more labor, blue-collar mindset" when asked why at least one dishwasher at that hotel had been in the same position for thirty years. A director of hotel operations was more explicit: "In part, it's what we pigeonhole them into."

Workers themselves were much more voluble on this point. One housekeeper did indeed feel pigeonholed: "[Management] considers us dumb dodos and dirty because of the kind of work we do." Another recounted that when she tried to bid for a server job, the restaurant manager repeatedly rebuffed her, saying: "Maids, never. I don't want any maids." Sometimes the unfortunate result is a self-fulfilling prophecy: because upward mobility rarely happens and because there are no formal mechanisms to pursue it, entry-level workers eventually stop bidding for better jobs—or even conceiving of getting them.

THE ROLE OF UNIONS AND UNION DENSITY

Thus far we have described recent changes in the hotel industry and the direct effects on low-wage workers' jobs. Since our research indicates that many of these effects are negative, the next critical question becomes: Are there factors that could make these industry trends more palatable for low-wage workers? Given the historic strength and relevance of unions in this service industry, we can also ask a more precise question: Do unions and/or union density mitigate the effect of these changes on workers?

Recent evidence suggests that, in some cases, unions have been able to negotiate not only higher wages but also deeper involvement in the firm's long-term decisions so that workers can contribute to the reorganization of the workplace in ways that benefit job stability and mobility opportunity as well as productivity (Black and Lynch 1997). Adrienne Eaton and Paula Voos (1992) argue that unions bring protections for workers and an organized collective voice to the workplace, both of which are necessary to ensure the success of the experimental programs (resulting from genuine worker participation and increased firm productivity). Dorothy Sue Cobble (1991) emphasizes the positive impact that unions have on women workers in terms of wage increases, decreases in gender and racial inequality, and other benefits such as job security and a greater voice in workplace decisions.

At the same time the pervasive image of intractable unions that resist change at every step has a not insignificant number of examples to back it up. In fact, research indicates that the simple presence of a union does not automatically guarantee higher wages or worker-friendly restructuring. One important mediating factor is the degree of unionization in the sector and in the region.

In their seminal examination of the impact of labor union density, Richard Freeman and James Medoff (1981, 561) documented that unions do in fact have a positive impact on union wages and even non-union wages, depending on the density of the relevant product market. H. Gregg Lewis (1983) also argued that the relative wage of each worker depends not only on his union status, sex, color, schooling, experience, and like variables but also on the extent of unionism in the workforce as a whole and the distribution of workers by union status among industrial sectors. In those cases where a correlation between union density and non-union wages is empirically observed, scholars do not agree on the direction of causality. On the one hand, the "threat effect" hypothesis posits that in high-density markets non-union firms will raise wages in order to prevent unionization efforts. On the other hand, the "crowding effect" hypothesis holds that an increase in the extent of unionization will restrict the demand for labor in the union sector and thus provide an excess supply of labor in the non-union sector, thus depressing wages in the non-union sector (see Moore, Newman, and Cunningham 1985; Curme and Macpherson 1991; Neumark and Wachter 1995; Waddoups 1999; Hirsch and Neufeld 1987). Still, there is no question that density is critical. In particular, unions may be able to leverage the power gained through density into projects that allow greater worker voice about reorganization and its impact on job quality. A lone union fighting for survival is unlikely to carry that kind of leverage.

The hotel industry offers a perfect setting for examining these issues. As shown in figure 2.2, national hotel union membership and coverage are currently just under 12 percent. Mirroring the national decline in unionization, coverage in the hotel industry has fallen substantially over the last two decades. Even with this decline, however, unionization in hotels currently exceeds the national private-sector rate of less than 10 percent. Metropolitan areas in particular have relatively high unionization rates: in 2000 metro-area hotel union membership was 13.8 percent (see first row of table 2.5), and in a number of large business and tourist destina-

Figure 2.2 Unionization Rates in the Hospitality Industry, 1983 to 2000

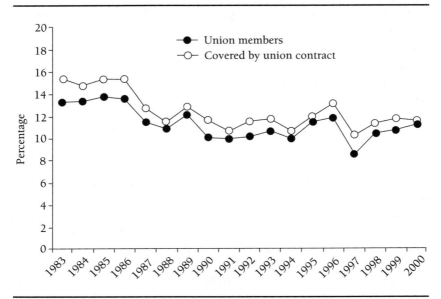

Source: Based on data from Hirsch and Macpherson (2001).

tions unionization rates can exceed 50 percent. Yet in other comparable cities, only a small handful of hotels are organized. As described at the outset, we explicitly captured this variation in our research design, studying both union and non-union hotels, in both high- and low-density cities.[24]

The question, then, is whether unions have been able to mediate the form that hotel restructuring has taken, under which conditions, and along which dimensions. As summarized in table 2.6, we focus on the following key aspects of industry restructuring: wages, work intensity, hours and scheduling, subcontracting, and career ladders. We examine each in turn and analyze the role that unions have played in negotiating the issue in the context of high and low union density, as well as union and non-union hotels. Taken altogether, we find that unions have been able to make significant progress on some fronts but not others, and that most often their success is a function of hotel union density in the region.

Table 2.5   Unions and Wages in the Hotel Industry in U.S. Metropolitan Areas, 1983 to 2000

	1983	1989	1995	2000
Union members	14.5%	15.0%	14.8%	13.8%
All workers				
Union median hourly wage	$8.87	$9.73	$9.04	$10.50
Non-union median hourly wage	$7.79	$7.65	$7.91	$9.00
Union/non-union wage ratio	1.14	1.27	1.14	1.17
Nonmanagerial workers only				
Union median hourly wage	$8.82	$9.73	$9.04	$10.37
Non-union median hourly wage	$7.09	$7.30	$7.35	$8.00
Union/non-union wage ratio	1.24	1.33	1.23	1.30

Source: Authors' analysis of CPS-ORG files.
Note: All wages in 2000 dollars.

WAGES

First and foremost, unions matter in this industry because they influence wages.[25] In 2000 overall unionized hotel workers in metropolitan areas earned 17 percent more per hour than non-unionized workers (see table 2.5). If we narrow the scope to frontline workers (the focus of our study), the union wage effect grows even larger, to 30 percent. It is a testament to the continuing strength of the Hotel Employees and Restaurant Employees International Union (HERE) and other unions in the industry that these differentials have not declined precipitously over the past several decades, as has occurred in other industries. It is also noteworthy that the union wage effect is strongest for the lowest-paid occupations. Janitors and food preparers stand to gain the most from representation, with a national union wage premium of 39.5 percent and 36.0 percent in 2000, respectively. For bartenders and baggage porters, who earn significantly more, the premium was 19.1 percent and 19.4 percent, respectively (Hirsch and Macpherson 2001).

Among our case-study hotels, union wages were higher than non-union wages, but just slightly so. (The premium within any one city ranged from $0.25 per hour to $1.70.) Far more important was union density. As a vice president of hotel operations for a major hotel observed: "In a union town, you pay if you're non-union. In a non-union town, you pay if you're union." The highest-

Table 2.6 The Effect of Unions on Firm Restructuring in Eight Case-Study Hotels

Dimension of Restructuring	Union Effect?	Degree of Effect	Relevant Conditions
Wages	Yes	Within markets, union wages are higher by $0.25 to $1.70 per hour.	Union density matters more than union presence—high-density wages are $3 higher than low-density wages.
Work intensity	Some	Work intensity is at the forefront of labor-management relations. Some union hotels have lower workloads (as measured by room quotas). Some hotels make sure that workers get paid for the added work (in the case of cross-training).	Strongest effects are seen in high-density cities, but they are not always apparent even there.
Hours and scheduling	Some	Hours and scheduling are at the forefront of labor-management relations. Successful protection of full-time jobs is seen in some cities.	Strongest effects are seen in high-density cities. Union attention to and prioritization of this area is critical.
Subcontracting	Some, but weak	In some cities subcontracting of restaurants has been resisted and/or effects on workers have been mitigated through negotiations. Most other forms of outsourcing are unchallenged.	Strongest effects are seen in high-density cities, especially where unions are making this a priority.
Career ladders	Little	Not relevant.	Only in germination stage where density is high.

Source: Authors' compilation.

paying hotels in our study, whether unionized or not, were located in high-density cities. In these hotels, housekeepers started at well over $10 per hour (and in one city both union and non-union hotels pay over $13). By contrast, the worst-paying hotels in our study were located in a low-density city, where housekeeping wages started between $6 and $7 per hour, regardless of whether the hotel was unionized or not.[26] Waddoups (1999) documents this density effect for Las Vegas, finding that non-union workers there earn wages approximately 19 percent higher than those of their non-union counterparts in other cities, other things being equal. Our case-study finding on the important wage effect of union density also echoes more representative studies across industries (Belman and Voos 1993; Neumark and Wachter 1995).

That unions matter for wages may seem a mundane point. But in this low-wage, heavily immigrant service industry, it is clear that many workers still see this as the principal role and benefit of the union. Union leaders themselves consistently pointed to higher wages as their key contribution to the workforce, and wages were consistently cited as a top priority in future contract negotiations. In fact, one union leader pointed out that the importance of wage demands in bargaining is increased by the diversity of hotel union membership: only the housekeepers (generally one-half or less of total union membership) care about room quotas, while only food and beverage workers care about restaurant subcontracting, but all workers can rally around wage increases. As a result, for both unions and their members, higher wages remain the central benefit and priority of the union.[27]

WORK INTENSITY

Since restructuring has often resulted in increased workloads for many frontline hotel workers, the issue has become a critical focal point for both unions and their workers. For example, housekeepers have witnessed a bewildering increase in amenities in recent years, from in-room coffee pots to ever more elaborate bedding and pillow schemes. We found that workers in union hotels had a much higher sense of awareness about increasing workloads and their rights in this process. For example, most union workers we interviewed could automatically recite the contract rules on workload and re-member precisely when certain amenities were added and how conflicts over their addition were resolved. This sense of history and awareness was clearly less present at non-union hotels.

In the end, however, the extent to which unions and/or union density have been able to stop the speedup of work is not clear. For example, all of the hotels we studied required that each housekeeper clean between fourteen and seventeen rooms per day. Still, three rooms a day can make a big difference, and it is no coincidence that the lower quota (fourteen rooms) was posted by a union hotel in a high-density city, and the higher quota (seventeen rooms) by a non-union hotel in a low-density city. But all the other hotels in our study required sixteen rooms per day. Similarly, the main work intensity issue in kitchens is cross-training, and unions have generally not been able to staunch the inroads of this practice. However, they have been able to ensure that workers are compensated fairly when assigned to another job (that is, get paid a higher rate when working a higher-level job), and that is often not the case in non-union hotel kitchens. For example, a worker classified as a basic cook at a non-union hotel expressed intense frustration that he is often required to do the same work as an advanced cook but is paid $4 less an hour.

Unions, then, have had the most success in bringing issues of workload to the forefront of labor-management relations, ensuring that speedup is at least negotiated and duly compensated. In a few cases (all in high-density cities), unions have successfully forestalled attempts to increase workload altogether. There are also signs that this issue will gain priority in the future: several hotel unions we interviewed have begun to conduct their own time studies of different housekeeping and food-prep tasks in order to prepare stronger arguments against workload increases.

Hours and Scheduling

For both workers and managers in our hotels, the issues of hours, scheduling, and staffing level are all closely intertwined. A predominant image of the past is that hotels kept staff around even in slack times, assigning busy work and deep-cleaning. But as firms have pushed to cut costs and increase productivity, staffs are kept leaner to begin with, and workers who may have once waited idle during slow times are now sent home without pay. At the same time firms are searching for ways of increasing the efficiency of the staff that remains on-site. It is not surprising, then, that scheduling and hours of work are central concerns of all workers in the industry, and ones in which unions have played a critical role.

In general, the scheduling strategy at union hotels has been to assign work hours, shifts, and stations on the basis of seniority. This traditional structure allows the most senior worker to take all the work she is interested in (up to forty hours), followed by everyone else on down the seniority list until the necessary work for the week is filled. Obviously, this system secures full-time, year-round employment for the most senior workers. By contrast, non-union hotels employ much looser seniority systems for scheduling. Tenure matters in non-union hotels, but managers report that they try to get their "best workers" the shifts they need and appreciate the flexibility and fairness that such a system allows. At these hotels workers do not pay as much attention to the rules of shift, hour, and station assignment, since it is simply an area of management prerogative. Although a number of workers we interviewed found fault with this system, often claiming favoritism, it had never occurred to them that it could be changed. As in the case of increasing workload, union workers' awareness of their right to fight the issue was much more acute.

The union's long history of negotiating over scheduling issues has also aided its fight against another recent trend in the hotel industry: the conversion of full-time jobs into part-time jobs. Recent contracts in cities with high union density have begun to shape the definition of "part-time" and the rules for employment of (as well as the numbers of) part-time workers. One contract, for example, required that everyone working two shifts or more a week would qualify for full-time benefits, to a large degree eliminating the advantages of converting full- into part-time jobs. In another city the union contract contained explicit language about the percentage of the workforce that could be classified as full-time, part-time, and "on call."

While managers in union hotels often extol the virtues of working with a contract (the rules are clear and everyone understands them), they also complain about the inflexibility that the rules bring. Clearly, from the management perspective, inflexibility in work rules, job definitions, and scheduling creates a formidable barrier to implementing desired workplace reorganization. On the other hand, from the workers' perspective, these rules provide protection and limits to their jobs.

SUBCONTRACTING

Even in union hotels, when jobs are outsourced or specific units or tasks subcontracted, the workers who take up the work are generally paid less and not covered by the union contract. As a result, union membership is reduced, as is the quality of employment offered by the hotel. Our research suggests that unions usually have little power to inhibit subcontracting altogether but can sometimes mitigate its negative effects on their members.

The hardest trend to fight has been the outsourcing of labor-intensive kitchen tasks—baking, cleaning and chopping produce, making stocks and sauces. The purchasing of prepared foods has become such a ubiquitous and fundamental business strategy in the industry that it has been almost impossible for unions to stop it. Because the outsourcing is usually done piecemeal, the union would have to fight over just one or two jobs at a time, and in the end the economics of using food prepared elsewhere is simply too compelling. However, when the number of jobs involved has been larger and the economic advantages less clear—for example, subcontracting an entire laundry unit—unions have achieved somewhat more success by focusing their efforts on slowing the process down or limiting it.

For example, unions in high-density cities have largely been able to resist the otherwise prevalent trend of subcontracting hotel restaurants.[28] And sometimes, even in low-density cities, they have been able to negotiate the terms of the subcontracting. In one such instance, an interesting hybrid emerged: the hotel's restaurant was subcontracted, but the staff remained employees of the hotel and members of the union. In another example, a union hotel wanted to reduce staff and operation hours of its upscale restaurant. Union leadership negotiated a transition process: the number of restaurant staff was decreased over time through attrition and reassignment. Although restructuring was not stopped in these instances, from the perspective of workers this type of "managed change" was a vast improvement over the way subcontracting normally proceeds—most often with the dismissal of large numbers of workers.

CAREER LADDERS

We have painted a bleak picture of the almost total lack of upward mobility for most housekeeping and entry-level food and beverage hotel workers. This picture, unfortunately, is characteristic of both union and non-union hotels; there are simply not many career ladders in this industry, and the mere presence of a union does not create more middle-tier jobs. In fact, union and non-union hotels alike have eliminated supervisory positions in recent years. In this context, it is difficult to secure advancement for workers, especially when bread-and-butter issues such as wages and job security require the union's constant attention.

Nevertheless, some hotel unions in high-density cities are beginning to focus on, and find ways of chipping away at, structural barriers to mobility. In one innovative program, for example, housekeepers are trained and employed as kitchen workers or servers during the winter season when room occupancy is low, thus potentially opening up routes to promotion. While such intelligent training and deployment might seem a perfectly obvious solution to immobility, it is in fact quite rare in the industry and is found only in high-density settings. In the next section, we take a closer look at innovative models that address career ladders and the myriad job quality issues in hospitality, and what it takes to make them successful.

STRATEGIES FOR CHANGE

The growth of the service sector challenges academics, policymakers, and practitioners alike to develop strategies, policies, and institutions that can begin to remake and upgrade the sector's ubiquitous low-wage, labor-intensive, dead-end jobs. Hotels offer insight into this challenge and these jobs because they have undergone familiar restructuring (consolidation, subcontracting, and so forth). Our in-depth case studies and background industry research document that hotels have reorganized their operations over the past two decades in ways that increased workload and work instability in housekeeping and food and beverage jobs while delivering stagnant, and very low, wages to the workers in the jobs. But we focus on hotels also because unions in the sector provide a lens through which to investigate the effects of a critical labor market institution on job quality for low-wage workers. Our research shows that both union presence and union density have important positive effects on frontline hotel workers. Far from being outmoded, unions have become a key part of the solution to improving job quality in the sector.

Given our deliberate selection of high-end, Class A hotels, the generally bad outcomes for workers should come as a bit of a surprise. With the largest size, the most substantial profit margins, and an apparent premium on service quality, these hotels should offer hope for higher job quality. However, wages for frontline jobs in these hotels do not dramatically exceed wages for the same jobs in lower market niches. Contrary perhaps to the "commonsense" equation of high market segment with high job quality, the high end of the hotel industry does not provide a model for high-quality jobs for frontline workers.

Market segment is insufficient to secure high job quality, but a combination of market segment and union representation can secure better outcomes for workers. The union payoff comes in the form of high wages for union workers, and higher wages for all hotel workers in high-union-density cities. The union payoff also comes in terms of worker awareness of and resistance to negative restructuring, especially when that restructuring increases workload or job instability in a hotel. Simply put, union hotel workers are, in general, better paid and better informed.

Moreover, not only are local unions in the sector paying attention to the basic concerns of wages and workloads, but increasingly they are embracing their immigrant workers and pursuing contract-based and public policy strategies that deal directly with immigrants' issues and rights. Nationally, HERE and many other unions have taken a strong pro-amnesty stand. And in one city the contract explicitly allowed workers time off to deal with the Immigration and Naturalization Service (INS). These strategies signal a substantial departure from labor's more protectionist history on immigration and prove that at least some unions are ready to represent their increasingly diverse ranks.[29]

Unions can make a positive difference for workers in the hotel industry, but their true strength is density. In our research, the power of density was clear: in high-density cities wages were higher (for union and non-union workers alike), work intensity was lower, contract provisions on workload were more constraining, and innovative bargaining was much more prevalent.

In some unique but inspiring cases, the hospitality industry has generated some of the most innovative solutions to "bad jobs" found in the country today. In addition to our case studies, we examined three projects in which unions and hotel management have joined forces to address critical problems facing both the industry and its workers. While none of these projects would have emerged without the high union density in their region, it is the innovation and leadership, especially from labor unions, that has made them successful. Replication is therefore not simply an issue of building a new training center or bargaining for a lighter workload; it requires a rather unique vision about labor's role in both workforce and economic development, one that is still relatively rare. Nevertheless, the programs we describe here provide promising models for an industry largely characterized by low-wage, dead-end jobs for workers as well as cutthroat competition and increasing financial pressure for hotel managers.

THE CULINARY AND HOSPITALITY
ACADEMY OF LAS VEGAS

The Culinary and Hospitality Academy (CHA) of Las Vegas was established in 1993 by a consortium of local hotel casinos and unions to provide job training for all union members as well as classes in ESL, GED (general equivalency diploma) preparation, and soft skills. Additionally, the academy works closely with the industry's hiring hall, so that graduates are first in line for new job openings at the hotels. Since the CHA's inception, more than sixteen thousand workers have graduated from the academy, and over 70 percent have been placed in jobs. Union hotels report that turnover is 50 percent lower among academy graduates as compared to off-the-street hires. Both the placement and retention statistics, as well as the sheer scale of the program, easily surpass other programs in the region.

The CHA is funded almost entirely by contributions from employers, who are getting a good deal. The training is highly tailored to the industry (an employer board gives advice on curriculum), and the cost is significantly cheaper than at the local community college ($780 versus $6,000 per graduate). The system works so well that at this point employers effectively treat the training center as their main source of entry-level workers—even non-union hotels want to hire academy trainees. The CHA has been able to secure this central role because it solves two critical problems facing the hotel and gaming industry, which is the primary employer in Las Vegas. First, the academy has solved severe recruitment and retention problems by providing a steady stream of workers to union hotels. Second, by successfully training recent immigrants and welfare-leavers, the academy has addressed the growing problems of lack of skills and work experience in the new workforce.

On the worker side, the CHA has become known as the premier source of training and good jobs in the region. The training is free to the workers, everyone qualifies for it, and at the end there's a decent paying job. From the workers' standpoint, it is this last point—the direct feeding of graduate students into the industry's hiring hall—that most distinguishes the academy.

Having gone to scale, the CHA is now focusing on broadening and diversifying its services. The bulk of the academy's training is currently focused on entry-level skills, but ultimately the goal is to provide advanced training in order to open up career ladders that have historically been closed to frontline workers. There is already scattered evidence of increased mobility for CHA graduates (for example, housekeepers who have become assistant managers, cooks who have become executive chefs). The challenge will be to systematize such career ladders and structure them as part of a formal training program.

THE SAN FRANCISCO HOTELS PARTNERSHIP PROJECT

Created in 1994, the San Francisco Hotels Partnership Project is part of a multi-employer contract between eleven first-class hotels and the largest union in the industry. The logic of the partnership is to continue to provide job security and solid compensation to workers while also allowing for increased competitiveness at the member hotels. These goals are achieved through the "living contract," which establishes an unprecedented structure for labor-management collaboration on productivity issues.

At the core of the partnership are problem-solving teams in the hotels that address long-standing workplace issues. These teams are staffed by workers, managers, and neutral facilitators and translators, always with the objective of developing joint solutions with sustained input from all sides. Often there is coordination or information sharing with teams at the other member hotels so that a partnership-wide standard emerges. An early initiative was to implement team-building and communication training at all levels of the hotels; this was critical to any future progress, given the history of hostile labor-management relations. Other initiatives include classes in vocational ESL and basic skills, alternative grievance resolution, and a welfare-to-work training center for housekeepers. Another project trained more than 200 entry-level workers to be higher-paid banquet servers, allowing the banquet hiring hall to have the best-ever performance in filling job orders for the holiday season. Funded with more than $1 million in state funds and an additional $500,000 from employers, these programs have offered more than 223,800 hours of training to more than 1,500 labor and management participants.

Finally, and perhaps most important from the perspective of our study, problem-solving teams at several hotels have focused on issues of work content and cross-training in the context of organizational restructuring. In one pilot project the entire kitchen area was restructured: twenty-seven kitchen job categories were collapsed into three, and two job titles were eliminated altogether. This reorganization spoke directly to one of the main concerns of the employers: that rigid job titles hindered flexibility in how workers were deployed, therefore putting unionized hotels at a competitive disadvantage with non-unionized ones. The union and its workers were involved in every part of the reorganization; wages were raised and seniority rules were renegotiated in the process. While such joint projects are not yet the norm, the direct and sustained participation of workers in decisionmaking is the hallmark of the partnership model in fully realized form.

THE HERE FOUR-CITY HOSPITALITY CAREER LADDERS PROJECT

In what is the youngest and most ambitious initiative in the industry, the San Francisco Hotels Partnership Project has recently started to work with employers, unions, and community colleges in San Diego, San Jose, and Los Angeles on a long-term program to solve the problem of upward mobility in the industry. This project is still in the planning stage. The ultimate goal is to create formal career ladders for entry-level workers, both within and across job categories, at the same time meeting the growing need for skilled workers in California's hotel industry (which is predicted to grow twice as fast as the overall economy in the next decade).

On the "demand side," labor-management teams in each hotel will work on redesigning jobs and promotion policies to eliminate existing structural barriers to mobility for entry-level hotel workers. On the "supply side," workers in participating hotels will receive paid training in a job category different from their own, complemented with education and career counseling and vocational English as a second language (VESL).[30] The project staff itself serves as a critical intermediary here, by providing hotels with the technical assistance to implement the workplace reorganization, facilitating the sharing of information among the twenty-nine participating hotels, and facilitating the complex process of working with local community colleges on training programs. As with the two foregoing programs, the project is supported by a combination of employer contributions and state training funds.

Even though each of these initiatives is at a different stage of development, they share several key characteristics. Management and labor are both at the table, industrywide problems are attacked jointly, and intermediary staff provide technical assistance and coordinate with outside funders and training institutions. The solutions that are developed also have a consistent structure: boosting productivity and competitiveness while at the same time guaranteeing good, secure jobs to workers. Although this model has most often been pursued in manufacturing, its use in the hotel industry shows that "win-win" or "mutual gains" solutions are possible in the service sector.

The trick, of course, is figuring out how to spread the model. Almost every industry faces problems in the organization of work and production that are best solved by collaborative structures that deliver collective answers. And low-wage workers and their representatives everywhere have a clear interest in stemming and reversing the loss of wage standards and career ladders. In other words, the incentives are there; translating them into action is the hard part. There are a number of new efforts across the country to systematize and disseminate the "high road" sectoral partnership model (by groups such as the Working for America Institute and the National Network of Sectoral Practitioners). These efforts must be continued and expanded, because while public policy supports at the national and local level are important, ultimately the struggle to rebuild the American employment relationship will be won or lost in the workplace itself.

The authors would like to thank the Rockefeller and Russell Sage Foundations for their generous support of this project. Our collaborators, Deborah Moy and Helen Moss, contributed an enormous amount of insight and direction at every stage of the research. For their invaluable comments, the authors would also like to thank Eileen Appelbaum, Rose Batt, Thomas Kochan, Eric Parker, Jeff Rickert, Joel Rogers, Jeffrey Waddoups, Howard Wial, and Erik Olin Wright, as well as the numerous participants in our case study research.

NOTES

1. On the impact of changes in labor market institutions, see Card and Krueger (1995) and Dinardo, Fortin, and Lemieux (1996). On skill-biased technological change, see Bound and Johnson (1992), Autor, Katz, and Krueger (1997), and Mishel, Bernstein, and Schmitt (1997). For reviews of the evidence on globalization, see Freeman (1995).

2. This research was quite intensive, covering hotel trade magazines, industry journals, industry analyst reports and surveys, newspaper articles, and Bureau of Labor Statistics (BLS) data and resulting in an eighty-page summary drawing on roughly four hundred articles, organized by topic. A sampling of sources includes *Lodging Hospitality, Hotel and Motel Management, Cornell Hotel and Restaurant Administration Quarterly,* and the websites of the American Hotel & Lodging Association (*www.ahma.com*), Hospitality Net (*www.hospitalitynet.org*), and Smith Travel Research (*www.str-online.com/info*).

3. We do not here present detailed data on the four cities in order to protect the identities of the case-study hotels. We did, however, conduct extensive regional research, which we used both in choosing the four cities and in analyzing our findings. This research included seventeen background interviews with local industry informants, as well as official data on trends in hotel employment, unionization rates, and wages and the labor force over time.

4. Note that with two hotels in each cell, some amount of validation is possible.

5. Three of the hotels were visited after September 11, 2001, a time when the industry was in deep crisis, and our fieldwork at these three hotels was significantly shorter.
6. This section draws largely on our background industry research.
7. The industry uses the terms "subcontracting" and "outsourcing" interchangeably, and the language of "core competencies" runs rampant.
8. That said, we should note a renaissance of sorts in hotel dining, especially in the themed restaurants with famous chefs at the upper end of the market. It is an open question whether this trend will spread beyond the small five-star segment.
9. This and the remaining sections draw largely on our case-study materials.
10. Workloads have increased in other parts of the housekeeping department as well. Houseman positions, for example, have been cut down or eliminated altogether at many hotels. This results in increased workloads for the remaining housekeeping employees.
11. One housekeeper recalled that when she started working nineteen years ago, the room quota was eight; now it is seventeen, the highest rate in her city.
12. On the other hand, several of our hotels strictly monitor overtime and try to avoid it because their state laws have stronger hours protections that mandate overtime pay either for working more than eight hours a day or for the sixth consecutive day of work.
13. In contrast, the 1999 median annual salary for general managers at luxury properties was $112,162. Other 1999 annual median salaries and wages (across all segments and property sizes) include: $52,409 for human resources directors; $30,000 for both front-office managers and room managers; $27,716 for executive housekeepers; $57,000 for F&B directors; and $35,133 for restaurant managers (Frabotta 2000).
14. Also shown in table 2.3 are the wages for supervisors and managers and for the front-desk division. We return to these positions in the next section but here simply note that most of them are out of reach for housekeeping and kitchen workers.
15. The severe labor shortage prevailing in the industry during the first part of 2000 may have something to do with the perception of housekeeper training as "sink or swim."
16. Furthermore, evidence suggests that the industry as a whole is strongly opposed to increasing Occupational Safety and Health Administration (OSHA) standards. The president and CEO of one large hotel chain notes (Higley 2000): "OSHA has lost what little sense it had left. The ergonomics issue is so alarming. It's incumbent upon

anybody that has a vested interest in this industry to fight this issue."

17. For example, in one housekeeping department we visited, only one manager had been hired from within. All of the other managers were hired from the outside.

18. One hotel maintained a chart of each housekeeper's English ability. At the time of our visit, according to the chart, all these workers knew at least rudimentary English, and many were at higher levels of fluency.

19. One manager wryly admitted that his instinct fails about half the time.

20. One hotel we visited, however, was in the process of developing a "Hotel University," which will provide management training for anyone who wants to move up into a supervisory job. This managerial training will be mandatory; before anyone is promoted to supervisor, they will have to graduate from the "university." Once they graduate, however, they can be a manager in any department.

21. Here we focus on discrimination based on race and ethnicity. But gender discrimination is alive and well. As one director of hotel operations said about housekeeping: "Men can't handle the job, they don't have the temperament. Women have stronger constitutions; they handle pain better." See also Bates (1999) and Moss and Tilly (1995, 2000). For a more in-depth examination of the ongoing segregation and discrimination based on both race-ethnicity and sex in the hotel industry, see Cobble and Merrill (1994).

22. A 1998 study (Whitford 1998) by the American Hotel Foundation on minorities in the hotel industry found that minorities account for 55.2 percent of line-level jobs but just 38.4 percent of supervisory positions and 21.5 percent of management.

23. Indeed, few whites and African Americans apply for housekeeping and dishwasher positions. But it is not necessarily the case that they avoid these jobs because they lack a work ethic. As an African American executive housekeeper observed: "Many African Americans grew up seeing their mothers and grandmothers doing domestic cleaning in private homes. Now the younger generation thinks they are better than this, that they are better educated and deserve more."

24. In each city, we worked with union leadership to identify geographic boundaries, the numbers of workers, hotels, and rooms in each market segment, and finally, the union/non-union breakdown on each count. We do not here present the exact density estimates (again, to protect the anonymity of the cities and their hotels), but on all measures two of the cities have high hotel union density and two have low hotel union density.

25. In our case studies we did *not* find that health insurance varied in any significant way. Among the hotels we visited, all workers were eligible for health benefits between 90 and 120 days after employment (and the time difference was not attributable to union density or the absence or presence of a union).

26. It is important to note that these wages do not simply line up with cost of living in the respective cities.

27. Furthermore, these higher wages may also indirectly benefit the hotels themselves by reducing turnover rates, which some industry insiders estimate costs hotels $5,000 per employee (see Worcester 1999). As the president of a large hotel corporation observed: "Unions buy long-term commitment. Once they're in, [the employees] generally stick around."

28. Both of our unionized hotels in high-density cities had no subcontracted restaurants.

29. Some have argued that the influx of immigrants has allowed businesses to pursue low-wage strategies in the sector, and they call for restriction of immigration to improve job quality. Realizing that it is unrealistic to stem or reverse global labor flow, hotel unions have set that question aside and instead have taken on immigrants as full members.

30. The emphasis on both lateral and vertical movement is important here. For example, a room cleaner who currently has almost no chance of moving into a supervisory position may move laterally into a kitchen position. With peer coaching, improved language skills, classroom training, and greater confidence, she may then be promoted from pantry to assistant cook to second cook.

REFERENCES

Andorka, Frank H. 1999. "Choice Certifies Housekeeping Operations." *Hotel and Motel Management* 214(8): 21–22.

Autor, David H., Lawrence F. Katz, and Alan B. Krueger. 1997. "Computing Inequality: Have Computers Changed the Labor Market?" Working Paper 5956. Cambridge, Mass.: National Bureau of Economic Research.

Barbee, Cliff, and Valerie Bott. 1991. "Customer Treatment as a Mirror of Employee Treatment." *Advanced Management Journal* 56(spring): 27–32.

Bates, Beth T. 1999. "No More Servants in the House." *Review of Black Political Economy* 26(3): 33–49.

Baumann, M. A. 1997. "Task Force Studies Lodging Sanitation Policies." *Hotel and Motel Management* 212(September 15): 4–5.

Belman, Dale L., and Paula B. Voos. 1993. "Wage Effects of Increased Union Coverage: Methodological Considerations and New Evidence." *Industrial and Labor Relations Review* 46: 368–80.

Bernstein, Laurence. 1999. "Luxury and the Hotel Brand: Art, Science, or Fiction?" *Cornell Hotel and Restaurant Administration Quarterly* 40(1): 47–53.

Black, Sandra, and Lisa Lynch. 1997. "How to Compete: The Impact of Workplace Practices and Information Technology on Productivity." Working Paper 6120. Cambridge, Mass.: National Bureau of Economic Research.

Bound, John, and George Johnson. 1992. "Changes in the Structure of Wages in the 1980s: An Evaluation of Alternative Explanations." *American Economic Review* 82(3): 371–92.

Canina, Linda. 1996. "Initial Public Offerings in the Hospitality Industry: Underpricing and Overperformance." *Cornell Hotel and Restaurant Administration Quarterly* 37(October): 18–25.

Cappelli, Peter. 1993. "Are Skill Requirements Rising?: Evidence from Production and Clerical Jobs." *Industrial and Labor Relations Review* 46(3): 515–31.

Cappelli, Peter, Laurie Bassi, Harry Katz, David Knoke, Paul Osterman, and Michael Useem. 1997. *Change at Work.* New York: Oxford University Press.

Card, David, and Alan Krueger. 1995. *Myth and Measurement.* Princeton, N.J.: Princeton University Press.

Cobble, Dorothy Sue. 1991. "Organizing the Postindustrial Work Force: Lessons from the History of Waitress Unionism." *Industrial and Labor Relations Review* 44(3): 419–36.

Cobble, Dorothy Sue, and Michael Merrill. 1994. "Collective Bargaining in the Hospitality Industry in the 1980s." In *Contemporary Collective Bargaining in the Private Sector,* edited by Paula B. Voos. Madison, Wisc.: Industrial Relations Research Association.

Consortium for Retention and Advancement (CORA). 2001. Executive summary. Seattle, Wash.: CORA.

Cranford, Cynthia. 1998. "Gender and Citizenship in the Restructuring of Janitorial Work in Los Angeles." *Gender Issues* 16(4): 25–51.

Curme, Michael A., and David A. Macpherson. 1991. "Union Wage Differentials and the Effects of Industry and Local Union Density: Evidence from the 1980s." *Journal of Labor Research* 12(2): 419–27.

Dinardo, John, Nicole Fortin, and Thomas Lemieux. 1996. "Labor Market Institutions and the Distribution of Wages, 1973–1992: A Semiparametric Approach." *Econometrica* 64(5): 1001–44.

Eaton, Adrienne E., and Paula B. Voos. 1992. "Unions and Contemporary Innovations in Work, Organization, Compensation, and Employee Participation." In *Unions and Economic Competitiveness,* edited by Lawrence Mishel and Paula B. Voos. Armonk, N.Y.: M. E. Sharpe.

Frabotta, David. 2000. "How Much Are You Worth?" *Hotel and Motel Management* 215(19): 1.

Francis, J. 1998. "After the Merger: Now What?" *Lodging Hospitality* 54(3): 33–34.

Freeman, Richard B. 1995. "Are Your Wages Set in Beijing?" *Journal of Economic Perspectives* 9(3): 15–32.

Freeman, Richard B., and James L. Medoff. 1981. "The Impact of the Percentage Organized on Union and Nonunion Wages." *Review of Economics and Statistics* 63(4): 561–72.

Gillette, Bill. 1995. "Best Western Convention Focuses on Change." *Hotel and Motel Management* 210(October 16): 3.

Higley, Jeff. 2000. "Lodging Industry Storms Capitol Hill for Summit." *Hotel and Motel Management* 215(6): 13.

Hirsch, Barry T., and David A. Macpherson. 2001. *Union Membership and Earnings Data Book: Compilations from the Current Population Survey (2001 Edition).* Washington, D.C.: Bureau of National Affairs, Inc.

Hirsch, Barry T., and John L. Neufeld. 1987. "Nominal and Real Union Wage Differentials and the Effects of Industry and SMSA Density: 1973–1983." *Journal of Human Resources*(winter): 138–48.

Kaestle, Paul. 1990. "A New Rationale for Organizational Structure." *Planning Review* 18(July–August): 20–22.

Lattin, Thomas. 1993. "Factory-Outlet Hotel Wakes Owners to Basic Needs." *Hotel and Motel Management* 208(April 26): 28.

Lewis, H. Gregg. 1983. "Union Relative Wage Effects: A Survey of Macro Estimates." *Journal of Labor Economics* 1(January): 1–27.

Lomanno, Mark V. 1998. "Is Take-out Taking Over?" *Hotel and Motel Management* 213(12): 22.

Marinko, Barbara. 1991. "Mardeck Holds Many Holiday Firsts: Push for 1990s Is Ultimate Customer Service." *Hotel and Motel Management* 206(March 11): 3.

McCann, Jen. 2000. "Privatization Helps Make Deals." *Hotel and Motel Management* 215(16): 79.

McCarthy, Michael J., and Jacqueline Simmons. 1995. "A Late Snack from Room Service?: Don't Count on It." *Wall Street Journal,* February 24.

Mishel, Lawrence, Jared Bernstein, and John Schmitt. 1997. "Did Technology Have Any Effect on the Growth of Wage Inequality in the 1980s and 1990s?" Washington, D.C.: Economic Policy Institute.

Moore, William J., Robert J. Newman, and James Cunningham. 1985. "The Effect of the Extent of Unionism on Union and Nonunion Wages." *Journal of Labor Research* 6(1): 21–44.

Moss, Philip, and Chris Tilly. 1995. "Skills and Race in Hiring: Quantitative Findings from Face-to-Face Interviews." *Eastern Economic Journal* 21(3): 357–74.

———. 2000. "Why Opportunity Isn't Knocking: Racial Inequality and the Demand for Labor." In *Urban Inequality: Evidence from Four Cities.* New York: Russell Sage Foundation.

Neumark, David, and Michael L. Wachter. 1995. "Union Effects on Nonunion Wages: Evidence from Panel Data on Industries and Cities." *Industrial and Labor Relations Review* 49(October): 20–38.

Nozar, Robert A. 1995. "Clarion Re-engineered for Profit." *Hotel and Motel Management* 210(October 16): 3.

Null, Christopher. 2000. "Hotels Go High Tech." *Ziff Davis Smart Business for the New Economy* 13(5): 56.

Reynolds, Dennis. 1990. "Managed-Services Companies: The New Scorecard for On-site Food Service." *Cornell Hotel and Restaurant Administration Quarterly* 40(3): 64–73.

U.S. Bureau of the Census, Department of Commerce. 1997. "Table 6: Concentration by Largest Firms, 1997." Accessed April 4, 2002, at: *www.census.gov/epcd/www/pdf/97conc/c97r72-sz.pdf.*

U.S. Department of Labor, Bureau of Labor Statistics. 2001. "Table 1: Incidence Rates of Nonfatal Occupational Injuries and Illnesses by Industry and Selected Case Types, 2000." Accessed January 25, 2002, at: *www.bls.gov/iif/oshwc/osh/os/ostb1001.txt.*

———. 2002a. "2000 National Industry-Specific Occupational Employment and Wage Estimates: SIC 701—Hotels and Motels." Accessed January 25, 2002 at: *www.bls.gov/oes/2000/oesi3 701.htm.*

———. 2002b. "National Employment, Hours, and Earnings: Average Weekly Hours of Production Workers: SIC 701—Hotels and Motels." Accessed January 25, 2002, at: *data.bls.gov/cgi-bin/srgate.*

Waddoups, Jeffrey C. 1999. "Union–Non-union Wage Differentials in the U.S. Hotel Industry." *Proceedings of the Fifty-first Annual Meeting of the Industrial Relations Research Association* 1: 161–68.

———. 2001. "Unionism and Poverty-Level Wages in the Service Sector: The Case of Nevada's Hotel-Casino Industry." *Applied Economic Letters* 8(3): 163–67.

Waldinger, Roger. 1996. "Who Makes the Beds? Who Washes the Dishes?: Black-Immigrant Competition Reassessed." In *Immigrants and Immigration Policy: Individual Skills, Family Ties, and Group Identities,* edited by Harriett Orcutt Duleep and Phanindra V. Wunnava. Greenwich, Conn.: Jai Press.

Watkins, Ed. 2000. "The Consolidation Conundrum." *Lodging Hospitality* 56(15): 2.

Webb, Steve. 2000. "More Hotel Mergers Comin' Up." *National Real Estate Investor* 42(8): 20.

Whitford, Marty. 1998. "Missing in Action: AHF Study Substantiates That Few Minorities Advance from the Front Line to Management." *Hotel and Motel Management* 213(14): 1.

Worcester, Barbara A. 1999. "The People Problem: Management Companies Struggle to Attract, Train, and Retain Employees." *Hotel and Motel Management* 214(4): 38–40.

Yetzer, Elaine. 2000. "Newcomer Tops ISHC's Latest Issue List." *Hotel and Motel Management* 215(11): 3.

CHAPTER 3

The Effects of Work Restructuring on Low-Wage, Low-Skilled Workers in U.S. Hospitals

Eileen Appelbaum, Peter Berg, Ann Frost, and Gil Preuss

Although commonly thought of as an employer of highly educated and technically skilled medical staff, the U.S. hospital industry also provides large numbers of low-skill, low-wage jobs. Food service, housekeeping, and nursing assistant jobs make up the largely invisible backbone of any U.S. hospital. These jobs have traditionally provided employment with benefits to some of the most economically disadvantaged participants in the U.S. labor force, including recent immigrants and residents of the inner city.

Over the past fifteen years the U.S. hospital industry has come under considerable pressure to reduce costs and streamline services while continuing to provide high-quality medical care to an increasingly demanding public. Recently hospitals have begun experimenting with alternative approaches to structuring low-skill, low-wage jobs. As hospitals exhausted other routes to cost-cutting and service improvement, some managers began experimenting with the redesign of these roles. At the same time, exceptionally tight labor markets in the latter half of the 1990s made recruiting and retention of even low-skilled workers an important concern. Some managers initiated the redesign of work processes with the goal of increasing job satisfaction among these workers and reducing turnover.

The purpose of this chapter is to explore the impacts of these changes on the current jobs of workers employed in housekeeping, in food service, or in patient care as nursing assistants in U.S. hospitals. These are low-wage jobs that generally require a high school degree or less to perform adequately.[1] We document the changes in work organization in these low-skill, low-wage occupations and analyze how these changes affect the turnover and job satisfaction of these workers. Despite these changes, within-hospital career mobility for workers in these low-skill occupations remains extremely limited. This chapter provides some limited evidence on what those paths look like and how they may be changing.

The research presented here was conducted in 16 U.S. community hospitals. We chose to focus on community hospitals because they make up the largest proportion of U.S. hospitals. We also chose hospitals of a similar size—between 200 and 400 beds for the most part—again, as the most representative size of community hospitals. Our research sites were chosen to provide insight into hospital practices throughout the country: we conducted fieldwork in hospitals based in the Northeast, the Midwest, the Southwest, and the South. At each hospital we met with and interviewed managers; in addition to an executive-level manager, we interviewed managers from human resources as well as the managers of food service, housekeeping, and hospital units in which nursing assistants were employed. In addition to this field research, the research presented here draws on completed telephone interviews with 746 workers employed in food service, in housekeeping, or as nursing assistants in 12 of these hospitals. Approximately 80 workers per hospital were randomly selected from employee lists supplied by the employer for the telephone interviews.

We present evidence on the changing nature of employment and careers in this sector. In interviews with hospital managers we gathered information on the pressures facing their hospitals. In addition, we heard from managers about strategies they had implemented (and that some had later abandoned) to cope with the need to continue to drive down costs while providing high-quality health care. We also heard from the employees about their careers to date and about their current jobs. We asked them where they had worked before, where they planned to be working in the next few years, and what they did now at work. We also asked about changes in their jobs, the skills and abilities they brought to the hospital, and the effects their jobs had on them.

We find that higher wages and staffing adequacy in departments are key management measures that reduce employees' desire to leave their current employers. However, as we discuss later in this chapter, hospitals face rising expenses and severe cost pressures that challenge their ability to raise wages and improve staffing levels. Changes in work processes for low-skilled workers, introduced in an effort both to improve quality and reduce costs, have been rather modest. In contrast to the traditional organization of low-skill jobs in hospitals, workers in enhanced jobs perform a broader range of work tasks and are assigned to specific departments. We find from the worker survey that these jobs are not more likely than jobs in traditional work settings to have any of the characteristics associated with high-performance work organization, such as participation in teams, pay contingent on performance, higher levels of training, and employment security. The emphasis on cost-cutting appears to have precluded more far-reaching changes in work redesign. And where we do find enhanced jobs, we also find that workers in these jobs are no more satisfied with their jobs than are other workers. However, we do find that enhanced jobs have been effective in reducing employees' intention to quit their jobs.

The evidence presented in this chapter is based on a combination of qualitative and quantitative data. The chapter begins with an overview of the U.S. hospital industry, the pressures facing the industry, and a description of the occupational groups that are the focus of this study. We also present data on the career patterns of the workers interviewed in this study, both where they have come from and where they plan to go. We then describe their current jobs and the primary models of work organization—traditional, enhanced, and contracted out—that employers appear to be adopting in their efforts to restructure low-skill, low-wage jobs in U.S. hospitals. In the next section, we explore the impact that unions are having on the choices that hospital managers make with respect to new models of work organization, and we describe the implications of these changes for these workers' careers. Finally, we analyze the empirical data on the impact of various models of work organization on the work lives of low-wage workers in the U.S. hospital industry. Using the worker survey data, we analyze work organization effects on employees' intention to leave their employer and on employee satisfaction. The chapter concludes with a discussion of our findings.

THE U.S. HOSPITAL INDUSTRY

In 1998 health care spending in the United States accounted for over 13 percent of gross domestic product (GDP)—the largest proportion of GDP of any other major industrialized country. The hospital industry accounted for one-third of this spending (Plunkett 2000). Over the decade 1986 to 1996, U.S. hospitals' expenses doubled, and these costs are expected to continue to grow at about 6.5 percent annually. In 2000 inpatient and outpatient hospital services accounted for 47 percent of the total increase in health care spending (Strunk, Ginsburg, and Gabel 2001).

In its attempts to stem this rampant cost escalation, the hospital industry has undergone a transformation over the past decade. One change in the industry is consolidation: hospital mergers and closures have reduced the number of hospitals by more than 10 percent, from 6,841 in 1986 to 6,201 in 1996 (Plunkett 2000). Even though the number of hospitals has declined, employment in the industry continues to grow. In 1996 the U.S. hospital industry employed 4.28 million people, an increase of more than 500,000 over the prior decade.

PRESSURES ON THE U.S. HOSPITAL INDUSTRY

The U.S. hospital industry is facing a number of pressures that are leading to the current consolidation as well as cost-cutting and changes in service delivery. Among the most important are those coming from the insurance industry, from continued shrinking of government funding, and from demographic changes.

The insurance industry poses several challenges for U.S. hospitals. The growing number of uninsured and the cost of their care are having significant financial impacts on many hospitals. In 2000 fully 18 percent of Americans (43.3 million people) had no health insurance at some point during the year (Plunkett 2000). When requiring hospital-based care, such patients are billed directly for services they receive. In many cases, such patients are unable to pay, with the result that in 2000 American hospitals wrote off, it was estimated, nearly $20 billion in bad debt.

Those patients with insurance also pose problems. Managed care plans have taken over the insurance of the majority of insured Americans. A common strategy adopted by health maintenance organizations (HMOs) is to place limitations on the delivery of specific care and to reduce reimbursement to hospitals in the delivery of specific procedures. As a result, many hospitals have found that they cannot deliver some services for the amount of reimbursement they receive from insurance companies (and so take a loss on the provision of certain services). In addition, some HMOs give bonuses to doctors not to use supplementary, specialty, and hospital services. Further, publicly funded health insurance has reduced hospital reimbursement, particularly following the Balanced Budget Act, which sought to slow the growth in Medicare and Medicaid expenditures. The forecast is for these programs to remain in tight financial circumstances through 2002 and beyond.

A final pressure on hospitals comes from the aging of the U.S. population. The over 65 age group accounts for a disproportionate amount of hospital expenditures. In 1996 Americans over 65 accounted for 4,679 days of care per 1,000 persons. In comparison, Americans aged 25 to 34 accounted for 360 days of care per 1,000 people. Not only does the over-65 demographic group use a disproportionate share of hospital resources, but it has also increased by 12 percent over the past decade—from 31.1 million Americans in 1990 to 34.9 million in 2000—and this group is expected to continue to grow over the next several decades, only exacerbating the cost pressures already faced by U.S. hospitals.

HOSPITAL RESPONSES

Hospitals are responding to these increasing financial pressures in a broad array of ways. Hospitals are high-cost operations. Therefore, measures have been taken to decrease overall hospital usage, both by sending less acutely ill patients to alternative sites for care and by shortening the stays of those who do require hospital admission. The last decade has seen dramatic growth in the use of home care and in long-term-care facilities. There has also been notable growth over the past decade in outpatient clinics. Patients who in the past would have required hospitalization are now seen at outpatient clinics for day surgery and the treatment of chronic disease. Outpatient visits grew from 295 million in 1986 to 506 million in 1996. Not surprisingly, the average daily census of U.S. hospitals has fallen 22 percent. Over the same time period, however, hospital personnel per 100 patients has increased by 51 percent—an indication of the rising acuity of patients in U.S. hospitals. Hospital length of stay has also shortened notably over the 1980 to 1996 period. In

1980 the average length of stay was just over a week (7.3 days); by 1996 that figure had fallen to 5.2 days.

There have also been significant changes in how patient care in hospitals is delivered. Most notable has been the reorganization of the work of nurses, which has occurred in several waves since the mid-1980s. The last and most recent wave of restructuring occurred in response to the cost pressures faced by U.S. hospitals in the mid-1990s. The result has been the replacement of registered nurses (RNs) with nursing assistants. Registered nurses have been asked to focus on care planning and more technically demanding tasks, while nursing assistants have been given greater responsibility over routine tasks, such as bathing and feeding patients, taking vital signs, and conducting basic sterile procedures. In addition, hospitals have engaged in numerous cost-cutting activities such as supplier consolidation, reengineering, and the implementation of cost-cutting teams. Recently hospitals have also begun to restructure the jobs of their low-wage, low-skilled workers in attempts to cut costs as well as to improve patient care and satisfaction (and thereby potentially improve performance in the marketplace).

LOW-SKILLED WORKERS IN HOSPITALS

Food service workers, housekeepers, and nursing assistants are the occupational groups that are the focus of this study. Food service workers are employed in all facets of food preparation, cafeteria operation, and food delivery in the hospital. Housekeeping staff clean and maintain patient rooms as well as hospital common areas and work areas (operating rooms, the emergency department, and so forth). Nursing assistants provide nontechnical patient care. In 2000, 48,334 people were employed in hospital food service occupations; 169,625 were employed in hospital housekeeping, and 375,939 were employed as nursing assistants (authors' analysis of the Current Population Survey, March 2001).

Wages for these groups tend to be at the bottom of the wage distribution. Food service workers and housekeepers in particular often earn close to the minimum wage. Nursing assistants earn slightly more. In 2000 the median wage for food service workers was $8.25 an hour, for housekeepers $8.15, and for nursing assistants $9.00. This reflects an increase in nominal wages of 6 percent, 16 percent, and 14 percent, respectively, for the three groups over their 1995 wages.

For the most part, these employee groups have relatively low levels of formal education. Thirty-three percent of food service workers and 28 percent of housekeepers have less than a high school education. The balance have at least a high school diploma, with a relatively small percentage of people in these occupational groups having attended at least some college (14 percent of food service workers and 18 percent of housekeeping staff). Nursing assistants are generally more educated: 86 percent have completed high school, and roughly half have also attended some college. This is probably explained by the education requirement for becoming a licensed nursing assistant.

Union coverage in these hospital-based occupations, hovering around 20 percent, is higher than in the U.S. economy as a whole. In 2000, 18 percent of hospital food service workers were covered by a union contract, as were nearly 24 percent of housekeepers and just over 21 percent of nursing assistants (authors' analysis of the Current Population Survey, March 2001). However, all of these rates had declined slightly over the 1995 to 2000 period.

The vast majority (more than 90 percent) of food service workers and housekeepers work full-time (more than thirty-five hours per week). Only a slightly lower percentage (about 80 percent) of nursing assistants work full-time. Thirteen percent of nursing assistants work twenty-one to thirty-five hours per week, while only about 4 percent of food service workers and housekeepers work twenty-one to thirty-five hours per week.

Data from our own survey of housekeepers, food service workers, and nursing assistants provide additional insight into the labor market experiences and career patterns of these workers. Prior to working at the hospital, most housekeepers held jobs doing housekeeping (26 percent), other low-end services tasks (25 percent), or working in manufacturing (15 percent). Most food service workers in our sample previously worked in low-end service jobs (32 percent), in retail (14 percent), or in restaurants (17 percent). The majority of nursing assistants, on the other hand, previously worked as nursing assistants in nursing homes (37 percent) or in other medical services jobs in hospitals, firms, or clinics (19 percent).

As part of our survey, we asked workers: In what type of job do you see yourself working in three years? Most housekeepers saw themselves working in the same job (40 percent), in another low-end service job somewhere else (18 percent), or in other slightly more high-paying jobs in health care (16 percent)—for example, as a dietary technician. Similarly, most food service workers saw themselves working in the same job (44 percent), in another low-end service job somewhere else (17 percent), or in other slightly higher-paying jobs in health care (15 percent)—again, as a dietary technician or nutrition specialist. Most nursing assistants, on the other hand, saw themselves working as registered nurses in three years (45 percent) or as continuing on as nursing assistants (30 percent).

These data from our survey reveal that the labor market and career patterns for nursing assistants, on the one hand, and housekeepers and food service workers, on the other, are very different. Nursing assistants move within a labor market in medical services. Most are recruited to hospitals from other health care organizations, and many hope to move into higher-paying nursing jobs with additional formal education. The jobs of nursing assistants are occupationally linked to the health care sector and its mission of care for the sick. Housekeepers and food service workers move within a labor market of low-end service jobs in retail, restaurants, and hotels. Hospitals recruit these workers out of this market, and workers return to these low-end service jobs when they leave the hospital. With few opportunities to move into higher-paying jobs within the hospital and with limited patient contact, housekeepers and food service workers are far less connected to the health care mission than nursing assistants. Thus, when compared to nursing assistants, housekeepers and food service workers are less likely to be committed to the hospital as a long-term career choice.

EXTERNAL CONSTRAINT OF EXTREMELY TIGHT LABOR MARKETS

Complicating hospital employers' plans for restructuring the jobs of their low-wage, low-skilled employees were the unusually low unemployment rates of the late 1990s. Beginning in about 1996, unemployment rates began to fall below the 4 to 5 percent range associated with full employment. In October 2000 the unemployment rate for the United States as a whole had fallen to a low of 3.9 percent. Many cities found themselves with still lower unemployment rates during this time. For example, Phoenix, Arizona, one of the cities in which hospitals in this study are located, saw its unemployment rate drop to 2.7 percent.

Thus, the higher levels of turnover experienced by hospitals during this period of extreme labor market tightness only served to exacerbate hospitals' worsening cost pressures. Annual turnover rates among these occupational groups at some hospitals approached 100 percent. Rates greater than 50 percent were common for many hospitals across all occupational groups examined in our study. The direct costs of recruiting and training became burdensome, as did the indirect costs associated with inexperienced job-holders delivering substandard levels of customer service. Moreover, most hospitals were financially constrained in their ability to raise wages to any substantive degree so as to alleviate some of this labor market pressure.

At the time of this study, hospitals found themselves faced by the twofold problem of untenable levels of turnover in their low-wage, low-skill occupations and the ongoing need to cut costs while continuing to deliver high-quality patient care. The subsequent restructuring of low-wage, low-skill jobs in U.S. hospitals has been driven by these two pressures.

EXPERIMENTS IN THE ORGANIZATION OF WORK

In response to increasing pressure from the labor market and to control costs and improve quality, hospitals have been searching for ways to reorganize traditionally low-skill, low-wage jobs. Overall, the pressure felt by hospital administrators has resulted in two distinct responses. On the one hand, because food service and housekeeping are not typically seen as distinct sources of hospital success or expertise, some hospital administrators have outsourced these functions or their management to external firms that specialize in these areas. On the other hand, food service workers, housekeepers, and nursing assistants all have direct contact with patients, and those contacts can affect patients' experiences in the hospital and satisfaction with care. In response, other hospital administrators have sought to improve employee skills within these jobs and ensure a more stable workforce through more careful selection, cross-training, and work reorganization.

This latter strategy stresses quality improvement more than cost control, but all hospital administrators are faced with both pressures as they adopt innovative work practices for low-skill workers. Moreover, the capacity to maintain a work strategy that integrated both of these objectives may have been limited by the increasing cost and labor market pressures faced by hospitals during the late 1990s as they were adopting alternative work practices.

Based on our interviews with hospital managers, we observed two strategies for low-skilled workers in addition to the historical model traditionally observed in hospitals: multi-skilling–cross-training and outsourcing. Prior to our formal analysis of these work practices, we first discuss the broad outlines, rationale, and tensions evident within each of the following sets of practices: traditional functional, multi-skilling–cross-training, and outsourcing. We discuss separately the strategies adopted by hospitals for housekeeping and food service workers and nursing assistants.

TRADITIONAL WORK ORGANIZATION IN HOSPITALS: HOUSEKEEPING AND FOOD SERVICE

Housekeeping and food service work in hospitals has traditionally been organized along narrow functional task responsibilities. Housekeepers work within environmental services and are typically assigned to a particular job or area that they cover on a regular basis, whether a unit of the hospital or a task such as mopping floors. Moreover, few promotion and training opportunities exist as employees move from Housekeeper I, a job in which they are responsible for emptying garbage cans and cleaning patient rooms, to Housekeeper II, which requires the use of some equipment, such as floor cleaners and buffers. Similar dynamics exist for food service workers, though some more horizontal movement is available. For example, cashiers might work in both the tray-line area and in salad preparation. In a few instances, housekeepers and food service workers are promoted to first-line managers.

Although these jobs have rarely been "enriched," hospitals have successfully recruited and maintained employees in these positions in the past because of the pay and benefits available in hospitals. With competitive wages and benefits that more closely resembled those of professional employees, hospital work was desirable compared to housekeeping or food service work in other settings. As the labor market tightened, however, other competitors increased wages to closely match or even exceed those available in hospitals. Moreover, hospitals faced increasing pressure to reduce the benefits they gave to low-wage workers. As a result, the relative benefit of housekeeping or food service employment in hospitals disappeared. Hospitals began losing employees to fast-food restaurants, casinos, and stores such as Wal-Mart or Home Depot as these employers paid competitive wages and benefits and offered work that did not require, for example, cleaning up after patients or dealing with blood. As a result, hospitals found it increasingly difficult to fill vacant positions.

One response of several of the hospitals we visited was to reduce job requirements for those being hired. Some hospitals that had required a high school diploma or its equivalent dropped this requirement. Some hospital administrators began to consider people with minor police records for employment. In one instance, we were told that the specific crime would be taken into consideration and people assigned appropriately; for example, someone convicted of theft would not be given access to patient rooms but could work in the laundry. Alternatively, hospital managers sought to adopt work practices that would result in more enriched jobs for employees, thus making the jobs more desirable.

ENHANCED HOUSEKEEPING AND FOOD SERVICE JOBS

One initiative taken by a few hospitals in our sample to reduce turnover and improve the patient experience was to adopt multi-skilled or enhanced positions for housekeeping and food service workers. The assumption underlying these enhanced jobs was that by broadening jobs and assigning employees to a specific unit, employees, patients, and the hospital would all gain.

In contrast to the traditional functional job, these new enhanced jobs included task responsibilities that had previously been held by employees in several functional areas, including housekeeping, food service, and transport. For example, a new service support associate (one commonly used title) would be responsible for housekeeping on the unit, delivering food to patients and assisting with their feeding, and transporting patients to Radiology for X-rays. Underlying such an assignment were several expectations: that the employee would be more satisfied by having broader and more varied job responsibilities; that patients would be more satisfied if they interacted with fewer employees during their stay; and that the hospital could both improve quality and reduce costs through increased employee flexibility. Although it is unclear how many hospitals adopted this enhanced model, several national consulting firms promoted this approach as a response to the cost and quality pressures faced by hospitals.

In our interviews, managers raised several potential problems with the implementation of the enhanced model for housekeeping and food services. First, because employees in the new multi-tasked jobs frequently received minimal training in the other job responsibilities, they tended, we were often told, to continue working in the tasks they felt most comfortable with rather than in the new areas of responsibility. Second, the new enhanced jobs increased patient contact dramatically. Housekeeping employees who may have seen patients only when they entered the room to empty garbage cans now also brought food to patients, transported them to Radiology, and performed other tasks as requested by the nursing staff. Managers reported that employees who did not want significant patient contact resisted these changes. Patients themselves also raised concerns about certain tasks being performed by the same person. Managers told us that some patients did not like having their food brought to them by the same person who cleaned their garbage cans.

Third, nurse managers frequently lacked the skills and knowledge to supervise the new employees in their units. In particular, though the service support associates were placed on the units under their supervision, nurse managers knew very little about housekeeping and could not effectively supervise the work and ensure its accomplishment. Finally, since the new employees were also the lowest-wage workers on the unit, they were frequently asked to do additional tasks, such as accompanying a patient going out for a cigarette or sitting in a patient's room to make sure the patient did not try to get out of bed. Although such tasks reduced the time available to employees to conduct their other tasks, they were still expected to complete them.

OUTSOURCING HOUSEKEEPING AND FOOD SERVICE

Outsourcing of housekeeping and food services is an important strategy adopted by some hospitals as they seek to reduce costs and improve the efficiency of these functions. In a recent survey conducted for the *Hospitals and Health Networks Journal,* nearly 25 percent of the respondents reported that they outsourced food services, and 15 percent reported that they outsourced housekeeping and janitorial services (*Hospitals and Health Networks* 2001). In our study, we found only one instance of the employees themselves being outsourced. In this case, hospital management was seeking to reduce food service costs. By outsourcing the employees, workers no longer received the benefits available to them from the hospital but rather the benefits that are more typical of food service workers (much higher health insurance copays, fewer vacation days, and so on).

More frequently outsourced in hospitals, however, was management. Several hospitals brought in managers from companies such as Sodexho or Servicemaster to direct food services or housekeeping. These companies have developed specific work routines, including training material, methods to determine worker efficiency, and other management tools. Moreover, hospitals were frequently able to bring in higher-caliber managers than would have been available through direct employment. Employment by Servicemaster would provide a housekeeping manager, for example, with a career ladder as he or she moved from a small hospital to a larger hospital, and then to managing several hospitals in a region. In contrast, managers employed directly by a hospital would have much more restricted promotion opportunities.

It is important to note that our interviews revealed no clear differences in work organization for employees when management was outsourced. In fact, when management was outsourced, jobs often remained traditionally organized. The primary difference may have been in better departmental management, including training material and task allocation.

TRADITIONAL NURSING ASSISTANT WORK ORGANIZATION

Nursing assistants in hospitals have traditionally been responsible for a relatively narrow set of task responsibilities, including bathing and feeding patients and assisting registered nurses as needed. Owing to the limited range of tasks over which they were responsible, nursing assistants worked with a wide set of patients on a unit.

While a registered nurse may have had primary responsibility for five to six patients, a nursing assistant worked with twenty patients in helping various nurses with their work.

The education and skills required to be a nursing assistant are typically higher than those for food service workers and housekeepers. Hospitals usually require at least a high school diploma or equivalent, and most request a certification that requires several months of additional training. Within hospitals, however, nursing assistants typically receive very limited training upon employment, ranging from one to four weeks.

ENHANCED NURSING ASSISTANT WORK ORGANIZATION

To improve outcomes and reduce costs, hospitals frequently redefined nursing assistant (and registered nurse) job responsibilities and sought to integrate nursing assistants more fully into the patient care team. Due to the wage and education differences between nursing assistants and registered nurses (registered nurses typically earn more than $20 an hour), many hospitals shifted routine tasks from registered nurses to nursing assistants, including taking vital signs, drawing blood, and conducting basic sterile procedures. The next change was integrating nursing assistants more fully into a specific team of care providers. As such, in contrast to the previous work organization model, nursing assistants may now work with a single registered nurse (or two) and conduct a broader set of tasks for these nurses' patients.

As with housekeeping and food services, the goal in enhancing these jobs was to broaden task responsibilities and make them more interesting for employees, thus reducing turnover and costs, improving quality, and increasing employee satisfaction.

UNION REPRESENTATION AND OUTCOMES FOR LOW-SKILLED WORKERS

Workers at six of the sixteen hospitals in our study were represented by a union. In two cases (and in two different cities), the unionized hospitals were virtually alone. The other four unionized hospitals were located in a city where the norm was to be unionized and union density in the hospital sector was extremely high.

Union representation of housekeepers, food service workers, and nursing assistants can bring important changes to the outcomes experienced by employees. On the one hand, unionization provides the opportunity for employee representatives to participate in the design and implementation of any work organization change initiative. Through this process, better models of work organization can be developed. On the other hand, hospitals are under strong market pressure to reduce care delivery costs. In addition, there are few clear models that have been shown to improve outcomes for the hospital and employees. As such, union leaders may face a difficult time in pursuing specific workplace strategies.

At the hospitals in the two low-union-density cities, the union has had very little impact on outcomes for employees or for the hospital.[2] In neither case has the union been able to raise wages substantially; pay has remained virtually the same as at non-union hospitals in the local area. Moreover, the union has had no substantive involvement in the workplace other than to negotiate a collective bargaining agreement every few years and process members' grievances as they arose.

In contrast, the union in the high-union-density city has had a significant impact on low-skill work in the city's unionized hospitals, owing partly to the extremely high levels of union density and partly to the politically savvy leadership of this union. Through its lobbying at the state level, this union has procured substantial additional funding for health care in the state, money that has translated into significant wage increases for its members. As a result, food service workers, housekeepers, and nursing assistants in these unionized hospitals earn significantly more than comparable non-union workers in the rest of our sample. Starting wages range between $11 and $12 an hour compared to $7 to $8 an hour in the other (largely non-union) cities we visited. Even controlling for the high cost of living in this large city, unionized hospital workers here are better off. Second, the union has also had an impact at the level of the individual hospital through the negotiation of labor-management cooperation committees. Through this joint process, the union was able to influence the pay and security benefits for housekeeping and food service workers whose jobs were redesigned into service support associate roles. As mentioned earlier, the service support associate role has been tried in many hospitals around the country, with mixed success. Despite its checkered record, management has remained keen to implement this model. The union in this city ensured, however, that workers had access to adequate training to acquire the necessary skills, and it also worked to protect their job security. In addition, the union negotiated higher wages for the support associate job.

The union also had an impact on shaping the nursing assistant job. Through the joint labor-management cooperation committee, the union played a significant role in redesigning nursing assistant jobs across the unionized hospitals in the city. By promoting skill upgrading and providing the funds for extensive training, the union ensured that existing nursing assistants were equipped to move into redesigned, expanded, and cross-functional jobs. Over the course of six to eight weeks, nursing assistants were trained in phlebotomy and equipped with the necessary skills to perform electrocardiograms. These changes in job content were accompanied by changes in overall work organization and a pay increase of over 20 percent. In addition, the union focused on the process through which employees were moved from the traditional work model to the enhanced model to ensure that those interested in pursuing skill development and a cross-functional job were given that opportunity. The work organization model adopted by the hospitals in this high-union-density city did not appear to differ dramatically from the model adopted elsewhere, but the union was able to promote broader skill development, greater wage increases, and a process that represented the interests of employees in the newly defined jobs.

Certain key characteristics of the union and the relationship between labor and management seemed to be important in work organization models that were successfully redesigned. First, the union maintained a very strong position in the region with high levels of union density and broad representation of employees across different occupational groups. Second, the union made significant funds available for use in the training initiatives. These funds were specifically used to train employees as jobs evolved from traditional to enhanced. Employees also used these funds for ongoing educational upgrading (for example, to complete a GED or to attend nursing school). In addition, the availability of union training funds placed unions in a position to promote broader training for employees. In contrast, in other hospitals where all training funds had to come from the hospital, the capacity to promote extensive training would have been limited. Third, labor-management relations in these hospitals have historically been cooperative, resulting in an openness to address work reorganization through an ongoing dialogue between the union and hospital leaders. All of these factors played an important role in changing work organization models with significant and supportive union involvement.

ENHANCED JOBS FOR LOW-SKILLED WORKERS? EFFECTS ON TURNOVER AND JOB SATISFACTION

By implementing different forms of work organization, such as enhanced jobs, hospital managers expected to increase the satisfaction of employees and reduce their intention to quit. Whether managers' expectations were realized remains an open empirical question. In this section, we utilize the results of our survey of hospital workers in low-skill jobs to examine the impact of hospitals' efforts to enhance jobs on turnover and job satisfaction. We begin with a brief review of the literature on turnover and satisfaction.

INTENTION TO QUIT

The literature on voluntary turnover suggests that two types of practices are available to organizations to reduce turnover rates: inducements such as pay and benefits and employer-employee relationships (Shaw, Delery, and Jenkins 1998). Organizational dynamics such as the organization of work, job design, and human resource practices can be shaped to reduce turnover (Arthur 1994). Such practices are more likely to be changed in situations where employers find it difficult to find workers with the necessary skills and attitudes to replace those who have left the organization. When the costs of replacing workers are low—that is, when the job is easily learned and does not require much in the way of firm-specific skills and employee behavior is easily monitored—organizations lack incentives to invest in retaining workers (for a discussion of transactions costs, see, for example, Williamson 1979).

It is generally assumed that workers in the low-skill food service, housekeeping, and nursing assistant occupations are easily replaced and that the costs of turnover for these workers are low. In traditional work organization settings, hospitals make little investment in training these employees, and managers rely on close supervision and monitoring to get the work done. In the past, management did not adopt workplace practices for these occupational groups that would build employees' organizational commitment and support a stable employment relationship. However, as tight labor markets from 1996 to 2001 increased the choice of jobs available to these workers, leading to high rates of turnover, some hospital managers began to adopt workplace practices intended to reduce turnover rates.

Previous research suggests that higher pay and benefits and greater employment security are practices that reduce workers' incentives to find another job and motivate their long-term commitment to the firm (Osterman 1987). Employees are less likely to leave a job with good pay and benefits because other jobs with these characteristics are more difficult to find (Zenger 1992; Powell, Montgomery, and Cosgrove 1994; Shaw, Delery, and Jenkins 1998). Employment security is also expected to reduce turnover, since a lack of job stability may reduce employees' commitment and attachment to the organization (Cotton and Tuttle 1986; Ashford, Lee, and Bobko 1989; Shaw, Delery, and Jenkins 1998).

High-involvement workplace practices are also expected to reduce employees' intention to quit, while those associated with a low-commitment environment are more likely to lead workers to quit (Arthur 1994; Huselid 1995). High-involvement practices, which build employees' firm-specific skills, include: selecting better-educated workers and investing in training; designing enhanced jobs that provide opportunities for challenge, creativity, and participation in decisions; and incentives such as high relative pay, greater job security, and trust. High-involvement practices may also be important in "interactive service work" (Leidner 1993) in health care, where the quality of the patient's hospital experience is shaped by employee behavior.

Employees value high levels of trust in the establishment in which they work and the intrinsic rewards they get from their jobs. These characteristics, which are usually associated with high-performance workplace practices and enhanced jobs, are not only important to workers but increase job satisfaction (Appelbaum et al. 2000). They also reduce turnover (Batt 2000) since, like high pay, these job characteristics are inducements for long-term commitment.

In contrast, low-involvement workplace practices follow the logic of traditional mass-production manufacturing. Jobs are narrow, and workers learn routinized tasks through repetition. Labor costs are minimized through low investment in selection of workers and training, monitoring of workers, and low relative pay. Low-involvement workplaces tend to have higher rates of voluntary turnover. Close supervision may increase job demands and is associated with lower levels of worker autonomy and trust. Too much work to do, too many demands on time, and low levels of trust have all been shown to increase turnover rates or intentions to quit (Leonard 1987; Batt 2000). Other characteristics of the organizational environment, such as conflict with coworkers or frequent overtime requirements, may also make work unpleasant and lead workers to quit.

Finally, fair treatment of workers has been posited to reduce voluntary turnover by increasing the attractiveness of the workplace. "Voice" mechanisms, such as the grievance procedures associated with unions, should reduce employees' intention to quit, as should employees' satisfaction with the fairness of their pay (Shaw, Delery, and Jenkins 1998).

JOB SATISFACTION

Job satisfaction, which represents a worker's overall evaluation of his or her job, is widely used as an overall measure of the work experience. Job satisfaction is assumed to be related to a host of positive consequences in both the work and nonwork aspects of life (for a review, see Kalleberg 1977). It is a subjective measure of individual well-being, but it is a particularly powerful measure since it exhibits strong correlations, in the expected direction, with mental health, life expectancy, heart disease, absenteeism, and turnover (Palmore 1969; Sales and House 1971; Freeman 1978; Wall, Clegg, and Jackson 1978; Clegg 1983).

The job design literature has emphasized redesigning work as a means to motivate workers trapped in routinized and alienating jobs (Hackman and Lawler 1971; Hackman and Oldham 1975, 1976, 1980). By expanding job tasks, organizing work into teams, or giving employees some discretion within their jobs, workers become more satisfied with their jobs and more motivated to put forth effort on the job. Thus, workplace practices that enhance jobs, require greater skill, and provide opportunities for challenge and creativity should increase job satisfaction.

Human resource practices associated with high-performance or high-commitment workplaces, such as training and employment security, are likely to be valued by workers. As a result, work settings in which these practices are present should also see higher levels of job satisfaction.

Recent research on job satisfaction has found that job satisfaction is increased in high-trust workplaces where jobs are intrinsically rewarding and stressors such as conflict with coworkers, too many demands on one's time, and more work than workers can handle are reduced (Appelbaum et al. 2000). Thus, practices adopted by hospital managers to reduce turnover should also be effective in improving job satisfaction for workers.

SURVEY OF WORKERS IN LOW-SKILL HOSPITAL JOBS

The collection of data for this study is still under way. The analysis reported here is based on a survey of 746 workers in 12 hospitals. The sample includes 164 food service workers, 305 nursing assistants, 219 housekeeper or environmental services workers, and 58 workers in miscellaneous low-skill jobs.

Fewer than 10 percent of the housekeepers in our sample are in enhanced jobs thus far, and the overall numbers of other low-skill workers are too small to analyze. Thus, the focus of our empirical analyses of the effects of enhanced jobs on worker turnover and job satisfaction is on food service workers and nursing assistants.

The sample we analyze includes a total of 164 food service workers, of whom 42 (26 percent) are in enhanced jobs, and 305 nursing assistants, of whom 182 (60 percent) are in enhanced jobs. Among food service workers, our sample is 59 percent white, 28 percent black, 10 percent Hispanic, and 3 percent other. For nursing assistants, the distribution is 66 percent white, 27 percent black, 3 percent Hispanic, and 4 percent other. Nursing assistants tend to be younger and better educated than food service workers. The average age of food service workers is 42.6 years, while for nursing assistants it is 36.3 years. About 30 percent of nursing assistants have a high school degree or less—fewer than 3 percent lack a high school degree—while 55 percent have some education beyond high school, and 14 percent have a college degree. Among food service workers, 12 percent have less than a high school degree, 52 percent are high school graduates, 31 percent have some education beyond high school, and 5.5 percent have a college degree. Food service workers in our sample earn on average $9.59 an hour, while nursing assistants earn $10.28. Working full-time, year-round, these employees earn less than $21,000 a year.

ENHANCED VERSUS TRADITIONAL JOBS

If enhanced jobs are to increase workers' job satisfaction or reduce the likelihood that they will leave their job in the near future, they must differ in significant ways from traditional food service and nursing assistant jobs. The worker survey provides an extraordinary level of detail that enables us to examine whether this is indeed the case.

Workers were asked about the characteristics of their jobs, their participation in problem-solving teams, and the extent to which they participated in decisions and communicated with other employees. They were asked about job characteristics that increase intrinsic rewards: Did they use their skills and creativity on the job? Did they find their jobs challenging? They were asked how difficult it was to learn to do their jobs, what amount and types of training they received, whether they were certified or had technical degrees, and whether there were opportunities for promotion to higher-paying jobs. The survey asked about workers' perceptions that management provided adequate staff to get the work done and their perceptions of employment security. Workers were also asked questions about the work environment: Were they treated fairly? Did they trust management? Did conflict or work demands create stress? Workers were asked whether they belonged to a union or were covered by a union contract. Finally, workers were asked about pay rates, hours, and overtime and about their satisfaction with the fairness of their pay and benefits. Thus, the richness of the data gathered in the worker survey enables us to examine the nature of the jobs that managers characterize as enhanced.

Enhanced jobs as described by managers are characterized by broader job tasks and assignments of employees to specific units. Surprisingly perhaps, the worker survey reveals that enhanced jobs done by food service workers and nursing assistants exhibit very few of the characteristics associated in the literature with high-performance jobs or high-commitment workplaces. Indeed, among food service workers, traditional jobs sometimes scored higher on the few indicators of high-performance practices where the jobs differed. Appendix 3.1 provides a full list of job and work environment characteristics and human resource practices. Here we report only the characteristics and practices that differed significantly between enhanced and traditional work settings. We report these separately for food service workers and nursing assistants. Mean differences are significant at the 5 percent level unless otherwise indicated.

Among food service workers, those in traditional settings were much more likely to participate in problem-solving teams—65 percent of workers in traditional jobs versus 47 percent of those in enhanced jobs. Consistent with managers' view that enhanced jobs are jobs in which workers perform a larger number of work tasks, classroom training was significantly higher for workers in enhanced jobs. Workers in traditional jobs were significantly more likely to report that management provided adequate staff to carry out the work at their hospital and that management would take steps to avoid layoffs if there were budget cuts. Conversely, workers in enhanced jobs—who performed a broader range of tasks—were more likely to report that they were often asked to do more work than they could handle. Traditional jobs in food service appear to be more intrinsically rewarding as well. Workers in traditional jobs are more likely to report that their jobs require them to learn new things (significant at the 10 percent level) and that they find their jobs challenging. These workers also report having more opportunities to move to higher-paying jobs (significant at the 10 percent level). Hourly pay was higher in enhanced work settings: these workers earned $10.03 an hour compared to $9.41 an hour on average for workers in traditionally organized food service jobs. Finally, workers in traditional work settings reported that managers treated them in a consistent and predictable manner and that management was open with them.

Comparing nursing assistants in our sample in enhanced and traditional jobs also reveals few differences. Nursing assistants in enhanced jobs spent significantly less of their time interacting with patients, were more likely to receive one-on-one training, and were less likely to receive training in quality improvement techniques. Consistent with being given responsibility for a broader array of work tasks, they also reported that their jobs were more complex and would take a new hire longer to learn (significant at the 10 percent level). Nursing assistants in traditional jobs were more likely to report that they found their jobs challenging (significant at the 10 percent level), but they also were more likely to report that they found their jobs stressful, too many different demands were made on their time, they were asked to do more work than they could handle, and there were not enough workers to carry out the work.

There were no significant differences in pay: nursing assistants in enhanced jobs earned on average $10.20 an hour, slightly less than the $10.40 earned by those in traditional jobs. Nevertheless, nursing assistants in enhanced settings were more likely to report that they were satisfied with the fairness of their pay. Finally, nursing assistants in enhanced jobs were more likely to report good relations between management and employees (significant at the 10 percent level) and less likely to be a member of a labor union.[3]

DO ENHANCED JOBS REDUCE TURNOVER OR INCREASE SATISFACTION?

Hospital workers in this study were asked, "All in all, how likely is it that you will try hard to find a job with another employer within the next year—very likely, somewhat likely, or not likely at all?" About 18 percent of both food service workers and nursing assistants reported that they were highly likely to quit. In response to the question "Overall, how satisfied would you say you are with your job—highly satisfied, somewhat satisfied, somewhat dissatisfied, or highly dissatisfied?" 31 percent of food service workers and 39 percent of nursing assistants reported that they were highly satisfied with their jobs. We created a job satisfaction index that includes, in addition to this overall measure of satisfaction, employees' satisfaction with opportunities for personal growth and satisfaction with the resources they have to do their jobs. Chronbach's α for this index is 0.79. In this section, we examine the effect of being in an enhanced job on the likelihood that a worker will try hard to find another job and on the index of job satisfaction. The mean values for key variables in our analysis are reported in appendix 3.2.

The 469 nursing assistants and food service workers in this analysis work in 58 departments in 12 hospitals. The workplace practices of interest—those related to enhanced jobs, training, and participation in teams—vary by department. Employees' observations of these practices are not independent, and workers employed in a department may vary systematically in some important but unobserved characteristics. We take this into account in the empirical analysis, clustering on department to adjust the standard errors. Sample size considerations led us to pool data for the 2 occupations and use a dummy variable for nursing assistants to examine differences between them.

In all of the models reported in tables 3.1 to 3.4, we control for basic demographic variables (not reported in the tables)—gender, race-ethnicity, education, and age[4]—and include a dummy for nursing assistants. We find that women are less likely to quit than men, workers with some college are more likely to quit than other workers, older workers are less likely to quit than younger workers, and black workers are more likely to quit than other workers. With respect to the effect of these basic variables on job satisfaction, we find that black workers are less satisfied with their jobs, while those whose race-ethnicity is "other" (not black, white, or Hispanic) are more satisfied with their jobs. Nursing assistants are consistently more satisfied with their jobs than food service workers.

Model 1 in table 3.1 examines the effect of having an enhanced job on the intention to quit, controlling for gender, race, age, education, and occupation. Model 2 adds the effects of hourly pay, and model 3 also adds union membership. Models 4 through 7 examine the effects of human resource practices that may reduce turnover— employment security, adequate staffing, formal training, and informal training.[5] Being in an enhanced job significantly decreased workers' intention to quit in each of these models (models 2 through 7), as did earning higher wages (models 2 through 7). Union membership has no effect on turnover in this analysis. The perception of employment security and the perception of adequate staffing both reduce employees' intention to quit. Both formal and informal training have no effect on the intention to quit.

In table 3.2, we find that enhanced jobs have no effect on workers' job satisfaction in each of the models (1 through 7). In model 2, we find that earning higher wages has a statistically significant positive effect on satisfaction for food service workers and nursing assistants. Union membership (model 3) has no effect on satisfaction for nursing assistants and food service workers. In model 5, however, the union variable becomes statistically significant and is negative. Lower reported job satisfaction of union members is a common finding and is usually attributed to the greater freedom that unionized workers have to voice their discontent without fear of being fired (Freeman 1978; Freeman and Medoff 1984; Meng 1990; Miller 1990). Employment security and staffing adequacy (models 4 and 5) both have a strong positive effect on job satisfaction. Both formal and informal training increase job satisfaction significantly.

The findings of tables 3.1 and 3.2 pose somewhat of an empirical puzzle in that workers in enhanced jobs report a lower intention to quit while at the same time not reporting any greater levels of job satisfaction. Although they provide no definitive answers, several other findings suggest some explanations. First, food service workers do earn more when they work in enhanced jobs. Despite being no more satisfied on the job, they may report being less likely to quit because they earn higher wages. Second, nursing assistants working in enhanced jobs report lower levels of stress on the job than their counterparts working in traditionally organized jobs. Nursing assistants in enhanced jobs also report having better relations with management. Thus, even though they do not find the jobs more satisfying, the lower levels of stress and better working relations with management may explain why nursing assistants in enhanced jobs report that they are less likely to quit.

Table 3.3 examines the relationship between high-performance workplace practices and enhanced jobs. In an analysis not reported here, we find that high-performance work practices as reported by workers are for the most part not associated with enhanced jobs as reported by managers. With the exception of perceptions of employment security, we find no association between enhanced jobs and participation in a problem-solving team, pay contingent on performance, training (either formal or informal), or perceptions of staff adequacy. Broadening jobs and assigning employees to specific departments, as managers do in enhanced work settings, have not led to the introduction of high-performance work practices.

In models 1 and 2 in table 3.3, we examine the effects on turnover and job satisfaction, respectively, of enhanced jobs, higher wages, and high-performance work practices. As before, we find that enhanced jobs reduce employee intentions to quit but do not affect job satisfaction. Higher wages and perceptions of employment security also reduce turnover for both groups of workers. Higher

(Text continues on p. 107.)

Table 3.1 The Effect of Enhanced Jobs on Turnover

	Model 1	Model 2	Model 3	Model 4	Model 5	Model 6	Model 7
Nursing assistant	-0.427**	-1.407	-0.262	-0.209	-0.505	-0.188	-0.172
	(.209)	(1.22)	(0.218)	(-0.413)	(0.653)	(0.211)	(0.221)
Enhanced	-0.277	-0.314**	-0.366**	-0.350*	-0.572***	-0.320*	-0.298*
	(0.180)	(0.158)	(0.177)	(0.188)	(-0.207)	(0.173)	(0.175)
Wage	—	-0.245**	-0.170**	—*	-0.165**	-0.172**	-0.185**
		(0.112)	(0.067)	(0.067)	(-0.077)	(0.069)	(0.077)
Nursing assistant × wage	—	0.120	—	—	—	—	—
		(0.127)					
Union member	—	—	-0.086	-0.225	0.005	—	—
			(0.276)	(0.278)	(0.307)		
Staff adequacy	—	—	—	-0.350***	—	—	—
				(0.130)			
Nursing assistant × staff adequacy	—	—	—	-0.003	—	—	—
				(0.156)			

Employment security	—	—	—	—	−0.492***	—	—
					(0.162)		
Nursing assistant × employment security	—	—	—	—	0.102	—	—
					(0.208)		
Formal training	—	—	—	—	—	−0.089	—
						(0.277)	
Informal training	—	—	—	—	—	—	−0.441
							(0.283)
N	447	401	397	394	372	400	400
Prob > Chi 2	0.0000	0.0000	0.000	0.000	0.000	0.000	0.000
Pseudo R-squared	.0419	.0538	.0540	.0712	.0811	.053	.058

Source: Authors' compilation.
Note: Control variables include gender, race-ethnicity, education, and age. Robust standard errors are in parentheses. Intention to quit job uses an ordered logit regression.
* .05 < p < .10.
** .01 < p < .05.
*** p < .01.

Table 3.2 The Effect of Enhanced Jobs on Job Satisfaction

	Model 1	Model 2	Model 3	Model 4	Model 5	Model 6	Model 7
Nursing assistant	0.563**	1.883**	0.559**	0.850*	1.263**	0.378*	0.490**
	(0.238)	(0.817)	(0.228)	(0.466)	(0.581)	(0.212)	(0.199)
Enhanced	0.124	0.075	0.076	0.076	0.231	0.069	0.056
	(0.187)	(0.196)	(0.185)	(0.170)	(0.175)	(0.200)	(0.181)
Wage	—	0.249***	0.173***	0.121**	0.127**	0.158**	0.178***
		(0.058)	(0.060)	(0.057)	(0.055)	(0.061)	(0.058)
Nursing assistant × wage	—	−0.132	—	—	—	—	—
		(0.082)					
Union member	—	—	−0.413	−0.227	−0.540*	—	—
			(0.338)	(0.324)	(0.285)		
Staff adequacy	—	—	—	0.885***	—	—	—
				(0.098)			
Nursing assistant × staff adequacy	—	—	—	−0.184	—	—	—
				(0.129)			

Employment security	—	—	—	—	0.745*** (0.140)	—	—
Nursing assistant × employment security	—	—	—	—	-0.289 (0.180)	—	—
Formal training	—	—	—	—	—	0.546** (0.240)	—
Informal training	—	—	—	—	—	—	0.861*** (0.159)
N	446	400	396	393	371	399	399
Prob > F	0.000	0.000	0.000	0.000	0.000	0.000	0.000
R-squared	0.050	0.071	0.074	0.259	0.168	0.082	0.114

Source: Authors' compilation.
Note: Control variables include gender, race-ethnicity, education, and age. Robust standard errors are in parentheses. Job satisfaction uses an OLS regression.
* $.05 < p < .10$.
** $.01 < p < .05$.
*** $p < .01$.

Table 3.3 The Effect of Enhanced Jobs and Other Human Resource Variables on Turnover and Job Satisfaction

	Model 1: Turnover	Model 2: Job Satisfaction	Model 3: Turnover
Nursing assistant	−2.05	2.73**	−0.301
	(1.475)	(1.04)	(1.70)
Enhanced	−0.511**	0.166	−0.483**
	(0.214)	(0.159)	(0.226)
Wage	−0.282**	0.250***	−0.121
	(0.131)	(0.071)	(0.150)
Nursing assistant × wage	0.181	−0.246**	0.022
	(0.149)	(0.091)	(0.171)
Union member	0.111	−0.339	−0.099
	(0.294)	(0.320)	(0.370)
Staff adequacy	−0.168	0.586***	0.130
	(0.126)	(0.091)	(0.147)
Employment security	−0.345***	0.240**	−0.250**
	(0.118)	(0.100)	(0.119)
Problem-solving team	0.104	0.376*	0.314
	(0.247)	(0.208)	(0.232)
Pay for performance	−0.049	0.215	−0.010
	(0.198)	(0.172)	(0.208)
Formal training	0.009	0.168	0.105
	(0.273)	(0.234)	(0.236)
Informal training	−0.398	0.404**	−0.228
	(0.285)	(0.177)	(0.288)
Job satisfaction	—	—	−0.535***
			(0.082)
N	345	343	342
Prob > F	—	0.000	—
R-squared	—	0.306	—
Prob > Chi 2	0.000	—	0.000
Pseudo R-squared	0.099	—	0.170

Source: Authors' compilation.
Note: Control variables include gender, race-ethnicity, education, and age. Robust standard errors are in parentheses. Intention to quit job uses an ordered logit regression. Job satisfaction uses an OLS regression.
* $.05 < p < .10$.
** $.01 < p < .05$.
*** $p < .01$.

wages increase job satisfaction for food service workers, but in this model they have no effect on nursing assistants' satisfaction. Perceptions of employment security and staff adequacy increase job satisfaction. In addition, those participating on a problem-solving team and receiving informal training are more satisfied. Finally, in model 3 we find that more satisfied workers are less likely to quit. Enhanced jobs still significantly reduce employee intentions to quit when job satisfaction is added to the model. Higher wages no longer have a direct effect on employees' intention to leave their jobs but rather reduce turnover indirectly through their effect on job satisfaction.

Table 3.4 examines the effects of variables that measure whether the workplace can be characterized as a high-commitment workplace—employees' trust in managers, stress, and intrinsic rewards of the job—on intention to quit and job satisfaction. Prior research shows that a high-trust environment, less stressful work settings, and jobs that are intrinsically rewarding can increase job satisfaction and reduce turnover (Appelbaum et al. 2000; Batt 2000). We measure trust as an index of four items: supervisors treating workers fairly; management being open and up front with workers; good relationships between managers and employees; and the extent to which respondents trust management (Chronbach's $\alpha = 0.84$). We measure stress as an index of four items: the extent to which respondents experience conflict with coworkers; how often respondents experience too many demands on their time; how often respondents are asked to do more work than they can handle; and how often respondents feel depressed about work (Chronbach's $\alpha = 0.72$). Finally, intrinsic rewards are measured by the following four items: "The job makes good use of my skills and knowledge"; "The job requires that I learn new things"; "The job requires me to be creative"; and "The job is challenging" (Chronbach's $\alpha = 0.80$).

Individual perceptions of trust have sometimes been criticized as inadequate since it may be difficult to distinguish between more trusting individuals and individuals who work in a high-trust environment. We address this issue by first calculating an average trust variable for each department, then constructing the deviation of each employee's perception of trust from the average value of trust for the employee's department. The deviations are positive for individuals whose perceptions of trust are above the average for their department, and negative for those for whom they are lower. In

Table 3.4 The Effect of Trust, Stress, and Intrinsic Rewards on Turnover and Job Satisfaction

	Model 1: Turnover	Model 2: Job Satisfaction
Nursing assistant	−0.280	0.133
	(0.264)	(0.160)
Enhanced	−0.238	0.117
	(0.217)	(0.129)
Wage	−0.148*	0.005
	(0.088)	(0.046)
Union member	0.125	−0.109
	(0.321)	(0.232)
Staff adequacy	0.325**	0.108
	(0.147)	(0.092)
Employment security	−0.077	−0.066
	(0.123)	(0.058)
Problem-solving team	−0.038	0.489***
	(0.260)	(0.133)
Pay for performance	−0.139	0.194*
	(0.178)	(0.109)
Formal training	0.272	−0.199
	(0.297)	(0.160)
Informal training	−0.102	0.069
	(0.279)	(0.130)
Trust	−0.187***	0.135***
	(0.052)	(0.035)
Stress	0.209***	−0.162***
	(0.040)	(0.026)
Intrinsic reward	−0.054	0.232***
	(0.056)	(0.039)
N	336	335
Prob > F	—	0.000
R-squared	—	0.554
Prob > Chi 2	0.000	—
Pseudo R-squared	0.181	—

Source: Authors' compilation.
Note: Robust standard errors are in parentheses. Intention to quit job uses an ordered logit regression. Job satisfaction uses an OLS regression.
* $.05 < p < .10$.
** $.01 < p < .05$.
*** $p < .01$.

empirical work not reported here, we examine whether personal characteristics or workplace characteristics predict these deviations. We find that personal characteristics, such as gender and race-ethnicity, do not explain differences in perceptions of trust. Workers with less than a high school diploma and older workers are more trusting than other employees. Importantly, as in other research (Appelbaum et al. 2000), high-performance workplace practices are important predictors of workers' trust in management. Participation in a team and receiving formal training lead to greater trust, as does the employee's perception that he or she has employment security and there is adequate staffing. Working in an enhanced job also increases trust. Notably, higher wages do not predict trust. It is not simply the case that better-paid workers like their managers better. As expected, trust and job satisfaction are highly correlated. Overall, the evidence suggests that it is not simply the case that more trusting people express greater trust in their managers, but that the trust variable captures objective conditions of individuals' jobs.

Models 1 and 2 in table 3.4 examine the effects of employees' trust in management (measured as the deviation from average value of trust in the employees' department), stress, and intrinsic rewards of the job on turnover and satisfaction. We find that higher trust reduces employees' intention to quit while greater stress increases it. Intrinsic job rewards do not affect turnover. Higher wages and adequate staffing reduce turnover, but neither enhanced jobs nor high-performance practices (participation in a team, pay contingent on performance, formal or informal training) affect turnover. Both higher trust and intrinsic rewards increase job satisfaction, while greater stress reduces it. As before, enhanced jobs do not affect employee job satisfaction. However, participation in a problem-solving team and pay contingent on performance increase satisfaction.

It is important to note that while many employees responded that their pay is contingent on unit or hospital performance, there is no evidence of a direct contingent pay system. Rather, the observed response arises from employees perceiving that they will earn more money, probably through better pay increases, if the hospital performance is better.

CONCLUSION

The analysis in this chapter suggests that hospital managers are correct in their view that changes in the work environment can reduce turnover and increase workers' job satisfaction. In particular, the enhanced jobs introduced by managers to reduce turnover are effective in accomplishing this goal. Broadening jobs and assigning employees to specific units reduces their intention to quit. Enhanced jobs do not, however, have an effect on job satisfaction. High-performance workplace practices, with the possible exception of perceptions of employment security, do not have a direct effect on turnover. However, participation in a problem-solving team, pay contingent on performance, and formal and informal training all have a positive effect on job satisfaction. Since employee satisfaction reduces turnover, high-performance workplace practices do have an indirect effect and lead to lower turnover. Finally, high-commitment workplaces—where workers report higher levels of trust and lower levels of stress—both reduce employees' intention to quit and raise satisfaction. Levels of stress are lower where staffing is adequate.

The message for managers is clear. Workplace practices—even the modest changes that enhanced jobs entail—can be effective in reducing turnover. Enhanced jobs have no effect, however, on employee satisfaction. High-performance workplace practices such as teamwork and training raise job satisfaction and indirectly reduce turnover. Bolder changes in the work organization of low-skill jobs and greater investment in the skills of the workers who fill them are effective in reducing turnover. Practices that increase employees' trust in managers also raise satisfaction and reduce turnover.

Other types of managerial practices are also important for reducing turnover. The analysis clearly demonstrates that higher wages and adequate staffing reduce turnover. Employees in low-skill jobs have less desire to quit when pay is higher and hospitals provide adequate staff. Adequate staffing reduces stress by enabling hospital workers to avoid having too many demands made on their time, being asked to do more than they can accomplish, and experiencing conflicts with coworkers.

It is probably not news to managers that higher wages and lower patient-to-staff ratios reduce turnover. But financial pressures on hospitals from the insurance industry, continued shrinking of government funding, and the aging of the population make it difficult for hospitals to act on this knowledge.

Hospitals and workers are caught in a kind of catch-22, and the quality of patient care is likely to suffer unless funding of the medical system is increased and a direct effort is made to raise pay and increase staffing levels. As the U.S. population ages, this will become an ever more acute public policy issue. Moreover, most hospitals probably would not direct any greater reimbursements they might receive toward increasing wages for low-skilled workers but rather toward addressing other pressures they face, including: labor shortages of nurses and pharmacists, investments in new technologies, and the development of better physician services. Although hospital managers might recognize that the enhancement of jobs for low-wage, low-skill occupations would improve outcomes, they might not be willing to invest the resources necessary to change the jobs. This investment would include raising wage rates for employees and providing sufficient staff. We saw a clear instance of widespread changes in enhanced jobs, including broad task responsibilities, extensive training, and higher wages, in the presence of a strong union in a city with high union density. With its willingness to devote independent resources to improving jobs, this union was able to work with hospital managers to design jobs that addressed both hospital and employee needs.

We would like to thank the Russell Sage and Rockefeller Foundations for their generous support of this research. We would also like to thank Danielle Young for her research assistance.

APPENDIX 3.1: VARIABLES USED TO COMPARE TRADITIONAL AND ENHANCED WORK ORGANIZATION

- Measures of job autonomy

- Measures of task variety

- Measures of task interdependence

- Participation in problem-solving teams

- Formal and informal training

- Quality improvement, interpersonal skills, and technical training

- Length of time it would take to train a person to do the respondent's job

- Education
- The extent of communication with coworkers and supervisor
- Employment security
- Adequate staffing
- Intrinsic rewards from the job
- Stress
- Participation in decisions
- Union membership and coverage
- Hourly wage
- Performance-based pay
- Measures of trust in management and supervisor fairness
- Promotion opportunities
- Relations with coworkers
- Relations with management
- Measures of organizational commitment
- Hours of overtime
- Satisfaction with pay and benefits

Table 3.A1 Mean Values for Key Variables (Nursing Assistants and Food Service Workers Only)

	Observations	Mean	Standard Deviation	Minimum	Maximum
Nursing assistant	469	0.65	0.477	0	1
Food service worker	469	0.35	0.477	0	1
Gender	469	0.84	0.367	0	1
White	456	0.64	0.482	0	1
Black	456	0.27	0.447	0	1
Hispanic	456	0.05	0.228	0	1
Other race	456	0.04	0.184	0	1
Less than high school	467	0.06	0.238	0	1
High school graduate	467	0.36	0.482	0	1
Some college	467	0.46	0.499	0	1
College graduate	467	0.11	0.318	0	1
Age	465	38.52	12.838	17	81
Enhanced	469	0.48	0.500	0	1
Wage	418	10.04	1.660	6.55	18.97
Union member	463	0.17	0.375	0	1
Employment security	429	3.01	0.995	1	4
Staff adequacy	464	2.73	1.092	1	4
Problem-solving team	461	0.58	0.495	0	1
Pay for performance	435	0.39	0.487	0	1
Formal training	467	0.66	0.473	0	1
Informal training	468	0.57	0.496	0	1
Trust index	456	12.44	3.359	4	17
"Supervisors treat workers fairly."	463	3.21	0.938	1	4
"Management is open and up front with me."	465	2.86	0.872	1	4
Management-employee relationship	464	3.21	1.170	1	5
How much do you trust management?	465	3.11	1.036	1	4

Table 3.A1 *Continued*

	Observations	Mean	Standard Deviation	Minimum	Maximum
Stress index	463	11.44	3.313	4	20
How often do you experience conflict?	468	2.41	1.024	1	5
How often do you have too many demands?	467	3.57	1.107	1	5
How often are you asked to do more than you can handle?	468	3.30	1.206	1	5
How often do you feel depressed at work?	467	2.15	1.112	1	5
Intrinsic reward index	461	12.94	2.741	4	16
"My job makes good use of my knowledge/ skills."	468	3.27	0.800	1	4
"My job requires that I learn new things."	467	3.29	0.869	1	4
"My job requires me to be creative."	467	3.06	0.938	1	4
"My job is challenging."	466	3.30	0.894	1	4
Intention to quit job	466	1.57	0.763	1	3
Job satisfaction index	465	9.45	1.859	3	12
How satisfied are you with your personal growth and development?	468	3.15	0.721	1	4
How satisfied are you with the resources to do your job?	467	3.08	0.765	1	4
Overall, how satisfied are you with your job?	468	3.21	0.743	1	4

Source: Authors' compilation.

NOTES

1. Housekeeping and food service jobs require no formal education; these jobs often do not even require the ability to read and write English. Nursing assistant jobs do require additional formal training. However, because such training often consists of little more than six weeks of community college or in-hospital training, we have put nursing assistants in our category of low-skilled workers.
2. The overall union density of these two cities was not particularly low; unionization in the hospital sector in both cities, however, was low.
3. This finding will likely change when we add to the study our analysis of the worker responses from the four unionized hospitals. All nursing assistants in those hospitals worked in enhanced jobs and were paid significantly more than their non-union counterparts in other cities.
4. Gender = male or female; race-ethnicity = white, black, Hispanic, or other; education = less than a high school degree, high school degree, some college, or college graduate.
5. We also examined whether part-time workers differed from full-time workers in their intention to quit or in job satisfaction. We found that work schedules did not have a significant effect. These results are not shown in the tables.

REFERENCES

Appelbaum, Eileen, Thomas Bailey, Peter Berg, Arne L. Kalleberg. 2000. *Manufacturing Advantage: Why High Performance Work Systems Pay Off.* Ithaca, N.Y.: Cornell University Press.

Arthur, Jeffrey B. 1994. "Effects of Human Resource Systems on Manufacturing Performance and Turnover." *Academy of Management Journal* 37(3): 670–87.

Ashford, Susan J., Cynthia Lee, and Philip Bobko. 1989. "Content, Causes, and Consequences of Job Insecurity: A Theory-Based Measure and Substantive Test." *Academy of Management Journal* 32(4): 803–29.

Batt, Rosemary. 2000. "Managing Customer Services: Human Resource Practices, Turnover, and Sales Growth." *Academy of Management Journal* 45(3): 587–97.

Clegg, Chris W. 1983. "Psychology of Employee Lateness, Absence, and Turnover." *Journal of Applied Psychology* 68(1): 88–101.

Cotton, John L., and Jeffrey M. Tuttle. 1986. "Employee Turnover: A Meta-analysis and Review with Implications for Research." *Academy of Management Review* 11(1): 55–70.

Freeman, Richard B. 1978. "Job Satisfaction as an Economic Variable." *American Economic Review* 68(2): 135–41.

Freeman, Richard B., and James Medoff. 1984. *What Do Unions Do?* New York: Basic Books.

Hackman, J. Richard, and Ed Lawler. 1971. "Employee Reactions to Job Characteristics." *Journal of Applied Psychology* 55(3): 259–86.

Hackman, J. Richard, and Greg R. Oldham. 1975. "Development of the Job Diagnostic Survey." *Journal of Applied Psychology* 60(2): 159–70.

———. 1976. "Motivation Through the Design of Work: Test of a Theory." *Organizational Behavior and Human Performance* 16: 250–79.

———. 1980. *Work Redesign.* Reading, Mass.: Addison-Wesley.

Hospitals and Health Networks. 2001. "2001 Contract Management Survey." *Hospitals and Health Care Networks* (October): 60.

Huselid, Mark A. 1995. "The Impact of Human Resource Management Practices on Turnover, Productivity, and Corporate Financial Performance." *Academy of Management Journal* 38: 635–72.

Kalleberg, Arne L. 1977. "Work Values and Job Rewards: A Theory of Job Satisfaction." *American Sociological Review* 42(1): 124–43.

Leidner, Robin. 1993. *Fast Food, Fast Talk: Service Work and the Routinization of Everyday Life.* Berkeley: University of California Press.

Leonard, Jonathan S. 1987. "Carrots and Sticks: Pay, Supervision, and Turnover." *Journal of Labor Economics* 5(4): s136–152.

Meng, Ronald. 1990. "The Relationship Between Unions and Job Satisfaction." *Applied Economics* 22(12): 1635–48.

Miller, Paul W. 1990. "Trade Unions and Job Satisfaction." *Australian Economic Papers* 25(55): 226–43.

Osterman, Paul. 1987. "Turnover, Employment Security, and the Performance of the Firm." In *Human Resources and the Performance of the Firm,* edited by M. M. Kleiner, R. N. Block, M. Roomkin, and S. W. Salsburg. Madison, Wisc.: Industrial Relations Research Association.

Palmore, Erdman. 1969. "Predicting Longevity: A Follow-up Controlling for Age." *Journal of Gerontology* 39: 109–16.

Plunkett, Jack, W. 2000. *Plunkett's Health Care Industry Almanac.* Houston: Plunkett Research.

Powell, Irene, Mark Montgomery, and James Cosgrove. 1994. "Compensation Structure and Establishment Quit and Fire Rates." *Industrial Relations* 33: 229–48.

Sales, S. M., and J. House. 1971. "Job Dissatisfaction as a Possible Risk Factor in Coronary Heart Disease." *Journal of Chronic Diseases* 23: 861–73.

Shaw, Jason D., John E. Delery, and G. Douglas Jenkins. 1998. "An Organizational-Level Analysis of Voluntary and Involuntary Turnover." *Academy of Management Journal* 41(5): 1–15.

Strunk, Bradley C., Paul B. Ginsburg, and Jon R. Gabel. 2001. "Tracking Health Care Costs." *Health Affairs* 20(6): 8.

Wall, Toby D., Chris W. Clegg, and Paul R. Jackson. 1978. "An Evaluation of the Job Characteristics Model." *Journal of Occupational Psychology* 51(2): 183–96.

Williamson, Oliver E. 1979. "Transaction-Cost Economics: The Governance of Contractual Relations." *Journal of Law and Economics* 22(2): 233–61.

Zenger, Todd R. 1992. "Why Do Employers Only Reward Extreme Performance?: Examining the Relationships Among Performance, Pay, and Turnover." *Administrative Science Quarterly* 37(2): 198–219.

PART II

Technology: Fewer Better Jobs?

CHAPTER 4

Computer-Based Technological Change and Skill Demands: Reconciling the Perspectives of Economists and Sociologists

David H. Autor, Frank Levy, and Richard J. Murnane

Two recent trends have rekindled interest in questions about the impact of technological change on the skills that workers use at their jobs and the wages these skills command. The first is the increase in education-related earnings inequality. Between 1980 and 1998 the college–high school wage differential rose from 48 to 75 percentage points, a 56 percent gain. The second trend is the remarkable proliferation of computers and information technology. After the spread of mainframe applications during the 1970s, the use of personal computers increased dramatically in the 1980s, followed by enormous growth in applications of networked computers in the 1990s. The coincidence of these trends has led many economists to hypothesize that computer-based technological changes have contributed to the worsening economic prospects (both relative and absolute) of workers with little formal education. Skill-biased technological change may occur by substituting computer-driven machinery for less-educated workers in the performance of some tasks and by complementing more educated workers in the performance of other tasks.

Many sociologists see the economists' argument as unduly deterministic. Based on analyses of case studies, they argue that equating computers with skill-biased technical change ignores management's role in job and organizational design and relies on simplistic definitions of skill.

In this chapter, we offer a potential reconciliation of these positions. We present a verbal model of the types of tasks that computers are suited to perform and describe the implications of the model for the changing task content of jobs performed by humans.

We then offer aggregate evidence from the period 1960 to 1998 that supports the model and its implications.

We next review the limitations of this type of economic framework that are frequently underscored by sociologists—in particular a vague definition of "skill" and an excessive technological determinism. We attempt to show how the economic and sociological viewpoints can be reconciled. As our task framework emphasizes, computers are *not* in all respects "skill-biased"; rather, their specific capabilities and limitations cut across many definitions of skill. Nor does our framework imply that the process of computerization fully determines the structure of work organization. A key insight of our approach is that while economic incentives generated by computerization have predictable and important impacts on the set of tasks that workers perform, work task *content* is not entirely synonymous with the *organization* of jobs. Managers may have considerable discretion—at least in the short run—in bundling tasks into jobs with attendant impacts on skill demands.

We show how this composite model of "technological task determinism" and managerial discretion over task organization helps to interpret the impact of the introduction of digital check imaging on the organization of jobs and skill demands in two back office departments of a large bank. The introduction of check imaging led to the computerization of certain tasks in both departments. The reorganization of the remaining tasks differed across the two departments, however, yielding qualitatively different impacts on the types of skills demanded.

A VERBAL MODEL OF WHAT COMPUTERS DO

We begin by conceptualizing a job from a "machine's-eye" view as a series of tasks: moving an object, performing a calculation, communicating a piece of information, or resolving a discrepancy. In this context, we ask: Which tasks can be performed by a computer? A general answer is that computers perform tasks that can be fully described as a series of explicit procedures or programs. This description includes a large number of tasks. And as human engineering prowess has improved and the price of computing power has declined, the variety of tasks that can be cost-effectively computerized has increased immeasurably. There are also numerous tasks, however, that cannot (yet) be described as a series of explicit procedures, and these tasks do not lend themselves to computerization. To illustrate these two categories of tasks, we first explore the application of computers to manual tasks and then discuss information processing (cognitive) tasks.

Many manual tasks that humans perform (or used to perform) at their jobs are readily specified in straightforward computer code and accomplished by machines—for example, monitoring the temperature of a steel finishing line or moving a windshield into place on an assembly line. However, a problem that arises with many tasks, as Michael Polanyi put it, is that "we can know more than we can tell" (Polanyi 1966, 4). Accordingly, it is difficult to develop machines that carry out these tasks. For example, it is a trivial undertaking for a human child to walk on two legs across a room to pick an apple from a bowl of fruit. This same task is presently a daunting challenge for computer science and robotics (see Pinker 1997).[1] Both optical recognition of objects in a visual field and bipedal locomotion across an uneven surface appear to require poorly understood algorithms—the one in optics, the other in mechanics.[2]

We refer to tasks requiring visual and manual skills as "nonroutine manual activities." We emphasize the phrase *nonroutine* because if a manual task is sufficiently well specified or performed in a well-controlled environment, it often can be automated despite the seeming need for nonroutine visual or manual skills—for example, industrial robots can work on an assembly line. It is this "routineness," or predictability—an engineered attribute of an assembly line—that makes automation of manual activities feasible.[3]

Machinery has substituted for repetitive human labor since (at least) the Industrial Revolution (see Hounshell 1985; Mokyr 1990; Goldin and Katz 1998). What computer capital uniquely contributes to this process is the capability to perform *symbolic processing,* that is, to calculate, store, retrieve, sort, and act on abstract representations of information. Although symbolic processing is conceptually straightforward, the remarkable generality of this tool allows computers to supplant or augment human cognition in a vast set of information-processing tasks that have historically been the mind's exclusive dominion. In economic terms, advances in information technology have sharply lowered the price of accomplishing procedural cognitive tasks. Accordingly, computers increasingly substitute for the routine information-processing, communications, and coordinating functions performed by clerks, cashiers, telephone operators, bank tellers, bookkeepers, and other handlers of repetitive information-processing tasks.[4]

The applicability of computers to cognitive tasks is circumscribed, however, by the need for an unambiguous, ordered sequence of instructions specifying how to achieve a desired end. Consequently, there is little computer software that can develop, test, and draw inferences from models, solve new problems, or form persuasive arguments—tasks that many jobs require.[5] In the words of the artificial intelligence pioneer Patrick Winston (1999):

> The goal of understanding intelligence, from a computational point of view, remains elusive. Reasoning programs still exhibit little or no common sense. Today's language programs translate simple sentences into database queries, but those language programs are derailed by idioms, metaphors, convoluted syntax, or ungrammatical expressions. Today's vision programs recognize engineered objects, but those vision programs are easily derailed by faces, trees, and mountains.

The capabilities and limitations of present computer technology make it more suitable, in our terminology, for routine than for non-routine tasks. By implication, computers are *relative complements* to workers engaged in nonroutine tasks. This complementarity flows through three channels.

First, at a mechanical level, computers increase the share of human labor input devoted to nonroutine cognitive tasks by offloading routine manual and cognitive tasks from expensive professionals. Second, an outward shift in the supply of routine informational inputs (both in quantity and quality) increases the marginal productivity of workers performing nonroutine tasks that rely on these inputs. For example, comprehensive bibliographic searches increase the quality of legal research; timely market information improves the efficiency of managerial decisionmaking; richer customer demographics increases the productivity of salespersons, and so forth.

Third, and perhaps most significantly, workplace computerization appears to increase the relative demand for solving nonroutine cognitive problems (see, for example, Bartel, Ichniowski, and Shaw 2000; Fernandez 1999; Levy, Beamish, and Murnane 1999). Because "solved" problems are intrinsically routine and hence readily computerized, the comparative advantage of labor in a computerized environment is specifically in handling nonroutine problems such as resolving production deficiencies and handling exceptions. In net, these arguments imply that price declines in computerization should augment the productivity of workers engaged in nonroutine cognitive tasks.

Table 4.1 provides examples of jobs in each cell of our two-by-two matrix of workplace tasks (routine versus nonroutine, manual versus information-processing) and states our hypothesis about the impact of computerization on the tasks in each cell.

EMPIRICAL EVIDENCE SUPPORTING THE MODEL

Since our approach conceptualizes jobs in terms of their component tasks rather than the educational attainments of the job-holders (a more conventional approach), examining the empirical implications of the model requires measures of tasks performed in particular jobs and their changes over time. We drew on information from the fourth edition and revised fourth edition of the U.S. Department of Labor's *Dictionary of Occupational Titles* (DOT) (1977, 1991). The details of our data construction are provided in Autor, Levy, and Murnane (2001). Here we discuss the main features.

The U.S. Department of Labor released the first edition of the DOT in 1939 to "furnish public employment offices . . . with information and techniques [to] facilitate proper classification and placement of work seekers" (U.S. Department of Labor 1939, xi, as quoted in Miller et al. 1980). Although the DOT was updated four times in the ensuing seventy years (in 1949, 1965, 1977, and 1991), its structure is largely unchanged. DOT examiners make firsthand observations of workplaces and use guidelines supplied by the *Handbook for Analyzing Jobs* to rate occupations along forty-four objective and subjective dimensions, including training times, physical demands, and required worker aptitudes, temperaments, and interests.[6]

We appended DOT occupation characteristics to the census and Current Population Survey employment files for 1960, 1970, 1980, 1990, and 1998. In measuring changes in task requirements, we exploited two sources of variation. The first consists of changes over time in the occupational distribution of employment econ-

Table 4.1   Hypothesized Impact of Workplace
Computerization on Four Categories of
Job Tasks

	Routine Tasks	Nonroutine Tasks
Visual and man-ual tasks		
Examples	Picking and sorting engi-neered objects on an as-sembly line	Janitorial services
	Reconfiguring production lines to enable short runs	Truck driving
Computer impact	Computer control makes capital substitution feasible	Limited opportunities for substitution or complemen-tarity
Information-pro-cessing cogni-tive tasks		
Examples	Bookkeeping	Medical diagnosis
	Filing and retrieving textual data	Legal writing
	Processing procedural inter-actions and transactions (for example, a bank teller)	Persuading and selling
Computer impact	Substantial substitution	Strong complementarities

Source: Autor, Levy, and Murnane (2001, table 1).

omywide and within industries, holding task content within occupations at its DOT 1977 level. We referred to this source of variation as the "extensive" (across-occupations) margin. Variation along this margin does not, however, account for changes in task content within occupations (see, for example, Levy and Murnane 1996). Accordingly, we exploited changes between successive DOT revisions in 1977 and 1991 to measure changes in task content measures *within* occupations, which we labeled the "intensive" margin.

To identify plausible indicators of the skills discussed earlier, we reduced the DOT measures to a relevant subset using their textual definitions and detailed examples provided by the *Handbook for Analyzing Jobs* (U.S. Department of Labor 1972), the guidebook used by the DOT examiners. Based on these definitions and an examination of means by major occupation for the year 1970, we selected five variables that appeared to best approximate our skill constructs.

To measure nonroutine cognitive tasks, we employed two variables, one to capture interactive and managerial skills and the other to capture analytic reasoning skills. The first variable, which codes the extent to which occupations involve direction, control, and planning of activities, takes on consistently high values in occupations that involve a substantial number of nonroutine managerial and interpersonal tasks. To quantify the analytic and technical reasoning requirements of occupations, we drew on a DOT measure of the quantitative skills demanded, ranging from arithmetic to advanced mathematics. We identified a variable measuring adaptability to work with set limits, tolerances, or standards as an indicator of routine cognitive tasks, and we selected a measure of finger dexterity as an indicator of routine manual activity. Finally, we used the variable measuring requirements for eye-hand-foot coordination as an index of nonroutine motor tasks.[7]

In summary, we attached to representative samples of workers for 1959 to 1998 the values of five variables indicating the extent to which each worker's occupation was intensive in each of our five types of tasks. Changes over time in the economywide average values of the task measures, which are illustrated in figure 4.1, reflect the extent to which changes in the occupational distribution of the nation's workforce altered the task content of work performed by the U.S. labor force.[8]

Figure 4.1 reveals three striking patterns. First, the fraction of the labor force employed in occupations that make intensive use of nonroutine cognitive tasks—both interactive and analytic—increased substantially during this period.

In contrast, the percentage of the labor force employed in occupations that are intensive in routine cognitive and routine manual activities has declined over the last three decades. Most notably, while routine cognitive and manual tasks were both *increasing* during the 1960s, each commenced a decline in the 1970s that became more rapid in each subsequent decade. Finally, we observe a steady downward trend against nonroutine manual tasks that predates the computer era.

Although trends at this high level of aggregation are only suggestive, they are consistent with our conceptual model. In particular, our model posits a decline in the task share of human input devoted to routine manual and cognitive activities—the tasks most readily substituted by computers—and concomitant growth in hu-

Figure 4.1 Economywide Measures of Routine and Nonroutine Task Input, 1959 to 1998 (1959 = 0)

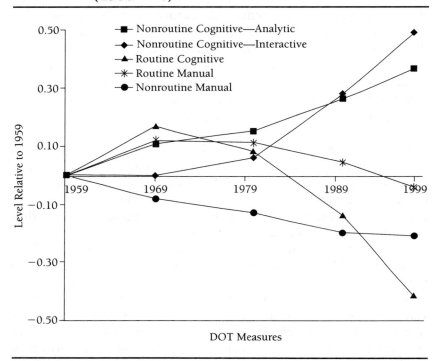

Source: Autor, Levy, and Murnane (2001, figure 1).

man task input of nonroutine activities, particularly nonroutine cognitive activities. We further expect computerization to have had little impact on trends in nonroutine manual task input (such as janitorial services), since computers neither substitute for nor complement these activities to a meaningful degree. This expectation appears consistent with the data.

As a further illustration, table 4.2 enumerates the DOT task measures by major educational group. Notably, while three of five task measures are monotonically increasing in educational attainment, the two measures of routine tasks—cognitive and manual—show a U-shaped relationship to education. High school graduates perform substantially more of both types of routine tasks than either high school dropouts or college graduates. These nonmonotonic patterns

Table 4.2   Means of *Dictionary of Occupational Titles* Job Content Measures Overall and by Education Group at Midpoint of 1960 to 1998 Sample

	Task Measure (0 to 10 Scale)				
	1. Non-Routine Cognitive/ Analytic	2. Non-Routine Cognitive/ Interactive	3. Routine Cognitive	4. Routine Manual	5. Non-Routine Manual
Overall	3.76	2.46	4.61	3.90	1.24
High school dropouts	2.55	1.32	4.93	3.72	1.80
High school graduates	3.34	1.75	5.30	4.09	1.26
Some college	3.97	2.45	4.87	4.02	1.10
College plus	5.36	4.76	2.86	3.57	0.87

Source: Autor, Levy, and Murnane (2001, appendix table 2). Current Population Survey 1980, all employed workers ages eighteen to sixty-four merged with *Dictionary of Occupational Titles* (1977).

suggest that the DOT measures are likely to provide information about job task requirements that is distinct from conventional educational categories.

In a detailed investigation described in Autor, Levy, and Murnane (2001), we show that the economywide trends illustrated in figure 4.1 consist primarily of within-industry shifts in the structure of work organization, reflected by changes in occupational structure. Moreover, these economywide changes are significantly more pronounced in the industries that rapidly computerized in these decades. Strikingly, those occupations that experienced the greatest increase in computer use during the 1980s and 1990s also underwent—according to measurements performed by DOT examiners—the greatest decrease in routine cognitive and routine manual tasks and the greatest increase in nonroutine cognitive tasks. These patterns support the hypothesis that the declining price of computing exerted a meaningful impact on the task structure of occupational employment in the United States during the past three decades.[9]

Although we focus here on the ability of computers to substitute for human labor in routine information processing, advances in electronic communications are potentially as important, a conclusion that is also consistent with our empirical results. These advances have enabled firms to profitably outsource and monitor routine production processes offshore, thereby reducing the demand for these routine skills domestically (see Feenstra and Hanson 1999, 2001; Autor 2001). Thus, while economists have hotly debated whether trade or technology is primarily responsible for rising inequality, this example suggests that the distinction is far from clear-cut.

ALTERNATIVE PERSPECTIVES

Although many economists would interpret this evidence as an indication that skill-biased technological change has helped to shape economywide skill demands, other social scientists, particularly non-economists, find the concept of skill-biased technological change troubling. For example, in a thought-provoking article, Paul Attewell (1990) delineates several conflicting ways in which to conceptualize skill. In the positivist tradition, skill is treated as an attribute of jobs, and jobs that are substantively complex are viewed as "skilled." A difficulty here is the arbitrariness of ranking along a single dimension of complexity jobs that are very different—for example, conducting biological research and managing a large organization.

A different research tradition, ethnomethodology, sees a variety of everyday activities—walking across a crowded room or carrying on a conversation with many voices in the background—as skilled tasks, even though humans master these tasks with little conscious thought. The ethnomethodologists' insight is validated by decades of research in artificial intelligence (Pinker 1997); as noted earlier, computer scientists have been relatively unsuccessful to date at programming computers to perform many of these "simple" activities. These different conceptions of skill raise questions about exactly what economists mean when they refer to "skill-biased technological change" and what the predictions are about the types of tasks that are the most likely candidates to be carried out by computer-driven machinery instead of by people. We believe that our simple conceptual model of "what computers do" provides some counterweight to these critiques.[10]

A different challenge to the skill-biased technological change idea comes from researchers who emphasize—sensibly enough—that the considerable discretion often exercised by managers in deciding how to implement new technologies has differing implications for the organization of work and skill demands (Hunter 1999;

Zuboff 1988). This observation raises the question of what factors influence managers' decisions about the organization of work. Assar Lindbeck and Dennis Snower (2000) propose a model in which managers create single-task jobs to take advantage of specialization when tasks are not complementary (for example, Adam Smith's pin factory) and combine tasks into broader jobs when tasks are complementary. In Autor, Levy, and Murnane (2001), we point out that workplace computerization often provides workers with vastly richer informational inputs—a process called "informating" by Shoshona Zuboff (1988)—and that this effect may increase the productivity of, and demand for, analytically skilled workers who can use this information effectively. Paul Osterman (1994) argues that "high performance job designs"—in which employees are involved in problem-solving, have responsibility for more than one task, and are paid for taking initiative—are likely to be present in organizations that value quality of service and in organizations whose management philosophy attaches importance to increasing the well-being of employees. Other scholars point to considerations of power and culture (Zuboff 1988); still others see government regulations as playing a role in some industries (Hunter 1999).

While agreeing that many factors may influence the technologies and forms of work organization adopted by firms in an industry at any point in time, many economists argue that in the long run competitive pressures lead to the dominance of the most efficient combination of technology and work organization—if there is indeed a single most efficient combination. Of course, the longer the "long run," the less interesting the long-run outcomes are relative to the potential diversity of medium-run forms of organization and technologies.[11]

We believe that it is possible to reconcile the arguments advanced by economists and sociologists concerning the impact of computer-driven technological changes on the organization of work and skill requirements. As argued earlier, rapid improvements in computer-based technology coupled with dramatically declining costs create strong economic incentives to substitute machinery for people in carrying out tasks that can be fully described in terms of procedural or "rules-based" logic and hence performed by a computer. Because of these incentives, computerization generates predictable (bordering on deterministic) changes in the task structure of jobs. For example, it is the rare accounting clerk who still hand-totals long columns of numbers and enters the results on paper ledgers. But the process of computerization is hardly all-encompassing; many tasks in the computerized workplace remain to be performed by humans. It is in the (re-)organization of these tasks that management decisions are likely to play a key role—at least in the short run—in determining how tasks are bundled into jobs, with potentially significant implications for skill demands. The interplay of these partly deterministic and partly discretionary forces is highlighted by our case study.

THE IMPACT OF NEW TECHNOLOGY ON CHECK PROCESSING AT CABOT BANK

In this section, we use our composite model to interpret the impact of a particular technological change on the organization of work and skill demands in two back office departments of a large bank.

CHECK PROCESSING

The steps that banks complete to process customers' deposits have not changed markedly since checks were introduced in the United States shortly after the Civil War. A bank must record ("capture") the amounts of individual checks, "proof the deposit"—that is, verify that the sum of the values of checks deposited by a customer is equal to the amount indicated on the customer's deposit slip—and then post the balance to the appropriate account. The bank then separates the checks into those written by customers of the bank ("on us") and those written on other banks (transit items). It debits the "on us" checks to the appropriate accounts and delivers the checks written on other banks to those banks. Banks must also have procedures to handle "exceptions." These include checks written on accounts that have been closed, checks written for amounts greater than the balances in the accounts on which they are drawn, checks that customers request stop payments on, checks written for large amounts that require signature verification, and fraudulent checks.

Fifty years ago banks did all of the sorting, balancing, posting, and handling of exceptions by hand with the aid of mechanical adding machines. The first major wave of technological change came with Bank of America's introduction of magnetic ink character recognition (MICR) in the early 1950s. Using MICR, a bank could provide its customers with checks and deposit slips with bank and account numbers imprinted at the bottom of the check in machine-readable magnetic ink. Companies, including General Electric, Remington, and IBM, developed reader-sorter machines that could read the information on the MICR line and sort checks according to the banks on which they were drawn (McKenney 1995). This reading-sorting was an early example of computers substituting for human labor input in performing a task that could be accomplished by equipment following a set of procedural instructions expressed in software.

Check Processing in Cabot Bank

"Cabot Bank" is one of the twenty largest banks in the United States. It has both large retail and large commercial banking operations, with branches in several states and in many countries outside the United States. The retail part of Cabot Bank has more than doubled in size over the past decade, primarily through acquisitions of smaller banks.

At Cabot Bank, as at most other U.S. banks, check processing is divided into two departments: Deposit Processing, which handles the checks that are not "exceptions," and Exceptions Processing. Cabot Bank's Deposit Processing Department, which occupies the first floor (downstairs) of a large urban facility, processes the 2.8 million checks deposited in the bank's branches and automatic teller machines each day. Until the mid-1990s, check processing at Cabot Bank centered on the position of the proof machine operator. As an example, the Cabot Bank processing center would receive a package of several hundred checks from Kmart. The package would include a deposit slip and an adding machine tape to show that the checks had been totaled correctly. The proof machine operator would then execute the following steps:

- Remove paper clips and staples from the checks and ensure that each faced in the same direction.

- Key in the amount of each check on the right-hand side of the MICR line.

- Add up the total of the Kmart checks and "proof" the deposit—that is, verify that the checks totaled to the amount on the Kmart deposit slip.

- If the total did not match the deposit slip, examine the adding machine tape and the encoded check amounts to find and correct errors. Possibilities included a keying error by the proof machine operator, a listing error by a Kmart employee, or a check lost in transit.
- Send the checks to the reader-sorter machine, which then sorted them by account number.[12]

During routine processing at Cabot Bank, approximately 3 percent of checks are identified as requiring individual attention. They are sent to the second-floor (upstairs) department, Exceptions Processing, of the same urban facility. Exceptions must be resolved rapidly both to satisfy Federal Reserve rules for returned checks and to provide good customer service.

Ten years ago Exceptions Processing was divided into a large number of narrowly defined jobs. For example, an employee who verified signatures on checks written for amounts greater than $2,000 first found the authorized signature card in a file. She then compared the signature to the signature on the check; if she discovered a discrepancy, she filed a paper form that led to further action by a worker with greater decisionmaking authority. A check could pass through three or four levels before reaching someone with the authority to make a final decision. Another group of workers processed stop payment orders, and still another group handled checks returned for insufficient funds. In each case, a significant portion of the day was spent shuffling paper to find the right checks in a box of newly delivered items or to move checks from one group to another. Since all work was done under deadline, it created substantial employee frustration.

Female high school graduates filled most of the jobs in Exceptions Processing. Turnover was 30 percent per year, a rate that was tolerable only because the skills required were minimal and could be learned quickly. Workers who stayed in Exceptions Processing developed expertise in one task but had little knowledge of the work outside their immediate area. As one manager commented, "We were in a situation where people checked their brains at the door."

As the daily volume of checks rose, the cumbersome workflow created both increasing delays and poor customer service. For example, some customers who were short of cash would buy time by writing multiple checks to creditors and then issuing multiple stop payment requests. Depending on the timing, each check might trigger an overdraft exception as well as the stop payment exception. If a check was large enough, it also would trigger a signature verification exception. Each of the three clerks involved would have only a partial picture of the problem, and each would have to locate the same paper check (in a large box of checks) to complete her processing. In the end, the customer might be (incorrectly) charged with both a stop payment fee and an overdraft fee. If the customer went to a bank branch to resolve the situation, there was no single person in Exceptions Processing for the bank to call.

While the tasks to be accomplished in Cabot Bank's Deposit Processing and Exceptions Processing Departments were different, the common characteristic was the need to handle and frequently move vast numbers of checks—pieces of paper that could be in only one place at one time and could easily be misplaced.

New Technology

Over time a set of forces was pushing Cabot Bank and its competitors to increase check-processing efficiency. The number of checks to be processed increased dramatically.[13] Nonetheless, processing had to be done quickly. Federal Reserve Bank regulations mandated that customers have access to their deposits within a specified period of time (two days for checks drawn on local banks), but regulations also required a bank to return paper checks to the banks on which they were drawn in order to receive payment. Rapid processing was necessary to minimize the costs of float. In addition, banking deregulation had increased competitive pressure to reduce cost and respond to customer demands for new and improved services (Mayer 1997).

To help address pressures on deposit processing and exceptions processing, Cabot Bank introduced "check imaging" into both departments in 1994. With imaging technology, a high-speed camera makes a digital image of the front and back of each check as it passes through the reader-sorter. Imaging eliminated the bottleneck that had existed because a check could be in only one place at one time. Stored on a central computer, check images were accessible to bank employees in both departments working at networked personal computers.[14]

Along with the introduction of check imaging, Cabot Bank adopted optical character recognition (OCR) software to scan and capture the amounts on check images as the checks passed through the reader-sorter. Deposit slips were scanned in a similar way. Computerized imaging and OCR could now accomplish two tasks that had been major bottlenecks hindering productivity improvement. The first was making information on individual checks available to employees in the two departments. The digitized check images stored on the bank's central computer did not need to be moved from one worker to another; they were accessible simultaneously to all authorized bank employees working at networked computers. The second bottleneck was reading and recording the amounts on legible checks and deposit slips, an extremely labor-intensive task when carried out by proof machine operators. Both of these tasks could be automated; indeed, doing so was the reason Cabot Bank adopted the new technology. This still left many tasks to be accomplished that did not lend themselves to automation because they could not be fully described in a sequence of if-then-do steps. Managers of the two departments were responsible for determining how these remaining tasks would be configured into jobs.

THE IMPACT OF NEW TECHNOLOGY ON THE DOWNSTAIRS DEPOSIT PROCESSING DEPARTMENT

Cabot Bank took the advice of the image-processing equipment vendor to reorganize deposit processing according to a standard job template.[15] Under the template, a check first goes to a preparation area where workers remove paper clips and staples and ensure that all checks face in the same direction. These workers then deliver the checks to a reader-sorter machine that magnetizes the ink on the MICR line of the item, reads it, sprays an endorsement and sequence number on the back of the check, microfilms the item front and back, and sorts it to a program-defined pocket based on the routing information on the check. As the checks pass through the reader-sorter, an image camera captures a digitized image of the front and back of the item. At the same time, OCR software scans machine-printed and handwritten numeric amounts in a designated location of the check. Successfully scanned information is stored along with the information on the MICR line of the check. As of

1999, the OCR software successfully "read" about 57 percent of imaged checks.[16]

When a digital dollar amount cannot be recognized, the image is sent first to the screen of a high-speed keyer, who tries to identify the check amount by looking at the numerical image written in the small box on the right side of the check. If the high-speed keyer is not sure of the amount from its numerical rendition, he or she passes the check image electronically to a low-speed keyer. This operator looks at the image of the whole check and, by comparing the numerical representation to the amount written in words, determines the value and keys it in. The keyed-in check amount is added to the electronic record for that check.

Once entered into the system, multicheck deposits are compared with deposit slips automatically. When discrepancies arise, a worker whose title is "image balancer" tracks them down. Using images rather than paper checks, the image balancer performs the error detection and correction that was once one of the multiple tasks performed by the proof machine operator. But the job of image balancer, like other redesigned jobs, now consists of a specialized task.

The introduction of the imaging and OCR technologies has resulted in an unbundling of the proof machine operator's tasks. Computers perform one of these tasks, and the remaining tasks are divided among specialized jobs. More specialized jobs have led, in turn, to a modest increase in wage dispersion among the several narrow jobs that now constitute the core of deposit processing. This specialization and associated wage dispersion is displayed in table 4.3. This table illustrates two points. First, the tasks that proof machine operators carried out before the introduction of image processing have been divided into four jobs, one of which is carried out by computers and three by humans. Second, the wage associated with each depends in part on the scarcity of the relevant skills within the workforce.

Removing staples and ensuring that checks all face in the same direction are tasks that most adults of average eye-hand dexterity can accomplish with no training. Consequently, the hourly pay for this job (check preparer), $9.51, is the lowest among jobs in the bank's two departments.

The job of image balancing requires somewhat scarcer skills.

Table 4.3 Reorganization of Check Processing at Cabot Bank, 1988 and 1998

Tasks	Employee Who Carried Out Task in 1988	Average Hourly Wage Rate in 1988	Number of Full-Time Employees in 1988 per Million Checks	Employee Who Carried Out Task in 1998	Average Hourly Wage Rate in 1998	Number of Full-Time Employees in 1998 per Million Checks
Prepare checks by removing staples and ensuring checks face in same direction				Check preparer	$9.51	16
Key in amount on checks with clear printing or handwriting	Proof machine operator	$10.03	67	Computer		
Decipher amounts on checks with poor handwriting and key in amount				Keyer	$10.00 plus incentives for speed and accuracy	15
Balance the deposit				Image balancer	$11.00	22

Source: Autor, Levy, and Murnane (2002).
Note: Wage rates are in 1998 dollars.

Like the earlier proof machine operator, the image balancer must be able to discover why some deposits do not balance. In addition, whereas the proof machine operator worked with paper, the image balancer must know how to use computers and how to do the work using electronic images instead of paper checks.

Managers in Deposit Processing recruited former proof machine operators to become image balancers because they had already demonstrated the requisite problem-solving skills. The bank provided thirty-six hours of classroom training followed by two weeks of support from an experienced image balancer.[17] In the end, most proof machine operators made the transition; apparently modest amounts of training imparted the requisite computer skills. In 1998 the average pay of the sixty-two image balancers was $11 per hour—16 percent higher than the pay rate for check preparers.

The department's highest wages were paid to the best keyers. While check preparers and image balancers were paid an hourly rate, keyers were paid an hourly rate plus an hourly bonus based on speed and accuracy. A keyer's speed could now be monitored by computer, a feature that simplified bonus determination. Counting the bonus, the best keyers earned $13.50 an hour, $2.00 per hour more than image balancers. This relatively high wage reflected a return to effort and to the skill of being able to recognize and record check amounts extremely rapidly and accurately.[18] As one bank official said, "There is always a demand for good keyers." In fact, "always" is too strong. Owing to improvements in OCR software, a growing fraction of checks are read without human intervention. One result is a decline in the demand for keyers at the bank per million checks processed.

To understand how check imaging affected deposit processing, it is useful to begin with a question. Given proof machine operators' large variety of tasks, why were these tasks originally bundled into a single job rather than assigned to separate workers? The tasks have a natural sequence and so lend themselves to a division of labor. Moreover, accomplishing some of the tasks (balancing) requires skills not needed in carrying out other tasks (removing staples). Although we do not have a definitive answer to this question, we suspect that an important reason for bundling tasks into a single job was to reduce the transactions costs associated with moving paper checks from one employee to another.[19]

The introduction of check imaging and the OCR software had

two effects on this task structure. First, it created strong incentives for management to reduce costs by computerizing the proof machine operator's rules-based task of "reading" and recording the amounts on legible checks. Second, although management had discretion in deciding how to organize the three remaining non-rules-based tasks, the reduction in the cost of moving the information on checks from one worker to another created incentives to divide the tasks into specialized jobs.[20]

In net, the changes in deposit processing were skill-biased. The introduction of image processing and OCR software led to the replacement of high school graduates by computers, thereby increasing the share of bank employees who had more formal education (primarily managers).[21] However, a closer look shows that not all of the changes in the distribution of jobs were skill-enhancing. In particular, check preparation, one of the jobs created when the proof machine operator's job was broken up into four specialized jobs, is a quite unskilled job.

Computer-labor substitution in deposit processing is likely to increase, not only because of further improvements in OCR software but because of potential changes in the regulations governing paper checks. State regulations currently dictate that bank customers can demand the return of their canceled paper checks at the end of each month. Currently, two-thirds of Cabot Bank's customers choose this option. Federal Reserve regulations require that paper checks written on other banks and deposited by Cabot Bank customers be returned to the original banks. Changes in regulations permitting banks to provide customers with paper images of their checks and other banks with digital images of checks would eliminate the jobs of many low-skilled workers who package checks for transit to customers and other banks.[22]

Image processing may ultimately have an impact on the geographic location of deposit-processing services as well. Since image keyers work with digital images, not paper checks, there is no technological reason why image keying needs to be accomplished at the site where the checks are digitized. Competitive pressure may push much of the back office clerical work to low-wage offshore locations, with a significant loss of jobs for less-educated workers in the parent plant.[23] Such geographic dispersion is happening in other industries as well.

THE IMPACT OF NEW TECHNOLOGY ON UPSTAIRS EXCEPTIONS PROCESSING

A central advantage of digitized files over paper files is that more than one person has access to the same information simultaneously. Had image technology been introduced into exceptions processing with no other changes, it is almost certain that productivity would have risen as employees spent less time searching for paper and more time resolving exceptions.

The vice president in charge of exceptions processing wanted, however, to accomplish more. He believed that a broader reorganization could achieve some measure of three goals: improved productivity, better customer service, and better jobs using more skills. In his words: "Fewer people doing more work in more interesting jobs."[24]

He also believed that involving employees in the redesign would both use their knowledge and gain their commitment to the new system. Managers held focus groups of exceptions-processing clerks, asking them what aspects of their jobs were irritating and what changes would make their jobs better. The consensus was that work should no longer be divided by exception type but by customer account, so that the same representative would deal with all exceptions—stop payment requests, overdrafts, and so on—connected to a given account. In this way, for example, a clerk who saw a stop payment order would anticipate a possible (incorrect) overdraft exception as well as other stop payment and overdraft exceptions from the same account. This reorganization would not be cost-free. A representative who had processed one type of exception for a number of years would have to learn how to process a variety of exceptions using networked personal computers. Nonetheless, management accepted the plan.

In deposit processing, the lowered transactions costs of moving information led to a greater division of labor, with the proof machine operator's job broken into several specialized jobs. As illustrated in table 4.4, the introduction of check imaging led to the *opposite* result in exceptions processing: narrow jobs were combined into new, broader jobs with responsibility for handling a variety of exceptions for a block of accounts.

The introduction of image processing eliminated the paper chase that had dominated work in exceptions processing. However, it did

Table 4.4 Reorganization of Exceptions Processing at Cabot Bank, 1994 and 1998

	Employee Who Carried Out Task in 1994	Average Hourly Wage Rate in 1988	Number of Full-Time Employees in 1994 per 65,000 Exceptions[a]	Employee Who Carried Out Task in 1998	Average Hourly Wage Rate in 1998	Number of Full-Time Employees in 1998 per 65,000 Exceptions
Verify signatures on checks written for large amounts	Exceptions processing clerk	$10.64	98			
Implement stop payment orders	Exceptions processing clerk	$10.64	98	Exceptions processing clerk	$13.50	470
Handle overdrafts	Exceptions processing clerk	$10.64	424			
Move information on checks from one exceptions processing clerk to another	Exceptions processing clerk	$10.64	30	Computer		

Source: Autor, Levy, and Murnane (2002).
Note: Wage rates are in 1998 dollars.
[a] There were 650 full-time exceptions processing clerks in 1994. To allocate these clerks among specialized jobs, we rely on a Cabot Bank manager's estimate that approximately 65 percent of clerks processed overdrafts, 15 percent processed stop payment orders, 15 percent verified checks, and the remainder moved boxes of checks from station to station.

not dictate the organization of the three nonroutine tasks: handling overdrafts, processing stop payment orders, and verifying signatures. Combining exceptions-processing tasks into multifunction jobs made sense to Cabot Bank managers and workers. However, some banks that have introduced check imaging have kept jobs in exceptions processing specialized by function.[25] This illustrates the importance of managerial discretion in organizing into jobs those tasks that are not readily described in terms of rules-based logic.

Although the new account-based workflow was designed in anticipation of check imaging, the bank began implementation before imaging technology came on-line. The immediate result—a surprise to managers—was a major improvement in productivity. Before the reorganization, 650 workers processed the 65,000 exceptions each day. By the end of 1995, after the reorganization of the Exceptions Processing Department but before the introduction of the image technology, this same workload was completed by 530 workers.

Achieving the productivity improvement was not costless. Employees underwent an eighty-hour round of initial training (forty hours in the classroom and forty hours on the job) to learn the skills needed to handle the full range of exceptions. The training began with learning to use a computer and moved to learning to handle the interrelationships among different types of exceptions. Managers reported that an important determinant of the effectiveness of the training was that workers who had volunteered to participate in the redesign of the workflow also played key roles in designing and implementing the training.

Although the reorganization of the workflow did result in a marked improvement in productivity, the time spent shuffling paper checks remained a significant bottleneck. For example, answering a query from a branch bank still involved a search for the right paper check. Check imaging removed most of these obstacles. By the end of 1996, a year after the introduction of the image technology, the number of workers in Exceptions Processing had fallen to 470.[26] Ultimately reorganization accounted for about two-thirds of productivity gains, with technology accounting for the other one-third.[27]

Given the productivity gains that Cabot Bank realized from reorganizing exceptions processing before the introduction of the image technology, we asked managers whether the bank had considered undertaking this reengineering during the late 1980s, when check volume was rising. The common response was that the bank was focused on absorbing newly acquired banks and did not consider the reorganization of exceptions processing. The managers also stated that other banks that do not use image processing still organize exceptions processing as a group of narrowly defined jobs. It is possible, though by no means certain, that the business case in favor of reorganization became compelling only when managers knew that the productivity gains from reorganization would be enhanced by the time savings from the elimination of paper shuffling that image processing made possible.

Because Exceptions Processing clerks now had more extensive training to handle a wider variety of tasks—skills valued by the bank's competitors—management decided it was prudent to pay higher wages. In 1993, before the reorganization of the department, 80 percent of the workers were classified as "nonexempt" (that is, their jobs did not require working independently, showing initiative, or supervising others). These nonexempt workers averaged $10.64 an hour (in 1998 dollars). As indicated in table 4.4, average wages in the unit were $13.50 in 1998. Most workers were moved up a pay grade when they successfully completed the training. In addition, management steadily increased the proportion of representatives who were "exempt," reflecting their new responsibilities. By 1998, 35 percent of the unit was in this category.[28]

Management also expanded the range within each pay grade. For example, the pay range in grade 23—a grade to which many representatives were initially assigned—had a 1993 range of $17,829 to $26,332 but a 1998 range of $18,900 to $37,100 (all figures expressed in 1998 dollars). The greater pay range reflected employees' greater scope for judgment and initiative in the redesigned job.[29] In particular, Cabot was one of the first banks to reorganize exceptions processing using check imaging, and management believed that motivated employees could recommend additional improvements. As the vice president said, "If you do your job, you get to keep your job—but you may not get cost-of-living wage increases. If you transform your job in a positive way, you will get a raise. If you transform your job and have a positive impact on the people around you, you will get a promotion."

The story of computerization in exceptions processing illustrates 2 patterns identified in quantitative studies of the consequences of computer-based technological changes. The first is the loss of jobs held by high school graduates. There was a 28 percent decrease in the number of workers needed to process 65,000 exceptions per night. A significant part of this reduction came through reorganization undertaken in anticipation of imaging technology rather than imaging technology per se. But this process—technology acting as a stimulus to reorganizing work routines—is likely to have occurred in many other industries and so may influence patterns in the Current Population Survey and other data sources used in aggregate wage studies. Because of high turnover in Exceptions Processing at Cabot Bank, layoffs were not required; but over the period, 180 positions were eliminated, almost all of them formerly held by high school graduates.

A second pattern identified by quantitative studies is a direct positive impact of computerization on skill demands. Reorganization of work and the introduction of image technology increased the skills needed in exceptions processing. Training went a long way toward increasing the supply of skills, particularly computer skills. Managers reported, however, that a more difficult skill to teach was the ability to "see the whole picture," that is, to understand the sequence of steps in processing a check and recognize the interdependencies among exceptions. Accordingly, Cabot Bank managers restructured the recruiting process. Under the revised procedures, managers asked candidates to describe problems they had encountered in previous jobs or in school and how they resolved them. The intent was to identify candidates who had a history of initiative and problem-solving. In addition, candidates were interviewed by supervisors from several groups and could be hired only if multiple supervisors vetted the hire. In the words of one manager, recruits "have to be right for the whole bank, not just for my area." Managers reported that the new recruiting process favored applicants who had completed at least some years of college.

There are at least two explanations for why managers tended to hire job applicants with some college education for the redesigned Exceptions Processing jobs, and we cannot distinguish between them. One is that completing college course work signals an ability to learn new things quickly, and managers found this to be a good predictor of success in adapting to changes in exceptions processing.[30] An alternative is that since a high school diploma was not a strong indicator of mastery of basic cognitive skills, the managers, perhaps unconsciously, felt that a risk-averse strategy was to hire applicants with college credentials for the recently upgraded jobs.

It is important to point out that college credentials did not become a necessary condition for obtaining a position in Exceptions Processing. Managers reported that in choosing among applicants for the redesigned jobs, they did hire some high school graduates with no postsecondary education. Many of these applicants had served as interns at the bank as part of school-to-career programs and had demonstrated initiative and an ability to learn quickly.

Management's redesign of the exceptions-processing job augmented the "skill bias" of the image-processing technology. Had managers retained the narrow task structure, computerization would have eliminated the jobs of many high school workers engaged in the exceptions-processing "paper chase." But the broader job design also spurred managers to recruit college graduates into the department, something they had not done before.

Was the new job design inevitable? Clearly not, at least in the short run. Management had considerable discretion to use the technology to either broaden the exceptions-processing job or leave the previous job design intact—with image processing improving efficiency by eliminating the paper chase. We do not know why Cabot Bank chose to reorganize the work of exceptions processing while other banks did not. One explanation may be that the relevant department was under the supervision of a vice president who had a strong personal commitment to improving job quality as well as reducing costs, a belief in the importance of involving line workers in the redesign process, and enough job security to assume the risks associated with such a significant change. However, in a case study of a single bank it is not possible to evaluate alternative explanations.

For the reasons outlined by Lindbeck and Snower (2000), we suspect that Cabot Bank's choice effectively leverages the complementarities among the exceptions-processing tasks and will be rewarded by the market in the long run.[31] But not enough time has elapsed to judge whether the different ways of organizing work in exceptions processing reflect multiple equilibria, or whether competition will reveal that one organizational form is more efficient than others.

CONCLUSIONS

Although there is considerable aggregate evidence linking computerization to changes in skill demands (some of it described in this chapter), we believe it is erroneous to assume that computers are in all respects "skill-biased" or that their impacts entirely determine the structure of work organization. As our conceptual model indicates, computers tend to displace certain types of tasks (routine cognitive and routine manual), complement others (nonroutine cognitive), and have little impact on yet another category of tasks (nonroutine manual). Evidence from the changing task structure of work over the past four decades indicates that the tasks performed by workers have indeed shifted along the dimensions predicted by this framework.

Yet it is important to observe that the set of tasks workers perform is not synonymous with the organization of jobs. As the Cabot Bank case illustrates, managers may have considerable discretion in bundling tasks into jobs, with attendant impacts on skill demands. Although in some cases the technology and information flow appear to largely dictate the structure of job tasks (as we believe occurred in the downstairs department of Cabot Bank), in other cases managers may choose among job organizations that either demand greater problem-solving skills (as occurred in the upstairs department) or primarily emphasize routine execution of narrowly defined tasks.

Of course, in the long run a dominant form of work organization may emerge, owing to technological dominance or social norms. Although it is our suspicion that computerized and information-intensive workplaces favor work organizations that emphasize problem-solving skills and flexibility, the evidence we have encountered to date indicates that other forms of organization are technologically and economically feasible at present.

The framework and evidence we have presented point to (at least) three questions meriting close investigation. The first concerns the workplace skills that computerization makes more important. Our framework posits that computerization has made skills in carrying out nonroutine cognitive activities increasingly valuable. But what specifically are these skills, and how can they be taught? Second, our case study evidence suggests that management discretion plays a key role—at least in the short run—in determining how noncomputerized tasks are organized into jobs, with attendant impacts on skill demands and working conditions. Understanding the factors that influence these managerial choices, aside from technological incentives, is a relevant question for workforce development policy. Our case study provides little guidance as to why managers choose to foster flexibility over mechanistic job organizations in workplace settings where both options appear economically viable.

Finally, our case motivates study of alternative channels by which advances in information technology affect the labor market. In this chapter, we have stressed computers' ability to substitute for human labor in routine information processing. Advances in electronic communications may be equally significant: firms can now profitably outsource and monitor routine production processes offshore, thereby reducing the demand for these routine skills domestically. Thus, while social scientists have hotly debated whether trade or technology is primarily responsible for rising inequality, this example suggests that the distinction is far from clear-cut. Here too, careful case studies of the changing organization of work will prove important for developing and enriching hypotheses.

NOTES

1. It is a well-known paradox of artificial intelligence that many tasks that programmers assumed would be negligible to program developed into formidable (and still unsolved) engineering problems, such as walking on two legs over uneven terrain. Conversely, many tasks that humans find formidable turn out to be minor programming exercises, such as calculating pi to the ten-thousandth decimal place.

2. It is a fallacy, however, to assume that a computer must reproduce *all* of the functions of a human to perform a human's job. Automatic teller machines (ATMs) have supplanted many bank teller functions although they cannot verify signatures or make polite conversation while tallying change. Similarly, domestic appliances take phone messages and make morning coffee but do not wear pressed black and white tuxedos and greet us at the door like the robots in Woody Allen's *Sleeper*. We nevertheless take it as axiomatic that if a job is traditionally constituted of nonprocedural tasks, it will be more difficult to computerize.

3. Note that the simple distinction between computer-substitutable and

computer-nonsubstitutable tasks is not absolute. For example, by calculating more efficient long-haul trucking routes, computers can "substitute" for the labor input of long-haul truck drivers. In reality, there is a nonzero elasticity of substitution between routine and non-routine tasks, a point we encapsulate in the formal model in Autor, Levy, and Murnane (2001).

4. See Bresnahan (1999) for further illustrations. In our study of the automation of check clearing, described later in the chapter (Autor, Levy, and Murnane 2002), we provide an example of this phenomenon.

5. Software that recognizes ill-structured patterns ("neural networks") and solves problems based on inductive reasoning from well-specified models ("model-based reasoning") is under development and has been applied commercially in several cases. These technologies have had little role in the computer-induced technical change of the last three decades.

6. While the DOT categorizes more than 12,000 highly detailed occupations, the DOT data we employ here are based on an aggregation of these occupations into detailed census occupations, of which there are approximately 450.

7. Definitions of these variables and example tasks from the *Handbook for Analyzing Jobs* are provided in Autor, Levy, and Murnane (2001).

8. In figure 4.1, each DOT measure is scaled from 0 to 10, with higher values indicating greater task input. Since these are not standardized metrics, it is potentially misleading to compare the magnitude of changes across dependent variables. In Autor, Levy, and Murnane (2001), we translate task demands into the more familiar metric of educational requirements.

9. Readers may ask two questions about the patterns displayed in figure 4.1 and table 4.2. First, to what extent are they sensitive to the limitations of the DOT described in Miller et al. (1980)? Perhaps the most salient limitation is that early editions of the DOT underreported the skills required in occupations dominated by women. Much of this problem was corrected by the publication of the fourth edition in 1977. Nevertheless, to examine the extent to which gender bias in the DOT variables may have affected our findings, we did the calculations that underlie figure 4.1 and table 4.2 separately by gender. The basic patterns are the same for both male and female workers.

Second, to what extent would our results be different had we chosen other plausible measures of task content from the list of variables available in the DOT? As reported in Autor, Levy, and Murnane (2001), the basic patterns hold when alternative plausible indicators of occupational skill content are used.

10. This model is developed more fully in Autor, Levy, and Murnane (2001).

11. See Adler (1992) for a thoughtful discussion of this issue.

12. In a limited number of cases, the reader-sorter could not read the MICR line because the check was damaged. These unreadable checks were carried to operators of check repair machines who keyed in the MICR information on a strip of paper, attached the strip to the bottom of the check, and returned the check to be read and sorted.

13. Recall that Cabot Bank processed about 2.8 million checks per night in its central processing facility. U.S. banks in total process about 320 million checks a night, and despite the increased use of electronic transfers, the Federal Reserve Bank projects that check volume in the United States will increase by 1 percent per year over the next 15 years.

14. Imaging was not a new technology in the 1990s; lawyers and accountants were already using it to make electronic copies of wills and estate documents. However, Cabot Bank was one of the first banks to use the technology to balance deposits, a high-volume daily activity that had to be completed under significant time pressure.

15. The production process in deposit processing was also quite constrained by regulations, most notably the requirement that paper checks be returned to the issuing bank.

16. The OCR software makes both type I and type II errors, in some cases misreading debit amounts, and in others rejecting as "illegible" checks that were in fact correctly read. Type I errors are particularly costly, because after they are caught by bank employees or customers, they require laborious downstream correction. With these facts in mind, the bank "tunes" the OCR software to minimize total check-processing cost.

17. Training began with playing games on the computer to develop facility in using a mouse. Substantial time was devoted to helping make the transition from working with paper checks to working with images of checks.

18. The bank faces a strong incentive to hire and reward workers who can key rapidly, since this reduces the number of keying workstations the bank has to purchase and maintain.

19. The job was designed long before any of the individuals whom we interviewed were hired by Cabot Bank.

20. The tasks could not be readily programmed in if-then-do instructions, either because they involved nonroutine fine motor skills (removing paper clips) or nonroutine cognitive skills (reading poorly formed handwriting, balancing deposits).

21. The employment impact was muted, however, because acquisitions led to rapid growth during the 1990s in the number of checks processed. In 1988, 67 workers in Deposit Processing processed 1.0 million checks per night. In 1998, 148 workers processed 2.8 million checks per night. Consequently, the 27 percent increase in average labor productivity between 1994 and 1999 was accomplished without layoffs.

22. See Minehan et al. (2000) for a description of probable changes in the regulations governing check processing in the United States.

23. One bank, Sun Trust, which operates in the Southeast, has already moved its keying operation to a central site. After it recognized that its keying operation outside Atlanta was particularly efficient, Sun Trust began transmitting the images of checks from many processing sites to the Atlanta site for keying. With similar ease, these images could be transmitted to another country. Examples such as this one underscore the difficulty in conceiving of "trade" and "technology" as distinct causes of declining demand for less-educated workers.

24. The goal of making jobs more interesting is consistent with the observation that changes in the tastes that accompany increased education of the workforce are a factor driving workplace redesign (Lindbeck and Snower 2000). Similarly, Osterman (1994) presented evidence that a concern with workers' welfare is one reason managers create high-performance workplaces characterized by interesting jobs.

25. A Cabot Bank manager provided this information to us.

26. The acquisition of another bank led to a subsequent increase in the number of exceptions processed by the bank and the number of employees in Exceptions Processing.

27. Implementation of the *paper* account-based workflow reduced by 120 the number of workers required to process 65,000 exceptions. The subsequent adoption of imaging technology reduced the number of needed workers by an additional 60.

28. It is possible that management increased the percentage of the workforce that was exempt from hourly wage rules in order to avoid paying overtime. However, we heard no mention of this in several rather frank interviews with workers in Exceptions Processing.

29. Of course, the expansion in pay grades may simply reflect the bank's response to market forces that were leading to greater wage dispersion throughout the economy during these years. There was no comparable expansion, however, of the compensation range within each pay grade in Deposit Processing.

30. The observation that college graduates function better than non-col-

lege graduates in settings undergoing change is consistent with the
work of Richard Nelson and Edmund Phelps (1966), Theodore
Schultz (1975), and Finis Welch (1970).

31. This view is consistent with Osterman's (2001) finding that the percentage of firms adopting high-performance workplace designs grew
during the 1990s.

REFERENCES

Adler, Paul S. 1992. "Introduction." In *Technology and the Future of Work,*
edited by Paul S. Adler. New York: Oxford University Press.

Attewell, Paul. 1990. "What Is Skill?" *Work and Occupations* 17(4): 422–
48.

Autor, David H. 2001. "Wiring the Labor Market." *Journal of Economic
Perspectives* 15(1): 25–40.

Autor, David H., Frank Levy, and Richard J. Murnane. 2001. "The Skill
Content of Recent Technological Change: An Empirical Exploration."
Working Paper 8377. Cambridge, Mass.: National Bureau of Economic
Research (June).

———. 2002. "Upstairs, Downstairs: Computers and Skills on Two Floors
of a Large Bank." *Industrial and Labor Relations Review* 55(3): 432–47.

Bartel, Ann P., Casey Ichniowski, and Kathryn Shaw. 2000. "New Technol-
ogy, Human Resource Practices, and Skill Requirements: Evidence from
Plant Visits in Three Industries." Unpublished paper. Carnegie Mellon
University, Pittsburgh, Penn.

Bresnahan, Timothy F. 1999. "Computerization and Wage Dispersion: An
Analytical Reinterpretation." *Economic Journal* 109(June): 390–415.

Feenstra, Robert C., and Gordon H. Hanson. 1999. "The Impact of Outsourcing and High-Technology Capital on Wages: Estimates for the
United States, 1979–1990." *Quarterly Journal of Economics* 114(3): 907–
40.

———. 2001. "Global Production Sharing and Rising Inequality: A Survey
of Trade and Wages." Working Paper 8372. Cambridge, Mass.: National
Bureau of Economic Research (July).

Fernandez, Roberto. 1999. "Skill-Biased Technological Change and Wage
Inequality: Evidence from a Plant Retooling." Unpublished paper. Palo
Alto, Calif.: Stanford University Graduate School of Business (June).

Goldin, Claudia, and Lawrence F. Katz. 1998. "The Origins of Technology-
Skill Complementarity." *Quarterly Journal of Economics* 113(3): 693–
732.

Hounshell, David A. 1985. *From the American System to Mass Production,
1800–1932: The Development of Manufacturing Technology in the United
States.* Baltimore: Johns Hopkins University Press.

Hunter, Larry W. 1999. "Transforming Retail Banking." In *Employment Practices and Business Strategy*, edited by Peter Cappelli. New York: Oxford University Press.

Levy, Frank, Anne Beamish, and Richard J. Murnane. 1999. "Computerization and Skills: Examples from a Car Dealership." Unpublished paper. Cambridge, Mass.: Massachusetts Institute of Technology, Department of Urban Studies and Planning (November).

Levy, Frank, and Richard J. Murnane. 1996. "With What Skills Are Computers a Complement?" *American Economic Review Papers and Proceedings* 86(2): 258–62.

Lindbeck, Assar, and Dennis J. Snower. 2000. "Multitask Learning and the Reorganization of Work: From Tayloristic to Holistic Organization." *Journal of Labor Economics* 18: 353–76.

Mayer, Martin. 1997. *The Bankers*. New York: Truman Valley Books/Plume.

McKenney, James L. 1995. *Waves of Change: Business Evolution Through Information Technology*. Boston: Harvard Business School Press.

Miller, Anne R., Donald J. Treiman, Pamela S. Cain, and Patricia A. Roose, eds. 1980. *Work, Jobs, and Occupations: A Critical Review of the Dictionary of Occupational Titles*. Washington, D.C.: National Academy Press.

Minehan, Cathy E., Paul M. Connolly, Sally G. Green, Krista M. Shields, and Chandler Perine. 2000. "The U.S. Retail Payments System: Moving to the Future." *Federal Reserve Bank of Boston Annual Report 2000*: 6–19.

Mokyr, Joel. 1990. *The Lever of Riches: Technological Creativity and Economic Progress*. New York: Oxford University Press.

Nelson, Richard R., and Edmund S. Phelps. 1966. "Investment in Humans, Technological Diffusion, and Economic Growth." *American Economic Review* 56(1–2): 69–75.

Osterman, Paul. 1994. "How Common Is Workplace Transformation and Who Adopts It?" *Industrial and Labor Relations Review* 47(2): 173–88.

———. 2001. "Work Reorganization in an Era of Restructuring: Trends in Diffusion and Effects on Employee Welfare." *Industrial and Labor Relations Review* 53(2): 179–96.

Pinker, Steven. 1997. *How the Mind Works*. New York: W. W. Norton.

Polanyi, Michael. 1966. *The Tacit Dimension*. New York: Doubleday.

Schultz, Theodore W. 1975. "The Value of the Ability to Deal with Disequilibria." *Journal of Economic Literature* 13(3): 827–46.

U.S. Department of Labor. 1939. *Dictionary of Occupational Titles*. 1st ed. Washington: U.S. Government Printing Office.

U.S. Department of Labor, Manpower Administration. 1972. *Handbook for Analyzing Jobs*. Washington: U.S. Government Printing Office.

U.S. Department of Labor, Employment and Training Administration. 1977. *Dictionary of Occupational Titles*. 4th ed. Washington: U.S. Government Printing Office.

————. 1991. *Dictionary of Occupational Titles.* 4th ed., revised. Washington: U.S. Government Printing Office.

Welch, Finis. 1970. "Education in Production." *Journal of Political Economy* 78(1): 35–59.

Winston, Patrick H. 1999. "Why I Am Optimistic." Accessed June 18, 2000, at: *www.ai.mit.edu/people/phw/optimism.html* (July).

Zuboff, Shoshona. 1988. *In the Age of the Smart Machine.* New York: Basic Books.

CHAPTER 5

"New Technology" and Its Impact on the Jobs of High School Educated Workers: A Look Deep Inside Three Manufacturing Industries

Ann P. Bartel, Casey Ichniowski, and Kathryn Shaw

The deterioration of the economic position of less-educated men is part of a well-documented increase in income inequality in the U.S. labor market between the late 1970s and early 1990s. During this time period the income gap between high school educated and college-educated men rose substantially (see Autor, Levy, and Murnane, this volume). Many analysts have advanced the idea of "skill-biased technical change" to help explain the declining position of high school educated workers (see, for example, Autor, Katz, and Krueger 1998; Bartel and Sicherman 1999; Berman, Bound, and Griliches 1994; Caroli and Van Reenen 2001; Greenan and Mairesse 1996; Katz and Murphy 1992; Krueger 1993). Researchers suggest that rapid advances in computerization spawned new production technologies during this time and businesses adopting these new computer-based technologies may well have increased the demand for more-skilled employees to work with these new technologies. Unfortunately, when researchers use the existing data sets of individual data or plant-level data, the measures of computer technologies are often very incomplete or imprecise. Existing research therefore provides very little direct evidence on the extent to which new computer-based technologies affect the demand for high school educated workers.

In this chapter, we turn to information gathered from plant visits to examine the impact of technology on the demand for high school educated workers. We use information collected from on-site investigations of plants within three narrowly defined indus-

155

tries—medical equipment manufacturers, steel, and valve manufacturers—to address the following three questions:

1. What new computer-based technologies have businesses adopted within these industries?

2. How, if at all, have these new technologies affected the jobs of production workers and the skills required in those jobs?

3. When businesses do require new skills of their production workers, do they adopt new human resource management (HRM) practices, such as recruiting, training, or compensation practices, to help ensure that workers have the desired skills?

We then combine the answers to these questions to address the overall question: How has the demand for high school educated workers changed owing to technological changes?

INDUSTRY SETTINGS AND SITE VISITS

We investigated these three questions about new technology and the jobs of production workers through plant visits in the medical equipment manufacturing, steelmaking, and industrial valve manufacturing industries.[1] We focus on these industries because they employ a large number of high school educated workers; because they cover a spectrum of growth patterns, from declining industry employment (in steel) to stable employment (in valves) to rapidly growing employment (in medical instruments); and because our access to practitioners in these industries allowed us to study several plants in each industry.

THE THREE INDUSTRIES AS LARGE EMPLOYERS OF HIGH SCHOOL EDUCATED WORKERS

In this study, we focus on the jobs of production workers in these 3 industries. Production workers in these industries need considerable amounts of skill, knowledge, and experience to operate million-dollar technologies in a steel mill, assemble a delicate surgical instrument in the medical industry, or produce a valve to exacting customer standards in the valve industry. Thus, these industries tend to provide reasonable, highly skilled, well-paying jobs for high

Table 5.1 Demographic Characteristics of Workers in the Three Industries, 1986 and 1996

Industry[a]	1986			1996		
	Union Members	Female	Average Education (Years)	Union Members	Female	Average Education (Years)
Medical, dental and optical instruments	8.7%	49%	13.0	4.2%	47%	13.6
Miscellaneous fabricated metal products	30.0	23	11.8	19.6	22	12.2
Blast furnaces, steelworks, rolling and finishing mills	60.4	9	11.7	50.1	11	12.6

Source: Hirsch and Macpherson (1997).
[a] These are the CPS industry groupings and are broader than the four-digit SICs used in tables 5.2 through 5.4.

school educated workers. As shown in table 5.1, the average years of schooling for steel industry production workers was 11.7 years in 1986 and 12.6 in 1996, while production workers in valves averaged 11.8 years of schooling in 1986 and 12.2 years of schooling in 1996. Education levels for production workers in medical equipment–making industries are about 1 year higher on average than they are in steel or valves—13.0 years in 1986 and 13.6 in 1996.[2] In 1992 these 3 industries employed upward of 370,000 U.S. production workers—170,885 in medical equipment, 134,500 in steel, and 63,711 in valves.[3]

These 3 industries differ markedly in terms of employment growth. Medical equipment manufacturing has been one of the fastest-growing industries in U.S. manufacturing. Industry shipments have increased by 5 to 6 percent a year in real terms since 1989, while the industry spent 8 percent of sales on research and development (R&D) in 1996, or about double the overall U.S. industry average (Standard and Poor's 1998). Accordingly, industry employment has grown rapidly. The number of production workers in this industry in 1992 (170,885) was nearly double the employment in 1972 (86,025), and some 30 percent more than the 1982 employment level (130,948). In contrast, the steel industry has witnessed a dramatic contraction of employment. While the mini-mill sector is fairly robust, with significant growth since the 1970s, contraction among integrated steel mills, especially in the early 1980s, resulted in large reductions in overall steel industry employment. Production worker employment in the steel industry in 1992 (134,500) was markedly below the number of production workers in 1972 (375,116) or 1982 (215,924). Valve making shows more stable employment over this time period, with employment levels for production workers of 60,224 in 1972 and 74,089 in 1982 before returning to its 1992 level of 63,711 (for more details on employment and wages, see tables 5.A1 through 5.A3).[4]

Therefore, by studying these three industries, we are investigating industries that employ well over one-third of one million high school educated production workers. Investigating how the jobs of these production workers have and have not changed with the advent of new production technologies provides one window on the changes in the situation of U.S. workers with relatively low levels of formal education.

WORKER DEMOGRAPHICS AND WAGES IN THE THREE INDUSTRIES

Statistics on business establishments and worker characteristics paint very different pictures of the workers and work sites in these 3 industries. Steel industry employees work in larger establishments (558 employees per establishment in 1992) than do employees in either medical equipment plants (44 employees per establishment) or in valve-making plants (63 employees per establishment).[5] Once inside the doors of these establishments, one observes production workers with different demographic characteristics. As shown in table 5.1, the medical equipment–making industry employs a large number of females (47 percent of the industry workforce in 1996) who are predominantly non-union employees (4.2 percent of the workforce was organized in 1996). In contrast, the steel industry production worker is much more likely to be a male union member: the steelmaking workforce is 50.1 percent organized and 89 percent male. The corresponding figures for the valve industry workforce for 1996 are 19.6 percent unionized and 78 percent male.

Average production worker wages in these three industries show that steel industry production workers earn the highest wages of the three ($23.44 an hour in 1982, $19.06 in 1987, $18.99 in 1992), and medical equipment industry workers the lowest production worker wages of the three industries ($9.90 in 1982, $10.74 in 1987, and $10.71 in 1992). Average wages of production workers in the valve industry fall in between the wages in the other two industries ($11.73 in 1982, $12.19 in 1987, and $12.11 in 1992).[6]

Plant Visits

We made extensive visits to plants in the three industries to investigate firsthand how technology has changed inside the plants and to conduct interviews about the effect of new technologies on production workers' jobs. In steel, we drew on many years of experience from recent research projects: we have personally visited forty-five finishing lines in integrated steel mills and thirty-four production lines in steel mini-mills. We have thus visited a significant portion of the entire industry's work sites. The information we report for the medical equipment industry is based on our observations and interviews at eight plants. For the valve-making industry, we conducted five plant visits but also made multiple visits to several plants. Our purpose was to obtain insights into our three questions about the nature of new technologies and their impact on jobs. Because no publicly available data on these questions exist, our plant visits were designed to enable us to observe new production technologies in these three industries firsthand and to conduct interviews with frontline personnel about how jobs have changed as a result.

During these visits we conducted interviews with several managers at each plant. Typically, these managers included the top plant or mill manager, an engineering expert, an operations manager, and the top HR staff person for the plant. Since we did not want to limit our interviews to getting "management's version" of the effects of new technologies on work, we also conducted start-to-finish production-line tours at each plant and discussed issues with production workers on these tours as well as off-line. Many of our interviews with production workers were conducted without managers present, and managers encouraged us to get the opinions and perspectives of production workers and union representatives in organized plants. The information and patterns reported in this chapter reflect the evidence collected during these interviews, discussions, and plant tours.

NEW TECHNOLOGY AND ITS IMPACT ON JOBS IN THE MEDICAL EQUIPMENT INDUSTRY

The medical devices industry is composed of four separate four-digit industries—SIC3841: Surgical and Medical Instruments; SIC3842: Surgical Appliances and Supplies; SIC3844: X-ray Apparatus and Tubes; and SIC3845: Electromedical Equipment—that make a wide variety of medical products.[7] Our plant visits to eight establishments documented this wide variety of medical products and production processes. We visited plants that produced relatively "low-tech" items (such as syringes, sutures, catheters, and elastic bandages), those that made medium-tech devices (such as anesthesia apparatus or drug pump and IV equipment), and those that made "high-tech" items (such as electrosurgical equipment and respiratory monitoring devices).

As we conducted our field research into the three questions about new technology, production worker jobs, and HRM practices in this industry, a clear difference in production processes and jobs was evident between medical plants with continuous, high-volume production processes and those with small-lot batch production processes. Therefore, we organize our evidence on our three questions from our visits to eight plants in this industry into two parts: conclusions for high-volume medical equipment producers and conclusions for batch medical equipment producers.

CONTINUOUS, HIGH-VOLUME PRODUCERS: SEEING TECHNOLOGIES AND JOBS OF THE PAST AND PRESENT

The Production Process   Among our many plant visits, one that offered some of the most dramatic and direct insights into the effects of new technologies on the jobs of production workers was a plant (in SIC 3841) that makes a low-tech medical product, such as biopsy needles or intravenous catheters.[8] To make a product such as a biopsy needle, a plastic plunger is inserted into a barrel, and then the needle is attached to the barrel. The specific steps in the production process are: molding the plastic into plungers and barrels; imprinting the barrel; assembling the barrel plunger and needle components; packaging and wrapping; and sterilizing packaged goods by radiation. The production process for catheters is similar, but in that case a needle is attached to a tube.

The high-volume plant we describe here provides especially direct answers to our three questions. Our evidence from this plant comes not only from interviews with managers and workers who have experience with new and old technologies, but also from direct observations of new and old production processes. In particular, this plant still operates a much older production line for specialty products that it produces in relatively small quantities. Our tours of this plant therefore took us from the technologies and jobs of the past to those of the present.

Examples of New Technology   When the plant opened forty years ago, production was 10 million units per year. Today the plant makes 6 million units per day. In the last decade output rose substantially while employment fell some 20 percent. New technologies that the plant has adopted underlie these dramatic changes in output and employment. Several examples demonstrate the causes for these changes.

Several new technologies in this plant helped raise productivity. Ten years ago, continuous motion machines replaced incremental motion machines in the step of the production process that assembles the component pieces—the barrels, stoppers, and plungers. The difference between the new and old machines is that in the new there are dials that feed the component parts together in a smooth continuous motion, whereas the older technology assembles component parts in a much slower, stop-start motion. Continuous motion machines increase assembly speed substantially, thereby generating dramatic productivity improvements. In packaging, sophisticated robots fill units into blister packs, wrap the packs, move the correct number of packs into boxes, and send boxes on to sterilization and shipping.

The "computer guts" of all of these assembly and packaging machines are programmable logic controllers (PLCs). Programs inside PLCs determine the precise, three-dimensional movements of robotic arms. They track how many times a machine stops and starts and maintain the synchronized, split-second movements in continuous motion assembly machines, while also detecting line malfunctions. The sophistication and capabilities of PLCs have advanced dramatically in the last twenty years, and with these advances have come corresponding advances in the speed and accuracy of medical equipment production at high-volume plants.

PLCs and computer chips embedded inside the newest production machinery automatically identify problems and abnormalities in the production. Units in the production line can be rerouted automatically to other normally functioning lines while a computer display shows a map of the machines that highlight the problem areas.

Another set of new technologies at this plant improves the quality of these medical products. Around the same time the plant introduced continuous motion machines, it also began to use computer numerically controlled (CNC) lathes to improve the quality of the tip of the needle. As a result of this new technology, tips can meet higher-quality tolerance levels. Another example of a quality-improving technological change is the use of computerized laser cameras that inspect the products during the manufacturing process.

Jobs and Skill Requirements   As the plant introduced these computer-controlled, high-speed, and high-volume technologies, the jobs of production workers changed dramatically. During our tours we often saw no employees at all in large areas of the plant. The new technologies are capable of operating on their own for long periods. At the old-technology packaging line of this plant, the picture was very different. Employees remained fixed at specific spots on the line. These workers fed the units into the blister packs, sorted the packs along the line, and stuffed the packs into boxes. On the high-volume lines, robots have automated all of these routine tasks.

If production workers on lines with older—and lower-output—technologies are tied to the lines performing routine tasks, and these tasks have been eliminated by PLC-controlled machinery, what do the jobs of production workers on new-technology lines

now involve? Our plant tour of the lines with state-of-the-art technologies revealed a relatively small number of workers who were
"dotted" around the plant rather than stationed at one spot next to
a particular machine. These workers responded to flashing lights,
buzzers, and computerized maps that indicated problems on the
lines (signals that are set off by sensors tied into PLCs). Otherwise,
these workers were conducting regular rounds, checking on equipment. Production employees now work with many more pieces of
equipment and do diagnostic, resetting, and repair tasks. As another example, under old technologies, workers needed to inspect
needles for quality imperfections based on predetermined sampling
procedures, while employees on newer lines inspect and diagnose
the operations of the laser cameras that automatically do the quality
control and inspection work.

These changes in the nature of the jobs of workers operating the
production lines have in turn changed skill requirements for workers significantly. Skill requirements have clearly increased. The
skills required for today's line technologies at this plant are trouble-
shooting skills, diagnostic skills, and knowledge for equipment
maintenance and repair. Because equipment repair and improvement often involve team problem-solving efforts, managers also
look for employees who have the interpersonal skills to operate in
teams.

New Human Resource Management Practices   How does management work to ensure that production employees have the required
skills for the plant's high-technology and high-volume production
process? One avenue is through the hiring and selection process.
The head of HR for the plant said they are looking for employees
who have diagnostic and interpersonal skills and are computer-liter-
ate rather than employees with only a specific technical ability to
operate a machine. However, the plant recruits in an often-tight,
not heavily populated, local labor market, and applicants generally
do not have these characteristics.

The plant therefore relies more heavily on a combination of
training and compensation policies to develop the desired skills in
employees. A centerpiece of these two HR practices is the plant's
skills matrix, which is consistent with the new skills workers now
need. Key elements in the matrix include the ability to operate a
wide range of production machinery, the ability to diagnose equip-

ment failures and errors, and skills in production coordination and planning and work group facilitation. Training initiatives are aimed at enhancing these skills. Training comes in the form of ever-evolving classroom computer training (on- and off-site), off-site classroom training at local area colleges that work in partnership with the plant, and apprenticeship periods in different areas of the production process. Trained "skill assessors" certify each employee's standing on the different dimensions of skill in the matrix. An employee's position in the matrix then determines a significant portion of his or her pay in the pay-for-skill pay component of compensation.

In addition to these HRM practices in the areas of training and compensation that are aimed at developing the requisite skills among production workers, other HRM practices have also changed. Most obvious is the change to broader, more flexible job definitions now that workers are required to work in many more areas of the plant with a broader array of equipment. Historically the plant has had as many as 150 job titles; it now operates with 30 titles. Problem-solving teams have also been introduced within the last 10 years. Workers are now organized into product-focused teams that operate as businesses. The teams visit their customers, monitor product quality, and are responsible for hiring, firing, and performance management. These teams also engage in problem-solving activity to address problems with the sophisticated technologies.

We are not able to document the dynamics of wage changes for production workers as technologies changed for this plant (or for the others we discuss here). New technologies were introduced unevenly throughout the plant over many years, and wage data over long periods were not available. However, the plant's HR manager does believe that wages for production workers at this highly automated medical equipment plant (whose jobs have become more broadly defined and now require broader sets of skills) are much higher than they are in other medical equipment plants where jobs remain narrow in scope and more limited skills are needed for specific tasks. This manager cited the example of another medical equipment plant in the company that makes a low-tech product and hires production workers to perform basic production and assembly tasks with pay at or near the minimum wage. A production worker who has made it to the top of the skills matrix at the continuous, high-volume medical equipment manufacturer would earn about three times the minimum wage. Recall that, as shown in table 5.A1, the typical wage in the medical equipment industry is $10 to $12 an hour.

Evidence from our plant tours and interviews at this plant clearly document that, even within the narrowly defined medical equipment industry, production processes vary considerably in the extent to which new computer technologies are used. Furthermore, new computer-based technologies lead to changes in the jobs and skill requirements of production workers. Finally, indirect evidence from interviews also suggests that wages in plants with new technologies and more skilled production workers can be well above the wages of other (less-skilled) production workers in the same industry who work in technologically simpler production processes.

Batch Producers in Medical Equipment: The Technology Is in the Product

The Production Process Several medical equipment manufacturers that we visited make products such as oxygen pumps, ventilators, automated IV drug pumps, or surgical instruments. These SIC 3845 plants make their products in batch production processes, and these share several characteristics. First, the production lines are themselves a series of tables typically arranged in a U shape with component parts nearby. Products go from one end of the U to the other, passing through a series of assembly steps along the way. The U-shape layout promotes communication among workers, and with modular tables, electrical outlets throughout the ceiling, and everything on wheels, the plant's architecture is easily reorganized. Second, the assembly work is generally performed by low-skill labor. A worker at one of the tables may be performing a task like attaching or inserting some component piece of the overall product. At each stage, these assemblers also typically check the quality of their own work and the work that precedes theirs, and they may also be aided in their assembly tasks by small pieces of automated equipment. Fourth, the products are made in batches to fill specific customer orders. For example, as certain features of a drug pump change, certain elements of the pump change as well and require different parts or setups. Fifth, labor costs account for about 10 percent of production costs.

Examples of New Technology   The central point described in our tours of these plants was that "new technology" for these plants is the technology imbedded in the products. Although production workers do make use of some automated equipment, such as mechanized tools for attaching equipment or computer programs to check tolerances on features of equipment, the products themselves often contain sophisticated computer technology. More specifically, ongoing improvements in computer chip miniaturization have allowed the plants to develop and produce new products. For example, the number of products made in one product area of a maker of advanced surgical devices increased from one to sixteen in less than a year—the most rapid rate of product innovation in that group ever. Surgical equipment evolves rapidly as surgeons request product modifications that will better meet their needs in the operating room. At another plant, managers indicated that over half of all sales are from products that are less than two years old.

At the same time, some examples of "new technology" are similar to those in the high-volume medical equipment plants. The clearest example here is that both the high-volume producers and these batch producers typically use sophisticated computerized irradiating equipment to sterilize their packaged products. The packaging technology of batch producers has also undergone technological improvements that have led to reductions in production costs, but these changes are not as extensive as the high-speed robotic processes used in the high-volume plants. Overall, the central observation about "new technology" in these medical equipment plants that make higher-tech products in smaller batch sizes is that new computer-based technologies are imbedded in the products themselves. These technologies are not focused on increasing the number of units produced per worker. Productivity gains are measured primarily in terms of improved product sophistication, and the success of the plants rests critically on how fast they can develop new product varieties.

Jobs and Skill Requirements   The impact of new technology on skill requirements in this segment of the medical devices industry is therefore quite different from the effect of technology on jobs in the continuous, high-volume plant. Unlike the latter type of plant, where new technology has eliminated routine tasks and now requires employees to apply diagnostic and problem-solving skills on a broader range of equipment, the production worker jobs in the batch manufacturers are still assembly jobs. As one manager pointed out, "Don't let the clean, bright appearance of the assembly plant fool you. These are basically low-skill jobs." Assemblers in these plants do not necessarily require a rich understanding of the equipment they are using. One manager commented that many of the assemblers would not know how to restart a testing program on the computer if it stopped.

Some subtler changes in skill requirements were noted in our interviews. The sophisticated nature of the products has made the assembly process more complex and checking for product quality is now an important component of the workers' jobs. Managers commented on the need for reliable workers who pay attention to detail. In addition, because products now change more rapidly than in the past, managers indicated that they need employees who are flexible and can adapt to frequent line changes. The plant managers also felt that communication and interaction skills were important because the assemblers were required to interact with engineers, design people, and quality supervisors.[9]

Notice that managers have used the word *flexibility* to describe the changes in jobs and skills of workers after new PLC-controlled equipment came on-line in the high-volume plant as well as the changes that took place in the batch manufacturer as product design changes occurred more rapidly. Our direct observations on these different production processes, however, reveal that the word *flexibility* refers to very different ideas. In the high-volume plant, workers are now more "flexible" because they work on many more pieces of equipment, in a wider range of tasks throughout the plant, and with higher skill requirements, including the ability to complete diagnostic and repair tasks. In the batch plant, workers are more "flexible" because the assembly routines change more frequently as the products change, but the workers are still performing a limited range of assembly tasks that are relatively easy to pick up.

New Human Resource Management Practices   All of the plants require a high school diploma for the assembler jobs, and many of them hire employees through temporary agencies in order to have time to observe whether a new employee is a good fit for the company. Because basic assembly skills are much the same as they have always been, this screening process involves identifying workers with fundamental literacy skills, problem-solving skills, adaptability, and willingness to learn.

Nevertheless, some plants are taking novel approaches to help workers develop other desired skills and traits. Because quality control on medical equipment is of paramount importance, workers need to pay attention to detail. Training to ensure the highest standard of quality control is a central HR focus. One plant has instituted a training program in which workers watch private broadcasts of surgeries using the plants' products. This practice has led to a greater appreciation on the part of employees of the need for equipment that performs perfectly. Note that these plants hire primarily women for this detailed assembly work. (As shown in table 5.1, 47 percent of all medical instruments employees are women, and for production workers the percentage is even higher.)

Outside of the area of selection and training for skill acquisition and development, these batch medical plants employ many innovative HR practices. Workers still do low-skill assembly work, but managers have attempted to create a team environment for them. The plants also employ job rotation. However, the main rationales for these practices are that workers need to know how to perform the job on the station before and after their own and that workers are more attentive if their assembly tasks change periodically. Although managers indicated that these practices are better for managing a workforce than more traditional practices, the technology-related story that characterizes the continuous, high-volume plants is much less applicable here.

NEW TECHNOLOGY AND ITS IMPACT ON JOBS IN THE STEEL INDUSTRY

We also visited a large number of mills in the steel industry (SIC 3312)—both integrated steel mills and steel mini-mills. The production processes in these mills, particularly the integrated mills, cover a very large geographic territory. Accordingly, our integrated steel mill visits focused on a specific finishing line technology; we visited a total of forty-five finishing lines. In the mini-mill sector, we visited thirty-four mills with an emphasis on rolling and shaping operations.

The Production Processes   The production processes in the two sectors of the industry are fundamentally different. To produce molten steel from material inputs, mini-mills use electric arc furnace technology, while integrated mills use the basic oxygen furnace technology. Because of the vast differences in production technologies, we describe the two production processes in turn.

Mini-mill production begins with scrap metal as the basic input into the electric arc furnace. Each "charge" from the electric arc furnace pot produces molten steel. Molten steel is then poured directly into the continuous casters, which take the stream of liquid steel and separate it into one or more strands of steel that cool and harden into steel billets (or long, thick rails of steels) after exiting the caster. Billets are then reheated, thinned in narrower and narrower bars, rods, or wires, and then shaped into a series of sequential "stands" through which the reheated steel passes.

In integrated steel mills, the raw materials are iron ore, limestone, and coal. Before reaching the steelmaking furnace, these raw materials are first transformed into molten iron by blast furnaces. The basic oxygen furnace transforms iron and additional inputs into molten steel, and then the molten steel proceeds to the continuous caster, as in mini-mill steel production. Our visits to integrated steel mills focused on finishing line operations. Once the molten steel has been processed into long sheets of very thin steel rolled into coils, many different finishing processes can be used. For example, "pickling" is the process that cleans the steel by removing iron oxides from intermediate steel products, such as steel coils. Cleaner steel permits higher quality and more reliable finishing-end treatments. The temperature of the acid bath used to pickle steel is critical to its effectiveness. We focused on one particular kind of finishing operation, but all finishing processes clean, treat, or coat the steel to give it the dimensions and properties required by the customer.

Examples of New Technology in Mini-Mills   Our mini-mill tours concentrated on the rolling and shaping stands near the end of the production process, but managers pointed out new technologies in earlier stages of production as well. In scrap metal processing, magnetic sensors and related computer programs analyze the content of the scrap metal and allow producers to select scrap that more closely resembles the desired chemical composition of the finished steel. This screening improves both steel quality and productivity by eliminating the need to alter the composition of steel by burning out impurities or by adding metal alloys to achieve the desired chemical properties.

The production process from the reheat furnace through the rolling and shaping operations has also changed. Formerly, based on personal observations, line workers were required to use manual controls to adjust the reheat furnace, which takes billets (the intermediate product) and heats them to the point where they are malleable enough for subsequent machines. Automation has also removed the need to have workers "walking the line" and setting controls for every motor and pump to desired settings. Rather, computerized sensors and controls now monitor the line, synchronize some pieces of equipment automatically, and relay information back to a central operator who issues computer commands to make additional adjustments from a central location. Finally, computer-aided automation has also allowed for coordination among the production steps in mini-mills. It is now possible to send a hot billet or steel bar emerging from the caster stage directly to the shaping and finishing stage. This coordination is only possible with computer-aided analysis of whether the hot output from the caster is suitable input for the reheat furnace.

An important distinction we observed was that the degree of this technological sophistication varies across mini-mills. More complex products require more technologically complex production processes. Some mills make simpler steel products with much less exacting specifications. Producing thick I-bar and reinforcement bars (used to strengthen concrete in large construction projects) is a relatively straightforward process compared to the process of producing a very thin steel product with various kinds of angles and bends. The former is a simpler rolling process that involves relatively few stands after the reheat furnace to reshape and narrow the diameter of the billet. In the latter process, many more stands and more elaborate shaping machines are required to make a thin, angled product to exacting shape specifications. Predictably, the latter processes involve more computer monitoring of the rolling stands and steel throughput.

Examples of New Technology in Finishing Lines at Integrated Mills
In our tours of steel finishing lines at integrated mills, we saw many

technological improvements. New steelmaking technologies have significantly enhanced product quality because computer-automated equipment constantly checks and adjusts throughput and intermediate outputs according to programmed production specifications. Productivity is dramatically higher as a result of new technologies because materials move much more rapidly through the process from the warehouses of steel coils to the shipping dock, and because, for a number of reasons, the lines experience many fewer line stops. Finishing lines are highly automated and very dependent on elaborate computer hardware and software systems.

Cleaning and finishing operations often run steel coils through an acid bath as part of the production line. Previously, workers adjusted the acid bath based on their own observations of steel output and the "feel" for the process they had acquired from years of experience. Now sensors relay information through computerized systems back to a central computerized pulpit where an operator can control both the acid content of the bath and the speed of steel through it. In addition, computer controls make automatic adjustments to the finishing process.

Computer programs also automatically allow the steel to be processed through these finishing lines in a continuous process. Computer software and programs are used to keep track of all steel coils in a warehouse. The characteristics of coils coming off a finishing line need to be matched as closely as possible with the next incoming coil. Computer programs call automatically for the next coils in the schedule, and automated machinery delivers the coil with little or no manual handling to the entry end of the finishing line. Computerized gauges also ensure accurate alignment of the outgoing and incoming coils as the two coils are welded at the entry end of the finishing line. Because of the size and gauge of two successive coils is better matched, welds between coils are more reliable, and line stops due to weld breaks are thus reduced. We also observed sophisticated automation in delivery, shipping, and packaging operations at the end of these lines. In some lines, steel coils are transported from the end of the line to the appropriate delivery and shipping area by computer-driven vehicles that wind their way unmanned through the plant.

Jobs and Skill Requirements   Several patterns emerge when we look at the effects of new computer-aided technologies on production worker jobs. First, because materials handling by operators has been reduced to a very low level, a number of the most demanding physical tasks have been eliminated. Machines move raw materials and finished product, often in accordance with computerized inventory and shipping programs. Prior to these changes, employees were responsible for the tasks now performed by the machinery and computer-aided sensors.

Second, employees are now less likely to be stationed at specific locations along a line performing very specific tasks. In some ways, employees previously acted as the computerized monitors of today's lines, making judgments based on experience about the way steel should look as it moves through the process. Employees were more likely to perform narrowly defined jobs, whether operating specific pieces of equipment or developing a rich knowledge about specific characteristics of the look of steel at particular stages of production.

A third pattern lies in how employees talk about their work. Employees in steel operations do not describe themselves as "machine operators" but rather speak of themselves as "monitoring" the equipment. One example from a finishing line illustrates this distinction. With the adoption of a larger number of sensors and gauges with automatic computer-generated information on the quality of the finishing operation, one employee now works from a central pulpit where all of this information is displayed. Previously, these aspects of this finishing process required two employees at both the entry and exit ends of the process.

The skills required of employees also change as jobs become broader, as employees work at more areas of a production line, and as computer-generated information increases substantially. Employees now need to be able to trouble-shoot problems on a wider array of equipment. They are no longer controlling routine actions but fixing disruptions and breakdowns when computerized machinery is no longer conducting the routine operations correctly.

Paramount in the changes in skills is the increased demand for group problem-solving skills. Statistical process control (SPC) technologies generate large amounts of information on operations. Not only does the SPC technology increase the demand for data analysis skills, but the computer-generated SPC data helps identify areas of the production process that are out of normal operating ranges. These data become the input into team problem-solving efforts. The problem-solving process requires a new set of analytical and interpersonal skills, and the ideas generated from these continuous-improvement activities are now a critical employee contribution to line performance.

As perhaps expected, the jobs at the mini-mills that make more basic I-bar or rebar products were the exception to this pattern of changing skill requirements. Managers there did not indicate a pressing need for problem-solving skills from their employees. In these lines, it is not hard to identify a production problem. Because there are fewer steps and the product has less exacting specifications, rectifying production problems does not require elaborate analyses of SPC data by problem-solving teams uncovering hard-to-identify sources of problems and devising elaborate measures for improving output. Again, product complexity is intricately related in this industry to production process complexity. In the mini-mills where the complexity of the production process and product is relatively low, the demand for these worker activities and skills was correspondingly low as well.

In sum, changes in jobs and skill requirements in many steel mills show close parallels to several of the changes observed in continuous, high-volume medical equipment makers. Computerization has freed employees from specific stations and broadened job descriptions. Workers monitor the line and the information on the line generated by computer technologies. Diagnostic skills are increasingly in demand, as are analytical and problem-solving skills. These changes were less noticeable in certain mini-mills that make less complex steel products.

New Human Resource Management Practices   Over the past twenty year all mini-mills and integrated steel finishing lines have become much more automated and rely much more heavily on computer hardware and software systems, but the extent of this automation varies from mill to mill. The capital equipment at the newest lines (those opened between the early 1980s and early 1990s) is the most highly automated and computerized. We therefore use examples from these more modern facilities in this section to illustrate the HRM practices that the mills are using to obtain workers with the skills to operate these technologically advanced lines.

Overall, these firms are looking for employees who have not only a high school education but a range of key skills and personal traits that only high-quality high school graduates would have. For example, one mill identifies the following specific skill dimensions: "Analysis (identifying problems, securing relevant information, relating data from different sources, identifying possible causes of problems); judgment (developing alternative courses of action and making decisions which are based on logical assumptions and which reflect factual information); interpersonal cooperation (working effectively with others on the team or outside the line of formal authority to accomplish organizational goals); and ability to learn (assimilating and applying new, job related information, taking into consideration information complexity)." This mill's list of skill dimensions includes ten additional personal skills. The mill also identifies a set of technical computer skills in the area of machinery operations, instrumentation services, mechanic services, and electrician services.

At this mill, applicants go through eight steps in the selection process, which includes tests, exercises, and interviews. Managers provided us with a detailed checklist showing the match between each of the eight screening devices and different subsets of the skills being sought. Such selection processes are important mechanisms at many such lines for identifying employees with the right skills.

Another reason selection processes tend to be very careful is that wage levels are quite high (about $20 per hour plus benefits) for jobs requiring only limited education. At a second steel production line, the selection process includes the following steps: a job fit survey to identify cooperative attitudes compatible with a team-based work environment; an attitude survey to identify ability to learn; a work history survey to identify past supervisory experience; a safety index test to identify more accident-prone employees; process and mechanics skills tests to identify diagnostic skills; electronics and maintenance skills tests to identify technical skills; and interviews by two current employees. Management at this production line also used academic specialists to validate any formal survey and test instruments.

Training opportunities to develop operation skills, diagnostic skills, maintenance skills, and interpersonal skills take many forms. On-site skill development exercises, off-site classroom training, tailor-made programs using outside consultants, and educational benefits are part of the array of programs used. Another interesting form of training for workers at many lines is the practice of regularly scheduled visits to customers. Managers and workers agree that this direct dialogue about customer problems is a critical source of employee knowledge.

These modern lines also tie incentive pay to skill acquisition through a pay-for-skills compensation plan. Employees advance to higher levels in the pay plan by taking tests that measure the degree to which they have mastered the use of different machinery and more general skills as well.

In addition to these skill-enhancing HRM practices, the most modern lines use other new work practices. Almost by definition, jobs are defined broadly with a very small number of job classifications. Active problem-solving teams are common to all of the newest production lines. These teams address recurring problems with an eye to making long-term improvements in line operations part of a regular continuous-improvement process.

Older steel production lines have fewer "innovative" HRM practices, but the trend in these plants has been to adopt more of the practices that are commonplace among the most modern lines. Problem-solving teams and skills training are now found in almost all of the production lines we visited, new or old. Skill requirements are met more often through training initiatives than through employee selection at these older lines, owing to the limited number of new hires. Again, the main exception we observed to the pattern of widespread use of teams and skills training is the mini-mill that makes low-complexity products. Elaborate problem-solving efforts are simply not needed to identify the source of problems in line operations when the product is simpler to make and equipment is technologically less advanced.

Thus, in almost all steel production lines we visited in the mini-mill and integrated sectors—save for mini-mills that make less complex products—we observed many examples of new computer-based technologies that have changed the jobs and skill requirements of production workers. These work environments relied heavily on innovative HRM practices to help ensure that workers had the new skills needed in these technologically sophisticated production processes. These conclusions for the continuous, high-volume steelmaking processes therefore mirror very closely the conclusions for the continuous, high-volume medical equipment makers.

NEW TECHNOLOGY AND ITS IMPACT
ON JOBS IN THE VALVE
MANUFACTURING INDUSTRY

The Production Process   Valves control the flow of liquid or gases through pipes. For example, in a bottling plant a valve controls the amount of the liquids passing through the pipes, which then combine the liquids as they feed into bottles. A simple valve is made by etching grooves at each end of a steel pipe (for screwing to pipes), boring holes at different spots to attach control devices, and then making and attaching the various devices that control the flow. Thus, the production process involves milling, grading, drilling and tapping, boring, and turning. Workers bore a hole down the middle of the block, etch grooves at both ends, bore numerous holes in different spots in the block for bolts or attachments, and produce protrusions that permit controls to be attached. Overall, manufacturing in valves or machine tools is organized into the stages of machining, welding, assembly, testing, and packaging. Valves are often produced in small lot sizes for specific customers. Thus, the valve-making industry (SIC 3491, 3492, and 3494) provides another example of a batch production process.

Examples of New Technology   In the past the steel block would be reshaped on a work bench with manual tools to chip or drill or bore holes. This very labor-intensive work was done by a skilled machinist who understood the use of the tools and the properties of the steel block that would enable it to be shaped to precise specifications. This process is still used in some areas of valve plants for complicated products or large products. In the 1950s this process was modestly automated with numerically controlled (NC) machines that used computer tapes to code instructions for the machines. In the 1970s production technology for making valves improved radically with the advent of the computer numerically controlled (CNC) metal working machines, which have spread gradually throughout the industry since that time and improved dramatically. In the overall machine tool industry, which is similar to the valve industry, NC and CNC machines were only 5 percent of the total machining base of equipment in 1983, 15 percent in 1987, and 32 percent in 1998. By 1997, 69 percent of machine tool plants used some form of these machines (Association for Manufacturing Technology 2000).

Between the 1970s and today the number of machines required to produce a valve has declined dramatically. In addition, the time required to produce a commodity valve product has declined from several days to one. It is computerization that has produced these productivity gains, by improving performance in three areas:

1. CNC machines have dramatically improved the metalworking phase of production. The CNC machines developed in the last ten years can perform a wider range of tasks on one machine and do so automatically with less programming by the operator. The extensive software that now controls the machine has been combined with technological improvements in metalworking. The newest software allows operators to run CNC machines through a simple graphical user interface, and the computer-generated instructions automatically move gauges and drills to precise spots for very accurate drilling and forming operations. Thus, these machines can not only produce a much greater range of products but produce them much faster. The setup time (the time required to program the machine for each type of valve produced) has been falling over time as CNC machines have become more technologically advanced. Because the setup time has declined, companies can switch products much more frequently and produce a wider range of products to suit their customers' needs.

2. Computer-controlled devices have now reduced the time it takes to inspect products. Each dimension of a complicated valve often must be produced to an accuracy rate of one-thousandth of an inch, so inspection is a critical part of the production process. For many years inspection was done with very time-consuming hand-measuring devices. In the last few years inspection machines have been introduced that use a laser probe technology: the operator touches each surface of the valve (interior, exterior, holes, and so forth) with a probe that develops a three-dimensional picture and measures all dimensions.

3. Computer software and high-speed personal computers have improved the product design phase. New product design is an important element of production—valve production is very specialized, and new valves are often designed for each customer. In the 1990s valve-producing firms began switching from two-dimensional CAD/CAM software programs to three-dimensional CAD/CAM software that shows the valve

as a solid model rather than a two-dimensional representation, thus substantially facilitating the rapid design of new products. Three-dimensional design software eliminates the need to produce a demonstration model and significantly improves the quality of the design by reducing production errors and the amount of rework after a valve is in production.

Jobs and Skill Requirements   Even before the introduction of the CNC machines, a machine tool operator was a skilled machinist, and that is still true today. Because the machinist at each station sets up the machinery to do the particular operation, he or she must understand the blueprints, set the metal cutting speed at feed, determine how much metal to take off and how much to chip, then use inserts and holders to do the milling, drilling, tapping, or turning. Machinists specialize in different tasks—some are skilled at the drill press, for instance, and others at the lathe.

Today the CNC operator must have not only machinist skills but problem-solving and computer skills. The CNC machine performs the operations much more automatically: the operator programs in the dimensions of the valve, and the computer software calculates the correct method of machining the valve. In the past these calculations were done by hand by the operator with blueprints. Thus, it would seem that the operator could be less skilled today, but employers have several reasons for continuing to hire highly skilled machinists for these jobs. First, because CNC machines cover a broader range of machining activities (drilling, tapping, turning, and so forth), today's operators need to be skilled in all these activities rather than specialize, as they did in the past. Second, the newer technologies require that employees be problem-solvers; thus, machinists must understand the machining technology even though the CNC does the calculations for them. Third, more computer skills are required, though these programming skills take a relatively short time to learn compared to machining skills because the graphical interface with the computer simplifies the programming tasks.[10]

Thus, skill demands within the metalworking part of production have probably increased overall. Owing to the computerization of machines, not only are valve manufacturers likely to hire skilled machinists with problem-solving skills, but they also are not hiring the less-skilled operators they used previously. In the past, when the production of valves required the use of six to ten machines, some of them were set up by skilled machinists but operated by much-less-skilled operators. Now CNC machines do far more tasks automatically on one machine, and thus very low-skill operating jobs are gone. This is not surprising: automation has caused overall labor demand to decline per unit of output.

Skill demand has also risen in the product design stage because draftsmen have been eliminated by the new software and only engineers are needed for design. With three-dimensional CAD/CAM machinery producing blueprints automatically, there is no need for draftsmen, and the three-dimensional nature of the program eliminates the need for the multiple drawings that used to be necessary. The use of the new machines has also resulted in a decline in the demand for engineers.

New Human Resource Management Practices   In the valve industry most plants are quite small. The work environment in many plants has long been characterized by a family feel. Still, HRM practices have changed considerably over time. In small shops everyone is part of the team and called upon when needed. New technology has changed the nature of the production worker's job in ways similar to what we observed in the continuous, high-volume plants in medical equipment and steel. Valve industry machinists participate more in problem-solving activities, very little of which occurs while operating the machinery. For example, if the machinery is worn down (as when the ball screw in the machine is too worn to turn the pallet properly or the hydraulics are clogged), the computer recognizes the problem instantly and will not continue the process. Employees do not need to solve this sort of problem through team activity. There are two reasons they are more likely instead to solve problems away from the machine. First, in designing new products, a team gets together to clarify a drawing, perhaps making changes (in space or tolerance) and suggesting equipment or production methods. Second, the machinist is involved in improving the approach to production. For example, to improve performance a certain area of operations might be videotaped. Machinists and others then brainstorm to improve the process. Machinists at these kinds of firms tend not to rely on incentive pay. Most are paid a flat hourly rate, with some bonuses to meet special targets.

Training is extremely important for machine operators. When

hired, they not only have graduated from high school but have acquired additional machining skills at a community college or technical institute. Thus, these jobs are held by individuals with a high school degree with some additional training. After they are hired, the firm trains them in running the specific CNC machines—either on the job or, if new machines are purchased, through the seller of the machine. Finally, firms also train workers to use the inspection machines. Overall, firms provide extensive training on these machines.

THE FUTURE OF WORK IN THE THREE INDUSTRIES

The rising income inequality of the last twenty-five years suggests that many workers have been "left behind"—that is, the real incomes of better-educated workers rose while the incomes of the less-educated declined in relative terms, possibly because of new technologies. In the three industries studied here, plants have adopted sophisticated new production technologies made possible by advances in computer hardware and software. These new technologies often led to fundamental changes in the jobs of production workers and the skills they need. In steel, valves, and high-volume medical instrument production, workers began to run the production process through computerized monitoring systems rather than through "hands-on" manual control of production. Only in low-volume medical instruments have jobs been relatively unchanged.

The key question is: Why have we retained these high-paying jobs in the United States? Will these jobs continue to be available to high school educated workers in the future? Our interviews with plant managers provided us with the opportunity to gather information about the types of jobs and plants in the three industries that are likely to remain in the United States or likely to be moved offshore. In this section, we discuss the factors that create comparative advantages for U.S. plants and thus increase the likelihood that these plants and their production worker jobs will remain in the United States.

Several factors affect labor demand. Technological changes can reduce the demand for labor as capital substitutes for labor—in other words, the substitution effect reduces labor demand. In addition, higher wages in the United States relative to other countries can reduce the demand for labor. However, if firms are able to either increase quality or reduce prices as a result of technological changes, these improvements will increase product demand and thus increase labor demand and retain jobs in the United States. This scale effect increases labor demand.

Jobs are retained because some firms value the high skill levels of U.S. workers, but this factor alone cannot account for the overall job retention. As summarized in table 5.2, several factors have combined to retain jobs in the United States. For the most part, jobs are retained because workers are skilled, the customers are close by, and firms are producing sophisticated products that are more efficiently designed and built in the United States. However, manufacturing plants may be staying in the United States but they are also producing with fewer workers per unit of output. Managers told us that the high costs of labor are inducing them to introduce labor-saving technological improvements. In all three industries new technologies are reducing labor demand per unit of output as capital substitutes for labor. However, it is the rising and higher-quality output that then increases the overall demand for these skilled workers, and proximity to customers and R&D that keeps jobs in the United States.

Finally, the jobs that remain in the United States are going to individuals who are relatively more able among the high school educated: they are literate, often use basic math skills, have good interpersonal and communications skills, often are good problem-solvers, and, in the case of manufacturing, often have strong mechanical skills. In other words, these workers may not be typical high school graduates. Our work tells us that this should change: high schools should educate students with the objective of teaching these "soft skills."

THE HIGH SKILL LEVEL OF THE LOCAL LABOR FORCE

In two industries, we heard evidence that production worker jobs will remain in the United States because of the high skill level of the American worker. The plant manager at the medical equipment plant with the continuous, high-volume production process felt that one of the reasons the plant would remain open was the good local labor pool, which had the skills (computer literacy, problem-

Table 5.2 Why Production Jobs Are Retained in the United States

	Medical Devices		Valves	Steel
	Continuous, High-Volume	Batch Production		
The skill level of local labor force is high	✓	—	✓	✓
Plant is close to R&D and/or engineering group	✓	✓	✓	—
Plant is close to customer	—	✓	✓	✓
Labor cost is small share of total cost	✓	✓	—	✓
Existing fixed capital stock is hard to move	✓	—	—	✓

Source: Authors' compilation.
Note: A check indicates that we judge this to be an important reason jobs are retained in the United States.

solving skills, diagnostic skills, and communication skills) required by the production process. Although this company operates a similar plant in Mexico, it is unlikely to close the U.S. plant and consolidate operations in Mexico because the requisite skill set is not available there.

In looking at why production worker jobs in the valve industry are likely to stay in the United States, it is important to recognize that many valve makers are specialty design firms. Working with engineers, they design for specific applications. The production of commodity valves in large batches is declining. As long as there is an adequate supply of skilled machinists in the United States, the specialty design segment of the industry will probably remain. This part of the valve industry would be hurt if developing countries were eventually able to supply these same skills in a lower-wage workforce.

PROXIMITY TO ENGINEERING AND R&D GROUPS

When new products are being developed, it is best to have the manufacturing process close to the R&D group so that the two groups can experiment with alternative production approaches and fine-tune the production process. Managers in virtually all of the plants echoed this idea. The low-tech medical product plant has an engineering group on-site that designs new products and designs and builds the production machines. The on-site location facilitates the design and testing of the new machinery. Similarly, R&D shops are located on-site at the plants that produce high-tech medical products as well. For many plants, the on-site engineering group interacts frequently with R&D personnel at U.S. headquarters. The fact that plants are fairly close to U.S. headquarters facilitates this interaction between production and R&D.

Thus, as long as the United States remains preeminent in the R&D phase of medical device manufacturing, some production worker jobs in this industry will remain in the United States. We can reach similar conclusions for the valve and steel industries. In valves, most producers in the United States are making customized valves to the specifications of individual customers. Thus, new valves are designed on the premises and then the process moves directly to production. The steel industry is constantly developing—usually on-site—new products with different specifications, shapes, and metallurgical compositions. In sum, it is in part the preeminence of the engineering and design workforce in the United States that contributes to maintaining high-quality production jobs in the United States. Thus, a high-quality engineering workforce is indirectly helping to keep high-wage production jobs in the United States.

PROXIMITY TO THE CUSTOMER

Proximity to the customer has been a key reason the small-batch medical equipment plants have remained in the United States. For example, in a plant that manufactures complicated surgical equipment we learned that ideas for new products and product modifications come from the customers (doctors, hospitals) and that there is significant interaction between the customer and the manufacturer during the design and manufacturing phases.

Proximity to the customer also influences location decisions in some parts of the steel industry. Finished steel products from integrated steel mills that are shipped to automotive assembly plants often come from steel mills that have close working relationships with those auto plants. Steel finishing processes are likely to remain close to auto plants. In fact, some Japanese steelmakers opened steel finishing facilities in the United States to serve the needs of auto plants opened here by Japanese car companies.

The location of steel mini-mills is also geographically constrained by the nature of the markets for their products. For example, mini-mills that produce rebar steel supply their products to metropolitan and regional construction markets. These mini-mills are also likely to remain in close proximity to their product markets because of the high transportation costs of their product and the wide availability of scrap steel. In most of the plants we visited in the three industries, being located in the United States confers a greater advantage than moving abroad because here plants interact closely with customers.

THE LOW LABOR CONTENT OF THE PRODUCTS

Products that have low labor content and need strong technical infrastructure support will continue to be produced in the United States. One company that makes drug infusion pumps is keeping these jobs in the United States but manufacturing abroad the disposable plastic tubes that are used in very high volume with the pumps. Similarly, another company that makes pumps keeps these jobs in the United States but the plastic injection-molded equipment that goes with the pumps comes from other countries. Steelmaking is also very capital-intensive. Even if steelmakers in other countries could employ lower-wage workers, most managers believe that this cost disadvantage for U.S. firms is not significant as long as labor costs are a fairly small part of steel production and as long as workers here are highly skilled. However, integrated U.S. steel firms are suffering under the huge overhead costs of pensions and health care owed to retired workers.

FIXED CAPITAL STOCK

In all three industries, especially steel, many plant managers indicated that jobs will remain in the United States because the current capital stock exists here and it would be very costly to move abroad.

CONCLUSIONS

A set of in-depth plant visits inside three industries helped us document how new technologies have and have not changed the nature of production worker jobs. Several conclusions about the relationship between new production technologies and the nature of production worker jobs emerge from this look inside these three industries.

First, narrowly defined industries contain plants making very different products with very different technologies. All of the medical equipment plants share the same three-digit SIC classification and span only three different four-digit classifications. The steel mills are all part of the same four-digit classification, and valve manufacturers are part of only three different four-digit industry classifications. However, plants within these three industries use very different technologies, and the extent to which plants have adopted new computer-based technologies varies dramatically from plant to plant within an industry.

Second, in all three industries new computer-based technologies have produced significant improvements in productivity and product quality—and thus, in some cases, falling product prices. Productivity has clearly risen in the continuous, high-volume manufacturing plants—in all three industries—and in some cases prices have fallen or product quality has risen. Productivity gains are less evident in medical equipment plants that use assembly workers in batch production processes and in some valve plants, but in these cases a greater range of products, and thus higher-quality products, has evolved from the technological improvements in design and production in these industries.

Third, changes in job tasks due to increased computerization have often, though not always, resulted in "up-skilling" in these industries.[11] The full range of changes in skill demand are summarized by industry in table 5.3, which shows the growing importance of the "soft skills." As is emphasized in Autor, Levy, and Murnane (this volume), computers are now doing the symbolic processing. Retrieving data and acting on it in systematic ways to run the production lines, computers are doing the routine work of production. It is the nonroutine work, like addressing production-line failures or correcting small errors in line performance, that neither computers nor less-skilled operators can perform. Thus, computerization causes firms to demand workers with good problem-solving and communication skills, and sometimes the reading and math skills to undertake problem-solving. In the high-volume steel and medical equipment industries, workers are much more mobile throughout the plant and now must apply diagnostic and problem-

Table 5.3 Skill Requirements in Response to Technological Change

| | Medical Devices | | | |
	Continuous, High-Volume	Batch Production	Valves	Steel
High school diploma	Yes	Yes	No	No
Mechanical or machine skills	No	No	Yes	Yes
Problem-solving skills	Yes	No	Yes	Yes
Diagnostic or monitoring skills	Yes	No	Yes	Yes
Communication skills	Yes	Yes	Yes	Yes
Ability to learn basic computer skills	Yes	No	Yes	Yes
Flexibility in learning new jobs	Yes	Yes	Yes	Yes
Statistical skills or basic motor skills	No	No	Yes	Yes
Dexterity or high attention level	No	Yes	No	No

Source: Authors' compilation.

solving skills to highly automated machines that have eliminated routine work tasks.[12] In contrast, while valve manufacturing is now much more computerized, the up-skilling is more modest. These firms still require skilled machinists as before, and less-skilled operators are rarely hired. Finally, in some establishments, such as minimills and medical instrument assembly plants, skill demands have hardly changed because technological changes in production have been more modest. In plants with technology that is less complex, in particular mini-mills that produce less complicated products, skill demand has changed less.[13]

Even though up-skilling in these industries has increased the demand for soft skills, there has been only a modest increase in the demand for computer literacy. Nearly all of the jobs in these industries (except for a subset of those in medical assembly) require the workers to work at computer keyboards or monitors. In virtually all cases, however, the plant managers said that if job applicants have basic literacy, math, and people skills, and some technical skills such as machining (for valves), then computer skills can be readily taught on the job. For example, workers in valves no longer need to run lathes; those jobs have been automated with the use of new CNC machines. Yet these workers still need to have machining skills because they must understand how the CNC machine works; these machining skills are in fact more important than the computer skills that can be taught on the job. Thus, these firms do not require computer training in school. Although skill demand has risen, these firms continue to hire high school educated workers with mechanical or machining skills and do not seek to hire college graduates who do not have the required technical skills.[14]

Fourth, when jobs and skill requirements change, newly adopted HRM practices help address the plants' need for workers with new, more demanding skills. Table 5.4, which summarizes the full range of changes in HRM practices by industry, shows that the key change has been the introduction of greater degrees of worker flexibility— more job rotation, more training, and also more problem-solving. However, though technological changes have increased the need for worker flexibility, the capital-intensive technology dictates how these jobs should be combined for the most part. Plants have very limited options for redesigning jobs by task (unlike the results of Autor, Levy, and Murnane, this volume). The precise set of work practices that a plant uses to ensure that its workers have the necessary new skills varies from plant to plant. But selection, training, and pay-for-skills compensation plans all offer interesting and frequently used ways for plant management to elevate skill levels.

Thus, our research indicates that plants within narrowly defined industries adopt new computer-based production technologies at very different rates, and that when they do, skill requirements for production workers generally increase. To some extent, high school educated workers who want these jobs need to have some amount of computer literacy, since plants with these jobs prefer to hire such workers. At the same time, training programs and apprenticeships in different jobs appear to be especially important methods for workers to acquire the kind of plant- and equipment-specific computer knowledge they need. The primary skills that high school educated workers must bring to the job are the "soft skills," or the people skills—the ability to communicate, a willingness to learn on the job, and diagnostic and problem-solving skills.

Fifth, all three industries have witnessed increases in produc-

Table 5.4 New Human Resource Practices in Response to Technological Change

| | Medical Devices | | | |
	Continuous, High-Volume	Batch Production	Valves	Steel
Increased worker responsibility	Yes	No	No	Yes
Job rotation	Yes	Yes	Yes	Yes
Extensive training	Yes	No	Yes	Yes
Cross-training	Yes	Yes	Yes	Yes
Problem-solving teams	No	No	Yes	Yes
Pay-for-skills	Yes	No	No	Yes
Self-directed work teams	Yes	No	No	No

Source: Authors' compilation.

tivity, product quality, or product variety as a result of technological changes. Changes in labor demand, however, have varied across the industries. Innovations in product design and higher productivity in the medical equipment industry have increased product demand and thus doubled labor demand over time. For valve makers and steel mini-mills, labor demand has remained roughly constant; these industries have achieved higher productivity with approximately the same workforce. In the steel industry there has been dramatic downsizing and rising productivity over the last thirty years, but these changes did not arise from making technological improvements but instead from closing out-of-date, poor-performing plants and improving productivity in those that remained. In all three industries, however, new technologies appear to be the major reason we keep these jobs in the United States: they enable American manufacturers to improve products and serve nearby customers using a highly skilled, local workforce. The competitive advantage of the United States in the future in keeping these jobs lies in technology, the high skills of engineers and workers, and proximity to customers as firms design and produce the high-quality products they want.

For researchers, the patterns we observed in these plants suggest that new computer-based technologies vary across plants within narrowly defined, three-digit SIC industry groups and that these new technologies have changed jobs and skill requirements. Building upon the insights gained from this research, however, will prove challenging. The "new technologies" we uncovered are specific to individual work establishments and even vary across plants in a given company. Simple survey questions (like "Do you use a PC at your job?") do not capture the technologies we found in these plants. In some cases, the computer technologies were invisible to workers. With PLCs residing in enclosed metal boxes on the walls of a medical equipment plant, for instance, it was not obvious to the workers that they worked regularly with "computers." Future research that seeks to understand the impact of new technologies on the jobs, skills, and wages of high school educated workers could benefit by incorporating this kind of hands-on knowledge of specific industries. Field research that goes deep inside plants can identify in very concrete terms what "new technology" really is and what production workers really do.

We would like to acknowledge the superb support of the Russell Sage and Rockefeller Foundations. In addition, we thank the Alfred P. Sloan Foundation and the National Science Foundation for supporting our research on the steel industry and related work. Our coauthors on the overall steel project have contributed very significantly to the research, though they are in no way responsible for the views expressed in this chapter. We are indebted to Brent Boning, Richard Freeman, Jon Gant, Morris Kleiner, and Giovanna Prennushi. Finally, we thank the many industry participants who contributed their valuable time and insights to this study.

APPENDIX

Table 5.A1 Employment and Wages in the Medical Industry, 1972 to 1992

Industry	Year	Number of Plants	Total Employment	Production Workers	Average Hourly Production Wage[a]
Surgical and	1972	357	34,018	71%	$9.85
medical in-	1977	456	42,630	67	10.04
struments	1982	708	56,393	68	10.02
(3841)	1987	975	72,163	62	11.25
	1992	1,121	97,183	59	10.93
Surgical ap-	1972	618	42,512	67	9.66
pliances	1977	773	52,686	68	10.24
and sup-	1982	1,126	67,507	66	9.25
plies	1987	1,295	77,732	65	9.95
(3842)	1992	1,458	94,556	64	9.91
X-ray, elec-	1972	75	11,006	58	11.36
tromedical,	1977	187	30,125	54	11.98
and electro-	1982	231	47,553	48	10.99
therapeutic					
apparatus					
(3693)[b]					
X-ray, appa-	1987	67	8,711	63	12.50
ratus, and	1992	112	14,239	49	12.83
tubes					
(3844)[b]					
Electromedi-	1987	209	29,154	45	11.30
cal equip-	1992	330	39,836	45	11.91
ment					
(3845)[b]					

Source: Longitudinal Research Database.
[a] Deflated by CPI.
[b] In 1987 SIC 3693 was reclassified into two separate industry categories: 3844 and 3845.

Table 5.A2 Employment and Wages in the Steel Industry, 1972 to 1997

Year	Total Employment	Production Workers	Average Hourly Production Wage[a]
1972	469,100	81%	$17.23
1977	441,900	79	20.99
1982	295,800	73	23.44
1987	188,100	78	19.06
1992	170,600	77	18.99
1997	144,080	79	20.14

Source: Census of Manufacturers (1972, 1977, 1982, 1992, 1997).
[a] Deflated by CPI (1992 dollars).

Table 5.A3 Employment and Wages in the Valve Industry, 1972 to 1992

Industry	Year	Number of Plants	Total Employment	Production Workers	Average Hourly Production Wage[a]
Industrial	87	369	45,808	64%	$ 12.42
valves	92	453	51,432	65	12.28
(3491)[b]					
Fluid power	87	346	27,352	65	12.45
valves	92	340	28,436	65	12.04
(3492)[b]					
Valve and	72	648	86,035	70	11.54
pipe fittings	77	764	107,892	70	12.03
(3494)[b]	82	1,063	113,984	65	11.73
	87	372	24,774	70	11.76
	92	225	15,942	74	11.76

Source: Longitudinal Research Database.
[a] Deflated by CPI.
[b] Prior to 1987 all valve plants were categorized as SIC 3494. Beginning in 1987, three categories are used: 3491, 3492, and 3494.

NOTES

1. In the Longitudinal Research Database (LRD), medical equipment manufacturers cover industries 3841, 3842, 3844, and 3845 in the Standard Industrial Classification (SIC) system. Prior to 1987, the two SIC industries 3844 and 3845 did not exist but were a single classification, 3693. Steel manufacturing is industry 3312. Valve manufacturing plants were part of industry 3494 through 1982 and have been industry classifications 3494, 3491, and 3492 since then.

2. Education statistics are from Hirsch and Macpherson (1997). They define industries using CPS industry definitions that are somewhat broader than the four-digit SIC code definitions from the Longitudinal Research Database.

3. These figures may be conservative estimates of the size of the industries' production workforces, since these statistics come from the LRD, which uses narrower industry definitions than the Current Population Survey (CPS). The medical equipment manufacturers cover SIC industries 3841, 3842, 3844, and 3845. Prior to 1987, the two industries 3844 and 3845 did not exist but were a single classification, 3693. Steel manufacturing is industry 3312. Valve manufacturing was in industry 3494 through 1982, and the three industry classifications 3494, 3491, and 3492 since then.

4. Statistics on employment levels are from the LRD.

5. Data on number of employees and establishments are from LRD.

6. Wage data are reported in Hirsch and Macpherson (1997). Wages are deflated by the consumer price index (CPI) and are reported in 1992 dollars.

7. Prior to 1987, SIC codes 3844 and 3845 did not exist. Plants in those industries were classified as SIC 3693: X-ray, Electromedical, and Electrotherapeutic Apparatus.

8. To protect the confidentiality of this company and others that we visited, the products we describe are representative of the types of products we observed but not the exact products.

9. This pattern would be contrary to the predictions of the models of Kremer and Maskin (1996) and Acemoglu (2000).

10. When CNC machines were more difficult to program, manufacturers would have a small staff of programmers to help program the machines for the operators. These programmers are no longer needed.

11. For detailed empirical evidence on up-skilling across industries, see Autor, Levy, and Murnane (1998) and Bresnahan, Brynjolfsson, and Hitt (2002).

12. For additional evidence on the steel and medical equipment industries, see Applebaum et al. (2000).

13. For a similar conclusion, see Ballantine and Ferguson (this volume).
14. In contrast, technological change in some other industries, such as banking, has increased their use of college-level employees (Autor, Levy, and Murnane 2002).

REFERENCES

Acemoglu, Daron. 2000. "Technical Change, Inequality, and the Labor Market." Working Paper 7800. Cambridge, Mass.: National Bureau of Economic Research (July).

Applebaum, Eileen, Thomas Bailey, Peter Berg, and Arne L. Kalleberg. 2000. *Manufacturing Advantage*. Ithaca, N.Y.: Cornell University Press.

Association for Manufacturing Technology. 2000. *Producing Prosperity—Manufacturing Technology's Unmeasured Role in Economic Expansion*. McLean, Va.: AMT.

Autor, David, Lawrence Katz, and Alan Krueger. 1998. "Computing Inequality: Have Computers Changed the Labor Market?" *Quarterly Journal of Economics* 113: 1169–1213.

Autor, David, Frank Levy, and Richard Murnane. 2002. "Upstairs Downstairs: Computers and Skills on Two Floors of a Large Bank." *Industrial and Labor Relations Review* 55: 432–47.

Bartel, Ann P., and Nachum Sicherman. 1999. "Technological Change and Wages: An Interindustry Analysis." *Journal of Political Economy* 107 (April): 285–325.

Berman, Eli, John Bound, and Zvi Griliches. 1994. "Changes in the Demand for Skilled Labor Within U.S. Manufacturing: Evidence from the Annual Survey of Manufacturers." *Quarterly Journal of Economics* 109 (May): 367–97.

Bresnahan, Timothy F., Erik Brynjolfsson, and Lorin M. Hitt. 2002. "Information Technology, Workplace Organization, and the Demand for Skilled Labor: Firm-Level Evidence." *Quarterly Journal of Economics* 117: 339.

Caroli, Eve, and John Van Reenen. 2001. "Skills and Organizational Change: Evidence from British and French Establishments in the 1980s and 1990s." *Quarterly Journal of Economics* 116: 1449–92.

Greenan, Nathalie, and Jacques Mairesse. 1996. "Computers and Productivity in France: Some Evidence." Working Paper 5836. Cambridge, Mass.: National Bureau of Economic Research (November).

Hirsch, Barry T., and David A. Macpherson. 1997. *Union Membership and Earnings Data Book*. Washington, D.C.: Bureau of National Affairs.

Katz, Lawrence F., and Kevin M. Murphy. 1992. "Changes in Relative Wages, 1963–87: Supply and Demand Factors." *Quarterly Journal of Economics* 107(February): 35–78.

Kremer, Michael, and Eric Maskin. 1996. "Wage Inequality and Segregation by Skill." Working Paper 5718. Cambridge, Mass.: National Bureau of Economic Research.

Krueger, Alan B. 1993. "How Computers Have Changed the Wage Structure: Evidence from Microdata, 1984–1989." *Quarterly Journal of Economics* 108(February): 33–60.

Standard and Poor's. 1998. *U.S. Industry and Trade Outlook*. New York: DRI and McGraw-Hill.

CHAPTER 6

Plastic Manufacturers: How Competitive Strategies and Technology Decisions Transformed Jobs and Increased Pay Disparity Among Rank-and-File Workers

John W. Ballantine Jr. and Ronald F. Ferguson

It is well known that earnings disparity increased among U.S. workers during the last quarter of the twentieth century. Less well known is that disparity grew even among workers who were *equal* in their years of schooling and employed *within narrowly defined industrial sectors* (see, for example, Levy and Murnane 1992; Murphy and Welch 1993; Federal Reserve Bank of New York 1995; Federal Reserve Bank of Boston 1996; McFate, Lawson, and Wilson 1995; Mishel, Bernstein, and Schmidt 1998; Dunne et al. 1999; Bradbury 2002). Economists' leading hypothesis for growing disparity is that expanded use of computer-based technologies increased the importance of cognitive skill and the premium that employers were willing to pay for workers who possessed it. Many studies over the past decade have found the predicted statistical patterns. However, detailed firm-level studies on precisely how technologies affect skill demands and compensation patterns inside particular industries are rare. In particular, there are very few studies to explain the growing disparity in some narrowly defined industrial sectors among workers who have equal years of schooling.

In response, this chapter is a study of compensation levels and associated human resource policies for rank-and-file workers among twelve firms in one narrowly defined industrial sector: manufacturers of plastic products, not elsewhere classified, whose four-digit standard industrial classification (SIC) code is 3089. The hourly wage rate for rank-and-file workers when we visited these firms in 1995 ranged from an average of $7.00 an hour among the three lowest-paying firms to an average of $11.22 among three that paid the most. Total compensation for rank-and-file workers, including wages plus benefits, ranged from a low of $8.77 an hour at the bottom three firms to $15.87 at the top three. In all twelve firms, typical rank-and-file workers were high school educated.

The chapter addresses three questions. First, why did some plastics firms adopt the most modern computer-controlled equipment in the 1980s while others continued using the industry's traditional technology through at least the mid-1990s, when we conducted firm-level interviews and collected data? Second, how did the adoption of new technologies affect rank-and-file job tasks? Third, did changing job tasks in some firms, but not others, contribute to growing disparity in earnings and other employment conditions for rank-and-file workers among the firms that we studied?

The technology for manufacturing plastic products dates to the early decades of the twentieth century. During the first fifty years or so, the technology changed gradually, and most production workers held one of two jobs. One was the *operator,* who loaded the machine with plastic resins, waited for the resins to melt and plastic to form in the mold, and then removed the plastic product. The other was the *inspector-packer,* who checked the product for flaws and packed it for shipment. Both were simple jobs, and very low levels of cognitive skill were sufficient. There was a high degree of technological uniformity across the industry.

This changed in the late 1970s, when some firms began adopting state-of-the-art, computer-controlled machines that automated and embellished the traditional operator's job. The computer-controlled machines were faster and more accurate at performing routine physical movements, such as injecting plastic resins into molds, and this enabled cost-effective fabrication of increasingly complex products. Our finding that computer-controlled machines displaced a job that mainly involved routine, repeated physical movement, and limited exercise of judgment is similar to what Autor, Levy, and Murnane (this volume) show using banking industry examples and what Bartel, Ichniowski, and Shaw (this volume) report for the sectors that they studied.

By 1995, when we visited the firms in our study, half had adopted highly sophisticated computer-controlled machines that used mechanical devices to load resins and statistical process controls to monitor production and product quality. In the firms that adopted these technologies most extensively, workers with high school educations who in the past had not used cognitive skills much on the job had become responsible for monitoring statistical controls, making judgments about production-line quality, and writing in production logs to communicate with supervisors and workers on other job shifts.[1] In addition, there was an increased emphasis on oral communication with coworkers and visitors.

Rank-and-file workers with skills sufficient to perform these functions were able to retain their jobs, but many others were not. Firms report that as they competed to attract and retain workers with adequate cognitive skills, wage differentials grew among rank-and-file workers in the plastics industry. Wages and benefits were lowest at firms where technologies and products changed the least, because the jobs at such firms remained simple. Indeed, at these firms, temporary workers became a larger segment of the workforce, for reasons that we discuss. Bartel, Ichniowski, and Shaw (this volume) report similar industry-level differences in degrees to which firms adopted sophisticated technologies and similar consequences for disparity in rank-and-file compensation and job quality.

HOW WE CLASSIFY FIRMS

Data for this study come from twelve firms that manufacture plastic products. They differ sharply in business culture and competitive strategy. Six of the twelve apply cutting-edge technologies and compete to supply the most innovative and defect-free products in the industry. In contrast, six supply relatively simple and standard products, using less complex technologies, and compete mostly to be the lowest-cost producers in their market segments. We label firms in the first category leading complexity (LC) firms and call the others standard complexity (SC) firms. Products of LC firms include those made in "clean rooms," such as compact discs (CDs) and disposable contact lenses, electronic parts made with specialty resins for automotive manufacturers, and silver chloride plastic sensors that conduct electrical currents for EKG medical tests. Conversely, the six SC firms in our sample supply relatively simple products that have few parts and require markedly less technical precision and customization than those produced by LC firms. For example, SC firms have no need for the sterile production environment of a clean room. Their products include home storage items such as wastebaskets and laundry baskets, plastic knives and forks and combs and brushes. We emphasize complexity in distinguishing these groups because complexity of both technology and products is key for understanding the implications for rank-and-file job tasks.[2]

The chapter's sections address technology, job characteristics, and human resource policies. In each section we address LC or SC firms as groups and highlight two exemplars—Inova from the LC group and Homepro from the SC group.[3] Inova and Homepro are large and successful injection molding companies. Their incumbent executives and key senior managers have been with them for more than two decades. Both companies focus heavily on customer service and product quality, and both have used technology, albeit to differing degrees, to create and maintain competitive advantages. Both employ high percentages of non-college-educated workers—some of whom are recent immigrants—among their rank and file. However, their business cultures, engineering capabilities, and competitive strategies are different. Inova strives to be a technology innovator that co-ventures with other technology-oriented firms and supplies specialty plastic products to other large manufacturing businesses. In contrast, Homepro uses standard technology and strives to produce high-quality plastic housewares for sale by large retail firms. It aims to be the low-cost producer among its competitors while also supplying the highest quality.

Inova and Homepro were once very similar firms. However, over the years managers have upgraded technology more at Inova than at Homepro. Jobs for rank-and-file workers at Inova have become more cognitively demanding. This helps to explain why Inova now pays a higher hourly wage to production workers, offers more fringe benefits, provides more training, and employs a smaller percentage of temporary workers compared to Homepro.[4]

The central importance of returns to skills as an explanation for growing disparity, even among workers with equal years of schooling, leads directly to our policy conclusion. Specifically, an important route to earnings growth for rank-and-file workers in the plastics industry is to improve the reading, communication, and basic math skills that managers say are prerequisites for rank-and-file jobs in LC firms, where wages and total compensation are higher. LC firms that do not have their own basic skills training programs claim that a shortage of job applicants possessing such skills is sometimes a bottleneck that prevents expansion.

Hence, it seems clear that LC firms would benefit from policies and programs to improve workers' reading, communication, and basic math skills. Just as important, workers with improved skills would benefit because LC firms would pay them higher wages. However, we are uncertain how the SC firms in our study would respond.[5]

Similarly unknown is whether LC firms, with their more advanced technologies, will someday displace SC firms in the product markets that SC firms now control. For now, LC and SC firms serve quite different markets. They use different technologies and have distinct human resource policies for rank-and-file workers. Based on what we learned from visiting firms and talking to various personnel, we expect these differences to persist for the foreseeable future, with associated consequences for compensation patterns and human resource policies for production-line workers.

METHODOLOGY

The data for this chapter come from an intensive series of on-site company interviews and forced-choice surveys of line managers, top executives, and human resources personnel at twelve firms. The sixty firms that we visited for the larger project represented a 75 percent response rate from among eighty randomly selected manufacturing firms from a single region of a northern state. The twelve manufacturers upon which this chapter focuses represent all of the firms in the sample that produced plastic products in SIC 3089. This was the largest cluster of businesses in our sample occupying a single four-digit SIC industry. All of the data in this chapter, both quantitative and qualitative, come from the visits, interviews, and surveys that we conducted in 1995 with these twelve firms.

The interviews and surveys focused on changes over the decade from 1985 to 1995, but several also included reviews of firm history reaching back to the beginning of the industry. The people we spent the most time with had been with their firms for at least ten years, and the majority for longer. They responded to a formal forced-choice survey that we administered in person. On each issue we asked to speak to the person best informed to address it. So it was not unusual for different people to respond to different parts of the survey. The survey covered a variety of topics, including trends over recent decades in business strategies, competitive pressures, products, customer demands, technologies, materials, product customization, investment, pricing policies, work organization, and company performance. Upon completing each section of the survey, we held an open-ended discussion of the issues that the forced-choice questions covered. Responses were tape-recorded, transcribed, and coded for analysis. Time spent at each firm ranged from half a day to one full day, usually in multiple visits.

TECHNOLOGY AND SKILL REQUIREMENTS

Injection molding and extrusion are the two generic technologies that firms use to make plastic products. Injection molding involves putting molten plastic resins into closed molds. The hardened plastic, when taken from the mold, is the product. Examples are plastic forks and knives, eyeglass frames, and plastic lenses. Extrusion technologies place molten plastic into hollow molds and then blow off the excess, leaving a product in the shape of the external wall of the mold. Extrusion is the technology for such things as plastic bottles and bags. The range of products to which injection and extrusion technologies are applied is much greater today than fifty years ago. Both types of technology are represented among the firms in our sample, but most, including the two firms we highlight, are injection molders.

Some firms in this study use base technologies that resemble early models dating to the middle of the twentieth century, while others apply (and sometimes invent) the latest advances in computer-aided plastics manufacturing and robotics. The two most important innovations at the end of the twentieth century were improved raw materials (plastic resins) and the introduction, beginning in the late 1980s, of automated molding machines with statistical process control (SPC) technology. With the standard mechanical machines, controls and monitoring mechanisms are mechanical. Operators change the temperature or pressure in the mold by turning a knob. Automated machines with statistical process controls have computerized sensors throughout the equipment to measure and report information such as resin temperature, thickness, clarity, strength, conductivity, and shape. Measures are reported numerically and graphically. In many cases, graphs show confidence intervals and record the reasons for variations. The shift from mechani-

Table 6.1 Rank-and-File Workers Performing Listed Job
Functions at the Twelve Firms, 1995

	Interpret Written Instructions	Maintain Production Logs	Use Basic Math Skills	Monitor Product Quality	Give Instructions to Computers
Leading com-plexity firms	90%	70%	87%	79%	48%
Standard com-plexity firms	63	10	33	81	17
Difference in means	27**	60***	54***	−2	31*

Source: Authors' compilation.
* $.05 < p < .10$.
** $.01 < p < .05$.
*** $p < .01$.

cal to computer-operated machines with statistical process controls
gave workers new responsibilities that play an important role in the
story that this chapter reports.

We begin by describing the changes in competitive strategies,
technologies, products, and jobs in SC firms, highlighting Homepro
among the SC firms and Inova among LC firms. A major purpose of
the discussion is to explain the LC/SC differences in rank-and-file
job functions shown in table 6.1.[6] There are some dramatic differences: 70 percent of LC workers but only 10 percent of SC workers
are responsible for maintaining production logs, while the percentages responsible for using math are 87 percent for LC firms but
only 33 percent for SC firms. There are smaller but still notable
gaps between LC and SC firms in rank-and-file responsibility for
interpreting written instructions and for giving instructions to computers. The final section contrasts SC and LC human resource policies and discusses how they relate to the technology and job complexity differences that the other sections address.

STANDARD COMPLEXITY FIRMS

Six of the companies in our sample are standard complexity firms.
They produce relatively simple products, many of which have not
changed much over several decades: combs, plastic knives and

forks, bird feeders, waste baskets, and other household goods. The injection molding technology for these products has evolved gradually from mechanical to automated machines. Larger companies like Homepro have invested more in new automated equipment, but sometimes SC firms simply modify older machines. Financial resources to invest in upgrading are often scarce because the close substitutability of competitors' products causes profit margins to be quite thin, especially in smaller firms. Given the scarcity of funds to invest in technology (and indeed, often no clear need to do so), SC companies emphasize price, quality, and service, not innovation.

Like LC firms, each SC firm has a distinctive history that shaped its recent strategy and market position. For example, the largest plastic cutlery manufacturer in our sample was purchased in the early 1980s by a major paper goods conglomerate. Financed by the conglomerate, the cutlery plant upgraded to new injection molding equipment to make customized knives, forks, and spoons for large retail suppliers, such as BJ's, Costco, and Sam's Club. In contrast, a small comb and brush maker has remained a family-owned business, and a second generation has taken over to keep it going. When the younger generation took control they focused on retrofitting used injection molding machines with multicavity molds that helped to double hourly production. Then they aggressively marketed their products to beauticians and other customers, sometimes customizing production for particular orders. By selling standard-quality products at competitive prices, this small company has survived and maintained sales levels—a major accomplishment in the owners' opinion.

Some other SC firms are family-owned as well. Their current owners learned the business when they were in high school and returned many years later to take over from their parents. They say that price and quality competition is much more intense than when their parents were running the businesses. Most, like the comb manufacturer, have upgraded equipment when they could afford to. As small and medium-sized injection mold "jobbers," they scramble to secure good contracts with medium-sized buyers. Small batch runs for such things as bird feeders and wastebaskets are common. Most of these SC companies are striving to generate more secure and predictable sales revenues with which to upgrade equipment and develop more customized and differentiated products.

RANK-AND-FILE JOBS AT SC FIRMS

Technology at SC firms has changed gradually over recent decades, and the consequences for rank-and-file workers have been modest. For example, the cutlery firm that was purchased by the conglomerate had invested in new equipment and a modest amount of skill upgrading. In particular, the firm was able to invest in automated equipment to produce utensils in a variety of colors. Only a few of the operators became involved with the new statistical process controls or with production logs. Most continued doing the same jobs they had before. Similarly, the packer's job remained simple and physically demanding and continued to require only minimal basic skills. Specifically, packers had to count the forks and knives correctly, read labels on boxes in order to pack the utensils in the appropriate containers, and stack the containers for shipping.

Smaller SC firms invested less than the larger ones and made do mostly with refurbished machines. Stories by line managers emphasize faster cycle times and redesigned production processes. One of the comb manufacturers doubled productivity by refurbishing some used injection molding machines to use molds with twice the number of comb cavities. It also reset the cycle time of the machines so that one operator could go back and forth between machines within the forty-second production cycle. With twice the number of combs and brushes coming off the production line, the packers had to reorganize their work so that the products could be put in the proper bags. Thus, increased productivity was achieved through faster cycle times, but the cycle times were achieved with little automation and only some tinkering with operations. Operator and packer jobs changed only slightly. Other small SC companies show some of the same basic patterns: some upgrading of equipment and productivity increases, but only small changes in job functions, including little or no increase in the need to use cognitive skill.

Most rank-and-file workers at SC firms had some responsibility for monitoring product quality by 1995 and for interpreting simple written instructions. However, the level of skill required was minimal, and the percentage of workers who had such monitoring responsibilities was generally lower than among firms in the LC category (see table 6.1).

HOMEPRO'S CULTURE AND BUSINESS STRATEGY

Homepro is our exemplar for the SC category. Two brothers who manufactured wooden heels for shoes founded Homepro in 1939 in collaboration with Earl Tupper, who later founded Tupperware. They believed that injection molding would be ideally suited for manufacturing heels made of plastic instead of wood. Unfortunately, the heels they produced stuck to sidewalks on hot days, so the product failed. Soon, however, the firm was making pocket combs, toothbrushes, and soap boxes for World War II soldiers. After the war they began making teacups and, by the early 1950s, a variety of polystyrene products for household use. By the late 1950s they were manufacturing wastebaskets, dishpans, laundry baskets, and a broad line of other housewares. Aside from more modern materials and designs, the product line has not changed much since the late 1950s. Management's primary focus has been production efficiency, product design customization (mainly colors), and customer service. The main change in the product mix has been rapid growth in the variety of home storage products to meet explosive demand for such products since the late 1980s.

Like virtually all plastics firms of the time, Homepro struggled through the oil price surges of the 1970s. Many of its competitors in housewares production sold out to other plastics firms, major chemical companies, banks, or business conglomerates. After the buyouts, few lasted through the 1980s.[7] Executives at Homepro believe that their firm survived because of tenacious and uncompromising attention to cost controls and quality. By the 1990s most large competitors from the 1970s were gone and Homepro was competing against only two or three other companies for its main customers—major chain stores, such as Wal-Mart and Kmart, that sell large volumes of houseware products. Homepro had a number of *small* competitors, but these were not of much concern because they lacked the capacity to compete effectively for large orders. Homepro in 1995 had the second-largest market share among plastic housewares producers—roughly one-tenth that of market leader Rubbermaid.[8]

Because chain stores were consolidating (even as the number of competitors for Homepro was shrinking), Homepro's market power seemed to lessen instead of grow. A Homepro executive told us that in New England alone a dozen chain stores that were Homepro customers in the early 1980s are no longer in business. Many were forced out of business or purchased by the large chains. Hence, by the mid-1990s Homepro was among a small number of large houseware suppliers competing for a small number of large chain-store customers.

In the face of stiff competition, Homepro's business strategy has been to use better materials and more refined designs to produce higher-quality products than competitors and to sell at prices 25 percent lower than the industry leader. Homepro officials claim that they can keep prices low because Homepro is the low-cost producer in the industry, even with high product quality. In addition, the firm prides itself on speed and responsiveness to sometimes fickle customers: "We have these large retailers looking for tremendous levels of service and aren't able to plan and forecast their needs. . . . They give us orders, then they'll call up and say, 'Cancel that order and ship something else instead.' There's more and more of that kind of confusion in the industry." Some customers want a revised order shipped in as little as two or three days, and Homepro prides itself on being prepared to respond to such requests. Large retailers expect even very large orders to be filled in half the time or less compared to the 1980s and earlier.[9] Just-in-time inventory practices among large retail firms and the high cost of shipping plastic products, which can be heavy, are key reasons that production in SC firms has remained on the U.S. mainland and the largest firms, including Homepro, have multiple production sites around the nation. According to Rachel Willis, Rachel Connelly, and Deborah DeGraff (this volume), the just-in-time demands of large retailers seem to be part of the explanation in the hosiery industry as well for production capacity in various sites on the U.S. mainland.

To summarize, the most important change for Homepro over the past few decades has been the share of its growing production that goes to a small number of large retail customers that want customized products manufactured and delivered with shorter and shorter lead times. Homepro officials believe that their success at maintaining and expanding market share in this environment comes from strict cost controls, high-quality materials, production planning that anticipates customers' just-in-time orders, and customized product designs.

RANK-AND-FILE JOBS AT HOMEPRO

At Homepro, just as at other SC firms, rank-and-file jobs have changed very little. Most of the burden of understanding statistical process controls and utilizing more cognitive skill fell to supervisors, not rank-and-file workers. Asked to compare 1985 with 1995 for typical rank-and-file workers, Homepro officials reported virtually no change in requirements to maintain production logs, to use basic math skills, or to use computers. For rank-and-file workers, the primary changes were requirements to read rudimentary written instructions and to monitor product quality in ways that do not require basic skills. These changes contrast significantly with those for rank-and-file workers at LC firms, whose responsibilities have changed more extensively.

Because about half of its machines were semi-automated by 1995, Homepro required a smaller percentage of rank-and-file workers to be full-time operators in 1995 than during earlier periods. The fact that machines were semi-automatic made the operator's job easier and less time-consuming. So operators began sharing more of the packers' job. Both operator and packer jobs remained simple. An official told us, "As long as they can read a label and distinguish between the item number and the color, we can train a good machine operator in about three hours to three days."

Homepro's emphasis on product quality as a source of competitive advantage is why all workers were asked to help monitor quality. However, managers emphasize that monitoring is basically just watching and reporting. One says, "Monitoring. That's the key word. Monitoring. They don't have a lot of control. We don't want them to have much. They are responsible for monitoring and reporting." Further, we were told at Homepro that keeping production logs is "more automated than ever. Less counting. They can't count. Nobody can count in case you haven't noticed. Send five people out to count a pile of boxes you get five different answers. The machines are monitored by computer. We used to do it manually." An official at Homepro emphasized that what they care about most in rank-and-file workers is a good attitude, punctuality, and willingness to follow directions and work hard.

Compared to the LC firms, SC firms used less sophisticated machinery, demanding less skill from rank-and-file workers, to produce an array of less complex products. Though some machines were automated and used statistical process controls, pressures to adapt and upgrade skills fell mostly on foremen, not the rank-and-file workers they supervised.[10]

LEADING COMPLEXITY FIRMS

As defined earlier, LC firms are more technologically sophisticated than SC firms. Through the 1960s and early 1970s, most of the LC firms were similar to the SC firms discussed here, because there was basically only one injection molding technology. However, each LC firm has a story regarding the impetus to become more technology-intensive and distinct. By the mid-1990s engineering capabilities and innovation had placed all six LC firms in our study near the cutting edge of design, production technology, and advanced materials utilization in the markets where they compete.

Two medium-sized LC firms report that demands from large customers were the strongest pressures driving them to upgrade. Managers responded first by redesigning products (for example, plastic bottles and car parts) and then by beginning to replace standard machines with more automated and expensive alternatives, some virtually dictated by the customer's product specifications. The plastic bottler in this group has the most automated plastic bottling equipment in the industry, codeveloped with major equipment manufacturers years before competitors had access to such machinery. For other LC firms, *ongoing* product and process innovation have become requirements. For example, one is a plastic parts supplier to the auto industry. Its auto company customers are partners with it in developing computer-assisted design (CAD) technologies and product development platforms. The firm's viability as a major automotive supplier depends on its product and process development capability (see also Helper and Kleiner, this volume). If it cannot design a method to build a particular part *at a price that the auto company sets,* then one of a small number of competitors is likely to get the contract instead. Similarly, another company had to innovate in order to survive: new engineers replaced wasteful and costly manufacturing processes with new ways of making sophisticated supplies for the electronics industry and telecommunications customers.

Each company in the LC group has a technology leadership story—sometimes driven by talented, entrepreneurial engineers, other times dictated by large buyers, like the auto companies. In each case, product design capabilities and production technology leadership are key to the firm's capacity to develop and produce complex plastic products or to produce relatively standard products (such as plastic bottles) in highly efficient ways. Developing such capabilities is the path-dependent outcome of decades-long processes of strategic business decisions, trial and error, and often luck.

RANK-AND-FILE JOBS AT LC FIRMS

All six firms in the LC category have upgraded to computer-controlled machinery and more complex production processes. Changes in *rank-and-file* job requirements are similar to what some *supervisory foremen* have experienced at the SC firms, where upgrading was less extensive and products were less complex. With the new machines and more automated production processes, rank-and-file workers at LC firms are increasingly responsible for watching computer screens, spotting statistical deviations, and recording data from statistical process technologies. In addition, workers in some firms have the authority to stop the entire production line. Several of these companies are moving towards ISO 9000 certification, and this too affects what workers are responsible for doing. ISO certification assures potential customers that the certified company has the capability to deliver state-of-the-art products. To earn certification, a firm's workers have to master a common set of procedures and operations and pass written tests. In addition, workers must speak with auditors visiting the plant. Therefore, the ability to communicate effectively with auditors is among the criteria that firms consider in hiring and retention decisions.

In our interviews, line managers mentioned that some workers could not meet the rising skill requirements. At one firm workers repeatedly failed some of the required statistical tests. One official told us that working with computers was not the biggest problem: "We've put in a system that makes it very easy for them. We try to keep the key punch to a minimum. [Instead,] it's math. To understand statistical process control; use of some equipment, like calipers, micrometers, precision weighing instrument scales; the ability to understand the principles—you can understand math, but that doesn't mean necessarily you'll understand when a process is out of control." At another firm non-English-speakers had difficulty learning to speak English well enough to operate in the new production environment. These small firms had few training resources and few job categories in which to accommodate workers who could not adapt to the higher skill requirements.

Officials at all of the LC firms talked about the complementarity of machines and workers in achieving very low error rates and the need to maintain an uncompromising culture in support of high quality. For example:

> The whole mind-set and mentality here is zero defects, on time, with everything that we do. So when we tell customers we want to ship to zero defect, we can't tell an operator or an inspector, "We can work to a certain quality level on this part and not the others." You need to have a certain philosophy that you're working to. We tell a customer we're willing to ship zero defects and offer them productivity improvements throughout the course of a contract.

Most of the LC firms require zero defects, or close approximations to it, in at least some of their products. Examples of products that require zero defects include compact discs, contact lenses, and various medical supplies.

One firm closed down, moved, and reopened, replacing its entire workforce in the process. In 1985 this firm was a declining, unionized company that had too many employees and produced poor-quality products for the electric power industry. By 1995 it had reopened about twenty miles from its old site with new workers and been transformed into what officials described as a team-oriented, efficient, and quality-oriented work environment. Managers say that the only alternative would have been to go out of business permanently. They told us they needed two things: workers with better reading and math skills, and more labor-management flexibility than they were able to achieve with the union at the original location. The reconstituted firm has a higher-skilled, lower-paid workforce, and no union.

For all of the LC firms, the adoption of automated computer-controlled machines eliminated the standard operator's job. In addition, more complex product designs and zero-defect requirements increased the need for sophisticated monitoring of quality, using statistical process controls. This affected the demand for basic skills among rank-and-file workers. Compared to Inova, with its training facilities, the medium-sized and smaller companies found it more difficult to retrain and retain existing workers who were lacking basic skills, though all the firms report that they tried.

INOVA'S CULTURE AND BUSINESS STRATEGY

Inova is the prototype for LC firms. Four eras in Inova's history have set the stage for its current status as a leading firm in the industry and the leading plastics firm in the region. During each era, we see the interaction of business culture, technical change, product development, and human resource policy decisions.

Inova's parent company was started in a garage during the late 1940s and produced nylon, using an injection molding process. During this first period from the late 1940s through the beginning of the 1960s, the company was profitable but quite similar to many other firms. The second period began in 1962, when a Cornell-educated plastics engineer from the Dupont Chemical Company joined as the general manager and began to change the firm's business culture to emphasize product innovation and sales growth. By 1969 he had become the majority owner and president of the company. Sales had grown from less than $1 million in 1962 to $4 million by 1969 and remained stable around that level through the early 1970s.

The beginning of the third period in Inova's history, during the early 1970s, was marked by two events. One was the president's explicit decision to build competitive advantage aggressively, based on the firm's engineering capacity to innovate. The professional engineering staff, which had already patented several distinctive technical processes, was strengthened even further. Even by the early 1970s the firm's product development capability had given Inova the ability to customize products in ways that competitors could not. For example, Inova became the exclusive maker of the nylon strings that apparel retailers use to attach price tags to clothing.

The second event was the first round of the 1970s oil price shocks in 1973. Processed oil is the primary ingredient in plastic, so high oil prices squeezed profits for the entire industry. Many firms, especially those headed by first-generation plastics-company owners who were near retirement, either failed or were sold to other companies. As the decade ended and the 1980s began, oil prices moderated and the industry consolidated. Like many other firms, Inova survived in the 1970s partly by purchasing other firms and taking over their customers. It was thus able to grow stronger by serving well-established customer demands during the late 1970s and early 1980s, when the fourth era in company history was beginning.

The fourth period was in full bloom by the late 1980s. By that time Inova was reducing its roster of customers to a smaller number of large firms, many from the Fortune 500. It began partnering with these larger, wealthier customers in a strategy that added globalization to its focus on technological innovation. This emphasis on innovation and partnerships with large customers in a globalization strategy remains the firm's core strategy.

Through each distinct period since 1962, Inova's culture and human resource policies have been skillfully aggressive, innovative, forward-looking, and independent. Inova hired local Puerto Ricans in the 1960s when no one else in the region did. Initially, the Puerto Ricans they hired were mostly army veterans from nearby Fort Devens. Then, building on its connections to the small Puerto Rican community in Massachusetts, Inova survived the 1970s by placing much of its new production capacity in Puerto Rico.[11] Later, based on its history with Puerto Rican workers and the success of the Puerto Rican operation, Inova aggressively helped Puerto Ricans migrate to the mainland to work in its Clinton, Massachusetts, plant.[12]

As part of Inova's firm history, the involvement with Puerto Rico and Puerto Rican workers was formative in two ways. First, the firm adapted to accommodate Spanish-speaking workers. By 1995 roughly one-third of the firm's global workforce spoke Spanish. Second, its success operating in Puerto Rico gave the firm confidence that it could expand both production and marketing away from the U.S. mainland, and the stage was thus set for the aggressively global strategy that was to come.

Even before it shifted toward globalization in the late 1980s, Inova had begun moving away from its status as a medium-sized, plastic-molding job shop. The shift started in the 1970s, when Inova pushed to become a technologically sophisticated and innovative plastics company. The firm received seed money from the Commonwealth of Massachusetts for a training institute, which it named the Inova Institute, to upgrade its labor force. It also received a subsidy from the federal Economic Development Administration (EDA) to upgrade its plant and equipment. The EDA grant helped finance a clean-room production facility that would later enable Inova to develop and produce sterile plastic products and deepen its ties to the pharmaceutical industry. The business relationships that had solidified initially in Puerto Rico in the early 1970s also played a part.

Eventually, Inova's clean rooms would produce soft disposable contact lenses, plastic shunts to keep blood vessels open, compact discs for the recording industry, and many other high-end plastic products. When the firm's first clean room was built, however, there were few uses for it. It was a speculative investment, characteristic of the firm's aggressive approach to business. As one adviser told executives: "This is beautiful, but you're ten years ahead of your time and . . . you're not going to get the markup for the cost of the room." In the short run, that adviser's skepticism was appropriate. In the longer run, however, the clean room made Inova an attractive partner for other firms.

Inova's competitive strategy focused increasingly on developing new products in strategic alliances with larger firms. Specifically, Inova's modus operandi was to identify the unmet needs of Fortune 500 customers and then to combine its own capacity with that of partner firms—including but not limited to the customer—to meet those needs creatively. For example, as early as 1980 Inova formed a partnership with a European firm that had the capacity to build customized, state-of-the-art, computer-controlled injection molding machines. At the same time Inova's own engineering capabilities were growing because the firm was hiring and developing more engineering talent.

The combined talents of Inova and its partners made for a formidable combination. Large business customers could present unsolved production engineering challenges, and Inova, working with partners, could solve them, *often with no money at risk*, because the customer would pay. An executive recalled: "We were in a situation where we had no money. So we would get somebody like [a Fortune 500 firm] to be a fifty-fifty joint venture partner." For instance, when one firm wanted to develop a high-quality audiotape, this executive explained, "they didn't have the technical know-how but they had the money. So we [and our technology partner] would provide the technical know-how. I don't know how many of those we've had," he told the interviewer, but he was certain that Inova had made a lot of such arrangements.[13] This capability to serve large customers with well-defined problems and the ability to pay for solution-building enabled Inova to expand its own capabilities and competitive advantages at a faster rate than would otherwise have been possible.

One consequence of these product development successes was Inova's growing effectiveness at attracting new customers and expanding existing accounts. Increasingly, Inova successfully induced large firms to outsource their injection molding business to Inova instead of producing in-house. It persuaded these firms that it could serve their product development and production needs better than they could themselves. During this period growth in sales to Fortune 500 companies allowed Inova to reduce the number of firms in its customer base:

> We used to have eight hundred customers, and now we have about a hundred, of whom fifty are our serious customers at more than a million dollars. The other fifty we're working with because we're looking to get them up to a million dollars. We don't have any customers that we know are never going to be a million dollars. . . . You do $150,000 for a product. By the time you've got the mold done, set it up, took it up, did the whole thing, learned their culture, you've got $150,000 long gone. Our customers are our partners. We share information, we trust them, they trust us. Without that, we're not the same company. You can't have a $150,000 partnership. But you can have a five-million-dollar partnership.

Its distinct managerial and engineering capabilities enabled Inova and its partners to design and produce complex plastic products with very low error rates that few other companies could match. Executives firmly believe that the company competes on quality and customization, not price. Because of its unique capabilities and trusting relationships, Inova's partnerships with Fortune 500 customers have expanded around the globe. By 1995 Inova was operating on the cutting edge of the plastics industry with regard to technological innovation and global business strategy.

RANK-AND-FILE JOBS AT INOVA

The standard machine operator job at Inova had almost disappeared by 1995 because the company had shifted in large measure to computer-controlled machines and a different division of labor. The workers who controlled the new machines were technicians, most with two-year degrees from colleges or technical training institutions (including the Inova Institute). Some were operators who had been retrained. However, most employees who were operators prior to the changeover had either left the firm or become inspector-packers. An official told us that when he joined the firm, about 15 percent of rank-and-file jobs were inspector-packers and the rest were operators. By 1995 the change and resulting shift in the operator's job had caused about 85 percent of the rank-and-file jobs to become inspector-packer jobs.

Being a successful operator had required only a series of manual functions that a person could learn quickly from coworkers. With the advent of statistical process controls, rank-and-file inspector-packers at Inova became responsible for recording and reporting data, filling out production logs, and monitoring the performance of machines. The transition to inspector-packer was difficult for some former operators because they lacked the skills (including language skills among immigrants) necessary for performing these tasks. Inova has endeavored to accommodate former operators by keeping the inspector-packer job relatively simple and helping to upgrade workers' skills. For example, engineers set up computer macros to reduce the number of keystrokes necessary for data entry.

Still, by 1995 the firm was getting to the point where only a small number of jobs were left for those who could not speak English and do basic math. In a few cases, officials have tailored jobs for specific people because of the firm's commitment to them. For example, some have been assigned to the few machines that still require active (manual) operators. The capacity to accommodate workers in this way is surely more limited at smaller firms. When possible, workers have been retrained at the Inova Institute. Some workers from the region's smaller firms also enroll at the institute, paying a fee. Courses include English as a second language (ESL) as well as general equivalency diploma (GED) and other courses that prepare workers to become skilled plastic technicians. Inova requires all of its workers to undergo some training at the institute each year.

Inova tries to retain existing workers and makes various accommodations to them in the process, but it makes little such effort for new applicants. For the most part, Inova in 1995 was not hiring workers who had weak skills in English or no apparent capacity for mathematical reasoning. Instead, it was hiring people with adequate English and math skills who managers expected could learn specific job skills and be promoted.

Beyond operators and inspector-packers, the maintenance mechanics who take care of the machines are the rank-and-file workers whose jobs have changed the most. Through job enrichment, maintenance mechanics have become the setup, maintenance, and process technicians, all rolled into one. In addition, people who show the ability to do more than their assigned jobs now encounter more informal flexibility and permeable job boundaries. For example, if an inspector-packer shows some mechanical aptitude, a supervisor might ask him or her to diagnose the problem with a machine or to help the maintenance or setup person. Workers who lack the basic math skills to understand measurements do not qualify for such opportunities. Inova's personnel office tries to hire people who have such skills. If they perform well in entry-level jobs, the firm aims to retain and promote them. Indeed, retaining and promoting talented people has become a core feature of the firm's competitive strategy.

Finally, it is interesting to note that Inova did in fact employ some very low-skilled workers in 1995. They were assembly workers who "just take the two things that were molded and stick them together and put them in a box." The products they assembled were not so heavy that they needed to be close to final markets because of shipping costs. Also, these products tended not to face the just-in-time delivery pressures that have kept low-skilled jobs in some other firms on the U.S. mainland. Consequently, Inova's low-skilled assembly workers are mostly in Mexico, Puerto Rico, Singapore, and other very low-wage nations.[14]

The differences in culture, technology, products, and job tasks between LC (such as Inova) and SC (such as Homepro) firms are key explanations for the disparities in compensation and other human resource policies that the next section describes.

HUMAN RESOURCE POLICIES

The plastics firms provided information concerning a number of human resource policies. Judging by how they rank on five policy dimensions, and ignoring any differences in job responsibilities, ta-

Table 6.2 Human Resources Policies in the Twelve Firms, 1995

Firm	Plant's Rank-and-File Workforce	Average Hourly Wage Rate	Benefits as a Percentage of Total Compensation	Total Compensation	Training Basic	Training Specific	Firm Paternalism[a]	Percentage of Temps at Any One Time	Hesitance to Lay Off Workers[b]
LC Firms									
Inova	850	$9.00	33	$13.43	Yes	Yes	4	10	3
LC2	135	8.00	30	11.42	Yes	No	3	0	3
LC3	200	8.00	35	12.30	Yes	Yes	4	15	4
LC4	37	10.00	32	14.70	No	No	4	0	3
LC5	150	13.65	30	19.50	No	No	3	2	3
LC6	23	10.00	25	13.33	No	No	1	0	3
SC Firms									
Homepro	300	$8.00	25	$10.66	0	1	2	50	4
SC2	320	7.50	40	12.50	1	0	4	40	3
SC3	34	7.00	20	8.75	0	0	2	5	4
SC4	35	8.00	20	10.00	0	0	2	15	2
SC5	70	7.00	15	8.23	0	0	4	1	3
SC6	190	7.00	25	9.33	0	0	4	40	2
Means and Differences									
LC mean		9.78	30	14.11	0.50	0.33	3.17	4.5	3.17
SC		7.42	24	9.91	0.17	0.17	3.00	25.2	3.00
Difference in means		2.36**	6*	4.20***	0.33	0.17	0.17	-20.7**	0.17

Source: Authors' compilation.

[a] Paternalism pertains to the appropriateness of attending to the private well-being of employees and their families. It ranges from a high of 4 to a low of 1.

[b] Layoff policy: 1 = lays off immediately when demand falls more than 10 percent; 2 = lays off after a brief delay; 3 = lays off after moderate delay; 4 = lays off after substantial delay.

* .05 < p < .10.

** .01 < p < .05.

*** p < .01.

ble 6.2 shows that LC firms seem to have more generous human resource policies. Compared to SC firms, they pay rank-and-file workers more and make less use of temporary workers. Further, even though there are only twelve firms in our sample, statistical t-tests show that these LC-SC differences in average compensation and use of temporary workers are statistically significant.[15] More LC than SC firms provide formal training, but this policy seems related primarily to firm size, not necessarily to the LC-SC distinction. Finally, LC firms hold a small but statistically insignificant edge over SC firms with regard to paternalism and layoff policies.[16] The LC-SC similarity in layoff policies is possible because the use of temporary workers stabilizes the core workforce in SC firms and helps them to avoid the need for layoffs.

WAGES AND BENEFITS

On average, total compensation for rank-and-file workers at SC firms is almost $3.00 an hour lower than at LC firms. Homepro, for example, ranks third highest in the SC group with total compensation in 1995 of $10.66 an hour, while Inova ranks third among LC firms, with an average of $13.43. The reason for the LC-SC earnings gap seems to be primarily that more LC workers use reading and math skills on the job and are responsible for maintaining written logs. Responsibility for maintaining production logs is an especially accurate predictor of compensation. The percentage of rank-and-file workers responsible for maintaining production logs accounts for virtually all of the LC-SC compensation gap in simple ordinary least squares (OLS) regression.[17] In addition, our interviews provided evidence that these wage and benefit differences are far from arbitrary. Instead, they represent strategic, firm-level decisions calculated to attract and retain workers with the skills, attitudes, and work habits that firms deem necessary for their business success.

For example, one firm noticed that many of the best workers hired were resigning within a week or two and taking better, higher-paying jobs at other firms. This caused the firm to raise the entry-level wage rate and adopt a more elaborate set of policies concerning reviews, raises, and benefits. These policies are reviewed regularly. Further, starting wages are higher for workers who have more experience with the types of equipment that the firm uses.

More LC than SC firms use pay raises as incentives. At every firm we interviewed, workers with greater seniority tended to earn more. However, pay raises at all six LC firms were performance-based, while this was true at only three SC firms. Even at Inova, executives recalled a few years when there were step increases for the hourly workers instead of performance-based raises. It was very unpopular with the managers, who regard the current performance-based system as much more effective.

Officials at Inova say that the wage rates they pay are the going market rates for the local labor market. However, the firm also pays attention to internal equity: "There are two separate scales [blue-collar and managerial]. If we're going to increase a wage scale we look at all of them. You can look at a salary survey, and they have their projections and their percentages and it's different [for blue-collar and managerial]. We don't. We tend to use the same percentages. If I'm going to increase the wage scale, I would be doing the same for both. Or actually all three, the third of which is the salaried office workers."

Inova also has profit-sharing, which averaged, during the period that we studied, about 3 percent of each worker's annual earnings. Officials believe that performance-based raises and universal profit-sharing create good incentives for productivity and also help minimize worker interest in union organizing. One maintained that profit-sharing is

> the biggest deterrent towards unionization. . . . [Profitability] is based on three factors: direct labor, material and supplies, and services, which those people can affect. And their profit-sharing is directly affected by how well they control those. So if some guy comes in hung over the next morning and can't do his job, they [the workers] take care of that. We [managers] don't have to worry about that. If there's a lot of waste, that's affecting the money in their pocket. So it's not only been a union deterrent, it's been a great motivator. It also enables us to get to the employees once every quarter. Every quarter there's a business meeting about firm profitability. So that's another factor.

The last attempt to organize a union at the firm was in the late 1970s.

Inova had little incentive to raise wages at the time when we interviewed them. Managers believed that Inova's growing reputation as a good employer helped to account for the improvement in the quality of applicants. As one said, "I think . . . there's a beginning of understanding that if you're going to work at Inova you've got to have those skills. So [underqualified workers] are not applying now because they can't fill out the application by themselves." He also reported that the firm is more diligent than before in checking references and doing some other things that have refined the selection process.[18]

TRAINING

Three of the six LC firms, including Inova, but only one SC firm provide formal basic skills training. Two LC firms and one SC firm provide job-specific training. Although one might have the expectation, based simply on rank-and-file job functions, that more LC firms would provide formal training, in fact half the LC firms provide none at all. Instead, these LC firms seek workers who already possess basic skills and are prepared to apply those skills in learning and performing new job-specific skills. Generally, it appears in this sample of twelve firms that whether a firm provides in-house formal training is mainly a function of firm size, not its LC or SC status.

Part of what makes Inova an attractive place to work is the Inova Institute, where workers get both basic and job-specific skills training. The institute enables Inova to hire and retain some workers whom other firms would not. For example, the owner of one much smaller firm in the past had always employed recent immigrants, many of whom lacked basic math and English-language skills. Now, she said, changes in technology make it more difficult: "When it comes to automation, I find they don't have those skills. They are wonderful people for rank-and-file jobs, but I don't find that they are that skillful, at least the [ones] around here. But they are interested, and they want you to teach them, and we don't have the time. We have the time to bring them along, but we don't want to teach them [English and basic math]." In contrast, the Inova Institute offers, in addition to ESL classes, GED and adult basic education (primarily math and English skills), so Inova has been able to compensate for skill deficits to a greater extent than many other firms.

However, this is true mainly for existing Inova workers. With new applicants, the Inova Institute increasingly emphasizes job-specific skills. As of 1995, Inova was seeking new hires who could be trained in job-specific skills without having to be taught the basic fundamentals of English and math. The firm wanted workers who were willing and able to learn what the Inova Institute could teach them beyond the basics of English and math and who had the potential to be promoted.

TEMPORARY WORKERS

The importance of reading and math skills is one reason Inova and other firms in the LC category hire very few workers from temporary help firms. Only two of the six LC firms said that temporary workers were an effective way to try out new employees. The president of one of these firms told us that he hires temporary workers when he gets recommendations from supervisors and other people such as, "This guy's golden," "This guy's good," or, "This woman is excellent." He acknowledged, however, that there were no temporary workers in the plant at the time we visited, and indeed, temporary workers were not an important source of new hires. Only one LC firm had a standard temp-to-perm hiring strategy—searching through temporary workers for potential permanent employees. A senior manager described the process. "We have a flux of about two to three temps some days, some days no temps. And you can use that as a screening process. . . . Some jobs are more difficult, some jobs are easier. It's not like a wholesale approach where we take in three, let two go. It's when we find a good temp that looks like they have the ability to learn, then we try to bring them on as a permanent and train them."

At the same time, there may be risks. The company's chairman of the board said:

> I think in the long run it costs more because you don't have the loyalty, the permanency. The permanency creates knowledge. It only takes one temp to make one big mistake for us, on a big safety item, and we could be sued into oblivion. . . . One could fool themselves and say, "The gap is growing and this and that, and here are the reasons. We've got to do it cheaper and cheaper. We must compete." . . . But one major event will put you under.

Officials at the four other LC firms said things like, "That's not our style," or, "We tried it and it didn't work out." About 10 percent of the workers at the Inova plant at any given time are likely to be temporary workers. We were told, "We do hire some of our temporaries, but it's not temp-to-perm. The companies that are having a hard time recruiting do a lot of that."

In contrast to the LC companies, temp-to-perm is a standard practice among SC firms. While the mean percentage of temporary workers on-site at any given time is 25.2 percent among SC firms, it is only 4.5 percent among LC firms (see table 6.2). Five of the six SC firms agreed that temporary placement firms are a good way to find and audition new employees. One might expect SC firms to use more temporary workers because cost-control pressures are high and temps are cheaper than regular employees, but only one firm acknowledged that low wage rates were an important motivation to use temps. Others said mostly that temporary workers are an effective way to manage fluctuations in production and to try out new employees.[19] Roughly half the workers at Homepro at any given time are employed by temporary help firms. According to the personnel manager, "We hire on a Homepro payroll what we feel is the absolute lowest amount of people we would have. We fill in beyond that with temporaries. We haven't had a layoff here in eight years because of that."

Because temporary workers in blue-collar jobs tend to have low basic skill levels, they are better matched to the machine operator and unskilled packer jobs that SC firms still have available. A manager at one SC company described his rank-and-file workers as having "no control over productivity." Instead, he pointed to the importance of machines. Speaking of productivity, he said, "The machine sets it. . . . The machine is the most important person I have. Absolutely." Reflecting his low regard for workers, he said that the machines "are the only ones that make any money for us. Workers all spend money. Right?" He explained how the firm's use of temporary workers started. The economy was strong in the 1980s, and few local workers were available. Temporary agencies provided a transportation network that brought in people from several distant communities. The practice of hiring temporary workers continued not only because the cost per labor-hour may have been lower, but also because the firm had learned it was a cost-effective way to manage fluctuations and screen new workers.

CONCLUSION

This chapter has explained how business cultures and shifts in technology changed job requirements for rank-and-file workers in the plastics industry and led to growing disparity in wages and working conditions. Among the six firms that we call the leading complexity group, business cultures are aggressively entrepreneurial and competitive strategies aspire to cutting-edge levels of technological sophistication. Products tend to be complex and tailored to the needs of particular customers. Many such products have no close substitutes and must meet zero-defect requirements. Between the mid-1980s and 1995, when we conducted our interviews, traditional machine operator jobs in LC firms were displaced in large numbers owing to the adoption of computer-controlled machines that required more technical skill to operate.

Only a small percentage of the operators at LC firms were able to qualify or be trained as technicians on computer-controlled machines. Instead, they left or took other positions in the same firms, usually as inspector-packers. Unfortunately for many, even the inspector-packer jobs in LC firms required that workers understand and utilize statistical process controls, maintain production logs, and communicate both orally and in writing with coworkers and supervisors. By 1995 workers who performed these functions successfully earned higher wages, received more fringe benefits, got more training, and experienced more stable employment compared to others. Their productivity supported their higher compensation levels. Conversely, workers who lacked the requisite skills or work ethic qualified only for less attractive jobs in the plastics industry, mostly in SC firms. Many worked as temporary employees with low compensation and no job security in SC firms that produced standard types of products and were under heavy pressure to keep costs low, including labor costs.

The plastic manufacturers we studied are not large firms with sustainable monopoly profits. Unions are rare, and compensation appears to be determined competitively among firms hiring from the same local market. In this market, employers pay more for workers who have better skills. Compensation for unskilled workers in the plastics industry will be difficult to raise without the skill upgrading that some workers, especially workers at Inova, have been able to acquire. It seems very unlikely, however, that training capacity will grow substantially in the types of firms we studied, since most are relatively small. Also, at least in the near future, there may be limited demand among SC firms for rank-and-file workers with the types of skills for which LC firms pay a premium.

Aside from improving public primary and secondary schools so that children will reach adulthood with better skills, public investments in training institutions to serve adult workers are likely to be the most effective mechanisms for upgrading skills among non-college-educated adults. Recall that even the Inova Institute originated with a public-sector grant meant to foster local economic development. Inova's success and its impact on the rest of the region—the workers it trained are now employed throughout the plastics industry—suggest that the grant achieved its intended effect. There are certainly other examples of investments in community colleges and other educational institutions for adults that have helped to fill gaps in the availability of education and training services. This study reinforces the idea that these are worthwhile public investments.

NOTES

1. See particularly literature on computer- and skill-biased technical change: Acemoglu (1998), Autor, Katz, and Krueger (1998), Autor, Levy, and Murnane (2002), Bresnahan, Brynjolfsson, and Hitt (2002), Dunne et al. (1999), Goldin and Katz (1998), and Howell and Wolff (1991).
2. See literature on technology and organization change: Adler (1992), Cappelli (1997), Fernandez (1999), Osterman (1994, 1999), and Snower (1998).
3. Firm names have been changed.
4. Further, in response to a forced-choice question, Inova managers said that attending to workers' personal and family welfare is "very appropriate" in the company's philosophy, while officials at Homepro agreed that it is only "a little appropriate" to do so.
5. In particular, we do not know the degree to which a more literate or math-savvy workforce might induce SC firms to use more skill-intensive production techniques.
6. Note that even though the sample is small, t-tests for differences in means show statistically significant differences in four of the five job functions.
7. People we interviewed suggested that once firms were purchased by companies from outside the plastics industry, they lost their focus

and the competitive edge needed to survive the industry's intense competition.

8. Having plants in multiple regions is important. By 1960 Homepro had a manufacturing location in Canada. It built plants in California in 1973 and in Alabama in 1979 and later moved a plant from California to Arizona in the mid-1980s. An official noted, "We've grown up in the industry in recent years with multiple plants to be able to serve our various markets. The products that we make are low in value and high in bulk, so we can't ship them very far."

9. One example we were given was a major order for back-to-school supplies. A Homepro official told us about an order for school supplies that was still unsettled in late June; in the past it would have been finalized by January or February.

10. See studies on longer-term job and occupational change: Hounshell (1985) and Penn, Rose, and Rubery (1994).

11. A major benefit of expanding into Puerto Rico was the island's tax-free production environment, which was part of the Operation Bootstrap development strategy. At that time Puerto Rico was becoming a haven for the American pharmaceutical industry. Johnson and Johnson, a major pharmaceutical firm with production facilities in Puerto Rico, quickly became one of Inova's primary customers. The combination of a tax-free environment and low wages helped Inova to survive the pressure on gross profit margins caused by the oil price increases.

12. As one executive recalled: "We actually sent people down and recruited people in Puerto Rico to come up here. We'd put them up at a hotel. They stayed here for three to six months. Then they'd go back, and we'd get somebody else to replace them. Some of them got up here and stayed. That was the way they got up here. Some just wanted to come up and work for a few months. We actually were recruiting down there."

13. The firm's annual report for 1995, for instance, features its technology partnerships.

14. It is interesting to note that while the products that SC firms produce do require packing, most emerge from a machine as a single piece and require no hand assembly.

15. Note that difference-of-means tests for statistical significance using the t-test are valid for very small samples, since the t-test includes an adjustment for degrees of freedom. Because the degrees of freedom are limited in the present example, only large differences will be found to be statistically distinguishable from zero.

16. Regarding paternalism, we asked, "What is the company's philosophy about how appropriate it is to try to help increase the well-being

of employees with respect to their personal and family situations?" Forced-choice answers ranged from 1 to 5 on a scale from "not appropriate" to "extremely appropriate."

17.   Simple OLS regressions predicting total compensation only as a function of a constant term and responsibility for keeping production logs has an R-squared value of 0.63. Adding a dummy variable for LC-SC to the equation adds absolutely no explanatory power at all. Conversely, the R-squared value when only the dummy variable for LC-SC and a constant term are included is 0.50.

18.   Managers also speculated that increases in the average quality of applicants might be due to recent layoffs in other high-technology sectors.

19.   For comments on trends toward temporary workers, see Cappelli (1997) and Osterman (1999).

REFERENCES

Acemoglu, Daron. 1998. "Why Do New Technologies Complement Skills?: Directed Technical Change and Wage Inequality." *Quarterly Journal of Economics* 113(4): 1055–89.

Adler, Paul S., ed. 1992. *Technology and the Future of Work.* New York: Oxford University Press.

Autor, David H., Lawrence F. Katz, and Alan B. Krueger. 1998. "Computing Inequality: Have Computers Changed the Labor Market?" *Quarterly Journal of Economics* 113(4): 1169–1214.

Autor, David H., Frank Levy, and Richard J. Murnane. 2002. "Computer-Based Technological Change and Skill Demands: Reconciling the Perspectives of Economists and Sociologists." Unpublished paper. Massachusetts Institute of Technology, Cambridge, Mass.

Bradbury, Katherine L. 2002. "Education and Wages in the 1980s and 1990s: Are All Groups Moving up Together?" *New England Economic Review* (1st quarter): 19–47.

Bresnahan, Timothy F., Erik Brynjolfsson, and Lorin M. Hitt. 2002. "Information Technology, Workplace Organization, and the Demand for Skilled Labor: Firm-Level Evidence." *Quarterly Journal of Economics* 109(May): 339.

Cappelli, Peter, ed. 1997. *Change at Work.* New York: Oxford University Press.

———. 1999. *Employment Practices and Business Strategy.* New York. Oxford University Press.

Dunne, Timothy, Lucia Foster, John Haltiwanger, and Kenneth Troske. 1999. "Wage and Productivity Dispersion in U.S. Manufacturing: The

Role of Computer Investment." Unpublished paper. Center for Economic Studies, U.S. Bureau of the Census, Washington.

Federal Reserve Bank of Boston. 1996. "Earnings Inequality: Spatial and Labor Market Contributions to Earnings Inequality." *New England Economic Review* (May–June, special issue).

Federal Reserve Bank of New York. 1995. "Economic Policy Review: Colloquium on U.S. Wage Trends in the 1980s." *Economic Policy Review* 1(1).

Fernandez, Roberto. 1999. "Skill-Biased Technological Change and Wage Inequality: Evidence from a Plant Retooling." Unpublished paper. Stanford University Graduate Business School, Palo Alto, Calif.

Goldin, Claudia, and Lawrence F. Katz. 1998. "The Origins of Technology-Skill Complementarity." *Quarterly Journal of Economics* 113(3): 693–732.

Hounshell, David A. 1985. *From the American System to Mass Production, 1800–1932: The Development of Manufacturing Technology in the United States.* Baltimore: Johns Hopkins University Press.

Howell, David R., Edward N. Wolff. 1991. "Trends in the Growth and Distribution of Skills in the U.S. Workplace." *Industrial and Labor Relations Review* 44(3): 486–502.

Levy, Frank, Anne Beamish, and Richard J. Murnane. 1999. "Computerization and Skills: Examples from a Car Dealership." Unpublished paper. Massachusetts Institute of Technology, Department of Urban Studies, Cambridge, Mass.

Levy, Frank, and Richard J. Murnane. 1992. "U.S. Earnings Levels and Earnings Inequality: A Review of Recent Trends and Proposed Explanations." *Journal of Economic Literature* 30(3): 1333–81.

McFate, Katherine, Roger Lawson, and William Julius Wilson, eds. 1995. *Poverty, Inequality, and the Future of Social Policy.* New York: Russell Sage Foundation.

Mishel, Lawrence, Jared Bernstein, and John Schmidt. 1998. *The State of Working America, 1996–1997.* Washington, D.C.: Economic Policy Institute.

Murphy, Kevin M., and Finis Welch. 1993. "Inequality and Relative Wages." *American Economic Review* 83(2): 104–9.

Osterman, Paul. 1994. "How Common Is Workplace Transformation in Who Adopts It?" *Industrial and Labor Relations Review* 47(2): 177–88.

———. 1999. *Securing Prosperity.* Princeton, N.J.: Princeton University Press.

Penn, Rojer, Michael Rose, and Jill Rubery. 1994. *Skill and Occupational Change.* New York: Oxford University Press.

Snower, Dennis J. 1998. "Causes of Changing Earnings Inequality." In *Income Inequality: Issues and Policy Options.* Symposium sponsored by the Federal Reserve Bank of Kansas City.

PART III

Career Ladders:
The Past or the Future?

CHAPTER 7

Too Many Cooks? Tracking Internal Labor Market Dynamics in Food Service with Case Studies and Quantitative Data

Julia Lane, Philip Moss,
Harold Salzman, and Chris Tilly

Core firms in the U.S. economy have traditionally had strong internal labor markets that provided opportunities for skill development and advancement. Through training or prospects for long-term employment that allowed for on-the-job training and returns to investment in education, workers starting out with low skill levels had opportunities to be hired for "good" jobs. Firms were able to provide these opportunities in part because vertical integration and the expansion of various support functions brought together a large and varied set of jobs under a single roof. It is widely perceived that these arrangements have largely been scrapped over the last twenty years (see, for example, *New York Times* 1996). However, there is a marked difference between the sweeping changes depicted by recent case studies and the small to negligible shifts reflected in large-scale quantitative data.

Case study research, ably reviewed by Peter Cappelli and his colleagues (1997), identifies two types of change, both dramatic: change in the organizational structure of firms and change in the structure of employment for workers. These are distinct but related shifts. Firms outsource, become "boundaryless," become embedded in networks, and change in other ways that lead to an altered employment structure. At the same time, businesses are weakening their employment relationships with workers to the point of dissolving internal labor markets (ILMs). Cappelli and his colleagues (1997, 4) conclude that with the breakdown of "traditional methods of managing employees and developing skilled workers inside companies . . . pressures from product and labor markets are brought

inside the organization . . . [establishing] market-mediated employment relationships." A key element of both changes is the replacement of vertical integration with outsourcing of all activities save a
few "core competencies" (Powell 2001).

Despite such case study evidence suggesting the devolution of
ILMs, most aggregate indicators of the vigor of ILMs have changed
relatively little (Bernhardt and Marcotte 2000). Declines in average
employee tenure are small (Neumark 2000), although some groups,
such as less-educated young men, have experienced more substantial drops (Bernhardt et al. 2001). The differential in tenure between large and small firms, which one would expect to narrow
over time if ILMs have significantly declined, shows no change between the 1980s and 1990s (Allen, Clark, and Schieber 1998). Estimates of the firm-specific components of wages, one way of assess-
ing the extent to which ILMs shelter wages, also show essentially
no change over the last couple of decades (Groshen and Levine
1998).

One interpretation of this apparent contradiction between case
study and aggregate data is compositional: the case studies represent changes that characterize only a small and perhaps atypical
subset of firms. In particular, it may be that processes that dismantle job ladders in one set of businesses create new job ladders elsewhere. And in a world in which firms intermittently tear down and
rebuild ILMs, such disparate findings would average out to little
change in the aggregate.

In this chapter, we take a close look at the evolution of ILMs
amid shifting business boundaries, using both new case studies and
a new quantitative data set that combines firm-level and worker-
level data. We focus on the food service sector, whose burger flipper
has become a symbol in public discourse for a rapidly expanding
category of low-end jobs.[1]

The case study research zeroes in on supply chain shifts, such as
outsourcing. Although the labor impacts of outsourcing have been
studied closely in a few industries—above all auto manufacturing
(Womack 1991)—it is important to broaden this base of knowledge. In contrast with much recent case study analysis of restructuring, we attempt to follow the trajectory of restructuring over a
relatively long time span, using retrospective questions to learn
about changes from the early 1980s to the present. We also compare the different organizational structures within which particular
functions took place before and after the restructuring. Thus, we

compare outsourcing firms and their suppliers. In effect, the comparison poses a counterfactual: *What if* the activities had not been outsourced? The quantitative analysis complements the case study findings by searching for generalizations on a large sample of workers and firms—indeed, nearly the universe of workers and firms for the state of Maryland during the years 1985 to 1996 in the industry under study. We analyze an unusual microdata set that links detailed longitudinal information on business establishments and workers, drawing on data from the unemployment insurance system. With these data, we are able to explore firm characteristics, such as turnover and earnings distribution, in terms of cross-sectional variation, samplewide trends (including entry and exit of firms), and firm-level trajectories. We can also examine individual worker mobility within the firm and aggregate up to firm-level or industry-level results.

Our case study and quantitative analyses highlight different aspects of change in food service: the case studies emphasize the results of employment shifts across food subsectors, whereas the microdata analysis spotlights trends over time within one key subsector. The case studies reveal that shifting functions to suppliers—in particular, food manufacturers—may actually embed them in a *stronger* internal labor market rather than a weaker one. The quantitative analysis focuses on food manufacturing, the endpoint of employment shifts. The evidence here is consistent with earlier findings in which we suggested that corporate restructuring is iterative, and that successive iterations may have diametrically opposed implications for internal labor markets (Moss, Salzman, and Tilly 2000). In line with this claim, our quantitative analysis shows both strong persistence in firm-level characteristics such as median earnings or turnover (consistent with the absence of bold shifts or the prevalence of successive adjustments that cancel each other out) and wide-ranging idiosyncrasy (indicating great variation in business-level strategies or the fact that businesses are at different stages of adjustment at any point in time). Quantitative findings also show *decreased* turnover for low-wage workers in food manufacturing between the 1980s and 1990s, along with slightly higher turnover for the highest paid. Two generalizations about the impact of restructuring on the workforce seem to hold:

1. Businesses still find it necessary to integrate substantial portions of their workforce into the firm through established internal labor mar-

kets, and outsourcing in food service appears to have reinforced this pattern.

2. New forms of internal labor markets, however, have on the whole reduced opportunities for the least-educated workers to enter the firm and to advance within the firm. In effect, the line between primary and secondary labor markets has shifted within and between firms to the disadvantage of less-skilled workers.

The rest of the chapter proceeds straightforwardly with a discussion of data and methods, a presentation of findings (first field-based, then microdata-based), and brief conclusions.

DATA AND METHODS

As already noted, this research couples qualitative company case studies with quantitative analysis of large, publicly compiled microdata sets to study food preparation and service.

Case Study Data

We conducted case studies of a small number of companies. To examine supply chain shifts, we looked at organizational clusters consisting of final food servers along with their suppliers, including distributors and manufacturers. We gained varying degrees of access to companies, but our goal—successfully realized in the large majority of cases—was to speak to top managers, human resources officials, and frontline managers at each site we visited. We learned about the trajectory of change in internal labor markets primarily by asking retrospective questions. Data-gathering extended from 1999 to 2002.

For the purposes of this study, our sample of cases includes ten firms at several points along the "food chain." Final food servers include Masterfood and Great Meals, two national institutional food service companies, the Ourtown School System, and Bellavista, a moderately expensive, independent restaurant. (All of these names are pseudonyms.) At the food distribution level, we are studying Food King and Quality Express, both national distributors, and two regional ones, Joe's Produce, which specializes in fruits and vegetables, and Jones Wholesaling, a very small independent. Finally, our study includes two food producers, Salads Supreme and Maritime Seafood. Most of these firms are part of three supply chains: Masterfood buys from Food King, which buys from Maritime Seafood; Great Meals buys from both Food King and Quality Express; the Ourtown School System buys from Joe's Produce; Salads Supreme sells to Quality Express, Food King, and Joe's Produce and buys from Joe's Produce as well. Total employment in these firms is about 360,000.

QUANTITATIVE MICRODATA

An alternative way of examining changing workplace practices is to examine changes in pay and turnover outcomes for large numbers of businesses over time. The ideal data set to address these issues would combine industry and firm information, together with geographic location and longitudinal information on the earnings and tenure profile of the workforce. Such a data set has not hitherto existed. In particular, household-based, demographic surveys, such as the Current Population Survey (CPS), are not appropriate to address firm-level issues, both because no respondents can be identified as coming from the same firm and also because no firm-level information is provided (other than the survey response to industry and size of firm). Administrative records, such as unemployment insurance (UI) system wage records, while ideal to address worker turnover and wage profile issues, do not have data on workers' demographic characteristics. The Economic Census microdata on firms, which cover all sectors of the economy, do provide detailed geographic information together with data on different facets of firm production and sales patterns, but they do not provide information on individual workers, wage profiles, tenure, or turnover and are only available every five years. The Census Bureau Business Register, which is the master sampling frame for the U.S. Bureau of the Census, is available every year and provides total employment, payroll, sales, and detailed geographic information for all establishments. The ideal data set would combine all of these sources of information, and it is just such a data set that we use.

This data set, derived from the precursor to the Longitudinal Employer-Household Dynamics (LEHD) program, contains quarterly information on the earnings and employment affiliation of the universe of workers in almost the universe of businesses in food manufacturing in the state of Maryland between the third quarter of 1985 and the third quarter of 1996, combined with demographic information on their characteristics. These data are particularly suited to the task because they permit two types of analyses: one that is business-based (have jobs for low-end workers *within a given firm* become more transitory?) and one that is worker-based (do the jobs workers get and hold *at the same firm* offer diminished prospects of earnings growth?). The unique strength of these data is that, for the first time in the United States, we can both calculate workforce composition for all the firms in a given industry and capture the dynamics of change in this composition.

Because these data were developed as part of a new initiative at the Census Bureau—the LEHD program, which is integrating data for a number of large states, covering some 60 percent of U.S. employment—and their characteristics are consequently not yet well known, it is worth discussing them in more detail here. Unemployment insurance data are state-level data filed each quarter by every employer who employs workers covered by UI legislation. These data cover about 98 percent of employment in each state, and each record consists of an employer identification number, an individual identifier, and the earnings associated with each job. An associated state file (the ES202 file) includes information on the employer's industry and location. These data are then integrated with Census Bureau data, under strict confidentiality protocols, to provide demographic information (date of birth, place of birth, race, and sex) on each worker in the sample.[2]

The data have a number of important advantages. The full sample size is extremely generous: there are roughly 1.5 million employees every quarter and over 100,000 reporting units; even after limiting our attention to food manufacturing and imposing all restrictions, we have over 600,000 records. The data also are longitudinal in 3 dimensions: we can track employees over time, employers over time, and the employer-employee match (which we refer to here as the "job"). In addition, because we have the universe of workers, we can create measures of employer workforce composition as well as job and worker flows for different groups of workers.

Even with the Census Bureau enhancements, there are some drawbacks to these data. First, we have no information about the hours or weeks worked; earnings measures reflect quarterly earnings. Second, the data are administrative in nature, and hence the employer can represent either an establishment or a firm, depending on how the business chooses to file the unemployment insurance record.[3] This problem is mitigated by the fact that about 70 percent of businesses are single establishments, and hence there is no difference between the two. However, for larger businesses with multiple establishments, the exact structure of the economic entity is often much more complex. Third, because employer identification numbers can change for administrative as well as economic reasons, firm births and deaths (including mergers and acquisitions) may be overstated by about 10 percent (based on research done at the LEHD program). This problem is minimized because of our focus on continuing firms. However, firms that have been acquired by other firms will not be included (because they are not true continuing firms), and firms that acquire other firms will show the workers from the source firm to be new hires.

We impose three primary selection criteria on our data: we select firms and workers from food manufacturing; we restrict jobs to full-quarter jobs; and we select continuing employers that at a given point had an annual employment of at least twenty employees and never had fewer than ten employees. We limit our analysis to food manufacturers in order to consider one relatively homogeneous subsector within the food supply chain. Since the case studies suggest that supply chain changes are shifting employment toward food manufacturing, this destination subsector seems most important to examine; our analysis does include some comparison with other food subsectors. To minimize the issues that arise as a result of the lack of hours information, we follow Topel and Ward (1992) as well as Burgess, Lane, and Stevens (2000) and restrict the data set to full-quarter jobs only. A job is considered a full-quarter job if the worker holding that job was employed by the same employer in the quarter preceding and succeeding the current quarter. We exclude firms that are very small or will last for a relatively short period of time, since they are unlikely to have internal labor markets and are not amenable to analyses of within-firm mobility and long-term trends.

Our final data set focuses on continuing firms that have at least twenty employees in at least one quarter in the period from the third quarter of 1985 to the third quarter of 1997 and that did not disappear for more than two quarters over the period. Although this criterion reduces the number of firms to 91, we keep the bulk of records—648,666 observations on a total of 87,366 workers.

CASE STUDY FINDINGS

AN INTRODUCTION TO FOOD PREPARATION

For our purposes it is useful to view the food preparation industry as composed of four segments, omitting the agricultural and fisheries sectors that supply the raw materials:

1. Retail: Supermarkets and groceries and nongrocery retailers such as Wal-Mart

2. Food service providers: Restaurants, food service in firms and institutions provided by the firms and institutions, and contracted food service providers

3. Food suppliers and distributors

4. Food manufacturers

In this chapter, we focus on industry changes in food service providers, food distributors, and food manufacturers. These three sectors combined accounted for nearly 10 million jobs in 2000. (Grocery stores employed another 3 million.) Entry-level pay in the relevant jobs ranges from $5.00 to $8.00 an hour, and the number of workers in the sites visited ranged from several to several hundred. None of the entry-level jobs require more than a high school education, and many do not even require this minimal credential. We first review the broad contours of the food industry and then turn to the results of these cases.

In the food service industry we are most interested in food preparation (as opposed to service) workers, who numbered about 2.8 million out of the 13 million food-sector (including grocery store) workers in 1999. Almost 20 percent of food preparation workers are between 16 and 19 years old, and about half are employed part-time. In grocery wholesaling, which imperfectly corresponds to the food distribution sector we studied, our field data cover warehouse workers, food preparation workers, food machine operations, supervisors, and drivers, totaling 364,000 workers in 1999. In food manufacturing, the relevant workers are food preparation workers, food machine operators, and their supervisors—a total of 41,000 workers in 1999. In each of the 3 segments—food manufacturing, food distribution, and food service—supervisors and managers of food preparation workers are a key point on the mobility ladder for food preparation workers. Such supervisors and managers, who are part of the above totals, numbered approximately 650,000 across all 3 segments in 1999.

RESTRUCTURING IN FOOD: CONSOLIDATION AND OUTSOURCING

All segments of the food industry have experienced significant consolidation. The top four firms account for 52 percent of sales among food service contractors; 28 percent among general-line grocery wholesalers; 20 percent among grocery stores; and 14 percent among food manufacturers. Sales from these top firms account for even higher proportions in specific food sectors: 35 percent in meat products and 29 percent in baked goods, for instance, though still only 7 percent among full-service restaurants (U.S. Bureau of the Census 2002a). Consolidation among broad-line food distributors (those supplying a wide variety of products) is particularly noteworthy. Technomic reported that among broad-line distributors (evidently defined somewhat more restrictively than the census definition), the share of the top three (Sysco, Alliant, and U.S. Food) grew from 32 percent in 1995 to 43 percent in 2000 ("Concentrated Power," 2000). (In 2001, U.S. Food acquired Alliant.)

The consolidation in each segment of the industry has fueled consolidation in the others. In food service provision, increased contracting business has generated growth among the larger firms and provided profitable opportunities for them to acquire smaller regional food service providers. Growth among the larger firms allowed them to achieve further economies of scale and scope that feed continuing growth. As the large players in food service provision grow and consolidate, they demand larger, more stable distributors to supply them, and they seek one-stop shopping to the extent possible. Sysco, U.S. Food, and other large distributors have thus grown with new business and acquired more and more regional suppliers. An executive in a Quality Express regional division stated: "There were thirty-eight competitors in [this] region when I started [in 1984]. In reality, we now have five, and only two that are real competitors."

Similarly, as distributors have grown and consolidated, they have sought ways to increase and stabilize the clients that they supply, providing further energy to the growth and consolidation of food service providers, chain restaurants, and supermarkets. The relationship between large distributors and large food service contractors has given both further advantages through mutually reinforcing economies of scale. This allows both to compete more effectively in their own markets, and that success encourages yet more outsourcing of food service and subsequent growth and consolidation in both market segments. The consolidation of restaurants into chains has also stimulated and been facilitated by the growth of large, full-service food distributors. And giant distributors have spurred manufacturing consolidation as well: in salad manufacturing, for example, "people are starting to buy each other up," according to the vice president of operations of Salads Supreme. The average food manufacturing plant grew from sixty-two employees in 1977 to seventy-three in 1997 (U.S. Department of Commerce 1977; U.S. Bureau of the Census 2002b).

In step with consolidation, three types of outsourcing have grown:

1. Institutional food service is increasingly provided by contractors.

2. Food preparation is being outsourced from food service to food manufacture (and food manufacturers themselves have outsourced).

3. Food-related services are also being outsourced: distributors now provide services to food servers.

Contracted food service firms serve more and more of the meals in firms and institutions. The food service contracting industry is only about thirty-five years old. That was when Aramark, which began as a vending machine contractor providing food service to sporting events, was established (Hoover's 2002). Sodexho (which now includes Marriott International) is a French company founded thirty-five years ago by Pierre Bellon "in borrowed space inside his uncle's anchovy factory." According to a recent Merrill Lynch report, the overall fraction of institutional food sales that are outsourced has now reached 51 percent (Hagerty 2002). Organizations are contracting out food service for a number of reasons, the most important of which are cost and quality. Food contractors can achieve economies of scale in buying food, machinery, and off-site food preparation that are not possible for independent food providers. Three firms currently dominate institutional food service: Sodhexo, Compass Group, and Aramark. Compass Group, currently number one, has sales of over $350 billion.

"'Our business is about economies of scale,' says Compass's Mr. Bailey. 'Frankly, the bigger you are, the more money you can make'" (Hagerty 2002). Such economies of scale can also help ensure consistency of quality. The benefits of economies of scale have been reinforced by the extraordinary growth of the largest service contractors, which are expected to grow by double-digit rates in the near future (Hagerty 2002). In addition, by contracting out, institutions can shed the costs of recruiting, training, and workers' compensation insurance and avoid pay comparability with non–food service employees in the firm.

The consolidation of food service providers, of restaurants into restaurant chains, and of food distributors has helped feed the second type of outsourcing—the shift of food preparation "upstream" along the supply chain from food providers in cafeterias and restaurants (and to a degree in supermarkets) to food distributors and especially manufacturers. Change across years in the numbers of food preparation workers within industry segments is difficult to gauge because the categories were modified in the Bureau of Labor Statistics Occupational Employment and Wage Estimates data in 1993, 1996, and 2000. We attempted to create consistent categories and found that between 1996 and 2000 food preparation workers within food service establishments declined by about 160,000 workers, while in food manufacturing the number of workers processing and preparing food increased by about 4,800.

Food service providers purchase greater amounts and varieties of pre-prepared food than before, shifting the preparation work to food manufacturers. A Great Meals facility manager explained:

There's more and more foods being done [by] the manufacturer than they are on-site. The reason for that is quality. There are things that you could buy that it would make no sense whatsoever for you to make. There's even some desserts out there that the finest pastry chefs in [this city] couldn't make them as good. You can pretty much

buy anything prefab now. . . . The other thing is all the precut vegetables. . . . You know, even entrées. I know folks that run hotels . . .
they're buying their chickens, chicken cordon bleu is already done,
and they're just baking them. And this is a hotel getting $50 and $60
a plate [for catered banquets].

Thus, giant food service providers achieve a scale at which it is
easier to plan and execute cost-effective outsourcing. But independent restaurants are outsourcing more as well. At Bellavista, an upscale restaurant, a line cook said that all meat comes into the restaurant precut and salad greens prepackaged. The pastry chef
indicated that improvements in production technology, such as
flash freezing, automated cake design, and improvements in transportation, had increased the purchasing of cakes and pastry by all
but some of the high-end restaurants.

Newly consolidated distributor firms help both their vendors
(food producers) and their food service clients coordinate planning,
generating larger shipments of prepared foods. The Quality Express
manager told us that his company's customers (primarily Great
Meals and a large number of independent restaurants) purchase
"more and more prepared foods, for lack of qualified personnel to
do that in-house for them." At distributor Food King, the executive
vice president of a regional division described the company's dis-
covery that purchasing salad preparations lowered transportation
costs compared to shipping component ingredients separately. He
and the owner of Joe's Produce pointed out that prepared food has
less weight and bulk because the waste is removed, and prepared
food is better preserved, reducing spoilage and easing shipping constraints by allowing greater latitude in delivery and logistical tolerances. According to the owner of Joe's, preparing carrots and onions
close to the growers reduces transport weight by 40 percent. (Interestingly, restaurants report that a significant cost savings of prepared food is in lower workers' compensation costs—fewer workers
are wielding large knives.) Joe's took an additional step and actually
moved into the food preparation business. The owner reported that
taking over the preparation of difficult-to-prepare items (such as
cauliflower) or highly labor-intensive foods (such as fruit salad) significantly increased the quantity sold to food servers. He claimed
that restaurants' preparation costs amount to three times the cost of
raw produce, but that his company's scale and mechanization, along

with lowered transportation costs, allows them to offer the same product to final servers at a significantly lower cost while reaping higher margins on the sale.

Like other manufacturers, food manufacturers themselves have outsourced. At Salads Supreme, where one of the main products is potato salad, the vice president spoke of the contrast between the late 1980s and today. "Back then, we brought the potatoes in, dumped 'em, peeled 'em, washed 'em, and made salad. Now a guy in [a nearby area] peels and washes them—all we do is cook. We don't want to bring bacteria into the plant." Sounding like any number of executives in other manufacturing sectors, she added, "Our philosophy is to do what we do best, and let other people do what they do best."

Finally, in addition to new goods, food distributors are providing new services to food servers. One goal is to facilitate the survival of small firms, because a stable firm is easier to service than a succession of firms—and is likely to grow as well. The other goal is to compete for new business. The services provided include general management consulting, marketing menu planning and product expansion, price setting, inventory and purchasing control, and worker training in safety and food handling. In the cases we heard about, these services are provided without charge, because the services pay for themselves by securing and helping to expand the business of customers. The largest food distributors are most active in providing such services. Food King has a large division devoted to providing this assistance. Similarly, Quality Express offers its customers management and menu planning services. However, some smaller, regional distributors are also pitching in; for instance, Joe's Produce trains clients in food handling.

Despite outsourcing's momentum, many of the companies in our sample have begun to encounter its limits, a subject to which we now turn.

JOB QUALITY AND MOBILITY IN FOOD: BEFORE AND AFTER

Industry consolidation, the shift of food preparation from food service providers to manufacturers and distributors, and the shift of business services from food providers and manufacturers to distributors have impacts on the quality of jobs in the industry as a whole.

We see three types of outcomes produced by these changes, all of them generally leading to higher-paying jobs:

1. Jobs are shifting to higher-paying industries.

2. Jobs are shifting to larger enterprises.

3. Jobs that once were done ad hoc or informally (such as menu planning and inventory management) are becoming more specialized and professionalized.

As food preparation shifts, work moves as well. For example, in salad preparation there are fewer jobs for low-skill food preparation workers on-site and more for machine operators using large machines at manufacturing sites, with significant changes in pay level and job conditions. Looking at pay by industry, the pay level in food manufacturing tends to reflect that of the manufacturing sector as a whole, with median wages of $11.80 an hour (SIC 20) compared to $6.70 an hour in the food service sector (SIC 580) (U.S. Department of Labor 1998). Looking, alternatively, at pay levels of occupations affected by the food preparation shift, food preparation workers in food service establishments average $7.25 an hour as compared to machine tenders and operators in the food manufacturing industry, who receive $10.88 an hour. In food distribution, where more food preparation is shifting, food preparation workers earn $8.68 an hour and food machine operators $8.72 per hour. Even for the same occupation, wage differentials between industries are striking: bakers in restaurants have median wages of $7.60 an hour as compared to $10.20 in the food manufacturing industry. Supervisors of food preparation workers also earn more in manufacturing and distribution than they earn in food service. Their wage rates are $16.29 in manufacturing, $16.47 in distribution, and $11.46 in food service (U.S. Department of Labor 1999). Moreover, the average food manufacturing establishment (fifty-five employees) is significantly larger than the average eating and drinking place (sixteen), suggesting more opportunity for career growth (U.S. Bureau of the Census 2002b).

Comparing jobs and wages for the Ourtown School System, a free-standing food service (table 7.1), with salad manufacturers Salads Supreme (table 7.2) suggests some of the changes involved. Both businesses are located in the same metropolitan area. Although

Table 7.1 Job Grid for Ourtown School System Food Service

Job Title	Wage	Requirements
Assistant cook–food preparer	$7.33 to $7.48 an hour	High school or less
Cook	$7.62 an hour	Zero to five years' experience
	$8.05 an hour	Six to twelve years' experience
	$8.90 an hour	Twelve or more years' experience
Food supervisor	Salaried, approximately $17,000 yearly	High school or less

Source: Authors' compilation.

entry wages start slightly higher at Ourtown, pay at higher occupational levels, opportunities for wage growth, and opportunities for movement into higher-level jobs are substantially greater at the manufacturer.

While shifting jobs from food servers to manufacturers improves job quality, it also alters the geographic locations and degree of geographic concentration of entry-level jobs. When Food King buys vegetables prepared near the farm—rather than selling unprocessed vegetables that are prepared by the restaurant—jobs shift from urban to rural areas (and presumably to the south and west of the country). For other prepared goods, ranging from pastry to prepared entrées, upstreaming food preparation shifts jobs scattered throughout urban areas, in the restaurants, to larger factory settings generally outside of the central city. Although the demographic characteristics of the two groups of workers might plausibly be quite similar—modestly skilled Latino immigrants in rural California work as produce processors or in suburban bakeries, displacing modestly skilled Latino immigrants in central cities—the implications for less-educated workers rooted in central cities may nonetheless be significant. Young people were 25 percent of food service workers in 2000, and food service jobs are often important first jobs through which workers gain more employability skills and establish an employment history.

The value of these jobs is significant in some urban areas where

Table 7.2 Job Grid for Salads Supreme

Job Title	Wage	Requirements	Upward Mobility
Hand packer	$7.00 to 9.50 an hour	Literacy not required	Yes
Assistant cook or mixer	$7.50 to $10.75 an hour	Literacy not required	Yes
Cook, mixer, lead person, ware-house worker, or assistant super-visor	$10.50 to $13.50 an hour	Literacy required	Yes
Supervisor	$10.00 to $20.00 an hour (nobody mak-ing $20.00)	No high school	Yes
Production man-ager	Not able to determine	No high school	Yes
Plant manager or quality control manager	Not able to determine	High school	Little
Vice president	Not able to determine	College	Little
President	Not able to determine	College	Little

Source: Authors' compilation.

there are few other available jobs (see Newman 1999). The shift in these jobs may be particularly significant to non-English-speakers: it reduces the number of jobs that do not require high levels of communication with either customers or coworkers (with notable exceptions, of course, depending on the location of the restaurant). Although mobility and job quality in the food service sector are not high, these jobs may provide launching pads for mobility outside the sector. However, such cross-sector mobility requires geographi-cal proximity to other industries with better job opportunities.

To take a preliminary closer look at geographic shifts in food preparation, we examine food industry shifts between 1977 and 1997 for California, our most populous state.[4] We limit our analysis to a single representative state because compiling county-by-county data is quite laborious. We have divided the food industry into three components: food manufacturing, grocery wholesaling, and

Table 7.3 Employment Growth for Total and Food Industry Employment in California, by Geographic Area, 1977 to 1997

	Total	Total Food	Food Manufacturing	Nondurable Wholesale	Eating and Drinking Places
Percentage increases					
California total	73	76	11	63	115
Agricultural counties	55	61	−7	60	103
Non-agricultural counties	110	100	36	67	91
Ratio of percentage increase to total for relevant area					
California total	1.00	1.05	0.16	0.86	1.58
Agricultural counties	1.00	1.11	−0.12	1.10	1.89
Non-agricultural counties	1.00	0.90	0.33	0.61	0.82

Sources: County Business Patterns data from U.S. Bureau of the Census (2002b) and U.S. Commerce Department (1977).

eating and drinking places. (To simplify the discussion we omit grocery stores, since our main concern is with the food *service* supply chain.) We have divided California geographically into agricultural and nonagricultural counties, defined by whether a county falls above or below the statewide proportion employed in agriculture in 1997. By this definition, twenty-one of California's fifty-eight counties are nonagricultural, accounting for 60 percent of the state's total employment and 55 percent of its food industry employment.

Table 7.3 shows that as California food *manufacturing* employment grew, it shifted dramatically from agricultural to nonagricultural counties, to the extent that the absolute number of food manufacturing jobs in agricultural counties actually declined. In food *wholesaling* employment, urban regions slightly outpaced their agricultural counterparts. Only eating and drinking place jobs grew faster in agricultural regions—exploding in rural areas, while only slightly exceeding population growth in urban ones. This growth presumably reflects the diffusion to rural America of the pattern of eating more meals outside the home—especially in fast-food restaurants—patterns already well established in urban areas by 1977. Thus, supply chain shifts do not appear to be leading to the ruralization of food preparation jobs. Data at the county level, however, do not permit us to distinguish adequately central city from suburban locations.

Our two manufacturing cases shed further light on geographic changes. Maritime Seafood is based in a remote coastal area, close to sources of the seafood it processes. Salads Supreme, on the other hand, is in a major metropolitan area. It was established in the mid-1980s in a working-class community neighboring the central city, but shortly afterward it relocated to a suburban community on a major peripheral highway. Salads Supreme is planning another relocation to a larger facility but is looking only within a ten-mile radius, since 60 to 70 percent of the workforce, according to the vice president, comes from an inner-city neighborhood in the central city or from the community in which it was originally located. The Salads Supreme workforce, she noted, is entirely made up of Latin American and African immigrants. The evidence from table 7.3 suggests that more workers are shifting to Salads Supreme types of locations than to isolated rural areas, as in the case of Maritime Seafood.

In addition to the industry effect, there is a firm size effect. Of course, the shift from food service to manufacturing itself entails a shift to larger businesses: in 1997 the average food manufacturing plant had seventy-three employees, more than four times the seventeen at the average eating place (U.S. Bureau of the Census 2002b). But in addition, with the outsourcing of food service provision and consolidation among food service providers, food preparation workers within food service itself are working for larger firms. Economic research in general indicates that larger firms pay better (Brown, Hamilton, and Medoff 1990), and this effect is evident in our field data as well. As shown by the job grids in tables 7.1 and 7.4, the Ourtown School System, an independent food service provider, pays lower wages for food prep workers than does Great Meals at the nearby site we studied ($7.38 to $7.48 an hour compared with $7.00 to $9.00) and much lower wages for cooks ($7.62 to $8.90 compared with $9.00 to $13.00) and supervisors ($17,000 a year compared with $13.00 an hour). Similarly, a comparison with a Masterfood facility in the same area as Ourtown (not shown) shows

Table 7.4 Job Grid for Great Meals Institutional Facility

Job Title	Wage	Requirements	Upward Mobility
Hourly line staff: dishwashers	$7.00 to $8.00 an hour	No high school, no experience necessary, good attitude, good ethic	Yes
Hourly line staff: prep cooks, some entry-level cooks, or some part-time cashiers	$7.00 to $9.00 an hour	No high school	Yes
Cooks and senior cooks; cashiers	$9.00 to $13.00 an hour; $9.00 to $12.00 an hour	No high school	Yes
Supervisors, cashier, faculty club	$13.00 an hour	No high school	Yes
Management: chef manager or assistant manager	$25,000 to low $30s; chef can earn up to $45,000	About seven years' experience, some college but not necessary	Yes, but limited
Food-service director	Not able to determine	Most have college	Some
General manager	$50,000 to $60,000	Most have college	Some

Source: Authors' compilation.

higher wages than Ourtown for cooks ($10.00 an hour or higher) and a higher wage ceiling for prep workers ($9.00 an hour). Wages at Great Meals and Masterfood come close to those at Salads Supreme, although they are still somewhat lower.

Distributor consolidation is also shifting distribution workers to larger enterprises. To see the result, compare wages for a regional division of Quality Express—a former regional company acquired two years before the interview—with those of Food King. While warehouse workers start at the same level ($8.00 an hour), Food King employees pull ahead within a short period of time (taking a large jump to $16.00 after three months) compared to Regional Foods (maximum of $12.00). Drivers also receive significantly better pay at Food King ($56,000) than at Quality Express ($35,000 to $40,000).

Although our data on manufacturing are limited, the example of Maritime Seafood suggests that there can be substantial consolidation-driven scale effects on wages in manufacturing as well. Maritime supplies the majority of its products through Food King and to a national chain restaurant. By increasing skills and changing production, Maritime developed what is, *for this industry,* a higher-road job with better pay and better working conditions. Training workers to separate different qualities of seafood (as opposed to processing all incoming seafood mixed into one batch), they were able to offer a premium grade at a higher price, unlike their competitors. They instituted teams and job rotation to fight the boredom and apathy that arises in typical seafood assembly line operations. The enthusiastic manager said, "Some years ago I created a team of core people that believed in accomplishment, in pride, that realized they were doing something better, and I now have an incredible group." The manager also increased average pay by going to a piecework system based on both quantity and quality. Workers are paid a base wage of $5.50 to $6.50 an hour, which is the industry standard, and they can increase their base wage 30 percent or more based on their piece rate. Currently two out of five Maritime workers make 20 percent or more above their base wage. All supervisors are promoted from the floor. Maritime has been able to develop the premium market that supports higher wages only by partnering with a large distributor with national reach; in fact, Maritime trains Food King salespeople so that they can promote the higher-premium products. Thus, the consolidation that created Food King created the opportunity for Maritime to take the high road.

Business services, such as menu planning, now provided by distributors to restaurants and food service contractors have created a class of jobs within distributors that do not seem to have existed as separate jobs in most restaurants. These tasks were most likely either taken on by restaurant personnel in less systematic ways or not done at all. With these services now provided by distributors, opportunities in the food industries have expanded and a new set of more professional and specialized jobs have emerged. The regional Quality Express warehouse, for instance, employs a chef solely to demonstrate alternative food preparation ideas to clients.

What are the implications for upward mobility for low-level

workers? The key effect here, once more, is scale: larger, national-level firms now employ a larger fraction of food processing and food distribution workers. We can characterize this shift very generally as a move from firms with smaller job pyramids (layers in the job hierarchy) and fairly frequent mobility up the pyramid to firms with larger pyramids but also with significant barriers between certain strata.

For instance, the job ladders for Great Meals and Masterfood have several more rungs of management than the job ladder for Ourtown. Added to this are the layers above the individual facility: in the case of Great Meals, resident district manager, district manager, vice president of operations . . . up to CEO. The many managerial levels have no parallel in the Ourtown School System, let alone in a free-standing restaurant like Bellavista. The same is true in comparing the Quality Express division—when it was an independent regional distributor—with the national hierarchy of Food King. Thus, the shift to larger national-level firms provides more *potential* mobility.

However, both the national food contractors and distributors tend to partition jobs into three main segments: line workers, facility-level managers, and managers above the facility level. The top two strata are difficult to penetrate from below. National firms tend to adopt corporate human resource practices and to seek managers from the outside who have more education (college or at least associate degrees) than supervisors promoted from within typically have. The managerial ranks have been made more professional by the corporate structure. The two managers we spoke with at Great Meals and the manager at Masterfood all have bachelor's degrees in food service management. Further, the district manager for higher education for Great Meals answered the question, "So what's the route into management? Get a college degree?" with, "That's probably the easiest, probably the most common. It's probably not the fairest way. . . . You can grab on to someone who's a great cook and can take responsibility. They might have a high school education. The next step into management is often very difficult for them. There's a high level of failure. By the same token, someone could be a great general manager, run a place really well, but it could be a tough step to running eight schools." The *Occupational Outlook Handbook* published by the Bureau of Labor Statistics is based on extensive field data and confirms that "most food service management companies and national or regional restaurant chains recruit management trainees from two- and four-year college hospitality management programs. Food service and restaurant chains prefer to hire people with degrees in restaurant and institutional food service management, but they often hire graduates with degrees in other fields." (U.S. Department of Labor 2002). The vice president at Salads Supreme, who has worked in food preparation in a grocery chain and two food manufacturers, stated that in manufacturing as well it has become more difficult to move up without a college degree.

Promotion from chef to manager in food service, from warehouse supervisor to manager in food distribution, or from shift supervisor to plant manager in food manufacturing appears to be more likely at smaller independent or regional firms. These smaller firms are more likely to choose managers from among shift or station supervisors in the establishment. Supervisors themselves typically have come from the workers they oversee.

A final change is that food distributors have raised the initial hurdle for entry-level jobs. Food distributors now service larger and more varied accounts. The larger accounts reflect the fact that the food service contractors and restaurants now depend on a smaller number of suppliers (usually one large one) for a much greater fraction of the food they serve. The Great Meals facility manager explained:

> Because we are such a large company, a lot of our purchasing decisions are made . . . at a corporate level. . . . Obviously, a company wants to make as few stops as possible, so they don't want to drop off a case of lettuce. Used to be years ago—again talking about a chain—you'd have fifteen different companies. One would just deliver your eggs. One would deliver your lettuce. One would deliver your cheese. One would deliver your meat. Now you have these big companies that pretty much deliver everything other than milk, because they're not allowed to deliver milk.

Hence, the customers of food distributors, the food service contractors and the restaurant chains, depend much more on the accuracy and timeliness of the deliveries they receive from the large distributors. Distributors have responded by increasing the skills they need from warehouse workers and supervisors and from drivers, both to maintain a high level of service to their clients and to push drivers to sell more.

The Food King executive told us that demand has heightened for a "perfect pallet" coming out of the warehouse. Warehouse workers must pay more attention to detail and must have more computer skill than in the past so as to be able to handle inventory scheduling, for example. We heard a similar story from Quality Express, where in the last few years clients have demanded and received more computer reporting of transactions. Quality Express has implemented a warehouse computer system to track expiration dates on products so as to guarantee clients at least four days' shelf life. To this end, they have increased training and provided computer instruction for warehouse workers.

Similarly, the large distributors in our sample have recognized that the driver not only provides transportation but is a strategic point of contact with customers to make sure customer needs (of a variety of types) are met and to sell new prepared food products. Consequently, at the large distributors drivers now do more and receive more training than before. Drivers at Quality Express receive extensive training in customer service, computers, and accounts receivable. At Food King, drivers are taking on more sales and accounts management tasks.

We did not observe a parallel trend in food service or in food manufacturing. As more food preparation is outsourced, the skill demands placed on food preparation workers have not increased, according to our field interviews. The major skill initiative by food service contractors, aside from government-mandated food safety instruction, is trying to boost customer service skills among employees. At Salads Supreme, despite the tighter federal food safety regulations, the vice president repeated several times that "illiterate workers are sometimes the best, because they don't get creative on you."

In summary, these case study findings in food subsectors provide no evidence of the disappearance of internal labor markets. As employment shifts toward manufacturing and toward larger firms, it appears to be shifting toward higher-quality jobs and more extensive job ladders. Within firms, the only evidence of curtailed mobility is increased credentialization of some promotion paths.

Variation in Managerial Strategy in Food

The discussion of food to this point may convey the impression of an unstoppable juggernaut driving the industry toward consolidation, toward shifting food preparation back along the supply chain, and toward the creation of credentialized job ladders. Such a uniform picture would be misleading, however. Every trend in food has exceptions, which may signal future countertrends.

In outsourcing there is often a trade-off between cost savings, on the one hand, and quality and timeliness, on the other. The Great Meals division manager described this trade-off:

> If I buy lettuce already sliced, the expectation is that I eliminate the person who's doing salad prep. We don't need a full-time person to just dump the lettuce in the bowls. Now, we're a people business. The [customers] see Betty Ann there every day cutting lettuce, and they feel like they have a relationship with her. They're not going to feel the same way about a machine somewhere cutting lettuce. So we're striving not to buy the products.

He concluded that despite the importance of Betty Ann, the overall trend "has moved to manufacturers preparing foods to make our lives easier." The trade-off sets limits, however, on what can be outsourced, and it has led to some "insourcing" of preparation as well. His own facility manager noted that fresh fruit preparations are rarely outsourced. That facility's kitchen buys fresh bagels from an independent local distributor, not because the frozen bagels supplied by Food King are inferior, but because the Great Meals site sells so many bagels that they would have to increase oven capacity significantly to warm the frozen bagels. At Masterfood the site manager told us that the costs of some fully prepared items, such as breaded frozen fish and canned soups, are rising and they have found that they can produce higher quality at lower cost in-house. Masterfood employees are now once more breading fresh fish, preparing soups, and even peeling carrots. And the Great Meals division manager himself referred to increasing demand for the "marché concept"—preparing food in front of the customer.

Similarly, in distribution outsourcing is not irreversible. Our interviewee at Quality Express pointed out that three years earlier they had outsourced the sorting and repacking of produce into smaller quantities. But four months before the interview, they had brought sorting and repacking back in-house because of quality concerns. He also reported that at his Quality Express site they are considering re-insourcing the custom-cutting of red meats and some fish processing so that they can cut down on the lead time currently required for customer orders.

Several factors—labor market tightness, the importance of specialized knowledge, and the determination of individual managers—limit the credentialization of managerial job ladders. Most of the interviews took place during the recent labor shortage, and we heard about companies' shortage-driven quest to "make" rather than "buy" a greater proportion of their managerial talent. At Great Meals the district manager told us: "For managerial workers the shortage has led to more promotions from within. . . . We recruited fewer from inside in earlier years. The market [of available workers] has shrunk. And the work has become specialized. . . . We have a strategic plan to keep those people. There's twenty-five to thirty hours of training for hourly workers [which is lost when a worker leaves]. That's multiplied by many factors more for the management ranks." In fact, Great Meals recently added the resident district manager category between the (facility-level) general manager and the district manager, in part as a way of gradually increasing a manager's level of responsibility to ease upward mobility.

The Great Meals facility manager, meanwhile, argued for promotion from within strictly in terms of firm-specific knowledge, without referring to the labor market squeeze.

> It is so much easier to move somebody up that already knows an operation than to move somebody in who [doesn't]. I have folks that know this operation inside and out that may not have the most experience as a manager. A very, very, very well seasoned manager coming in from [another institution] may have more experience than the person that I promote, but it would take him so long to learn [my institution] that it's a trade-off.

Although himself a graduate of a culinary institute, he dismissed the importance of schooling for chef work: "The school gives you a foundation. . . . But it doesn't tell you what to do when four people are out sick and you have a function for 150 people." He reported that all his supervisors and managers save one were promoted from within, and he proudly recounted that his assistant manager and one of his chef managers had both started out as dishwashers in the facility. Regardless of the Great Meals corporate policy, a site manager like this one has the power to create mobility opportunities.

QUANTITATIVE FINDINGS

Since the case study information comes from a small sample of firms, it is difficult to determine the generalizability of the results. Taking a completely different, yet complementary, approach to the same industry, this section uses a very large employer-employee data set to compare earnings, mobility, and turnover patterns over time for workers in different parts of the within-firm earnings distribution.

We begin by using the firm as the unit of analysis to establish some basic facts about food manufacturing. We then examine turnover as an (inverse) indicator of the vigor of ILMs and track the correlates of a firm's average earnings level. We turn to individual-level data to examine the evolution of promotion in firms. Finally, we compare food manufacturing with other food subsectors. Unless otherwise specified, all data are computed from the precursor to the Longitudinal Employer-Household Dynamics (LEHD) program, for firms and workers in the state of Maryland.

BASIC FACTS

We begin by explicitly categorizing workers by their position in the earnings distribution in the business for which they work.[5] As table 7.5 reveals, there is a substantial gap in earnings between the bottom and top quartiles. We cannot distinguish between the effects of hours differences and hourly wage differences, but since part-time employment is relatively uncommon in manufacturing (Tilly 1996), we presume that much of the earnings gap is due to hourly wage disparities.

The dual labor market literature has observed that women, minorities, and youth are much more likely to be in the bottom part of the *overall* earnings distribution than are white, prime-age males. This evidence comes from worker-based surveys, however, not from firm-based evidence. Our ability to describe the workforce composition of firms at a very detailed level permits us to determine whether

Table 7.5 Quarterly Earnings Distribution, Food Manufacturing

		Earnings Distribution of Median Firm		
		Bottom		
Average Size	Average	Quartile	Top Quartile	Ratio of Top
of Workforce	Earnings	Earnings	Earnings	to Bottom
128	$5,498.16	$2,537.71	$9,888.67	3.90

Source: Authors' compilation.

these types of workers are also at the bottom of *firms'* earnings distribution. Table 7.6 shows women as a proportion of the bottom earnings quartile workforce and contrasts this to the proportion in the top quartile. As in the overall earnings distribution, women are overwhelmingly represented in the bottom part of the firm earnings distributions, and men are overwhelmingly represented in the top part.[6] The same holds true in all industries for younger workers (not shown): they are much more likely to be in the bottom than in the top portion of the earnings distribution (presumably reflecting lower levels of human capital and experience). Interestingly, however, by the late 1990s food manufacturing saw growing numbers of women in the top quartile and fewer women in the bottom quartile.

DISMANTLING AND REBUILDING: CHANGES IN TURNOVER OVER TIME

Do firms dismantle and rebuild their internal labor markets? Firms in the food manufacturing industry have had ample opportunity to change their workforce structure, and our data demonstrate just how pervasive job changes are. To understand this, it is worth noting that worker change (worker flows) can come from two main sources: job reallocation, which happens when jobs are created or destroyed at the firm level; or worker churning—different workers churning through the same set of jobs.

In reporting average job and worker reallocation rates—together with the standard deviation of each—over the period for which we have data, table 7.7 demonstrates that there are huge amounts of worker reallocation. Worker reallocation exceeds job reallocation: for example, even though 21 percent of workers had either left or

Table 7.6 Women in the Top and Bottom Earnings Quartiles in the Food Manufacturing Workforce, 1985 to 1997

Earnings Quartile	1985	1990	1997
Bottom	52.88%	52.74%	51.67%
Top	11.59	14.17	18.53

Source: Authors' compilation.

begun work in this quarter, only 9 percent of jobs were new or destroyed. The churning rate reconciles these two kinds of reallocation: it measures the amount of worker flows in excess of job growth or decline, and that also paints a picture of substantial turnover, averaging 12 percent per quarter. Again, it is worth noting that the standard deviation is very large, suggesting widespread differences in turnover choices by firms. It is also worth noting that these reallocation figures are not directly comparable to either the monthly or annual turnover rates reported in other sources, because longer measurement periods lose information on intermediate turnover. Thus, annual rates will always be much less than four times the amount, and monthly rates much more than one-third.

While table 7.7 reports results for the entire set of firms and all workers within our data set, we are particularly interested in examining turnover patterns for continuing firms, as well as the churning of workers at the bottom end of the earnings distribution. We would expect churning to be higher for low-wage workers, and we find this in fact to be the case. Figure 7.1 describes churning rates for the different quartiles of the income distribution (bottom, top,

Table 7.7 Worker Flows, Job Reallocation, and Churning (Quarterly)

	Mean	Median	Standard Deviation
Worker flow rate	21.39%	13.28%	28.09%
Job reallocation rate	9.11	4.00	17.50
Churning rate	12.28	7.84	20.25

Source: Authors' compilation.

Figure 7.1 Churning Rates in Food Manufacturing

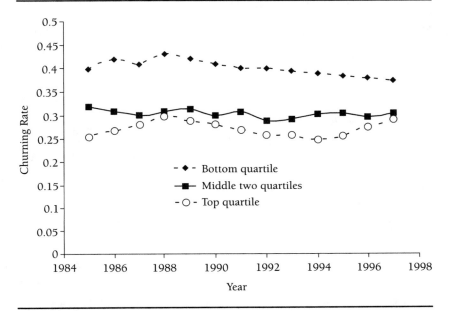

Source: Authors' calculations.

and the two middle quartiles grouped together) and for different industries over time. It is clear that they are much higher—indeed, almost twice as high—for the bottom end of the distribution as at the top.

But these are industry-level aggregates, and the internal labor market story is a firm-level, not an industry-level, story. We now fully exploit the richness of our data set, which enables us to track firms over time and examine in more detail one of the standard stories of the devolution of internal labor markets—that of rising job instability. Since this should manifest itself as a powerful trend toward increasing turnover, particularly at lower wage levels, we can directly test the hypothesis by estimating a set of regressions, with the firm as the unit of analysis and the churning rate as the dependent variable. Because we want to examine trends over time, controlling for the base churning rate at each firm, we include firm fixed effects. We capture firm-level persistence by including the lag of the dependent variable on the right-hand side, and since we are also interested in the effects of firm growth, we include firm size as

Table 7.8 A Firm-Level Analysis of Churning Rates in Food Manufacturing

Variable	All Quartiles	Top	Bottom
Lagged churning	0.21910	0.49788	0.37194
	(15.50)**	(31.16)**	(22.37)**
Time trend	−0.00139	−0.00152	−0.00249
	(6.47)**	(5.46)**	(6.59)**
Employment size (log)	0.00279	0.00510	0.00926
	(1.23)	(1.45)	(1.95)
Constant	0.11612	0.18977	0.42103
	(10.05)**	(12.11)**	(18.88)**
Observations	5,366	3,187	3,254
R-squared	0.0521	0.2450	0.1471

Source: Authors' compilation.
Note: Absolute value of z-statistics in parentheses.
** Significant at 1 percent level.

an independent variable (which, in a fixed-effect model, can be interpreted as changes to the firm base size).

An examination of the first sets of columns in table 7.8 reveals several trends that fit poorly with the standard story of ILM devolution. First, firm-level churning rates are strongly persistent (as shown by the statistically significant coefficient on the lagged dependent variable), indicating that businesses have not in general dramatically altered their turnover patterns. Second, food manufacturing shows a statistically significant *decrease* over time in churning rates, as shown by the negative time trend coefficient. In addition, the explanatory power of the regression for all quartiles is quite low, at .05, indicating wide-ranging firm-level idiosyncrasy in churning.

The divergence from the standard story widens still further when we examine turnover patterns separately for workers at the top and bottom of the earnings distribution, as shown in the "Top" and "Bottom" columns in table 7.8. The persistence that we documented with the overall firm churning rate becomes much more marked, and the explanatory power increases substantially, suggesting that firms are much less idiosyncratic in their treatment of workers at the top and bottom ends of the earnings distribution. In addition, the negative time trend on churning that was seen in the overall regression decomposes into a relatively large decrease in the churning for low-wage workers and a much smaller decrease in churning for high-wage workers. Indeed, in a separate analysis, we find that when exiting and entering firms are included, churning actually increases for high-wage workers—which might be consistent with reduced job security and increased cross-firm mobility for managers.

The finding of persistence suggests little net dismantling of internal labor markets in food manufacturing, consistent with our (admittedly limited) case study evidence from this subsector. Indeed, the negative turnover trend for low-wage workers suggests that in recent years reconstruction has outweighed dismantling. Complicating these findings are the high levels of firm-level idiosyncrasy in turnover (large variation in turnover rates within the industry, much of which cannot be accounted for by our statistical models). This idiosyncratic pattern, while possibly due to a wide variety of omitted variables, is also consistent with the wide variety of firm practices that was noted in the case studies.

GROWTH EFFECTS AND AVERAGE EARNINGS

We have noted that food manufacturing plants are growing larger. At the level of the individual plant, what is the connection between changes in firm size and changes in the average pay level of the firm? We find that changes in pay and changes in firm size are negatively related, suggesting that in general firms add and shed workers disproportionately at the bottom (table 7.9). The fixed effects specification controls for cross-sectional differences in firm size, so this does not contradict the familiar finding that larger firms offer higher pay. Also interesting is the finding that increases in turnover are strongly negatively correlated with average pay. Most of the other results are not surprising: average payroll falls as the proportion of women in the firm increases, and rises the higher the proportion of prime age and older workers. Increases in sales per worker, which is a rough proxy for productivity, are unsurprisingly consistently associated with greater earnings growth. Quarterly earnings have fallen over time (by 0.3 percent a quarter, or over 1 percent per year).

Table 7.9 Determinants of Average Quarterly Earnings in Food Manufacturing

Worker characteristics	
Female	−0.554
	(7.60)**
Prime age (twenty-five to fifty-four)	0.457
	(4.74)**
Older (fifty-five and older)	−0.032
	(0.28)
Firm characteristics	
Size of firm	−0.047
	(2.72)**
Age of firm	0.030
	(0.84)
Time	−0.003
	(5.06)**
Churning rate	0.041
	(1.84)*
Sales per worker	0.030
	(2.99)**
Constant	8.437
	(55.83)**
Observations	2,789
R-squared	0.80

Source: Authors' compilation.
Note: Absolute value of z-statistics in parentheses.
* Significant at 5 percent level.
** Significant at 1 percent level.

THE RELATIONSHIP BETWEEN FIRM CHARACTERISTICS AND PROMOTION

What determines the probability that workers at the bottom end of the distribution will move up within food manufacturing firms? We focus on two cohorts of new hires from 1985 and 1991 and examine the likelihood of workers moving up and down the earnings distribution of their individual firm. The first cohort (referred to as the 1985 cohort) includes those workers who were hired by a given firm between the fourth quarter of 1985 and the third quarter of 1986, excluding any workers who disappear for more than two quarters while continuing to work for the same firm. We follow those workers until 1991 or until they stop working for the firm, whichever comes first. Analogously to the 1985 cohort, we follow workers in the 1991 cohort until 1997 or until they stop working for the original firm. Part of the resulting story is one of exit: one-third of workers are no longer with the original firm five years later. There is also less mobility than one might expect—most stayers do not change quartiles. In fact, the probability of promotion from the bottom tier for 1991 hires is only .49, down from .6 for 1985 hires (if the worker stays).[7]

To scrutinize the relationship between firm personnel practices and the probability of moving up in the firm, we correlate the probability of promotion with both worker characteristics and firm personnel practices. Table 7.10 shows results with a worker fixed effect, which controls for all unchanging worker characteristics that affect the probability of promotion. These results suggest, not surprisingly, that younger and less senior workers are more likely to move up than older ones. (Twenty-five- to fifty-four-year-old workers are less likely to advance than the baseline group of workers age twenty-four or less, though the results do not attain statistical significance.) Firm characteristics are very important: after controlling for individual unobserved heterogeneity, higher-churning firms provide more opportunity for promotion. This is not surprising, since vacancies are necessary for promotions to occur (unless a firm is growing), but the strength of the relationship is interesting. Working for a high-productivity firm (high sales per worker) also boosts the likelihood of promotion.

One might expect to find a "new establishment effect," which we have identified in other industry case studies not discussed in this chapter. There is ample room for promotion in a new plant or office, but this upward mobility decreases as the business ages. It is not possible to observe the correlation of firm age with promotion probability, since firm age effects would be confounded with worker tenure effects. However, increases in firm size could be viewed as an alternative way to track the aging of a firm. As table 7.10 shows, larger firms are much less likely to promote than smaller firms. This size effect persists after controlling for worker fixed effects, suggesting that it is driven primarily by changes in firm size rather than cross-sectional differences, lending support to the new establishment effect.

A view that internal labor markets are in dramatic decline would predict major differences between the two time cohorts, but there

Table 7.10 Probability of Promotion from the Bottom Earnings Quartile in Food Manufacturing

	1985 Cohort	1991 Cohort
Tenure	−0.011	−0.007
	(1.76)	(1.12)
= 1 if age of worker is twenty-five to fifty-four	−0.024	−0.161
	(0.14)	(0.80)
= 1 if age of worker is fifty-five or older	0.153	−0.003
	(0.36)	(0.01)
Quarterly firm churning	0.501	0.724
	(1.49)	(2.88)**
Firm size (log)	0.035	−0.533
	(0.12)	(2.84)**
Sales per worker (log)	0.143	−0.511
	(1.52)	(1.97)*
Observations	8,464	14,688

Source: Authors' compilation.
Note: Absolute value of z-statistics in parentheses. Worker fixed effects included.
* Significant at 5 percent level.
** Significant at 1 percent level.

are few such systematic differences. The one notable change, again, cuts against the standard story. Bottom-quartile workers hired in 1985 became less likely to move up with each added year of tenure. This suggests a sorting process in which those who are likely to move up do so quickly. Among 1991 hires, however, the likelihood of advancement climbed with tenure, indicating that rising rewards to longevity have offset the sorting process.

COMPARING FOOD MANUFACTURING WITH OTHER FOOD SUBSECTORS

These quantitative explorations have been limited to food manufacturing, since case study and aggregate evidence indicate that food preparation jobs are shifting toward manufacturing. It is worthwhile, however, to compare food manufacturing with the other components of the food preparation industry. Table 7.11 makes this comparison. It is not strictly comparable to earlier tables because it includes all firms—not just continuing firms with twenty or more employees—and therefore reports higher rates of churning and

Table 7.11 Worker Flows and Earnings for Food Subsectors in Selected States, 1994 to 1998

	Food Manufacturing	Grocery Wholesaling	Food Stores	Eating Places[a]
Total worker flow rate				
1994	0.312	0.411	0.517	—
1996	0.306	0.373	0.517	—
1998	0.357	0.402	0.724	1.760
Churning rate				
1994	0.311	0.405	0.510	—
1996	0.295	0.372	0.510	—
1998	0.356	0.380	0.669	1.252
Average quarterly earnings				
1994	$7,767	$7,856	$4,386	—
1996	8,348	8,470	4,455	—
1998	9,050	9,207	5,030	$2,830
Average quarterly earnings, new hires				
1994	$5,530	$5,540	$2,275	—
1996	6,117	6,016	2,256	—
1998	6,790	6,515	2,761	$2,529
Ratio of average earnings to new-hire earnings				
1994	1.40	1.42	1.93	—
1996	1.36	1.41	1.97	—
1998	1.33	1.41	1.82	1.12

Source: Authors' compilation.
Notes: Includes all firms. Combines Florida, Illinois, Maryland, and North Carolina.
[a] Eating places data restricted to a subset of these four states.

lower quarterly earnings than in the more restricted sample of firms we examined earlier. However, it has the advantage of incorporating several other states in addition to Maryland, yielding a large sample.

In showing higher quarterly earnings and lower churning (turnover) dates, table 7.11 confirms that food manufacturing jobs are higher-quality than other jobs in the food sector. In fact, the more large-scale, automated, and "factory-like" the setting for food jobs, the better they are. The ranking goes from food manufacturing to wholesale groceries to retail food to eating places. Part of the difference in quarterly earnings, however, is surely due to hours differences, since grocery stores and eating places have high proportions of part-time employees.

The one exception to this ranking is opportunity for earnings growth, as crudely measured by the ratio of average wages to new hire wages. Here wholesale shows a slightly higher ratio than food manufacturing. Food stores show a much higher ratio, but this may reflect widespread two-tier wage structures in which incumbents are grandfathered in at a higher rate and new hires come in at a lower rate with no prospect of ever making the higher rate. Eating places still show the lowest ratio.

Overall, the differences between the food subsectors are quite substantial, suggesting that additional quantitative analysis of the other food subsectors would be informative.

CONCLUSIONS

Both case study and quantitative evidence indicate that internal labor markets are alive and well, despite significant shifts and changes. The case studies demonstrate that, in the case of food service, removing internal labor markets in one place involves expanding them in another. Food preparation job ladders are disappearing in final food service organizations (restaurants, cafeterias, food service contractors), but these functions are being shifted to food manufacturing firms with job ladders of their own. Our case study findings on the nature of ILMs in food manufacturing are limited, but there is certainly evidence that food preparers in the manufacturing sector enjoy better-paid jobs, embedded in larger organizations, than their counterparts in food service organizations. The story is not simply one of outsourcing a fixed set of food preparation activities. Food distributors' aggressive marketing, coupled with manufacturers' economies of scale, have greatly expanded eating places' offerings and presumably fueled the growing number of meals purchased rather than prepared by Americans. In addition, consolidation grafts the limited management ladder of local or regional operators onto national or international management structures.

In earlier work on electronics manufacturing and financial services, we argued that corporate restructuring is iterative, often alternating between deconstruction and reconstruction of internal labor markets (Moss, Salzman, and Tilly 2000). The case for iteration is less clear in food preparation, where consolidation and supply chain shifts appear to be continuing—at a heightened pace—a twenty-year trend. In particular, the consolidation of food distribution, which has helped to propel outsourcing as well as consolidation in other food sectors, has accelerated rapidly in the last several years, resulting in the dominance of two industry giants that are beginning to reshape the practices of their newly acquired affiliates, vendors, and customers. Nonetheless, we do find some movements toward re-insourcing, driven primarily by concerns about quality and customer service. Many of the outsourcing initiatives are quite recent—for instance, the contracting of produce breakdown and repackaging by the Quality Express division beginning in 1998—and companies may in time reevaluate and reverse them (as Quality Express did in 2001). The question is whether quality and service concerns will indeed compel companies to reverse direction, or whether they will open new niches for competitors adopting a different structure. One clear pattern is that managerial and corporate strategy constantly shapes the restructuring of ILMs. Food service managers weigh the trade-offs between reducing cost and adding value. Food distributors invent markets—for chopped vegetables, soups, sauces, pastries, entrées—where none existed before.

The microdata evidence confirms the continued importance of internal labor markets and is consistent with either relatively little change in ILMs or with iterative restructuring—although it also reminds us that the reach of ILMs has been and remains limited. Firm-level persistence in turnover suggests that dramatic shifts in turnover strategy are exceptional. Turnover idiosyncrasy may be generated by divergent managerial strategies or by firms being scattered across different points in an iterative process. Turnover at the low end has decreased over time, contrary to expectations of shortened job tenure. However, this does not mean that today is a great time to be a low-wage worker. Turnover remains much higher for those at the low end, and firms' tendency to add and shed workers at the low end translates into a higher risk of layoff. The most common five-year mobility outcomes for low-end workers are stagnation—remaining in the lowest quartile—or exiting the firm rather than moving up. Microdata evidence for the "new establishment effect" tells us that while there are exceptional opportunities for workers who are present at the opening of an establishment, those possibilities diminish as the establishment grows.

We also claimed at the outset of the chapter that new forms of internal labor markets have reduced opportunities for the least-educated workers to enter and advance within the firm. Our food industry findings provide evidence for this proposition as well. The credentialization associated with consolidation in large corporate structures appears to have reduced the opportunities for entry-level workers to rise to management. (In fact, in the case studies it is difficult to distinguish between this size-driven effect and the new establishment effect.) The geographic relocation of less-skilled food preparation may have diminished urban entry-level job opportunities. The microdata do not measure skill (but see Abowd, Haltiwanger, and Lane 2001). They therefore do not address the question of entry requirements directly. However, they do reveal that despite lower turnover, the probability of moving up from the lowest quartile declined between the 1980s and 1990s.

Combining quantitative and qualitative data to examine these questions has yielded payoffs, but also frustrations and unanswered questions. The key payoff is the ability to link stories—such as the persistence of ILMs—to aggregate data. But the frustrations are significant as well. Supply chain shifts move jobs across the borders of the industries defined in quantitative data, making it difficult to track the relevant changes. Quantitative data lack the descriptive detail that would be needed to fully compare with case studies, whereas case studies tend to lack precision, especially in retrospectively viewed changes. Significant questions remain: Above all, to what extent are the quantitative and qualitative results actually capturing the same processes?

Despite these unresolved issues, the combination of qualitative and quantitative analysis is fruitful. Both methods raise significant challenges to the notion of a dramatic devolution of internal labor markets—at least in the food industry. Our findings point to the promise of future research drawing on the two approaches in tandem.

We wish to acknowledge Adela Luque and Radha Biswas's participation and invaluable research assistance throughout this project. We also thank the Russell Sage and Rockefeller Foundations for financial support.

NOTES

1. This study of food service is part of a larger set of industry case studies that also cover electronics manufacturing, financial services, and retail sales.

2. Specifically, all analysis must be for statistical purposes only, and only for approved projects that also serve a Census Bureau Title 13 purpose. All output is disclosure-proofed by Census Bureau staff before release. All identifiers are removed and replaced by anonymized keys. Individuals working with the data are subject to a $250,000 fine and/ or five years in jail if there is a breach of confidentiality.

3. Work is ongoing to match the state data to the Census Bureau Business Register to further inform our knowledge of these issues.

4. After 1997 County Business Patterns data shifted from the Standard Industrial Classification (SIC) system to the North American Industrial Classification System (NAICS), making accurate time-series comparisons with earlier years considerably more difficult.

5. This is for the third quarter of 1990, in 1990 dollars, and is calculated for firms with more than ten employees. All earnings are quarterly.

6. Recall that these are quarterly earnings, so they incorporate both lower wage rates and fewer hours.

7. These findings are from pooled analysis of food manufacturing, electronics manufacturing, financial services, and retail with no store. Unfortunately, changes in the LEHD program data make it extremely difficult to replicate these results for food alone. However, comparison of the results of table 7.10 for the four industries combined and for each industry separately indicates that differences in mobility patterns across the industries are relatively small.

REFERENCES

Abowd, John, John Haltiwanger, and Julia Lane. 2001. "From Workshop Floor to Workforce Clusters." Report to the Sloan Foundation. Washington: U.S. Bureau of the Census.

Allen, Steven G., Robert L. Clark, and Sylvester J. Schieber. 1998. "Has Job Security Vanished in Large Corporations?" Paper presented to the National Bureau of Economic Research Summer Workshop, Cambridge, Mass. (July 27–31).

Bernhardt, Annette, and Dave Marcotte. 2000. "Is 'Standard Employment' Still What It Used to Be?" In *Nonstandard Work: The Nature and Challenges of Changing Employment Arrangements,* edited by Françoise Carré, Marianne A. Ferber, Lonnie Golden, and Steve Herzenberg. Champaign, Ill.: Industrial Relations Research Association.

Bernhardt, Annette, Martina Morris, Mark S. Handcock, and Marc A. Scott. 2001. *Divergent Paths: Economic Mobility in the New American Labor Market.* New York: Russell Sage Foundation.

Brown, Charles, James Hamilton, and James Medoff. 1990. *Employers Large and Small.* Cambridge, Mass.: Harvard University Press.

Burgess, Simon, Julia Lane, and David Stevens. 2000. "Job Flows, Worker Flows, and Churning." *Journal of Labor Economics* 18(3): 473–79.

Cappelli, Peter, Laurie Bassi, Harry Katz, David Knoke, Paul Osterman, and Michael Useem. 1997. *Change at Work*. New York: Oxford University Press.

"Concentrated Power." 2000. *Refrigerated and Frozen Foods* 11(10): 18.

Groshen, Erica L., and David I. Levine. 1998. "The Rise and Decline (?) of U.S. Internal Labor Markets." Research Paper 9819. New York: Federal Reserve Bank of New York.

Hagerty, James R. 2002. "Aramark Aims to Gobble up Business from Rivals in Europe." *Wall Street Journal*, January 24.

Hoover's. 2002. Available at: *www.hoovers.com/premium/profile/8/0,2147,40038,00.html*.

Lane, Julia, and Adela Luque. 1998. "Low-Wage Workers and the Future of Work: Firm Personnel Policies and Job Outcomes." Unpublished paper. Washington, D.C.: Urban Institute.

Moss, Philip, Harold Salzman, and Chris Tilly. 2000. "Limits to Market-Mediated Employment: From Deconstruction to Reconstruction of Internal Labor Markets." In *Non-Traditional Work Arrangements and the Changing Labor Market: Dimensions, Causes, and Institutional Responses*, edited by Françoise Carré, Marianne Ferber, Lonnie Golden, and Steve Herzenberg. Madison, Wisc.: Industrial Relations Research Assocation.

Neumark, David, ed. 2000. *On the Job: Is Long-term Employment a Thing of the Past?* New York: Russell Sage Foundation.

Newman, Katherine. 1999. *No Shame in My Game: The Working Poor in the Inner City*. New York: Alfred A. Knopf and Russell Sage Foundation.

New York Times. 1996. *The Downsizing of America*. New York: Times Books.

Powell, Walter. 2001. "The Capitalist Firm in the Twenty-first Century: Emerging Patterns in Western Enterprise." In *The Twenty-first-Century Firm: Changing Economic Organization in International Perspective*, edited by Paul DiMaggio. Princeton, N.J.: Princeton University Press.

Swinnerton, Kenneth, and Howard Wial. 1995. "Is Job Stability Declining in the U.S. Economy?" *Industrial and Labor Relations Review* 48(4): 293–304.

Tilly, Chris. 1996. *Half a Job: Bad and Good Part-time Jobs in a Changing Labor Market*. Philadelphia: Temple University Press.

Topel, Robert H., and Michael P. Ward. 1992. "Job Mobility and the Careers of Young Men." *The Quarterly Journal of Economics* 107(2): 439–73.

U.S. Bureau of the Census, Department of Commerce. 2002a. "1997 Economic Census—Concentration Ratios." Available at: *www.census.gov/epcd/www/concentration.html*.

———. 2002b. "County Business Patterns." Available at: *www.census.gov/ epcd/cbp/view/cbpview.html*. See also website of Fisher Library, University of Virginia: *fisher.lib.virginia.edu/cbp/county.html*.

U.S. Department of Commerce. 1977. *County Business Patterns: California*. Washington: U.S. Government Printing Office.

U.S. Department of Labor, Bureau of Labor Statistics. 1998. "Statistics from Industry-Occupation Employment Matrix for 1983–1995." Unpublished data provided by BLS staff.

———. 1999. *Occupational Employment and Wage Estimates*. Available at: *www.bls.gov/oes/oes—data.htm*.

———. 2001. *National Industry-Occupation Employment Matrix*. Available at: *www.bls.gov/oep/nioem/empiohm.jsp*.

———. 2002. *Management, Business, and Financial Occupations*. Reprinted from the *Occupational Outlook Handbook, 2002–2003 Edition*. Bulletin 2540–2 (February): 36–37. Available at: *www.bls.gov/oco/reprints/ ocor002.pdf*.

Womack, James P. 1991. *The Machine That Changed the World: How Japan's Secret Weapon in the Global Auto Wars Will Revolutionize Western Industry*. New York: Harper Perennial.

CHAPTER 8

How and When Does Management Matter? Job Quality and Career Opportunities for Call Center Workers

Rosemary Batt, Larry W. Hunter, and Steffanie Wilk

The dramatic growth of call centers in the last two decades is an important labor market phenomenon for low-wage service workers. Whereas historically service provision was personalized and service labor markets were local, advances in information technologies and new business strategies have made possible the emergence of call centers in which service and sales transactions are mediated through telephone and computer technologies. Firms in manufacturing and service industries alike increasingly view call centers as their primary vehicle for interacting with customers. The phenomenal growth of call centers has created an industry comprising thousands of technology vendors, information technology specialists, industrial engineering and management consultants, and companies that manage some seventy thousand call center operations in the United States. While data on the size of the industry are difficult to procure, estimates are that call centers grew at 20 percent annually in the 1990s and that they now employ at least 3 percent of the workforce in the United States, 2 percent in the United Kingdom, and 1.3 percent in Europe (Datamonitor 1998, 1999).[1] Moreover, many cities view call centers as a centerpiece in their economic development strategies.

The growth of call centers has important implications for the quality of jobs and mobility opportunities for low-wage service workers. First, call centers introduce principles of mechanization and industrial engineering into a much wider array of service transactions than was hitherto possible. Service jobs once characterized by variety and personal relationships between employees and customers have been transformed into routinized jobs featuring impersonal customer relations, sales quotas, and continuous electronic monitoring of workers. Second, the decoupling of service jobs from local service markets has left the jobs of low-wage service workers much less secure. Call centers represent the consummate "disposable workplace": call volumes to one center can be redirected at a flick of a switch, making call center workers potentially more vulnerable to plant closings than manufacturing workers. The competition for jobs between call center workers in New York and those in Phoenix, Ireland, and India puts downward pressure on wages and makes union organizing much more difficult. Third, call center technology helps create dead-end jobs by facilitating the relocation and outsourcing of service work to remote areas. For example, a bank teller with a high school education could once enjoy a good job, security, and promotion opportunities, but entry-level banking jobs are increasingly call center jobs, separated geographically from internal promotion opportunities.

Call center jobs, however, do not have to be low-wage, dead-end jobs. In this chapter, we argue that the quality of jobs and mobility opportunities depends importantly on managerial choice and union presence. Union representation in call centers is rare except in traditionally unionized service industries such as telecommunications and airlines.

We first provide the conceptual framework for our study and analyze how and why changes have occurred in labor markets for customer service and sales workers. We then draw on qualitative case material at the workplace and organizational levels to analyze how call center management practices vary in unionized and non-unionized primary sector firms (in telecommunications and financial services) and at subcontractors offering call center services to firms in these sectors. To further assess the importance of management practices, we move to the individual level of analysis and utilize quantitative data from the "best-case" unionized telecommunications company to demonstrate how variation in management practices influences the quality of jobs, attitudinal outcomes, and perceptions of mobility among workers. The chapter ends with conclusions and policy implications.

LABOR MARKET TRENDS FOR CALL
CENTER WORKERS

We define the quality of jobs along four dimensions. Better jobs use technology as a complement to rather than a substitute for labor, feature more investment in skills and training, offer greater opportunities for discretion and collaboration with coworkers, and offer relatively high pay and employment security. The quality of call center jobs depends on management strategies, which are shaped by the interplay of several factors, including new technologies, product market regulation and deregulation, and union institutions. Together these factors influence, but do not determine, managerial choices. We distinguish here between call center strategies that have become widespread—where there is evidence of a fairly clear trend or pattern—and those whose net effect in light of countervailing forces is as yet unclear.

Among the most prominent of trends affecting call center workers is center differentiation—by function, product, or customer segment. The availability of call center technology has allowed firms to consolidate local service functions into large remote centers dedicated to a particular purpose. They have essentially created white-collar factories that produce a specialized product. Examples of functional differentiation include the separation of "outbound" centers that manage direct-dial telemarketing from "inbound" centers that handle customer inquiries. Telecommunications companies have created separate centers for telephone operators, repair, dispatch, customer billing and sales, and collections. Banks have differentiated centers by product: credit cards, retail banking, mortgages, insurance. Companies have also used call center technology to create centers dedicated to distinct customer segments—for example, residential customers, small businesses, and tiers of medium, large, and global businesses.

The separation of work into distinct centers by function or segment also allows firms to adopt different business strategies and employment models for each center. At the low end, for example, firms may compete entirely on the basis of price, maximizing volume and minimizing costs. To do so firms apply industrial engineering principles to service interactions, mechanizing and automating where possible; they use Taylorist principles to create a detailed division of labor and time and motion studies to standardize work processes. In addition, because customers introduce uncertainty into the service production function, employers establish behavioral routines (Leidner 1993), such as scripting, to further standardize customer-worker interactions. When employers design jobs to minimize skills, discretion, and job cycle time, they also typically create incentives built on fear of job loss or on piece-rate pay systems (commission pay in service and sales centers). Classic examples of this type of call center management include telephone operator and telemarketing centers. A typical telephone operator handles one thousand calls per day and has a job cycle time of twenty-one seconds—one-third of the job cycle time of an auto assembly worker. The typical telemarketing rep handles hundreds of calls per day.

At the opposite extreme are business and employment models that compete on quality service and customization. Referred to in the literature as customer relationship management (Gutek 1995), this approach draws on the logic of professional service providers. Firms that offer high-quality service and customization can compete on the basis of customer loyalty, and loyal customers tend to buy more and to buy higher value-added products (Heskett, Sasser, and Schlesinger 1997; Reichheld 1996). The logical employment model to achieve this business strategy includes the use of technology as a complement to labor, the hiring of employees with relatively high levels of formal education, and investment in firm-specific skills. Managers design work to provide opportunities for independent decisionmaking and collaboration with colleagues, and they reward employees with high relative pay and employment security.

This type of organizational restructuring is well developed in the telecommunications industry and has led to greater labor market and wage inequality by customer segment within the occupational group (Batt 2001).[2] For example, a 1998 national survey found that median annual base pay was $19,382 for telephone operators, $27,281 for residential service representatives, $34,786 for small-business representatives, and $61,603 for large-business representatives. Other characteristics that varied significantly by customer segment served included skill levels and investment in training, discretion and use of teams, use of part-time and contingent workers, and percentage of the workforce that was female (Batt 2000). Other industries use similar segmentation strategies. In financial services, for example, banks and brokerage firms provide differentiated levels of service, directing the bulk of calls to mass-market, high-volume centers with standardized approaches and reserving relationship-management strategies and low-volume service for an elite stratum of high-revenue customers (Hunter 1999).

Organizational restructuring by function, product, or customer segment leads to labor market segmentation. This segmenting in turn raises questions about career mobility, which we define to include horizontal and vertical mobility inside organizations as well as external opportunities. Segmentation matters especially when workers in low-end jobs cannot make their way into high-end jobs—when routes to advancement inside organizations are foreclosed. Barriers to such kinds of movement include locating low-end call centers far from other job opportunities, outsourcing centers altogether, or requiring a college education as a prerequisite for jobs in higher market segments. There are incentives to make the kinds of decisions that create such barriers, but not all firms do so: approaches vary across and even within the firms in our study.

In the telecommunications industry, unions in the former Bell System affiliates have had limited influence on these market segmentation and organizational restructuring strategies. However, the dominant union representing call center workers, the Communications Workers of America (CWA), has negotiated substantial wage increases for the call center workforce and insisted on a relatively compressed wage structure across customer segments. Unionized customer service and sales workers enjoy a 20 percent wage premium over their non-unionized counterparts in addition to comprehensive benefits (Batt 2001). Workers also gain access to better jobs through job posting and bidding by seniority and through company-paid tuition programs. In some companies, such as Verizon, the union has succeeded in negotiating a no-layoff clause and a clause prohibiting the outsourcing of call center work.

CONTESTED TERRAIN

There is also considerable opportunity for managerial choice within each product or customer segment, particularly among call centers that serve the mass market of consumers and small-business enterprises (Batt 2001; Hunter et al. 2001). Many firms in the mass market have hedged or even oscillated between strategies, seeking to minimize costs while also providing a level of service quality and customization that will not drive away business. It is here that the contested terrain of business strategy and management practices is likely to shape the quality of jobs and mobility opportunities for most call center workers. In the remainder of this section, we examine the market and technological changes that are driving price competition, then analyze the forces creating incentives to compete on customization and quality.

Sources of Low-Quality Jobs   Advances in information technologies, globalization, and the deregulation of service industries such as banking, telecommunications, and airlines have created unrelenting incentives to mechanize, automate, and outsource work. First, on-going advances in call distribution systems have made it possible for call centers to cover larger and larger geographic territories. Telecommunications companies—unionized and non-unionized alike—have consolidated local service bureaus into large megacenters, and banks have shifted work done in branch offices to call centers. The deregulation of both industries has facilitated this process. For example, falling long-distance telephone rates made 1–800 call centers at a national or international level more economically feasible. New entrants to the telecommunications industry were unconstrained by unions or by state public service commissions (PSCs) regarding where they located new operations. In financial services, deregulation has sparked consolidation within commercial banking and across industry subsectors, making possible further economies of scale. The centers themselves can be quite large: great scale economies may be achieved in call centers with several hundred employees or more, but only through high levels of mechanization and standardized work rules, which typically create greater alienation, absenteeism, and turnover.

Second, call distribution systems facilitate the fragmentation of jobs. With more primitive technology, or in face-to-face service encounters, service workers handled a wide range of inquiries: in telecommunications they handled orders, transfers, billing, and repairs; in banking they dealt with multiple financial products. Today "skill-based routing systems" can be programmed to send calls, by function, to specific groups of workers defined by firm-specific skill sets (for example, those handling a special promotion). Job fragmentation makes it easier to standardize work processes and to shift information processing from workers to software systems. The greater functional division of labor also tends to reduce the skill requirements of jobs: less knowledge of IT systems, narrower substantive or product knowledge, and less diverse social interaction skills are required of service workers.

Third, with the automation of call distribution systems, workers, who once controlled the pace of answering calls, now automatically receive a call as soon as the last call ends. This automation creates an assembly line of calls and shifts control over the pace of work from the worker to the IT system. Supervisors discourage employees from asking questions or interacting with coworkers because these activities are considered a waste of time. The fragmentation of work coupled with the automation of calls has led to reductions in job cycle time (the average time a worker spends with a customer). The reduction in job cycle time increases the number of customers handled per employee per day—the typical performance metric that call center managers use to estimate labor efficiency. Higher call handling loads make work more routine and customer interactions more difficult. Customers facing standardized call menus or long waiting times are more likely to lash out at workers, who must in turn absorb this wrath politely. This type of "emotional labor," however, is not typically valued as a "skill" and hence is not remunerated.

Fourth, the availability of electronic performance monitoring creates more onerous working conditions by exposing employees to constant monitoring and discipline. A series of careful studies at the University of Michigan have shown that the intensity of electronic monitoring is significantly related to higher levels of work-related stress and depression (Carayon 1993). Nevertheless, firms use electronic monitoring as a substitute for indirect labor. The systems provide ongoing data to enforce adherence to rules by recording both the content of customer-employee interactions and the time employees spend in each type of work activity: for example, on-line open to receive a customer, on-line with a customer, on hold with a customer (checking information, for example, or completing an order), or closed (completing paperwork, going to the restroom, going to lunch). Company-developed algorithms provide targets as to the amount of time allowable in each type of activity, and managers at a central control panel watch for flashing lights (green, blue, red, and so forth) that indicate whether employees have gone beyond the allotted time in any one area. Supervisors may counsel or discipline employees who are working at variance from the targeted time allotments (known as "out of adherence"). The newest monitoring technologies can track employees' keystrokes, mouse clicks, and screen navigation as well as voice interactions, enabling supervisors to re-create interactions exactly without real-time listening.

Fifth, the shift from local to remote centers has put downward pressure on wages. Jobs once clearly located within the telecommunications or banking industry, for example, now function as call center jobs in a distinct industrial sector, albeit one that is nearly impossible to identify from national labor market or productivity statistics. This sector is detached from the higher-skilled technical and professional jobs in the primary-sector industry. In telecommunications and banking, for example, historically firms have come under pressure to maintain internal equity between the lower-wage, predominantly female jobs of telephone operators or bank tellers and the higher-wage technical or professional jobs traditionally held by males. In telecommunications the unions in particular used their bargaining leverage to equalize pay; in banking "employer-of-choice" initiatives with attractive benefits packages extended far down the job ladder.

Increasingly, however, comparison groups for call center workers in primary-sector firms are low-wage call center workers in nonunionized or outsourced locations. Call center workers today are exposed to national and increasingly global competition. As borders have become more permeable and the cost of telecommunications has fallen, U.S. workers compete against call center workers in Ireland, South Africa, or India—countries with attractively lower wage rates.

Finally, the shift to remote centers with mechanized operations has also eroded the employment security of service and sales workers. Call distribution systems make it possible to shift work from one center to another in an instant. The ease with which equipment can be packed up and moved makes call centers potentially more vulnerable to plant closings than manufacturing plants. These low fixed costs also make union organizing particularly difficult. In recent failed union drives at Sprint's "La Conexion" call center in San Francisco (Frost and Campbell 1997) and Amazon.com's call center in Seattle, both companies simply closed their centers without adverse repercussions. Thus, at a time when successful union organizing among some service occupations has increased, organizing efforts in call centers are much more unlikely to succeed.

Incentives for Higher-Quality Jobs   In contrast to the changes in market institutions and technologies that facilitate price competition, other changes create opportunities for better jobs. First, the shift from local to remote service puts a greater premium on abstract or cognitive skills that require more formal education. For example, a telephone operator in the past could rely on her local knowledge of businesses and institutions to find telephone numbers quickly; in a remote center she must rely heavily on the computer database to figure out matches between the local name for a business and the official or corporate listing, which frequently differ. Similarly, in bank branches and telephone service bureaus, workers could rely on personal networks and tacit knowledge to answer customer inquiries. In remote centers, by contrast, workers must know how to access information from a complex system whose designers invariably fail to engineer answers to the full range of idiosyncratic customer inquiries.

Second, technological change creates incentives for firms to compete on the basis of product and service innovation. To the extent that firms choose this route, the skill requirements of their call center jobs are relatively higher. Workers need more product knowledge, because new products often involve more complex features, and with rapid innovation they must also be constantly learning new information about products. To be capable of handling product options that are more complex, varied, and subject to change, workers have to make more sophisticated use of information databases and order processing systems. For example, automating the orders for complex products or services typically lags behind their introduction; the call center workers must therefore know how to process the order and learn new routines each time a new product comes on-line. More complex products and services, in turn, require that workers have a broader range of social interaction skills—the ability to interpret, to persuade, and to negotiate with customers. Marketing innovations in themselves may have an independent effect on job complexity. To the extent that firms use marketing strategies to compete, ongoing changes in packaging and pricing, even of the same products, lead to ongoing changes in the information that call center employees must learn and manipulate. Competition on the basis of service also provides a force that in part mitigates the trend toward megacenters: managers may be less interested in large, impersonal factories where greater alienation results in relatively poor levels of service.

New Internet technologies are a third influence on the quality of jobs. In the mid-1990s most analysts assumed that the Internet would be a substitute for call center workers as self-service, Internet-based commerce and banking reduced the demand for labor. However, most industry analysts now view the Internet as a complement to labor, because the majority of customers cannot complete their transactions online. The Internet has therefore increased the demand for call center workers, and the call center industry is experimenting with "multichannel" contact centers that allow customers to use fax, e-mail, web, and telephone connections to make transactions. The more complex and varied jobs in multichannel centers are less vulnerable to machine-pacing and electronic monitoring and should command higher pay.

The deregulation of service industries has also introduced a fourth set of complexities. Deregulation has led firms to shift their focus from service to sales, in turn putting a greater premium on customer interaction skills. Deregulation has led to a collapse of industry segment boundaries as well. In financial services, for example, firms compete to sell products across categories: some customers carrying large credit card balances are excellent candidates for home equity loans, while customers with retail banking deposits are candidates for investment products. Pressure to "cross-sell" requires workers to be familiar with a wider array of product features. A parallel process in telecommunications is the attempt to shift to service bundling—one firm offering local, long-distance, wireless, and Internet services. Firms vary considerably in the extent to which they choose to fragment or bundle the provision of customer service and sales for these products. To the extent that firms provide integrated service and sales for more products, the complexity of call center jobs increases along the three dimensions we have discussed. The interactive effect of deregulation coupled with the use of remote call centers also has increased the complexity of some jobs because regulations vary from state to state and product to product. In call centers that handle customers across several states, workers need to know several sets of regulations and their impact on the company's products and services.

As discussed earlier, union institutions also play an important role in shaping managerial choices, and in turn the quality of jobs and mobility opportunities. The threat of unionization has managers' attention in low-end centers across the industry; while call center capital is mobile, moving is inconvenient enough that vulnerability to organizing campaigns can influence human resource practices and wage policies (as well as call center location decisions) at the margins. Although most call centers are not unionized, unions represent 33 percent of call center workers in the telecommunications industry, where union workers enjoy a 23 percent wage premium, according to 2001 CPS data. Beyond compensation, other management practices also vary significantly by union status. For example, a 1998 comparison of unionized and non-unionized call centers serving residential customers showed that unionized centers made significantly greater investments in skills and training, made less use of contingent and part-time work, offered greater employment security, and had lower quit rates.[3]

The CWA has also negotiated contract provisions that limit managerial prerogative in such areas as electronic monitoring, discipline for failure to meet performance standards, "adherence to schedules," forced overtime, and outsourcing and subcontracting. Model contract language on electronic monitoring, for example, effectively bans secret call sampling, restricts the number of times per month that employee calls can be sampled, limits sampling of calls to employees who are not meeting performance objectives, and pushes companies to use monitoring primarily for developmental rather than disciplinary purposes. Joint union-management committees designed to address stress, health and safety, or performance measures are functioning at Verizon, BellSouth, and the SBC companies of Southwestern Bell, Pacific Bell, Ameritech, and SNET. Forced overtime became a key issue in 1998 and 2001 bargaining, and the unions gained contract language restricting (but not eliminating) its use at Verizon, SBC, Ameritech, BellSouth, and GTE-Southwest. In 2001 the CWA also won "closed time" provisions at these companies, guaranteeing employees thirty minutes of time off-line each day for work-related tasks such as following up on customer orders or reading e-mail (Keefe and Batt 2002).

The CWA has also used its political leverage before state and federal regulators to force former Bell affiliates to provide better service quality—for example, by requiring minimum staffing levels in call centers. The union's strategy increasingly has been to link quality service to quality jobs. In addition, it has organized thousands of new call center workers into the union by winning card check and neutrality clauses with the former Bell affiliates in exchange for supporting their corporate merger activity before regulators (Katz, Batt, and Keefe 2003).

In sum, there is evidence that the rise of call centers is associated with a decline in the quality of jobs and mobility opportunities for a large segment of service workers; while unions improve call center wages and working conditions, the mobility of call centers seriously undermines the potential for unionization. At the same time ongoing advances in information technologies and changing market institutions are influencing the direction of call center management in contradictory ways, and as a result, future labor market outcomes are unclear.

VARIATION IN JOBS AND MOBILITY ACROSS FIRMS

To develop a more detailed analysis of how jobs and mobility opportunities vary across distinct organizational setups, we focused on four firms with multiple call centers—two firms in the primary sector and two subcontractors.[4] Management practices and employment outcomes vary in important ways within and across these firms. The two primary-sector firms in this study are a non-unionized financial services firm and a unionized telecommunications firm, both of which draw on some of the same regional labor markets and have historically offered good jobs with well-developed internal labor markets. Both firms have restructured service and sales operations along the lines described earlier, with dedicated call centers. The centers are organized by product market in financial services (retail banking, credit cards, home mortgages, auto financing) and by function and customer segment in telecommunications (operator services, collections, residential service and sales, small-business service and sales, and large-business customer service).

The two subcontractors in the study provide services to firms in many industries, including financial services and telecommunications. The teleservices firm was formed in 1997 to provide telemarketing sales; by 2001 it had grown to manage twenty-two telemarketing centers employing nearly five thousand workers. It competes on price and takes a classic mass-production approach to organizing work. The second subcontractor is a professional services firm that organized its first call centers in 1996 to handle human resource benefits administration for the employees of large companies. By 2001 it operated four call centers employing fifteen hundred workers. In keeping with its traditional professional culture, it has adopted a quasi-professional model of call center organization.

In each of the four firms we visited multiple call centers, interviewing workers, supervisors, and upper-level managers and observing work. We eventually interviewed or conducted focus groups with nearly two hundred fifty workers and managers in eighteen sites. To provide a framework for analysis of the data we collected on these site visits, we have categorized the quality and mobility of call center jobs along three dimensions—low, medium, and high—as depicted in figure 8.1. Job quality is affected by managers' approaches to market segmentation, the extent to which they separate activities by function, their deployment of mechanization, and union presence. Mobility opportunities, which can link together jobs of varying quality, are also shaped by managerial decisions: outsourcing, segmentation, and co-location of activities. Unionization can affect these opportunities as well. Table 8.1 provides additional details regarding the differences in jobs and mobility opportunities within and across these firms.

THE QUALITY OF JOBS

The skill requirements of call center jobs depend on the product or customer segment served as well as the degree of functional fragmentation: whether firms define the job as providing a service, engaging in sales, or both. We identified three types of skills required for call center jobs: computer-related, social interaction, and product or service knowledge. Computer-related skills include knowledge of general applications (such as word processing), ability to use firm-specific databases and systems, and the ability to "navigate" efficiently between and among screens and databases to pull records, enter data, and the like. For example, the telecommunications firm continues to rely on an old AT&T legacy system that requires knowledge of codes and processes that more current technology would not. The bank, similarly, has historically employed a

Figure 8.1 Job Quality and Internal Mobility Opportunities at the Four Firms

Internal Mobility Opportunities

Job Quality	Low	Moderate	High
Low	Teleservices subcontractor: • Telemarketing sales	Telecom: • Telephone operator service Financial services: • Mass-market credit card service • Mass-market retail banking service	
Moderate		Financial services: • Segmented credit card service and sales • Segmented retail banking service	Financial services: • Mortgages • Auto financing Telecom: • Collections • Residential service and sales • Small-business service and sales
High	HR benefits subcontractor: • Customer service jobs		Telecom: • Large-business customer service

Source: Authors' compilation.

host of systems and screens supporting different products, services, and functions, and while recent innovations have reduced the clumsiness of some of these interfaces, navigation skills remain important. The HR benefits administrator has developed a user-friendly system that nonetheless allows employees access to a rich database of customer information.

Social interaction skills include the ability to "read" the customer

(*Text continues on p. 288.*)

Table 8.1 Variation in Jobs and Mobility Across the Four Firms

	Teleservices	HR Benefits Administration	Retail Financial Services	Telecommunications
Job type	Telemarketing: sales; simple inbound service	Customer service	Retail banking: service Credit cards: segmented service and sales Mortgage: service Auto financing: segmented service and sales	Operators: service Residential: service and sales Small-business: service and sales Large-business: service
IT and work design				
IT: machine-paced calls	Yes	No	Retail banking: 100% Credit card, auto financing: 100% in service, 0% in sales Mortgage: 100%	Operators: 100% Residential: 100% Large-business: 0%
IT: electronic monitoring	Yes	No	Yes	Operators: 100% Residential: 100% Large-business: 0%
Customers per employee per day	In the hundreds; depends on amount of time clocked in	25	Retail banking, credit card: 200 Mortgage: 100 Auto financing: 75	Operators: 1,000 Residential: 75 Large-business: 20

Script use	High: mandatory	None	Short mandatory scripts in retail and credit card services; moderate, based on regulatory requirements in all segments	Moderate, based on regulatory requirements
Team organization	No	Yes: high levels of on-line and off-line teams	No on-line or off-line teams; some use of ad-hoc task forces; workers grouped in "teams" for incentive purposes	No on-line teams; some use of off-line teams
Compensation				
Pay range	Low: minimum wage	Moderate: $28,000 to $33,000	Moderate: $20,000 to $40,000	High: $30,000 to $50,000
Benefits	None or low	Moderate	Moderately high ("employer of choice")	High
Variable pay	Modest sales commissions	None	Modest sales commissions in some segments	Sales incentives
Skills and training				
Formal education	Low: diploma not required	High: 50% have college degrees	Moderate: diploma required; some have college; college sought and preferred in all segments	Moderate: diploma required; some have some college
Initial training	Low: two weeks or less	High: six weeks	Moderate: two to four weeks	High: twelve to sixteen weeks

(*Table continues on p. 286.*)

Table 8.1 *Continued*

	Teleservices	HR Benefits Administration	Retail Financial Services	Telecommunications
Ongoing training	None	Low to none	Moderate: extensive programs, not always accessible	Low
Employment security				
Company tenure	Low	Low	Moderate	High; union presence
Use of contingent, part-time staffing	Nearly all workers are formally "part-time"	Low to none	Low use of contingents; some part-time with benefits	Low to none
Outsourcing	NA	NA	Outsources outbound and some inbound sales (telemarketing); not customer service	Outsources outbound telemarketing; not customer service
Mobility				
Turnover	High: up to 400%	Moderate: 30%	Moderate to high: 30 to 100% by location	Low: less than 10%
Internal: job steps within call center	Entry-level; supervisor or trainer	Entry-level; specialized jobs; supervisor	Entry-level; sales specialists; supervisor or trainer; high-level staff	Entry-level; ad-hoc specialists; supervisor or trainer

Internal: job opportunities in higher segments or departments	None	Almost none	Moderate: line banking and staff jobs in other functions; computer-technical; college strongly preferred	Operators: modest; other segments: high; service, sales, technical: college degree for account executives, management
External advancement opportunities	Low; no marketable skills attained	Moderate; college-educated use this as stepping-stone to better employment	Low for retail and credit card; moderate for other segments; experience with bank is valuable	Moderate because most alternatives do not pay as much, even for somewhat higher-skilled jobs

Source: Authors' compilation.

and communicate information using only verbal cues and inferences. These skills vary in complexity, from giving information and
listening to customers to persuading and negotiating with customers, to calming irate customers. When sales rather than just
service is a part of the job, the mix of social skills becomes more
complex, and the ability to negotiate and persuade becomes more
critical for success. Product knowledge includes the product or service features, the range of offerings, the ways in which products
and services "go together" (bundling), rates, special promotions,
and, if applicable, the regulatory environment. If firms compete on
the basis of product innovation or marketing promotions, then
these strategies introduce further complexity (ongoing change) into
the product knowledge requirements of these jobs.

In sum, firms have considerable latitude in how narrowly or
broadly they define a product or customer segment to be served by
a given call center and whether to define the job to include service,
sales, or both. They also choose how to design their information
systems, how much to rely on off-the-shelf versus firm-specific
computer programs, and the extent of automation and electronic
monitoring. The interaction of the firm's multiple decisions therefore shapes the complexity of call center jobs.

Jobs with the lowest level of skill requirements and complexity
and the highest levels of routinization and electronic monitoring
are in telemarketing sales and telephone operator services. However, these jobs differ significantly along other dimensions of job
quality, primarily owing to the effects of unionization in the latter
case. The telemarketing subcontractor does not require a high school
diploma, though it does employ college students and even some
college graduates, since it is willing to offer jobs to workers with
spotty work histories. The firm provides less than two weeks of
introductory training, uses high levels of part-time and contingent
staffing, pays at or near state-mandated minimum wages, and offers
few or no benefits. Workers are paid only for the time they are
logged on to the computer. Turnover in these lousy jobs reaches
400 percent annually in some local labor markets. In the unionized
telecommunications firm, by contrast, the employer requires a high
school education and provides two to three weeks of initial training, and the union contract provides roughly $30,000 in annual pay
plus a full slate of benefits. Turnover is less than 10 percent. It is
worth noting that typical pay for non-union telephone operators is

less than two-thirds of union pay (Batt 2001), calling into question whether the union model for telephone operators is sustainable.

The financial services firm in our study runs several call centers designed to provide services to the mass retail market. Call centers with identical technology and similar work design (though separated by hundreds of miles) support the firm's credit card products; other centers serve retail banking customers. Entry-level jobs in each of these centers are heavily routinized and monitored electronically; workers must answer and complete calls quickly. Entry-level pay varies with conditions in local labor markets but does not exceed $25,000 annually for full-time workers, even those with college degrees.

The financial services firm also offers call center jobs with moderate levels of complexity and correspondingly higher pay. Such jobs include specialized lines of service in credit card and retail services as well as most call center positions in mortgages and auto financing. Comparable jobs in telecommunications are those in collections services. Jobs in residential and small-business service and sales in telecommunications are somewhat more complex and stressful because they combine service and sales; financial services jobs have very recently begun to incorporate these features as cross-selling becomes more central to the firm's strategy. These jobs have moderate to high levels of automated call distribution and electronic monitoring, and workers handle seventy-five to two hundred calls per day. For these jobs, firms require at least a high school education, but a considerable number of employees have completed some college.

The financial services firm does little outbound sales or telemarketing in-house, subcontracting most of this work to specialist telemarketing firms like the one in our study. One exception is sales work directed specifically at existing customers. Some workers in credit services do outbound customer calling to encourage existing customers to retain or increase their use of the bank's credit card products. These require higher levels of product knowledge and more ability to interact with customers than do entry-level jobs and thus command higher pay. Similarly, the auto financing group has a division that makes outbound calls to customers whose auto leases are near their expiration date; these callers are charged with negotiating with customers and, if possible, convincing them to purchase (with bank financing) the vehicles they have been leasing.

These jobs also pay more than those in inbound servicing in the auto financing area. Inbound representatives and their supervisors argue that the inbound servicing jobs require more knowledge of the intricacies of auto financing and its supporting IT systems; nevertheless, "remarketing" jobs generate revenue for the bank and are therefore paid better.

Differences in financial services and telecommunications jobs clearly reflect the presence of the union. For roughly similar kinds of jobs, the unionized telecommunications firm invests more than twice as much in initial training, pay, and benefits as the financial services firm; turnover rates range from 30 to 100 percent across the financial services call centers but less than 10 percent in telecommunications.

We found the highest levels of job complexity in call centers that serve large-business customers in telecommunications and in the HR benefits subcontractor. Compared to residential and small-business call center workers, those serving large businesses have considerably greater discretion and are less subject to electronic monitoring or machine-pacing, but they have no greater formal education requirement or training. There are informal opportunities to collaborate with other workers, but workers are not organized into explicit team-based structures. This is in contrast to the HR benefits subcontractor, which has developed an explicit, quasi-professional model for call centers. It targets college-educated individuals for recruiting by locating call centers near colleges or in suburban areas, where the labor pool has a greater concentration of college-educated workers. It has designed work so that employees not only handle customer calls but are responsible for maintaining and updating the computer information system. It has adopted an explicit team-based organization of work to foster learning and problem-solving. However, the unionized telecommunications firm pays considerably higher wages ($45,000 to $50,000 compared to $28,000 to $33,000) and benefits and has turnover rates that are less than 10 percent compared to over 30 percent in the HR benefits subcontractor.

Mobility Opportunities

We began our study defining advancement as movement into jobs that improve the pay and/or responsibilities of the worker. Most of the workers we interviewed also saw another form of advancement:

improvements in working conditions by reducing cycle time or increasing the time they spend off the phone. Steffanie Wilk and E. F. Craig (2003) found that the usefulness of mobility for matching workers and jobs depended in part on the relationship between inside and outside mobility, and the characteristics of the worker and the environment. Thus, we examined perceptions of both internal and external mobility opportunities.

The firms we studied offer workers two types of opportunities for internal advancement: those that allow the worker to advance within the call center and those that allow advancement outside the call center but within the organization. In our interviews we also asked workers and managers about potential external advancement opportunities—that is, the role of call center work as a stepping-stone to better employment elsewhere.

The Subcontracting Firms Jobs in the teleservices firm provide few mobility opportunities of any kind. Some supervisors were promoted from within, but others entered as supervisors from outside. There are also few opportunities for internal upward mobility in telemarketing call centers because they run very lean. The supervisor-to-worker ratio on a shift is one to twenty, with the extensive use of part-time workers implying that a worker's probability of being promoted is much lower than twenty to one even if inside candidates are preferred. Subsequent external opportunities are also scant. The firm's minimal hiring standards allow workers with weak or inconsistent work histories to accumulate work experience. This advantage is somewhat offset by the very high burnout and turnover rates; rather than serving as a stepping-stone, a short stint in telemarketing may offer further evidence of an individual's inability to hold a job.

Although the quality of jobs in the HR benefits subcontractor is high, the internal advancement opportunities are low. The better jobs in the consulting firm require a professional degree. The organization is quite flat, with only one layer of team coordinators between frontline workers and the general manager. Recognizing this problem, the company redesigned its organization in 2001 and created a job ladder in which workers could progress from associate to senior associate to team coordinator. In addition, it made more explicit a series of informal steps to promotion for gaining more experience and knowledge in special off-line projects, coaching and training new hires, and starting up new teams (as the company gains new clients). Associates may also switch to quality assurance and process analyst roles in plan management—the function responsible for maintaining and updating the information system.

To date, few workers have moved through these roles. In general, the company has tried to create an opportunity structure, but the internal mobility opportunities are relatively few because the call centers are sharply separated from the company's other main lines of business. In sum, this model provides an example of good jobs but few internal mobility opportunities. External mobility opportunities are stronger. The educational backgrounds of the workers coupled with valuable substantive knowledge in benefits administration provide a stepping-stone to better employment opportunities elsewhere; workers find it relatively easy to leave the call center environment. Steffanie Wilk, Laura Burris Desmarais, and Paul R. Sackett (1995) found that indeed workers will gravitate to jobs that match their abilities. Thus, in the case of employees in the HR benefits subcontractor, their higher skill levels more easily lend themselves to mobility to more complex jobs elsewhere as compared to the lower-skilled workers in the teleservices firm.

The Financial Services Firm   In the financial services firm, entry-level jobs in mass-market call center services offer three typical routes to advancement. First, employees can move up within the call center by acquiring product expertise. Each line of business has jobs that are filled by more skilled or experienced employees. In retail services, for example, each call center has an "escalation" line (for dealing with calls that entry-level reps cannot resolve), a set of call center jobs that handle more complex products, and a specialized line dedicated to wealthy customers. The credit card business features upper-level jobs, including a customer retention group that places outbound calls to encourage customers to retain or increase their use of the bank's credit card products. These better jobs generally offer higher pay than the entry-level positions, though pay is embedded in organizational compensation systems and new positions sometimes emerge more rapidly than the system can accommodate them.

A second opportunity for upward mobility in mass-market segments is provided by supervisory positions. Supervisor positions have clearly higher status and command 30 to 50 percent higher earnings than the best-paid positions on the floor, though these differences appear less substantial when it is noted that most supervisors work significantly more than forty hours a week without overtime pay. Most supervisors in the call centers are promoted from within.

Third, retail and credit card call center jobs also provide points of entry to other jobs in the bank outside of those lines of business or within the line of business outside the call center. A number of employees we interviewed were pursuing various kinds of technical certification (with the help of the bank's tuition programs), hoping to move into IT jobs. Prospects for this kind of advancement are heavily influenced by geography. The bank relocated many of its operations from its Northeast base to a large metropolitan area in the Southeast between 1997 and 2001 and continues to do so. Correspondingly, many of the southeastern call center employees post for (and obtain) jobs in other parts of the bank after one to three years of work in the call center. Employees in the call centers near the headquarters city continue to have opportunities, including those associated with working in the head office, but these have decreased proportionally. In fact, one of these call centers itself closed recently. (Employees were offered opportunities to take jobs in the new southern locations; only a small number accepted such a move.) Employees in call centers in the Southeast do not have the same access to opportunities: while they can see the positions being posted on the bank's system, it is difficult for them to interview for these positions, and jobs do not typically offer enough to motivate employees at these levels to consider relocation.

Jobs in the other lines of business—mortgage and auto financing—resemble more closely second- and third-level jobs at the retail and credit card call centers. Entry-level jobs in these lines of business command higher pay on the internal wage scale, entail more complex customer interactions, and are subject to less direct monitoring and attention to call handling time. These lines of business, however, do not feature similar sets of diverse jobs located within a hierarchy of skills and experience. Rather, call center workers perform jobs that are less differentiated from one another. Supervisors handle escalated or complex calls when necessary, but the representatives are strongly encouraged to acquire the skills to handle these calls. Internal advancement here is typically associated with movement into supervisory positions or to other jobs in the bank.

The Telecommunications Firm   The deregulation of the telecommunications industry and the strong presence of the union have created changes in mobility opportunities in this sector. These changes have had mixed effects on opportunities, and the firm we studied is representative of other former Bell affiliates. Our site visits identified a number of alternative mobility paths. Traditional paths take workers from operator services to mass-market customer service rep jobs, to supervisory positions, or to service rep positions in business markets. For this path, workers typically begin by undertaking a number of informal roles, working on special projects, coaching or training new hires, or assuming the role of acting supervisor for a small hourly pay raise. As a result, supervisors play an important role in facilitating informal opportunities on the job that may ultimately lead to formal promotion opportunities.

A second alternative is to move into technical positions, either as an outside field technician or an inside diagnostic technician. As the network has become fully digitalized, most diagnostic and repair work is done at computers rather than on telephone poles. For women trained as customer service reps to process information in firm-specific computer systems and databases, it is not a far step to use a different set of systems and databases to do diagnostic work on the lines. This promotion away from customer interaction also brings higher pay.

Some national data supports this interpretation. An analysis of establishment data from the Equal Employment Opportunity Commission (EEOC) from 1982 to 1998 found that the proportion of women and minorities in higher-skilled technical, professional, and managerial jobs has increased in the postderegulation world, a trend due perhaps to a disproportionate rate of early retirements by white male employees with higher levels of seniority (Batt and Keefe 1999). In this industry there has been a decline in race and gender occupational segregation.

Union contractual obligations have helped maintain seniority-based promotion ladders in the company we studied, although greater weight is now given to performance and skills. The unions have also helped maintain internal mobility structures by negotiating agreements that limit the outsourcing of work and relocation of centers to other states.

Other factors have eroded internal job ladders. First, office consolidation and reengineering have led to some relocation of centers in this company, although not as much as in many others. Where this has happened, job ladders are short-circuited; where it has not, internal mobility opportunities remain more fully intact. Second, jobs in operator services are less likely to serve as points of entry leading to better jobs. Although some operators continue to take the next step on the traditional ladder to customer service positions, the ladder is not as well traveled as before. Operator jobs have been redefined as data or information processing jobs with little need for social interaction skills. Customer service jobs have in the same period expanded their sales content, increasing the need for social interaction skills. Also, the firm has defined newly created sales jobs serving large-business clients as managerial positions requiring a college degree, which presents a barrier to entry.

On balance, workers in service and sales positions in the call centers of former Bell affiliates probably enjoy a broader set of opportunities than they once did. This is true in part because the strategic importance of customer service and sales operations has increased. While jobs serving the residential mass market are more routinized, employees learn a body of firm-specific knowledge and a set of skills that are highly valued in the company. These include firm-specific knowledge regarding the service order process, the range of departments responsible for fulfilling different functions, and the types of products and bundling of services that are offered. The skills include customer interaction and in some cases negotiating skills and familiarity with computer systems and databases.

In addition, in the 1990s the labor policies pursued by the Bell companies had unintended consequences. Many companies downsized heavily in the early 1990s, only to find a dramatic upswing in demand from the mid-1990s to 2001. Having laid off many of their most experienced workers, the companies scrambled to hire new employees, who quickly found opportunities for higher positions that had been vacated by workers who took early retirement. As a result, in general there were robust opportunities for new workers in the large telecommunications companies until the economic downturn in 2001.

MANAGERIAL STRATEGIES AND CHOICES

Call center jobs, as shown in figure 8.1, vary both in quality and in opportunities for mobility. Job quality follows strongly from the choices that managers make in confronting the product market, particularly how they decide to segment customer groups and services and how they deploy technology to accomplish this segmentation. Managers typically make these choices in response to their strategic goals in serving customers, trading off economies associated with segmentation and standardization against imperatives for customization and service quality. Managers with responsibility for call centers located clearly at neither the high nor the low end are faced with considerable uncertainty about the costs and benefits of these different strategies. Managerial consideration of the connections between job quality and their other goals, however, is often peripheral to these decisions.

Mobility opportunities follow from similar sets of managerial decisions. One benefit of market segmentation and product or service specialization is that these approaches provide opportunities for firms to establish internal job ladders. There is a sort of conundrum here for those interested in both quality and mobility: segmentation both supports ladders and results in the creation of jobs that are more routine, are lower-paid, and demand fewer skills. At any rate, ladders become real only when other managerial decisions also support rather than undermine internal mobility. Segmentation and the associated outsourcing of outbound sales efforts or telephone operators, for example, not only produce jobs of very low quality but also cut off workers in those jobs from both possible internal job ladders and the external opportunities that might arise from experience with primary employers.

Interactions between geography and managers' approaches to segmentation are also influential with respect to mobility. When a firm locates a call center in an area that is geographically isolated from the rest of the organization, internal mobility opportunities decline. In contrast, co-location of other services in the same building or near call centers, or locating call centers in areas near other centers or firm offices, provides more opportunity for workers to advance internally. The range of services offered within call centers and lines of business are also important influences on mobility, since broader ranges result in greater possibilities for segmenting jobs in ways that provide for meaningful advancement.

EFFECTS ON WORKERS

In 2001 we surveyed over five thousand workers and supervisors in five different business lines in the large telecommunications firm described earlier: operator services, collections, residential service, small-business service, and large-business services. Nearly all of the hourly workers in this firm are members of an international union with considerable bargaining power, and the firm serves both high- and low-end market segments. The company therefore provides an example of a best-case scenario for call center jobs and for mobility.[5] In this section we draw on the survey data to illustrate a range of jobs and mobility opportunities, workers' reactions to their experiences, and ways in which managerial strategies and decisions influence these outcomes.

The survey data, beginning with table 8.2, illustrate in more precise detail the important differences in jobs across the lines of business described earlier. Table 8.2 shows that workers in operator services perform highly routinized work. Operators' pay is low relative to other segments inside the firm (but high relative to low-end call center jobs generally, as in the telemarketing or mass-market banking centers described earlier). Workers serving residential and small-business customers earn higher wages and perform less routinized jobs than do operators. Residential representatives take more, shorter calls, and their interactions with those customers are slightly more scripted than those working with small businesses, though they do report having more discretion in dealing with these customers. The highly paid large business representatives perform more complex, less scripted calls and report the lowest levels of emotional exhaustion across the segments. Their relatively low levels of discretion with customers reflect their service roles and the absence of sales responsibilities (split off to a separate, mobile sales force).

Workers' assessments of the complexity of their jobs are consistent with our earlier account: operators' jobs are the least complex, followed by collections representatives. There is no statistically significant difference between the complexity of residential and small-

Table 8.2 The Telecommunications Firm:
Job Quality and Worker Characteristics,
by Market Segment

	Operators	Collections	Residential	Small-Business	Large-Business
Customers per day[a]	1,017	195	57	31	15
Time on phone per customer (seconds)[a]	54	272	452	846	711
Weeks of initial training for job[a]	2.1	5.0	11.6	12.4	6.9
Use of scripts (higher score = less scripting)[b]	1.96	2.71	2.96	3.23	3.54
Discretion with customers (higher score = more discretion)[b]	1.34	3.30	3.50	3.27	2.65
Expectation of layoff (higher = greater chance of being laid off)[b]	2.68	2.53	2.48	2.24	2.66
Emotional exhaustion (higher score = more fatigue)[b]	2.51	2.09	2.26	2.31	1.74
Job complexity (higher score = more complex)	2.85	2.98	3.15	3.13	3.52
Annual base earnings					
Workers	$31,485	$38,180	$41,391	$42,447	$47,440
Supervisors	59,145	59,695	60,701	61,040	57,153
Mean annual bonus					
Workers	2,941	4,840	2,704	3,396	5,410
Supervisors	5,973	6,103	5,856	6,085	7,050

Table 8.2 *Continued*

	Operators	Collections	Residential	Small-Business	Large-Business
Worker charac- teristics[c]					
Female					
Workers	86.0%	80.1%	78.6%	74.7%	80.3%
Supervisors	83.3	84.3	78.1	72.5	71.6
Minority					
Workers	25.7	30.9	43.8	37.5	33.5
Supervisors	23.2	29.6	31.1	28.2	34.3
Mean tenure (years)[d]					
Workers	12.4	9.6	6.7	7.9	13.9
Supervisors	20.0	19.0	14.8	15.2	17.4
Finished college[d]					
Workers	8.4%	17.8%	25.3%	28.7%	23.8%
Supervisors	33.3	23.5	36.2	49.2	22.6
Number of workers	717	198	992	310	220
Number of su- pervisors	108	68	155	64	34

Source: Authors' compilation.
[a] Drawn from mean responses to questions to workers on survey administered 2001. Because these are self-reports they are more useful for making comparisons across lines of business than as point estimates.
[b] Drawn from mean responses to questions on worker survey that make up multiple-item scales (responses range from 1 to 5).
[c] Drawn from company archival records.
[d] Taken from worker survey.

business reps' jobs, and large-business reps' jobs are the most complex.

Table 8.2 also displays characteristics of workers by customer segment served. The vast majority of workers in these call centers are women, and ethnic minority workers are overrepresented in this firm in comparison to the labor force as a whole. Operators are slightly more likely to be female, and slightly less likely to be members of ethnic minority groups, than in other lines of business. Along with large-business representatives, operators have the highest average length of service with the company. Most workers in each of the call centers have not completed their college education.

Earlier we noted that the varying complexities of call center jobs require different sorts of skills. Our survey documented supervisors'

Table 8.3   The Telecommunications Firm: Selected Skill Requirements, by Market Segment

	Operators	Collections	Residential	Small-Business	Large-Business
Social interaction skills					
Listening	6.7	6.9	6.9	6.8	6.7
Persuading	4.3	6.3	6.2	6.3	5.1
Negotiating	4.1	6.7	6.3	6.6	5.3
Computer skills					
Word processing	2.2	3.9	2.5	3.5	4.4
Spreadsheet	1.8	3.5	2.3	3.1	4.5
E-mail	1.5	3.1	2.7	4.4	6.4
Navigating be- tween screens	3.0	6.7	6.9	6.7	5.7
Product knowledge					
Features	4.7	5.5	6.8	6.6	6.1
Rates-pricing	4.7	3.7	6.6	6.4	5.6
Bundling	3.4	5.0	6.6	6.6	5.7
Number of supervisors	108	68	155	64	34

Source: Authors' compilation.
Note: Skill requirements are rated by supervisors on a scale from 1 (not important for the job) to 7 (very important). Ratings taken from 2001 survey of supervisors.

assessments of these requirements by market segment, and table 8.3 displays some of these results. Operators' supervisors clearly assess their jobs as having lower overall skill requirements in the three categories we focused on. The middle-segment jobs—collections, residential service, and small-business—require more social interaction skills and more ability to navigate between the various "screens" and computer systems. Jobs in the large-business segment, in contrast, require more extensive general computer skills (such as word processing and spreadsheets).

In table 8.4 we turn our attention to workers' career patterns and expectations. Operators typically occupy entry-level jobs; over two-thirds of these workers report having held only one position with their employer. Residential services positions are also entry-level positions: here three-quarters of the workers surveyed are in their first position with the employer. Small-business representatives and those performing collections are slightly less likely to have entered the firm in that job and more likely to have advanced to their positions internally. Collections jobs in particular are a haven for expe-

Table 8.4 The Telecommunications Firm: Internal Labor Market Patterns and Perceptions of Opportunity, by Market Segment

	Operators	Collections	Residential	Small-Business	Large-Business
Workers' number of different positions held with this employer	1.5	1.8	1.5	2.0	3.3
Workers who have held only one (current) position with employer	69.9%	63.1%	75.3%	53.8%	24.0%
Supervisors promoted from within	92.5	92.7	94.2	87.1	90.3
Workers' perceptions					
Career satisfaction	2.72[bc]	2.82[bc]	2.99[ac]	3.07[a]	3.19[ab]
Ease of "finding another job that is just as good as this one"	2.07	2.10	2.00[c]	2.15	2.35[b]
Present experience "would help me get a higher-paying job"	2.69[bc]	3.00[a]	3.02[a]	3.04[a]	3.18[a]
"Ease of internal movement"— finding another job inside the organization	2.47	2.53	2.49	2.44	2.69
Number of workers	717	198	992	310	220
Supervisors' expectations					
Likelihood that supervisees will move into better-paying job	3.68	3.75	3.64	3.56	3.70
Likelihood of promotion to management for supervisees	2.85[bc]	3.50[a]	3.47[a]	3.54[a]	3.47[a]

Table 8.4 *Continued*

	Operators	Collections	Residential	Small-Business	Large-Business
Number of supervisors	108	68	155	64	34

Source: Authors' compilation.

Notes: Figures represent mean responses to survey questions. "Career satisfaction" and "ease of internal movement" are summed scales with multiple items, responses ranging from a low of 1 to a high of 5. "Ease of finding another job" and "helpfulness of experience" are single-item responses ranging from a low of 1 to a high of 5. Supervisor expectations are also single-item responses ranging from a low of 1 to a high of 5. For workers' perceptions and supervisors' expectations, we report statistical comparisons of means across three groups. Where there are no indicators, the mean response in that category does not differ significantly from responses in *any* other categories.

[a] Indicates that the mean response for the group differed significantly from the mean response for the operator services group at $p < 0.05$.

[b] Indicates that the mean response for the group differed significantly from the mean response for the residential services group at $p < 0.05$.

[c] Indicates that the mean response for the group differed significantly from the mean response for the large-business group at $p < 0.05$.

rienced workers who did not want to live under the day-to-day pressure of sales quotas and so refused to become sales workers when the residential service bureaus shifted their emphasis from service to sales.

Three out of four large-business representatives have held multiple positions in the company. These positions represent higher rungs on internal job ladders and have been especially important destination jobs for less-educated workers: as table 8.2 shows, the large-business representatives are actually less likely to have finished college than the small-business or residential representatives. This is probably due to the fact that recent hires tend to have more formal education compared to the past, yet small-business and residential jobs continue to serve as entry points. It remains to be seen whether internal opportunities will remain available to less-educated workers. In our survey small-business representatives with a college education perceive significantly greater ease of internal movement (2.78 on a five-point scale) than do those who have not finished college (2.41), though differences by education are salient neither within other segments nor in the sample as a whole.

The survey data also allow us to examine workers' own perceptions of their opportunities and careers. Table 8.4 shows that workers' overall satisfaction with their careers is directly correlated with market segment: it is highest among the large-business representatives, lowest among the operators, with the others between these extremes. Workers' perceptions of their opportunities outside the firm are not as directly correlated with market segment. Here we note that workers across the levels generally do not think they would be likely to find equally good jobs in other firms; they are slightly more confident that their experience would help them find better-paying jobs if they chose to leave. This is further evidence that the union is influential with respect to job quality and that we are indeed examining a "best-case" scenario for call center jobs. With respect to these outside opportunities, operators are less likely than others to believe their experience would be helpful elsewhere, and large-business representatives are the most likely to believe they could find similar jobs.

Table 8.5 suggests that this firm's internal labor market provides opportunities for call center workers across each line of business. There are no differences across the various segments in workers' perceptions of their chances of advancing inside the organization. Rather than giving more advantages to higher-level workers, the internal labor market structure and union contracts enable workers to perceive their chances to advance inside the organization as independent of the segment in which they are working. The supervisors perceive workers' opportunities similarly. In fact, nearly 70 percent of supervisors believe that it is "likely" or "very likely" that the employees they supervise will have the opportunity to move into higher-paying jobs inside the company. Operators' supervisors are less likely to believe that their workers will advance to management jobs, but other than that, there are no differences across the lines of business. Generally, supervisors in all segments find it equally likely for their employees to advance internally.

Tables 8.2 and 8.4 suggest generally that this firm has in the past provided opportunities for workers who have not completed a college education to advance to relatively high-quality jobs. This is not to say that education does not matter; in fact, it is quite important. College education provides a route that enables workers to avoid "promote-from-within" requirements. For example, 31.3 percent of supervisors who were promoted from within the firm had finished college; in contrast, 69.7 percent of the supervisors hired from outside the firm had college degrees. Table 8.5 further illustrates how education provides access to jobs and advancement as a substitute for experience with the firm. In each market segment better-educated workers have held fewer total positions with the employer and have been with the organization for less time. This is consistent

Table 8.5 The Telecommunications Firm: Education and Internal Labor Markets

	Operators	Collections	Residential	Small-Business	Large-Business
Number of different positions held with this employer					
Finished high school or less	1.5	2.3	1.9	2.5	3.8
Some post–high school education but no college degree	1.5	1.7	1.5	2.0	3.6
College graduate	1.5	1.6	1.3	1.6	2.4
Tenure in years with this employer					
Finished high school or less	15.2	9.9	10.0	11.3	13.9
Some post–high school education but no college degree	9.3	7.1	6.1	7.6	9.3
College graduate	8.9	7.5	4.8	5.2	9.7
Number of workers	717	198	992	310	220

Source: Authors' compilation.

with observations from the case studies: newer workers are more likely to be screened for college education; education helps workers move through levels internally more quickly; and it also enables them to skip through typical entry-point jobs entirely.

Job ladders are not specified explicitly either within or across market segments. Our survey asked supervisors, in open-ended questions, to describe two "likely promotion sequences" for entry-level workers. Supervisors' answers to these questions ranged across dozens of job titles and positions. The most frequently mentioned sequences focused on advancement to team leadership or supervisory positions, followed by promotion to managerial jobs inside the call centers (perhaps because supervisors are themselves most familiar with these paths). Many supervisors listed "special projects," "acting" positions, and training jobs as intermediate steps on the way to such higher-level jobs (and as we see in table 8.4, 90

Table 8.6 The Telecommunications Firm: Geography and Internal Labor Markets

Number of Different Kinds of Company Offices Located "in This Building or Office Complex"	Share of Workers	Mean Number of Different Positions Held with Employer	Mean Number of Different Positions Held with Employer: Women Only	Mean Tenure with Organization in Years	Perceived Ease of Internal Movement
One	21%	1.38	1.39	7.4	2.41
Two	28	1.60	1.64	9.0	2.56
Three or more	51	1.89	1.98	9.8	2.43

Source: Authors' compilation.

percent of the supervisors we surveyed were promoted to their jobs from within the company). But the supervisors also mentioned many other jobs and sequences that move workers both within and outside their current lines of business. This is true even of operators' supervisors, though our interviews suggested that operators are finding it increasingly difficult to move into other kinds of services.

Decisions around the geographic locations of call centers affect workers' ability to move through these different kinds of jobs. Workers do not often find new call center jobs worth relocating for, and so colocation of multiple opportunities is particularly important. Table 8.6 illustrates this by comparing the number of positions held by workers in centers that have different levels of co-location. Our survey asked supervisors to identify the different kinds of offices located in the same building or office complex as the call center in which they worked. Consistent with the strong relationship between geography and internal advancement and retention of workers that we suggested earlier, we found that workers in call centers with more co-located offices have held more jobs and have been with this employer longer. This relationship is slightly stronger for women, suggesting that co-location might be especially important to workers who are more likely to be balancing responsibilities at work and home.

We note that there is little evidence that workers actually put the effects of geography on their mobility into perspective. Table 8.6

shows that workers' perceived ease of movement to other internal jobs is not affected by geographic co-location. This lack of salience helps to explain why managers do not put more emphasis on co-location in siting decisions. Although there are some benefits to managers in locating new centers near existing centers in order to establish internal job ladders that would give advantages to the existing local workforce, such benefits are reduced to the extent that workers do not perceive advantages from these decisions. Such managerial decisions must also be weighed against the costs of increasing internal transfers and turbulence, as well as against any other advantages that might accrue from establishing centers in more remote sites.

CONCLUSIONS AND POLICY IMPLICATIONS

Jobs in customer service have been fundamentally transformed by the availability of advanced information systems, the application of industrial engineering models to service activities, and new business and marketing strategies. Our evidence suggests that there is considerable managerial choice in the design of call centers and, as a result, variation in the content of jobs and mobility opportunities for call center workers.

On the one hand, mass-production models have been successfully applied to jobs such as those in operator services and outbound telemarketing. These "lousy jobs" in the new economy are typically characterized by bad pay and high turnover except where unions are present. There are large obstacles to unionization, however, owing to the technological ease of closing centers and moving work. At the other end of the spectrum are good jobs for service and sales workers who serve business customers. Our case studies show that these jobs command relatively high pay and are designed to allow workers considerable discretion and ability to collaborate and learn on the job through peers. The profitability associated with serving business customers, combined with these customers' insistence on high levels of service, encourages companies to compete in these markets by focusing on quality customer service and long-term relationship management.

Between the transactional and business-oriented jobs are the bulk of call center jobs, which employ workers who serve the mass market. It is for these jobs that managerial choice matters most, because here firms can decide to pursue a cost- or customer-driven focus. Although product complexity matters, it is clear from our case studies that firms can either choose to accept the complexity of the product and design quality jobs to fit that complexity, or they can reduce complexity by fragmenting the delivery of service and thereby reduce the skill content of jobs.

In these settings, unions have maintained high relative wages, benefits, and employment security; they have limited the use of contingent and part-time work and prevented the outsourcing of jobs. They have had little success in limiting the rationalization of work, although they have negotiated constraints on the more onerous practices, such as electronic monitoring. As a result, customer service jobs in unionized firms resemble their mass-production counterparts in manufacturing: workers accept high relative pay, job security, and benefits in exchange for repetitive jobs and onerous working conditions. The difference from manufacturing is that most of these call center jobs involve a contradictory mix of factors: on the one hand, machine-pacing and routinization, pressure to sell, and exposure to ongoing electronic monitoring; on the other hand, the requirement of a fairly broad and deep array of social, emotional, and cognitive skills.

Mobility opportunities for call center workers have also changed, but not in ways that are entirely predictable. Our best-case telecommunications company provides insight into how new forms of internal stratification have given rise to a new kind of internal labor market. In the past vertical mobility tended to occur within gender-segregated occupational families, with operator and clerical jobs viewed as entry-level positions that could lead to higher-paid customer service and sales or supervisory positions. There is some evidence that gender segregation is eroding, not only because of the successful EEOC case against the AT&T system in the 1970s but also because of the transformation of work in recent years. Customer service and sales workers learn firm-specific skills in product knowledge, information systems, and social interaction skills, and these are viewed as valuable and transferable to other technical and higher-paid sales jobs in the companies.

One surprising conclusion from our telecommunications case is that market segment does not represent fate for these workers. The nature of jobs varies systematically across segments, and these call centers are not formally linked together in a coherent internal labor market in which workers can expect to work their way from one segment up to another. But the extent to which workers perceive differences in internal mobility opportunities does not vary nearly as systematically by segment. Operators, for example, are no less likely than workers in other segments to expect future job opportunities. This scenario, however, depends importantly on corporate decisions to keep work in-house and to locate call centers close to other functions. Most companies, like the financial services firm in this study, do not follow this path. They tend to locate call centers in remote, low-wage areas or to outsource them altogether.

Several policy implications emerge from this study. First, we believe there are relatively few opportunities for labor market policies to shape better call center jobs. One exception is in cities with large concentrations of call centers, such as Phoenix, Albuquerque, Kansas City, Omaha, San Antonio, Jacksonville, Florida, and Hagerstown, Pennsylvania. Where cities view call centers as a promising economic development strategy, it is possible to imagine the creation of public-private partnerships focused on training, employment placement, and multi-employer job ladders. Employers would have incentives to participate in order to reduce the costs of high quit rates. Community colleges could develop curriculum geared toward creating a customer service professional associate's degree. Some cities, such as Los Angeles, are discussing these possibilities.

Second, it is clear that unionization provides a major vehicle through which call center workers enjoy not only higher wages and benefits but also less onerous working conditions and greater mobility opportunities. However, unions currently are limited to a minority of regulated service industries, such as telecommunications, airlines, and utilities. In these industries it is not only unions that have influenced the quality of jobs but federal regulators and state public service commissions as well, by being the guardians of service quality, which translates into better and more stable jobs. In telecommunications, states still require former Bell affiliates to answer calls within twenty seconds, which sets a standard for the industry, and most companies, even new entrants that do not fall under federal and state regulations, more or less follow the standard for competitive reasons. Similarly, unions—and to a lesser extent consumer groups—have used the PSCs to put pressure on companies to maintain quality standards, eliminate high pressure sales tactics that are likely to lead to fraud, maintain adequate staffing levels to meet the twenty-second rule, and keep jobs within their state boundaries. The unions have opposed rate hikes and mergers of telecommunications companies unless they produce better wages, working conditions, and neutrality of companies in union organizing campaigns (Katz, Batt, and Keefe 2003). As we have pointed out, however, unionization rates in call centers are likely to remain low in other industries.

On a more widespread level, it is more likely that the quality of jobs will depend on demand side factors, particularly consumer demand for quality and the ability of firms to develop business models that compete on quality and innovation. One possibility is consumer activism, or consumer-labor coalitions, against bad service. This has begun in the world of telemarketing, where consumers have rebelled against the invasion of their privacy by telemarketers. Twenty states have passed "do not call" legislation, which creates registries of consumers who must be excluded from direct-dial calling. National legislation was pending on this topic in 2002. This type of action may indirectly affect the quality of jobs in several ways. First, with the elimination of unwanted calls, workers are less likely to have to absorb the venom of irate customers. Second, with fewer calls and more opportunities to sell, it is likely to increase call length and reduce the level of tedium in these jobs. Third, it may improve the ratio of completed calls to attempted calls, thereby increasing the revenues per call. Telemarketers who work with sales incentives or earn commission pay may see their compensation rise. Fourth, it may push telemarketing firms to enlarge the scope of their business to include inbound service as well as outbound calls, thereby increasing job complexity and reducing the repetitiveness of customer interactions.

For mass-market centers that provide inbound customer service, there is growing evidence that consumers are fed up with touch-tone self-service menus, fragmented service, long waits, and inadequate information. Although companies typically believe that they need to maintain customer service ratings of over 90 percent in order to keep customers, surveys of call center customers put satisfaction ratings at little more than 50 percent (Purdue University 1999). Given this low level of satisfaction, it is not clear why more companies are not attempting to compete on the basis of quality. It could be that market information is inadequate. For example, whereas most products are rated by consumer organizations on a wide range of features and services, customer service is not. Marketing focuses on price, not, for example, the speed and accuracy of customer service. Thus, it could be that better marketing and consumer information would provide an impetus for companies to develop business models that compete on a broader array of quality indicators.

There is initial evidence, however, that mass customization also provides a better business model. Several studies of call centers have found that performance (measured by absenteeism and quit rates and by sales growth) is significantly higher when companies adopt such practices as more investment in skills and training, work designed with opportunities for discretion and collaboration, and high relative pay and employment security (Batt 1999, 2002; Deery, Iverson, and Walsh 2002). To the extent that financial markets permit and encourage managers to invest in these higher-end business models, it is possible that over the longer term both job quality and mobility opportunities will improve for many call center workers. Should markets and managers continue to focus on lowering short-run costs at the expense of service and job quality, and should consumers and regulators accept these decisions on the other end, the outlook for workers in this industry is less hopeful.

This research was funded by a generous grant from the Russell Sage and Rockefeller Foundations' Future of Work Program. We are grateful for the able research assistance of Lisa Moynihan, Monique Valcour, Jennifer Stevens, Jennifer Folger, Krista Knout, and Sidath Gunawardena.

NOTES

1. Accurate employment data are extremely difficult to find. The Current Population Survey (CPS) does not have a category to capture customer service and sales representatives because it is a mix of order-takers (defined as clerical workers in the CPS) and sales workers, and both of these positions may be based in call centers or in local service bureaus. Datamonitor is an industry consulting firm that has undertaken national surveys and developed a wide range of growth indicators for the industry. It reported that the sale of call center software

grew 21.5 percent annually in the 1990s (Datamonitor 1998). A recent survey by Purdue University (1999) reported annual growth in call center budgets of 18.5 percent in the late 1990s.

2. The resulting labor market segmentation increases variation in job structures and wages within occupational groups and within large primary-sector firms. This segmentation fundamentally differs from prior labor market organizing principles based on firm size, primary-secondary firm location in production chains, core-periphery models based on employment status, or race and gender (see, for example, Doeringer and Piore 1971; Osterman 1988; McCall 2001).

3. Unionized centers in this market segment invested twice as much in initial training as did their non-unionized counterparts (nine weeks versus four on average). In unionized centers it took twice as long to become proficient in the job (six and a half months versus three and a half months), an indication of higher levels of job complexity. There was greater pay compression across customer segments in unionized firms. Individual commission pay (a form of at-risk pay) averaged 7 percent of earnings in unionized centers and 15 percent in non-unionized centers. Benefit costs averaged 34 percent of median pay in unionized centers versus 23 percent in non-unionized centers. Employment security was also higher for union workers, with contingent and part-time workers comprising 9.5 percent of the workforce in unionized centers but 15.1 percent in non-unionized centers. The percentage of work outsourced was 11.8 percent in unionized centers but 21 percent in non-unionized centers. Reported layoffs as a percentage of the current workforce were 8 percent in unionized establishments but 34 percent in non-unionized centers. Quit rates in unionized centers were less than one-half the rates in non-unionized centers.

4. Fieldwork for this portion of the study included site visits to eighteen call centers. For each site visit, we used a forty-page protocol to guide the discussion and gather data on such topics as call center strategy, markets, HR practices (such as training, career paths, and compensation), working conditions, skill requirements, and absenteeism and turnover. Interviews were conducted with the center manager, middle managers, supervisors, and call center workers. Focus groups with employees of varying levels of seniority and skill and job shadowing of workers provided detailed data on the job characteristics and working conditions experienced by call center employees.

5. We administered surveys in 215 different call centers across 5 lines of business and obtained responses from at least 1 worker or supervisor in 202 of those call centers. We had 2,437 usable responses from the 4,381 workers we surveyed, a response rate of 55.6 percent. We

also had 429 completed surveys from the 940 supervisors we surveyed, a response rate of 45.6 percent.

REFERENCES

Batt, Rosemary. 1999. "Work Organization, Technology, and Performance in Customer Service and Sales." *Industrial and Labor Relations Review* 52(4): 539–64.

———. 2000. "Strategic Segmentation and Frontline Services: Matching Customers, Employees, and Human Resource Systems." *International Journal of Human Resource Management* 11(3): 540–61.

———. 2001. "Explaining Intra-occupational Wage Inequality in Telecommunications Services: Customer Segmentation, Human Resource Practices, and Union Decline." *Industrial and Labor Relations Review* 54(2A): 425–49.

———. 2002. "Managing Customer Services: Human Resource Practices, Quit Rates, and Sales Growth." *Academy of Management Journal* 45(3): 587–97.

Batt, Rosemary, and Jeffrey Keefe. 1999. "Human Resource and Employment Practices in Telecommunications Services." In *Employment Practices and Business Strategy,* edited by Peter Cappelli. Oxford: Oxford University Press.

Carayon, Pascale. 1993. "Effect of Electronic Performance Monitoring on Job Design and Worker Stress: Review of the Literature and Conceptual Model." *Human Factors* 35(3): 385–95.

Datamonitor. 1998. *Call Centers in Europe 1996–2001: Vertical Market Opportunities.* London: Datamonitor.

———. 1999. *Opportunities in U.S. and Canadian Call Center Markets.* New York: Datamonitor.

Deery, Stephen, Roderick Iverson, and Janet Walsh. 2002. "Work Relationships in Telephone Call Centers: Understanding Emotional Exhaustion and Employee Withdrawal." *Journal of Management Studies* 39(4): 471–96.

Doeringer, Peter, and Michael Piore. 1971. *Internal Labor Markets and Manpower Analysis.* Lexington, Mass.: D. C. Heath.

Frost, Ann, and Dan Campbell. 1997. "Sprint—La Conexion Familiar (A) and (B)." Case 9-97-C001 and 9-97-C992. London, Ont.: Richard Ivey School of Business, University of Western Ontario.

Gutek, Barbara. 1995. *The Dynamics of Service: Reflections on the Changing Nature of Customer-Provider Interactions.* San Francisco: Jossey-Bass.

Heskett, James L., Earl W. Sasser, and Leonard A. Schlesinger. 1997. *The Service Profit Chain.* New York: Free Press.

Hunter, Larry W. 1999. "Transforming Retail Banking: Inclusion and Segmentation in Service Work." In *Employment Practices and Business Strategy*, edited by Peter Cappelli. Oxford: Oxford University Press.

Hunter, Larry W., Annette Bernhardt, Katharine L. Hughes, and Eva Skuratowicz. 2001. "It's Not Just the ATMs: Firm Strategies, Technology, Jobs, and Earnings in Retail Banking." *Industrial and Labor Relations Review* 54(2A): 402–24.

Katz, Harry, Rosemary Batt, and Jeffrey Keefe. 2003. "The Strategic Initiatives of the CWA: Organizing, Politics, and Collective Bargaining." *Industrial and Labor Relations Review* 56(4): 573–89.

Keefe, Jeffrey, and Rosemary Batt. 2002. "Telecommunications Services: Union-Management Relations in an Era of Industry Re-consolidation." In *Collective Bargaining: Current Developments and Future Challenges,* edited by Paul Clark, John Delaney, and Ann Frost. Madison, Wisc.: Industrial Relations Research Association.

Leidner, Robin. 1993. *Fast Food, Fast Talk: Service Work and the Routinization of Everyday Life.* Berkeley: University of California Press.

McCall, Leslie. 2001. *Complex Inequality.* New York: Russell Sage Foundation.

Osterman, Paul. 1988. *Employment Futures: Reorganization, Dislocation, and Public Policy.* New York: Oxford University Press.

Purdue University. 1999. "Benchmark Study 1999." West Lafayette, Ind.: Center for Customer-Driven Quality, Purdue University.

Reichheld, Frederick F. 1996. *The Loyalty Effect.* Boston: Harvard Business School Press.

Wilk, S. L., and E. F. Craig. 2003. "Should I Stay or Should I Go? Person-Occupation Matching Within and Across Firms." Working paper, Management Department, Wharton School of the University of Pennsylvania.

Wilk, S. L., L. B. Desmarais, and P. R. Sackett. 1995. "Gravitation to Jobs Commensurate with Ability: Longitudinal and Cross-Sectional Tests." *Journal of Applied Psychology* 80: 79–85.

PART IV

Temps: Part of the Solution or Part of the Problem?

CHAPTER 9

A Temporary Route to Advancement? The Career Opportunities for Low-Skilled Workers in Temporary Employment

David Finegold, Alec Levenson, and Mark Van Buren

The rapid growth of the temporary staffing industry in the 1990s has posed a paradox to understanding the labor market for low-skilled workers. During this period, with the U.S. economy operating for several years at greater than what had been considered the rate of "full employment," employee bargaining power and job options increased. Even the lowest-skilled indviduals were able to find jobs, and millions were able to move from welfare into work. During this period one of the most rapidly expanding sectors of employment was temporary staffing. Conventional wisdom views temps as "contingent" workers, implying that the jobs are insecure and marginal and thus not desirable to employees (Polivka 1996). This chapter explores why low-skilled workers entered temporary employment in the 1990s, when other jobs appeared plentiful, and the attendant impacts on their labor market outcomes, including:

- Why do low-skilled workers accept temp jobs? Is a temp job a preferred route or a last resort?

- Does temping enhance labor market outcomes through opportunities to upgrade skills, get promotions and wage increases, and move into a permanent job?

- What factors explain which low-skilled temporary workers advance into higher-skill and higher-paying positions? How do the work settings in which they are placed affect their career outcomes?

317

- How do the experiences of lower-skilled workers in temporary jobs compare with those of lower-skilled permanent employees in similar positions, or those of higher-skilled individuals doing temporary work?

- What strategies do firms use when employing low-skilled temporary workers to remain competitive in their markets? What impact do these strategies have on firm competitiveness and labor market outcomes for low-skilled temporary workers?

In this chapter, we answer these and related questions through three types of analysis. We begin with an overview of trends in temping and the reasons for its growth. We then analyze a unique data set consisting of five years of payroll records for several U.S. temporary agencies that employ hundreds of thousands of individuals. We match these data with a survey of a nationally representative sample of temps at these agencies. We follow up those analyses with detailed case studies of three firms that extensively use temps. These case studies provide both more detail on temps' motivations and experiences and insights into the effects of firms' employment strategies and human resource practices on the skills, careers, and wage mobility of temporary versus permanent employees. Two of the three cases allow us to compare and contrast temps' experiences with those of permanent workers at the same sites.

The results from these multiple data sources suggest that temporary workers are diverse, with a wide range of skills, work experiences, and employment objectives. A high percentage of those who temp for two weeks or more receive some form of labor market benefit: free training, a wage increase, and/or a permanent job. We also identify ways in which temporary staffing firms could enhance the labor market outcomes of lower-skilled workers. Finally, the cases illustrate the importance of the client firm's policies and work environment in determining whether temporary workers experience any upward mobility.

OVERVIEW OF THE TEMPORARY STAFFING INDUSTRY

Temporary jobs traditionally have been concentrated in clerical and lower-skill, low-wage, industrial occupations. A significant shift occurred, however, within temporary employment between 1989 and

1994: white-collar positions (predominantly clerical and adminis-trative) dropped from 58 to 49 percent of total temporary jobs, while blue-collar occupations grew from 30 to 40 percent; the larg-est growth occurred among laborers and electronic assemblers (Bjurman 1995). The concentration in lower-skilled occupations may have begun to change in the 1990s, as U.S. firms moved away from traditional full-time, long-term employment toward the use of more flexible staffing arrangements, including part-time workers, job-sharing, consultants, and independent contractors (Abraham and Taylor 1996; Houseman 2000). Temporary agencies expanded their recruitment of more highly skilled technical, professional, and managerial workers in order to meet new demands (American Staff-ing Association 2001).

One sign of the changing labor market is the difficulty of defin-ing the opposite of a "temporary job." It is not a permanent job: there are few if any of these left in the private sector. Nor is it a full-time job: temps often work forty hours or more per week. It is also often difficult to differentiate temporary employment from out-sourced or contract work: many agencies staff, employ, and manage whole segments of a client's operations (for example, a call center, a factory shop floor, or an office pool). Sometimes the same individ-uals are in the jobs for years, only the employer changes from the client firm to the agency. (One result of the Supreme Court's deci-sion in the Microsoft case, however, is that many firms now insist that the agency dismiss anyone working for a year, to avoid co-employment claims; Prencipe 2001). Despite the definitional issues, we use the temporary-permanent distinction here for lack of a bet-ter alternative.

Wage differentials are a main reason for the concerns raised about the growth of temporary jobs: temp job wages in the period 1983 to 1993 averaged about 22 percent less than permanent job wages. This differential narrows considerably for most temps—falling to as low as 3 percent—when differences in education, experience, industry, and occupation are controlled for (Segal and Sullivan 1997a), and it fully disappears for managerial and professional temps (Economic Policy Institute 1997). Yet these analyses do not control for benefits, which temps rarely receive. Temporary workers are much more likely to be young, female, nonwhite, unmarried, and inexperienced than the rest of the workforce and to spend more time out of the labor force and unemployed (Segal and Sullivan 1997a).

Temporary jobs are typically transitional in nature (Houseman and Polivka 2000; Farber 2000). Louis Segal and Daniel Sullivan (1997a) find that about one-quarter of temps appear to maintain that status from one year to the next in the Current Population Survey (CPS). Moreover, despite rapid rates of growth in the 1980s and 1990s, temps still make up a small fraction of all workers in the U.S. economy at any point in time. By 1999 average daily employment in the temp industry stood at approximately 2.4 million people (Brogan 2000). Temporary jobs accounted for about 2 percent of all jobs in the mid-1990s and for an even smaller fraction of primary jobs among multiple jobholders—only about 1 percent (U.S. Department of Labor 1999).

The number of people who temp during a year, however, is much larger. Segal and Sullivan (1997b) found that the percentage of people who temp over a one-year period is approximately twice as high as those who temp in a quarter. Alec Levenson and David Finegold's (2001) analysis suggests even greater cycling in and out of temping: the individuals employed at a large agency on an average day represent only one-fifth to one-quarter of all the people employed by that agency throughout the year. If this pattern is representative, then scaling up average daily employment in the entire temp industry suggests a national figure of about 9.6 to 12 million people who probably worked as temps at some time during the year in 1999—or up to 10 percent of the labor force. This is most likely an upper bound estimate, however, since many people sign on at more than one agency to improve their chances of finding work.[1] Moreover, most people spend only a small fraction of the year working as temps.

Companies' use of temps may be associated with superior financial performance. Nandkumar Nayar and G. Lee Willinger (2001) find that firms with larger fractions of contingent workers have greater stock returns and better balance sheets. They attribute this to the impact of contingent work on the bottom line. While that may be true within a limited range, it is not likely to hold in the extreme—only one regular employee (the CEO) with all others contingent. Nayar and Willinger's result may also be due to a correlation between contingent work and other management practices that lead to superior financial performance (for example, rapid market response). Regardless, this evidence, coupled with managers' willingness to try any practice perceived to offer competitive advantage, suggests that firms' use of temps will continue to grow.

CAREER PATTERNS OF LOW-SKILLED AGENCY TEMPS: STUDY METHODS

Our data are drawn from multiple temporary agencies in the United States that account for a small but significant fraction of all U.S. temps for 1995 to 2001.[2] The data cover every state and all major metropolitan areas, ensuring a geographically diverse picture of the industry. Our initial data consist of all U.S. employment records, including wages and hours worked for each assignment. We use these data to analyze assignment length, the nature of the work performed, and the relationship of these factors with wages.

To help preserve anonymity for the agencies, the exact number of observations for many of the calculations from the payroll data is not reported. However, in most cases there are well over one hundred thousand observations, ensuring a high degree of statistical precision. This holds even in cases where a subset of the temps under consideration accounts for a relatively small fraction of the observations in the sample. Our discussion of the payroll records results is drawn from Levenson and Finegold (2001). We refer the reader to that paper for a detailed discussion of the payroll data and how those analyses were constructed.

SURVEY DESIGN

The payroll data contain no information on temp demographics. To obtain this and data on motivations, work experience, and attitudes, we surveyed a sample of all employees at these agencies. We surveyed people who were most likely to have been affected by temping—that is, those who had temped for at least eighty hours in a six-month period. This excluded about one-third of temps at these agencies and introduced a bias: people who temp for longer durations are more likely to have had positive outcomes.

The surveys were mailed 2 months after the end of the qualifying period; for example, when the period was August through January, the survey was mailed at the end of March. A total of 27,098 surveys were mailed in 2000 to 2001: 20,598 to industrial and clerical temps and 6,500 to professional and technical temps.[3] Included among the industrial and clerical group is an oversample of 5,250 temps who probably had fast wage increases during the qualification period.[4] The remainder of the industrial and clerical sample was drawn from a random national sample (from among all temps working at the agencies) and two-stage random sampling using a representative group of offices.[5] To induce as high a response rate as possible, all survey respondents were entered in a drawing for a bonus payment.[6]

In all, 4,500 usable surveys were returned, for a 16.6 percent response rate.[7] Among those who returned surveys, over 70 percent worked for the agency at which they were surveyed in the two months before the survey mailing date; only about 55 percent of those not responding worked for the agency during this period. Thus, the transient nature of temp employment contributed to the low response rate.

This conclusion is bolstered by the results of follow-up phone calls made to a subset of the industrial and clerical temp nonrespondents. The calls were made about eight weeks after the survey mailing date. The results suggest that an additional 22.5 percent of the survey nonrespondents should be excluded from the total because they were not at the address to which the survey had been mailed. Doing so yields an adjusted response rate of 21.4 percent (4,500 out of 21,001) for the entire sample (for details, see Levenson and Finegold 2001).

Because the surveyed temps were sampled from archival wage records, we can use those records to compare the respondents and nonrespondents. Respondents on average had greater hours (538 versus 464), greater total income ($7,385 versus $5,794), and average hourly wages ($12.61 versus $11.37) during the presurvey qualification period. Average growth in base pay was very similar for respondents and nonrespondents (3.73 percent versus 3.21 percent). During the preceding four and a half years, the respondents similarly had larger values for hours (1,568 versus 1,137), total income ($21,540 versus $14,910), average hourly wages ($12.32 versus $11.18), and growth in base pay (13.17 percent versus 11.03 percent).[8] Thus, respondents were better paid and temped more hours than nonrespondents.

LIMITATIONS OF THE DATA

With the exception of two of the case studies, we have no control group of low-skilled permanent employees to compare directly with low-skilled temps' experiences. In addition, though our quantitative analyses are based on data from a very large national sample of temps, it is drawn from only a small number of agencies. We believe the temp agencies we studied are typical of most agencies that employ low-skilled workers, but we must be cautious in generalizing our results. Furthermore, the survey results are applicable only to understanding the experiences of individuals who spent a significant time (two weeks or more) temping. This group is far more likely to have experienced wage growth or to be trained than the approximately one-third of individuals who signed on with an agency but then temped for less than two weeks. Because those who had positive outcomes were more likely to return the questionnaire, this introduced additional positive bias in our survey results.

Defining "Low-Skilled"

One problem that bedevils our study—as it does all the contributions to this volume—is defining "low-skilled" worker. We utilize the richness of our data to compare results from three different ways of conceptualizing "low skill": based on education, based on occupation, and based on wage. In addition, we analyze other factors—for example, prior work and computer and Internet experience—that may be considered part of temps' skills.

The first skill measure, based on formal educational qualifications, compares those with a high school diploma or less to those with some college and to those with a bachelor's or advanced degree. In our sample almost one-third of respondents have a high school diploma or less; about one-quarter have at least a four-year college degree. In addition, 18 percent also were students at the time of the survey. The problem with this measure, however, is that years of schooling is a crude proxy for individuals' skills and abilities.

A second categorization of individuals' competencies comes from the agencies' payroll data, which provide job codes for each assignment. We use these codes first to look at broad occupation categories that are consistent with the standard classifications used by the government and other national data sets: (1) industrial, (2) office, and (3) technical and professional assignments, with the last category serving as a proxy for "high skill." For some occupations the payroll data also differentiate level of skill (for example, basic versus advanced word processor); where we have sufficient data, we analyze these dimensions as well.

Table 9.1 Demographics of Temporary Workers

	Total Sample	Education			Occupation			Wage		
		Some High School or HS Diploma	Trade Certification, Some College, or AA Degree	Bachelor Degree or Higher	Industrial	Clerical	Professional or Technical	Earning $8.00 an Hour or Less	Earning More Than $8.00 an Hour	Fast Wage Progressor Oversample
Number of respondents	4,171	1,006	2,042	1,093	1,105	1,870	1,169	1,277	2,867	915
Age (mean)	37.9	37.4	37.4	39.1	36.7	37.3	40.0	36.2	38.7	36.9
Female	56.7%	59.6%	57.5%	52.6%	37.3%	83.0%	32.6%	61.2%	54.5%	64.5%
Student	17.6	5.6	24.0	16.6	12.1	20.8	17.6	15.1	18.7	15.8
Working another job while temp	18.6	16.2	18.7	20.9	20.2	18.3	17.8	19.1	18.5	20.4
Temp contribution to family income (mean)[a]	3.4	3.3	3.3	3.5	3.3	3.2	3.7	3.1	3.5	3.3
Earning $8.00 an hour or less	30.8%	55.7%	29.4%	9.9%	61.6%	28.5%	5.4%	—	—	46.3%
Earning more than $8.00 an hour	69.2	44.3	70.6	90.1	38.4	71.5	94.6	—	—	53.7
Industrial	26.7	54.9	23.0	6.8	—	—	—	53.3	14.8	44.8
Clerical	45.1	36.3	52.1	40.9	—	—	—	41.7	46.6	53.4
Professional or technical	28.2	8.8	24.9	52.3	—	—	—	4.9	38.6	1.8

Source: Authors' compilation.
[a] Mean score based on a five-point scale: 1 = very little; 2 = some; 3 = about half; 4 = most; 5 = nearly all.

The third way of defining "low-skilled" is based on wages, an approach frequently used by labor economists. We define lower-skilled temps (whom we refer to as "lower-wage" to avoid confusion) as those earning $8.00 an hour or less at the time of our survey. This corresponds to roughly 120 percent of the poverty line for a three-person family, assuming the temp is the sole income earner, working full-time, for a full year at that wage. One problem with using wage as a measure for skills is that it is also often a poor proxy: people with very similar skills may earn very different wages depending on the type of organization where they are placed and other constraints they face in the labor market or on preferences they may have for focusing on work versus other activities.

CHARACTERISTICS OF LOW-SKILLED TEMPS

Table 9.1, which contains the demographics, shows that the survey respondents have quite varied backgrounds. Temping is part of a dual strategy for many: almost one-fifth attend school, and a comparable number work at another job. On average, temp income accounts for a majority of family income.

There were some significant differences in the educational background of temps in the broad occupational and wage categories (see table 9.2). Not surprisingly, office workers and professional temps had much higher levels of formal educational qualifications than those in industrial positions. Lower-wage temps were also much less educated, yet 47 percent of them had some college education.

The differences in prior work experience were interesting (table 9.2). Professionals, higher-educated, and higher-wage temps worked for more of the three years prior to temping. Professional and technical workers were slightly more likely to have been laid off, but less educated, lower-wage, and industrial workers were much more likely to have been unemployed and looking for work immediately prior to signing on. Office workers were more likely to use temping to return to the workforce.

Less-educated, low-wage, and industrial temps were less likely to own a computer or use the Internet. They also indicated (results not reported) that their prior work experience had done a worse job preparing them for their temp assignments. This same pattern is apparent when comparing within specific occupations. For example, advanced computer operators spent far more of the prior three

Table 9.2 Prior Education and Work Experience of Temporary Workers

	Total Sample	Education			Occupation			Wage		Fast Wage Progressor Oversample
		Some High School or HS Diploma	Trade Certification, Some College, or AA Degree	Bachelor Degree or Higher	Industrial	Clerical	Professional or Technical	Earning $8.00 an Hour or Less	Earning More Than $8.00 an Hour	
Number of respondents	4,171	1,006	2,042	1,093	1,105	1,870	1,169	1,277	2,867	915
Education										
Some high school	4.6%	18.9%	—	—	14.0%	1.3%	0.9%	10.9%	1.8%	6.5%
High school diploma	19.7	81.1	—	—	36.4	18.2	6.6	33.3	13.8	27.6
Trade certification or apprenticeship	6.9	—	14.0	—	10.7	5.9	5.2	9.2	6.0	7.0
Some college	32.0	—	64.9	—	27.0	40.3	23.1	31.5	32.1	34.1

Associate's degree	10.4	—	21.1	—	5.0	10.4	15.1	6.6	12.0	8.3
Bachelor's degree	20.7	—	—	78.3	5.3	19.3	37.4	6.4	27.1	13.4
Graduate degree	5.7	—	—	21.7	1.5	4.6	11.6	2.1	7.4	3.1
Percentage time working in three years prior to temping	77.1	72.4	79.1	77.9	75.1	74.4	83.1	72.1	79.2	73.9
Laid off in three years prior to temping	32.8	32.3	33.8	30.9	33.3	29.6	37.0	30.7	33.5	31.5
Unemployed just prior to temping	41.9	50.4	41.4	34.9	52.5	38.1	37.5	49.6	38.2	46.5
Own a computer	66.7	42.4	69.0	85.2	39.4	69.6	87.8	46.2	75.8	54.8
Use the Internet	71.6	44.4	74.8	91.1	41.3	78.0	89.9	47.8	82.1	60.1

Source: Authors' compilation.

years in paid work (89 versus 61 percent) than basic computer operators and were less likely to have lost a job.

How Temporary Is Temporary Employment?

Temping is a very brief experience for many people: about one-quarter of all temps worked one week or less with these agencies; 5 percent worked a day or less. Most temps had only one or two assignments in a year. Only about 10 percent of all spells lasted thirteen weeks. Temps who were paid less tended to also work fewer hours. This is partly due to greater overtime pay among those who work more hours. But a certain proportion is due to higher base pay as well.

Why so many short-term assignments? Agencies have relatively little control over assignment duration. If they refuse to fill requests for very short assignments on which they lose money—for example, a day or less—they may risk alienating many good customers who submit requests for both long and short assignments. Short assignments can also serve as a screening mechanism to identify the better temps.

Despite the transitory nature of temp jobs, long-term temping may be a viable part of a career path for some workers. As firms continue to move to project-oriented modes of production, certain jobs may be available only to those willing to work as temps and independent contractors. As one of our case studies shows, temp agencies are beginning to take on the management of entire functions or facilities that their customers wish to outsource. Temping also may be a viable option for workers looking to improve their skills through the free training provided by many agencies (Autor, Levy, and Murnane 1999). Less-educated workers may not have access to training in nontemp jobs because most U.S. firms spend training dollars on those who are most highly educated (Lynch and Black 1998).

Employment Objectives

The disparate backgrounds of the survey respondents suggest that they have different motivations for temping. We analyzed individuals' primary reason for temping along two dimensions: whether someone views temping as worth pursuing on its own merits ("temps") or as a means to getting a different job ("perms"), and whether their outlook is immediate ("short-term") or more open-ended ("long-term/selective"). This yields four different categories of temps:

- Short-term temps who want to find short-term work as a temp (14 percent of sample)

- Long-term temps who want to find good temp assignments on an ongoing basis (25 percent)

- Short-term perms who want to use temp assignments to find a permanent job as quickly as possible (23 percent)

- Selective perms who want to use temping to find the right permanent position to meet their needs (38 percent)

Thus, just over 60 percent of our sample view temping as a way to find a permanent job.

We find the selective perm group to be the most interesting in certain respects. In the face of rising litigation costs for firing regular workers, firms may be increasing their use of temp assignments to audition workers for regular jobs (Autor 2000; Houseman 2000). Thus, for employees seeking these core jobs, working first as a temp may be the only way to get hired. In many cases the temps are screening as well, deciding for which firm or manager they want to work. This indicates a potential for sticking with temping over an extended period. In contrast, the Bureau of Labor Statistics classification of "involuntary" temps does not recognize the duration dimension: it groups together short-term and selective perms because they both hope that temping will lead to a permanent job (Levenson 2000). The selective perms' longer-term outlook suggests that they are more likely to take advantage of training and other skill-building opportunities while temping.

"Long-term temporaries" may seem like an oxymoron, but this type of arrangement appears to be a good fit for certain types of workers. These include college students who want to earn extra money while in school, and those—typically women—whose childcare and family responsibilities make temporary assignments viable as an alternative to regular, part-time jobs.

Lower-skilled temps—by all three of our definitions—are more

Table 9.3 Employment Objectives of Temporary Workers

Reason for Temping	Total Sample	Education			Occupation			Wage	
		Some High School or HS Diploma	Trade Certification, Some College, or Associate's Degree	Bachelor's Degree or Higher	Industrial	Clerical	Professional or Technical	Earning $8.00 an Hour or Less	Earning More Than $8.00 an Hour
Number of respondents	4,171	1,006	2,042	1,093	1,105	1,870	1,169	1,277	2,867
Short-term temping	13.8%	9.0%	13.1%	19.6%	9.8%	17.6%	11.8%	13.8%	13.9%
Long-term temping	25.5	21.4	24.6	31.0	17.7	29.0	27.7	21.7	27.3
Short-term perm	22.6	30.0	21.7	17.6	31.6	17.7	21.6	26.9	20.6
Selective perm	38.0	39.5	40.6	31.8	41.0	35.6	39.0	37.5	38.2

Source: Authors' compilation.

likely than office or professional temps to view temping as primarily a route to permanent employment. In particular, they are more eager to get a permanent job as quickly as possible (table 9.3). They are also more likely to agree that "temporary work is the only work I could find."

There are two aspects of the employment objectives that bear noting. First, the survey asked retrospectively about the person's reason for becoming a temp. Thus, there is a significant potential for bias due to ex-post updating. This is a concern for those who signed up looking to temp for only a short time yet ended up temping longer than they expected, as well as for those who initially were only looking for a permanent job but later came to appreciate the positive aspects of temping. Second, the respondents were forced to choose only one response out of four. Yet many people undoubtedly had multiple reasons for temping. So someone whose primary motivation is to find the right permanent job, for example, probably also wants good temp assignments until they secure that job. Thus, the categories more accurately describe shades of difference in motivation across individuals.

CAREER PROGRESSION—SKILL DEVELOPMENT

Human capital theory predicts that firms will not pay for general skills training. By definition, employees can use these skills to earn a higher wage on other jobs (Becker 1964). At first glance, this logic would appear to be particularly applicable to temp agencies, given their very high turnover rates. Yet the agencies in our sample, like others in the sector (Autor 1999), provide free training in a range of transferable skills—typing, introductory office skills, advanced computer programming, and so forth. One reason they do so is that the returns to the firm from such training appear to be high: the costs are low (the training is all computer- or video-based and individuals are not paid while training), and the payback is rapid (the firm can charge a higher margin on more qualified individuals). Agencies also offer free training to prepare people for positions for which there is a shortage of qualified individuals, including the specific skills requested by an employer (for example, Microsoft Office 2000) and to provide an inducement for individuals to sign on with their agency. In our study, access to training was a slightly more important motivation for lower-wage and less-

Table 9.4 Training Participation of Temporary Workers

	Total Sample	Education			Occupation			Wage	
		Some High School or HS Diploma	Trade Certification, Some College, or Associate's Degree	Bachelor's Degree or Higher	Industrial	Clerical	Professional or Technical	$8.00 an Hour or Less	$8.00 an Hour or More
Number of respondents	4,171	1,006	2,042	1,093	1,105	1,870	1,169	1,277	2,867
Offered training (percentage)	42.9	37.1	45.0	44.1	30.9	50.0	42.6	38.1	44.9
Took training (percentage)	53.7	54.0	55.6	50.6	52.3	59.2	44.4	55.6	53.0
Mean hours of training	21.0	25.7	20.7	18.5	30.4	17.3	21.3	29.6	17.1

Source: Authors' compilation.

educated workers, but only 4 percent of all temps indicated that training was their "main reason" for signing on.

In theory, free training is available to all temps we studied. Yet in practice only about one-quarter of our sample used the training. The level of participation can be explained in two stages (table 9.4): less than half report that they were offered free training, and only just over half of those offered training elected to take it. By comparison, about 21 percent of the general workforce reports receiving training from their employer in a given year (National Center for Education Statistics 1995).

Lower-wage individuals were less likely to be offered training but were more likely to take it when offered; they also took significantly more training per year. A similar pattern holds for education levels. Individuals in industrial positions also were much less likely to be offered training but were less likely to participate when it was offered. Yet industrial temps who got training spent significantly more hours in training than either office or professional temps. Within specific occupations we found that the more advanced workers—whether data entry workers, secretaries, or computer operators—were more likely to be offered training and recorded significantly more hours of training.

A number of factors appear to contribute to the relatively low participation rate in free training:

- Some offices have an unwritten policy that temps have to work at least forty hours before being eligible.

- Access is often limited because smaller offices typically have only one computer. That computer is also used for skill assessments and other office tasks. Internet-based training could have expanded access. But it was only just being introduced by one agency at the time of the study.

- Much of the computer-based training (CBT) curriculum is not modularized, requiring individuals to complete half- or full-day training in order to be certified as having passed the course.

- Temps have to train on their own time. (Most permanent employees train on company time.)

- Many lower-skilled individuals may not have been able to afford the transportation costs of getting to the training and the opportunity cost of spending full days in training without pay, although the slightly

Table 9.5 Factors Affecting Training Participation of Temporary Workers

	Offered Training[a]	Training Participation[a]	Hours of Training
Low education	−.05**	−.03	1.27
Computer experience	.02***	−.03***	−3.08***
Age	.00	.00	−.07
Female	.08***	.08***	−4.33**
Also a student	.01	.00	−1.26
Long-term temporary	.07**	.13***	4.51*
Short-term permanent	−.02	.07	8.64***
Long-term permanent	.06**	.11***	4.14
Fast wage progressor oversample	.04*	.03	2.08
Pseudo R-squared (columns 1 and 2);[a] R-squared (column 3)	.02	.01	.03

Source: Authors' compilation.

[a] The offered training and training participation results are from binary probits; the values in columns 1 and 2 are changes in the probability of the dependent variable from a one-unit change in the independent variable.

* $p \leq .10$.
** $p \leq .05$.
*** $p \leq .01$.

higher training take-up by those earning under $8.00 an hour suggests that this is not a major barrier.

The regression results show that skill and education levels are related to training, though the relationship is modest and the R-squared is low (see table 9.5; see also table 9.A1). Less-educated temps were less likely to be offered training but showed no difference in participation or hours. Those with greater computer experience were more likely to be offered training but took much less. In other results (not shown), we find that low-wage workers were also less likely to be offered training but took more hours when they did participate. Thus, the agencies' staff may not fully understand and actively promote the training for low-skilled temps—the group who perhaps could benefit the most (see impact of training in table 9.7).

Yet formal training is only one way in which individuals' skills may be enhanced. The respondents generally felt that the temp experience itself had improved their skills, and they rated the opportunities "to learn from other people at the workplace" and "to learn new things on the job" significantly higher than the opportunity to learn through training.

Labor Market Outcomes: Wage Growth and Obtaining a Permanent Job

A significant fraction of the temps we surveyed had positive career outcomes, defined as finding a permanent job or significant wage growth (10 percent or more) in the year the person temped the largest number of hours.[9] The fourth row of table 9.6 gives the percentage of those having one or both of these outcomes. It is less than the sum of the first and third rows because some people had fast wage growth and found a permanent job.

Less-educated, lower-wage, and industrial temps were more likely to move into a permanent job; the same held for lower-skilled clerks and customer service representatives (CSRs), relative to higher-skilled clerks and CSRs. It should be noted that the percentage of temps who found a permanent job is a lower bound: others temping at the time of the survey undoubtedly found permanent jobs subsequently. Moreover, anyone who was using temping to supplement a "regular" job should be excluded from this group as well.[10]

On the flip side, not everyone who found a permanent job indicated that the job came through a temp assignment with the agency. Only about one-quarter of short-term temps and long-term temps who found permanent jobs did so through a temp assignment with the agency. A much higher fraction—about half—of both short-term perms and selective perms who found permanent jobs said that the agency was directly responsible, a response that is consistent with their stated reasons for becoming a temp.[11] There was no clear pattern as to whether lower-skilled temps were more likely than their higher-skilled counterparts to find their permanent job through the agency; the results differ depending on the measure of skill used.

Better-educated temps earned a higher wage (table 9.1). Not surprisingly, office and industrial temps' average wages were much lower than those of technical and professional temps. They also had slower wage growth during this period (Levenson and Finegold 2001), a finding that is consistent with industry reports of much faster growth in the demand for professional workers (American Staffing Association 2001). Despite this, gains in wages for most

Table 9.6 Career Outcomes of Temporary Workers

| | Total Sample | Education[a] | | | Occupation[a] | | | Wage[a] | | Fast Wage Progressor Oversample |
		Some High School or HS Diploma	Trade Certification, Some College, or Associate's Degree	Bachelor's Degree or Higher	Industrial	Clerical	Professional or Technical	$8.00 an Hour or Less	More Than $8.00 an Hour	
Number of respondents	4,171	698	1,596	944	697	1,384	1,153	856	2,378	915
Permanent job	31.1%	34.4%	31.1%	31.6%	36.7%	32.2%	29.0%	35.6%	30.7%	28.1%
Permanent job through temp assignments	17.0	22.3	17.0	15.8	20.9	18.2	15.6	19.0	17.4	14.2
Wage growth 10 percent or more	30.2	28.9	25.9	21.9	25.4	29.7	20.7	21.7	27.0	47.3
Permanent job and/or wage growth 10 percent or more	53.9	57.4	50.4	47.1	55.1	54.3	44.8	51.9	50.8	64.7
Negative wage growth	11.1	10.1	9.1	6.1	11.5	10.0	4.6	12.4	7.0	20.7

Source: Authors' compilation.
[a] Data exclude oversample.

occupations outpaced inflation during this period, mirroring trends in the economy (Mishel, Bernstein, and Schmitt 2001). Median nominal annual wage rises for lower-skilled temp jobs, for example, included 6 percent for administrative or receptionist, 5 percent for casual laborers, and 6 percent for drivers (Levenson and Finegold 2001).

The amount of time individuals work as temps is directly related to their likelihood of obtaining a raise. Those working short periods of time experienced virtually no wage growth: only about 1 percent on average for those working one-quarter of the year or less. In contrast, wage growth for those working the longest (nine hundred hours or more a year) averaged 7 to 8 percent between the first and last weeks worked during the year; 25 percent of these temps had raises of greater than 10 percent. About half of all temps with large wage growth achieved this while working on only one assignment during the year (Levenson and Finegold 2001).

Table 9.7 presents regression results that analyze the factors associated with finding a permanent job and with (significant) wage growth. In each case three specifications are reported:

1. The base regression with our primary low-skill descriptor, educational attainment; also included are demographic controls for age, gender, and student status (first and fourth columns)

2. That specification with the other two low-skill descriptors added— low-wage status and industrial or clerical temp assignments (second and fifth columns)

3. The further inclusion of whether training was taken and other skill-, preference-, and experience-related factors that might influence labor market outcomes (third and sixth columns)

The results indicate that male temps, clerical workers, those earning over $8.00 an hour, and those who took training were more likely to obtain a significant wage increase. Consider now the profile of the "typical" temps of central interest to this volume: low-education, low-wage, clerical female and industrial male temps were 3 percent and 1 percent less likely, respectively, to experience significant wage growth, all else equal. Taking training helped offset this, bringing low-skilled women even with other temps (significant wage

Table 9.7 Explanations for Career Outcomes of Temporary Workers

	Permanent Job			Wage Growth 10 Percent or More		
Low education	.01	−.01	.00	.01	.03	.03
Wage at time of survey ($8.00 an hour or less versus more than $8.00)	—	.00	.02	—	−.07***	−.07***
Occupation (clerical versus others)	—	.02	.03	—	.07***	.06***
Occupation (industrial versus others)	—	.04*	.05*	—	.04*	.03
Age	−.01***	−.01***	−.01***	.00	.00	.00*
Female	.00	.00	.01	−.03*	−.05***	−.05***
Also a student	−.11***	−.10***	−.09***	.02	.01	.02
Training taken	—	—	−.04**	—	—	.04**
Working another job while temping	—	—	−.05**	—	—	.03
Contribution of temp income to family income	—	—	.01	—	—	.00
Percentage time working in three years prior to temping	—	—	.00***	—	—	.00
Laid off in three years prior to temping	—	—	.00	—	—	−.01
Unemployed immediately prior to temping	—	—	.03**	—	—	.00
Computer experience	—	—	−.01	—	—	.00
Own a computer	—	—	.05***	—	—	−.01
Use the Internet	—	—	−.01	—	—	−.03
Fast wage progressor oversample	−.05***	−.06***	−.06***	.13***	.13***	.13***
Pseudo R-squared	.03	.03	.04	.02	.02	.03

Source: Authors' compilation.
Note: Results from binary probit estimation. The values in the table are changes in the probability of the dependent variable from a one-unit change in the independent variable.
* $p \leq .10$
** $p \leq .05$
*** $p \leq .01$

growth was 1 percent more likely) and giving low-skilled men a boost (3 percent more likely).

The only skill-related measure that was significantly correlated with finding a permanent job (in terms of economic significance) was working in industrial assignments. However, the effect was significant only at a 10 percent level of confidence, below the cutoff (5 percent level of confidence) commonly used to determine statistical significance. Thus, unlike for wage growth, skill does not appear to play a large role in determining whether a temp finds a permanent job.

Interestingly, taking training was *negatively* associated with finding a permanent job.[12] We do not think this has the paradoxical implication that training makes someone less attractive to prospective employers. Rather, this probably represents a timing issue: anyone who reported finding a permanent job had to do so by the time of the survey, which in some cases was within three to four months of the person's first temp assignment. Taking training probably is a signal that the person postponed finding a permanent job while focusing on skill building or opted for training after realizing that his or her preferred permanent job would not materialize immediately. This would produce the observed negative relationship in table 9.7.

Finally, note that we do not know precisely why the wage increases occur. Some explanations we observed in our case studies include: successfully completing the screening period, prenegotiated increases based on tenure and performance, improved matching, skill building, and the random nature of assignments. If a temp takes the first assignment offered to earn money right away, improved matching can occur in later assignments. In the case of screening periods, it is the agency or client firm that may restrict access to higher-paying assignments until the person has proven himself or herself in an initial lower-paying assignment. In some large-scale partnerships between agencies and their customers, there is a regular schedule of wage increases based on time in the position and successful performance.

A final look into the nature of employment and advancement as a temp is provided in the last row of table 9.6. This shows that wages declined for roughly 11 percent of temps in each group in the year they worked the most hours (out of 1999 or 2000). This is not surprising if one considers that some temps may feel the need to take whatever assignment is available. Negative wage growth may also indicate a lucky initial assignment (or unlucky ending assignment) during the year. This is a reminder that wages and skill are not synonymous. Thus, the results in column 2 of table 9.6 should be discounted. One way is to assume that the degree of randomness that produces wage growth is comparable in both directions, negative and positive. This would reduce the fraction of temps with rapid positive wage growth by about one-third.[13]

CASE STUDIES

These analyses provide key insights into temps' wages and career mobility, but from the vantage of the temps only. They lack the perspective of the other actors in this unique employment relationship: the agencies and the client firms. From the data analyzed thus far, we know little about firms' use of temps, why certain settings offer greater wage and career progression, and how temps' experience compares to that of permanent employees doing the same work. The third phase of our research, the case studies, explores these issues in three very different firms. To maintain anonymity, we refer to them as Office Supplies, HealthTech, and We Deliver. In choosing these sites, we focused on clients that employed large numbers of lower-skilled temps but differed significantly from each other in work settings and types of temps. In each case, the client has a formal contract with an agency in our study.

Each case featured structured telephone and on-site interviews, a site visit, and a survey (see table 9.A2 for descriptive statistics on cases). The survey was a version of the questionnaire we administered to the larger sample of temps, with additional questions on the design of the temp's job (for example, level of autonomy, control over work, intrinsic job rewards) and the relationship between temps and permanent employees. The survey response rates ranged from 15 to 50 percent, and the number of respondents from 93 to 138. The response rates were lower for the 2 cases where the surveys were mailed back.[14] At the other site respondents handed them back to the on-site temporary agency representative in a sealed, blank envelope (to preserve anonymity). As an incentive, all case study survey respondents were entered into a drawing for a $500 bonus.

Before discussing the wage, skill, and career outcomes of temps in these companies, we offer a brief description of each case study site. Statistical profiles of all three are in the appendix.

OFFICE SUPPLIES: ADJUSTING FOR A CYCLICAL WORKLOAD

Office Supplies is a global supplier of office products. Our site was a manufacturing facility located in a rural area of the southern United States. This site runs 3 shifts, using about 150 temps per shift. However, the production volume varies widely throughout the year: at times as many as 800 temps work at the site. Office Supplies uses temps primarily to achieve flexibility in its head count. Because of the unpredictable and customized nature of its product orders, head count can vary by several hundred within a 2- to 3-week period. Using temps allows Office Supplies to protect core worker jobs and save up to 50 percent on labor costs. Temps are used to a lesser extent to fill in for absent or vacationing employees.

Temp jobs at Office Supplies are typical industrial assignments: machine operator, forklift driver, bailer, casual laborer, receptionist, data entry, and computer technician. The work setting is clean, and excellent safety precautions are taken, but the work itself is highly routinized. Both temps and permanent employees are rotated from job to job to relieve stress and minimize injuries. Temps and permanent employees work side by side in teams on the same production process.

The temps at Office Supplies are predominantly African American women. Many are single mothers, and 10 to 15 percent came from welfare-to-work programs. Another 25 to 30 percent are college students, most of whom work during the summer—the site's peak production season. Of the workers at the three case-study sites, Office Supplies temps are the least educated: over one-third of those surveyed have only a high school diploma or less education. Nearly two-thirds were unemployed and looking for work before taking the assignment. Using our typology, the largest group (34 percent) wants to find a permanent job as quickly as possible. Another sizable group (31 percent) is looking for the right permanent position. With the lack of high-paying alternative jobs locally and the relatively good working conditions at this site, almost all of these temps would take a permanent job at Office Supplies if offered.

HealthTech: Internal Pool of Temp Workers

HealthTech is a rapidly growing manufacturer of medical technologies and provider of services to the health care industry. We surveyed temporary employees used by HealthTech at its central offices near a major midwestern city, where it has thousands of employees. The company is widely known for its family-friendly policies and was once recognized as the state's "Employer of the Year."

In 1996 HealthTech discontinued a long-standing internal "overload" pool of permanent employees, outsourcing them to a temp agency. Today between 140 and 230 temps are at sites across the central office's multiple buildings throughout the year. HealthTech uses temps to protect its core employees and achieve flexibility in its head count. According to one HealthTech manager, it "gives us the flexibility to manage the size of the organization." Managers use temps when they cannot increase permanent head count. Using temps yields relatively small direct cost savings for HealthTech but helps lower the official turnover, since changes in temps are not counted in these statistics. Temps are also used to screen candidates for permanent jobs, although there is no formal, companywide policy on the matter.

Temp assignments are typically short-term, such as filling in for employees who are out sick or on leave. For example, a temp may do clerical work for three days, then pack boxes for two days. Some jobs involve project work lasting six months or more. Assignment type varies widely, from clerical (receptionists, customer service representatives, mail clerks) to industrial (packers, shippers, and drivers) to technical (laboratory workers). The work environment is clean and attractive; the workdays are standard. The work varies greatly, from monotonous and stressful (warehouse) to routine with some autonomy (clerical) to some variety (lab). Temps often work in teams with permanent employees. Requests for temps are decentralized and made separately by individual managers and departments. The agency fills these requests by advertising using HealthTech's name rather than its own.

A large majority of the temps we surveyed prefer temping as either a short- or long-term option, although HealthTech managers indicated that most who sign on as temps want a permanent job there.[15] Only 20 percent were unemployed and looking for permanent work before taking their HealthTech assignment. The temps are mostly female (90 percent) and about one-fifth are students. They are the most highly educated of the temps in the three case studies: only 15 percent have a high school diploma or less, and 28 percent have a college degree or higher. They are also the most computer-savvy: 83 percent own a home PC, and 87 percent use the Internet.

WE DELIVER: THE MANAGED SERVICES MODEL

We Deliver ships packaged materials worldwide. The site we examined is outside a large city in the southeastern United States. Previously an outbound call center processing cash-on-delivery (COD) payments, the site has recently made the transition to handling "exceptions" to standard payment procedures, with less call center work. About 270 people work there, with only 8 permanent employees.

The temp agency in this case uses a "managed services" model. Anecdotal evidence suggests that large firms increasingly are entering such arrangements. Under this model the temp agency acts as an outsourced human resources (HR) function for the organization, working closely with the client's management team to increase productivity, quality, and retention.[16] Typically, the arrangement is limited to a particular location, division, or type of work (for example, the mailroom, warehouse, or call center). The agency often provides on-site managers who handle temp recruitment, selection, scheduling, discipline, coaching, performance reviews, motivation, and compensation. As we show later in the section, the experiences and attitudes of temps here differ from those of temps in the other types of arrangements.

We Deliver entered a managed services contract with its temporary agency in 1996, when it began consolidating and automating COD call center operations. The firm's primary motivation for using temps was to achieve cost reductions, particularly in the area of benefits. Although non-unionized, We Deliver offers excellent benefits to its permanent employees to compete with its unionized competitors. Because labor constitutes up to 80 percent of We Deliver's costs at the facility, according to the senior manager, "if we can outsource our entire employment costs to a temporary agency and avoid paying benefits, it's a winner." We Deliver managers also saw temps as a way to minimize risk while automating the COD process, because they could quickly release the temps if needed.[17]

In 2001 the work shifted away from order processing and toward exceptions handling. At the time of our study, temp jobs at We Deliver were mostly clerical. Although some entailed outbound calling, most involved data entry, problem resolution, check verification, customer service, or package tracking. Some jobs were relatively routine (such as check verification), while others offered a great deal of variety (problem resolution, for example). Most temps worked independently rather than in teams. Temps who had been promoted to a supervisory level supervised the day-to-day work. The agency's on-site representative managed the entire temporary staff. The other permanent agency employee on-site was a training coordinator. All work occurred between 5:30 A.M. and 8:00 P.M., with no work on weekends. The working environment was pleasant, modern, and clean.

As with Office Supplies and HealthTech, most of the temps at We Deliver (89 percent in our survey) are women. More than three-quarters have some college education. A majority have a PC at home and use the Internet. Many are single parents looking for a flexible work schedule; about one-fifth are students. The vast majority are looking for permanent work and classified themselves as either "short-term perms" or "selective perms" (one-third and one-half, respectively). Like the temps working at HealthTech, many came to We Deliver expecting a permanent job in large part because the agency used We Deliver's name in recruiting. In our focus-group interviews, nearly every single temp wanted to obtain a permanent position at We Deliver.

SKILL, WAGE, AND CAREER GROWTH OPPORTUNITIES

Our analyses of the agency data from across the United States found that many temps who remain with an agency for at least two weeks experience wage progression, skill development, and/or find a permanent job. In the case studies, we examined how employers and temp agencies influence the attainment of these outcomes. We found that the degree to which these outcomes are attained is not uniform across settings and is heavily influenced by factors such as employers' motivations and strategies for using temps, the type of work, the working environment and organization of work, local labor market conditions, and the degree of latitude managers have in making decisions about temps and their work.

SKILL DEVELOPMENT

Skill development ranked in the top five out of seventeen possible features that temps want from their assignments at all three sites (see table 9.A3). Yet for less-educated temps at HealthTech and We Deliver, skill development is a lower priority: temps with no more than a high school diploma at these sites rated it in the bottom half of the list of features. At HealthTech and We Deliver, about three-quarters of the respondents said they were offered training—a much higher percentage than our national survey average of 43 percent (tables 9.4 and 9.A3). By contrast, only 36 percent of temps at Office Supplies reported being offered training—a proportion that is still higher than the national survey average for industrial temps of only 31 percent.

Skill development opportunities at We Deliver are clearly the most extensive and widely utilized. Of the three firms, temps at We Deliver participate the most in the training when it is offered to them (over 93 percent), and the rate does not differ by level of education. In fact, less-educated temps are the most likely to indicate that they have received an opportunity to enhance their skills through formal training. The high level of training participation no doubt results from the extensive training curriculum customized by the temp agency for We Deliver. The agency provides a dedicated on-site trainer and training center with a variety of courses. In the first three to six months, temps receive orientation and courses in basic computer skills, phone skills, Windows, and We Deliver's computer systems. Temps can also elect to take courses on supervisory skills, coaching, and listening skills.

As a signal of its commitment to retaining its temporary workforce, We Deliver encourages the agency to occupy any idle time that temps might have with paid training time. This was especially important at the time of our interviews, because the workload had been lower than anticipated. Not all temps felt they were fully employed and preferred to receive more hours than time off. They were pleased to have an opportunity to further develop their skills while also being paid for a full workweek.

In addition to its formal training program, the temporary agency for We Deliver also offers a mentoring program developed in 1999. According to a temporary agency memo, the mentoring program provides new temps "with accurate information concerning policies, procedures and benefits in a personable, one-on-one manner," using coaches "who are well versed in our operation, dedicated to [the temporary agency] and proven to have an excellent work ethic." The purpose of the program is explicit: to combat "turnover, absenteeism, tardiness, failure to complete full shift, and no-call no-shows." Although the program appears to be well designed, the temps we interviewed reported little familiarity with the program, and those who knew of it reported very little contact with their mentors.

Formal opportunities for skill development at Office Supplies are the most limited of the three. The temps we interviewed claimed that new temps receive very little formal training (two to three days of mostly orientation) and that they frequently have to push for learning opportunities. Only one-quarter of these temps claimed to have taken training offered by the agency. Our interviews with managers suggested that Office Supplies provides a higher level of training, with about 80 percent of entry-level temps getting one week of training, while the rest receive two to four weeks. A great deal of this training appears to occur informally on the job and is conducted by Office Supplies team leaders. New skills are most likely acquired as temps rotate from one job to the next. Since much of this training is specific to the work at Office Supplies, it is not surprising that their temps are the least likely of temps at the three firms to agree that they have obtained marketable skills (see table 9.A4).

At HealthTech a large proportion said that they are offered training by their temp agency and most take advantage of it, but the median hours of training among those taking it is extremely low (five hours). Some temps said that they are overqualified for their assignments and do not need the training, a fact that might explain the lower volume of training. This is especially true for technical and professional assignments, consistent with the lowest training participation rates for this group on our agencywide surveys. Unlike Office Supplies, HealthTech offers no formal training to its temps, preferring to leave such training to the agency. Our survey results from HealthTech confirm this: temps at HealthTech are least likely to agree that they have had opportunities to enhance their skills through formal training.

Another factor in the low reported hours of training is that much of it is likely to have been focused on orientating temps to Health-Tech's e-mail system. This training is provided by the agency as a prerequisite for any temp working at HealthTech. But anyone who has used the e-mail system on previous assignments—a large percentage, given HealthTech's penchant for requesting temps with HealthTech experience—undoubtedly needs no more than a refresher on how to use the system.

Wage and Career Progression

Just as our three case-study sites vary in the amount of skill development temps receive, the opportunities for wage growth and career advancement differ too. Although it was not evident which site offers the best combination of wage and career growth, by most measures Office Supplies trails the other two sites in both areas.

From the temps' standpoint, there is a clear and strong preference for wage growth over career mobility. As shown in table 9.A3, competitive pay is the single most important benefit sought by temps at all three sites, far outranking any of the sixteen other outcomes covered in our survey. At We Deliver the preference for good pay is accompanied by a strong desire for good benefits. Rapid advancement (career mobility) is not one of the top five benefits sought by temps at any of the sites; instead, many are focused on moving from a temporary to a "permanent" job. Whether the permanent job offers any chance of future career mobility appears to be less crucial than just getting out of temporary work.

Of the three case-study sites, HealthTech offers the greatest earning opportunities. Temps at HealthTech have the highest starting wage range ($9.50 to $15.00 an hour), and they are eligible for wage increases at their annual performance reviews, at which time their wages can rise by 4 to 5 percent. HealthTech also does not set a maximum wage for temps. The wage rates are set by either the HealthTech manager placing the order or the agency's on-site manager, with a contractually agreed markup rate charged by the agency. The HealthTech temps are the most likely to report fair pay and benefits (see table 9.A4).

The evidence on career progression at HealthTech is mixed. Our interviews suggested a high conversion rate to permanent employee status. Managers at HealthTech, for instance, reported that anywhere from 33 to 70 percent of perms used to be temps, depending on the department. Over one-quarter of the HealthTech temps we surveyed had landed a permanent job by the time of the survey, although the job may not have been with HealthTech. At the same time, however, the temps we surveyed at HealthTech, in particular those with a high school degree or less, are the least likely to agree that they have received chances to move into higher-level positions. This apparent discrepancy may be a result of a relatively high conversion rate, which is highest for temps with the most education. Those who were still temps at the time of the survey were more likely to report fewer advancement opportunities.

HealthTech managers reported that temps wanting a permanent job left within three to six months if they had not found one at the company. They also said that those seeking to be long-term temps are the most productive. The latter observation seems to apply primarily to clerical and administrative temps, who have substantially more opportunities for career growth. Although more the exception than the rule, some of the more advanced administrative assistants have developed this position into a career job. They have years of experience temping at HealthTech, are highly sought after for fill-in jobs throughout the company (particularly when senior executives' assistants are absent), and repeatedly turn down permanent job offers. Their high level of performance guarantees them ongoing employment and greater variety as they move among departments, building extensive personal networks within the firm.

In many ways the rates of wage and career mobility at We Deliver are similar to those at HealthTech, with one major difference: while 28 percent of those surveyed at We Deliver reported getting permanent jobs, none made such a report at We Deliver. This finding was not unexpected because there are few permanent jobs at the facility. Temps at We Deliver appear to have extensive skill development opportunities, acquire relatively marketable skills, and frequently list We Deliver's widely known name as their employer when applying for jobs. An overwhelming majority of those accepting permanent jobs said they are obtained because of their temporary work assignments (see table 9.A4).

To compensate for the lack of permanent job opportunities on-site, We Deliver's temporary agency offers "career pathing," an internal labor market that offers a sense of career mobility within the call center. The career ladder positions run from associate to coach to supervisor. In addition to the career ladder, the agency provides a formal set of periodic performance reviews (at thirty, sixty, and ninety days, and then at six-month intervals). The performance reviews are linked to opportunities for wage increases and/or promotions to higher levels. The agency created this development plan to address clients' concerns with the often high turnover at call centers, which can run 60 to 70 percent annually. (At We Deliver, the voluntary turnover rate averages between 1.5 and 1.8 percent a week). Career pathing is more commonly used in call centers with high-skilled temps, but a senior manager of the temp agency indicated that as many as 25 percent of the lower-wage call centers it manages have adopted it. Despite the career pathing, We Deliver temps reported no difference in their perceived career opportunities compared with those at the other two sites. This may be because the actual amount of mobility has been fairly limited: out of 260 temporary positions at the site, only nine are supervisors, and between fifteen and twenty are coaches.

We Deliver also provides opportunities for wage progression. Temps start at $8.25 an hour, and they are eligible for twenty- to fifty-cent raises at six months, then every twelve months thereafter, with no maximum wage. Temps can also receive up to a $1.00-an-hour raise with the recommendation of their supervisor. However, a recent wage rate study of the local labor market by the agency found that their wages lag behind those for similar jobs elsewhere. The temps at We Deliver are keenly aware that neither their wages nor their benefit packages are comparable to those of permanent We Deliver employees.

Starting wages at Office Supplies are by far the lowest of the three sites ($5.50 to 5.75 an hour, depending on shift). Wage growth is also on a smaller scale: temps can receive twenty-five- to fifty-cent increases at performance reviews every three months, but wages are capped at $6.75 to 7.00 an hour. Temps typically reach the wage cap in six months. Those with a high school degree or less reported significantly more satisfaction with opportunities to increase pay and benefits. Wage mobility also occurs for a relatively large minority of temps coming from welfare-to-work programs simply because they obtain a position temping with Office Supplies.

In addition to finding some wage growth at Office Supplies for less-educated temps, we also found that they have more opportunities for upward mobility across temp assignments within the company. Temps with less education are more likely to say they have chances to move to higher-level positions. The primary route of advancement for more-educated temps is landing a permanent job at Office Supplies. According to one manager, about 60 percent of the firm's current permanent workforce used to be temps. He estimated that each year about 20 percent of temps become permanent. The actual percentage may be lower: only 16 percent of the temps we surveyed reported a permanent job, and only a small fraction of those jobs came through their temporary assignments (see table 9.A4).

Explaining Variations in Skill, Wage, and Career Growth

As our case studies illustrate, there is no single reason why temps experience skill, wage, or career growth. Rather, the explanations lie in the tangled nexus of the objectives and needs that all three actors bring to the employment relationship. Within occupations, the variations seem to be driven more by where the temp is placed (that is, the client) than by the actions of the temporary agency or the temp.

All three firms we studied use temps as some part of a core-periphery staffing strategy, but their approaches vary. Office Supplies, for instance, is reluctant to invest in developing the skills of a workforce in a highly cyclical business. Instead, it relies on a good working environment and the chance of a permanent job to attract temps. Wage growth is limited.

At HealthTech, motivations for using temps vary across the firm. Temps are often used to screen potential candidates for permanent positions. Through temping, HealthTech is able to provide people with relevant experience before they are hired. Where temps are used for short-term work, little development or wage growth occurs. Only in a few cases involving mostly long-term clerical temps does HealthTech provide wage and career growth to retain them.

We Deliver, meanwhile, uses temps as a semipermanent workforce to handle a variable workload. Opportunities for skill development are provided both as a retention tool and a way to develop temp supervisors. The development opportunities give temps a sense of upward mobility that is better than what most temps experience, but short of what similar permanent employees experience. Wage progression is also used to retain the workforce, but only begrudgingly. As the senior We Deliver site manager put it, "Wage progression is not an outcome I desire, but a necessary one to keep employees from turning over." However, We Deliver's management also recognized that offering skill and wage mobility can be a double-edged sword. We Deliver walks the fine line between retaining temps who want permanent work through good jobs and skill and wage growth, on the one hand, and frustrating them by not offering permanent jobs. With the skills temps gain at We Deliver, many easily find work elsewhere.

Another source of variation in temps' labor market outcomes is the type of work they perform. This is clearest in the case of We Deliver. The senior manager at the facility believed that wage progression and career growth are effective and economical as long as the work is relatively low-skill, such as the COD processing that used to be performed at the site. But because the new tasks require more highly skilled employees, he was concerned about the cost of providing them with marketable skills.

According to our survey, temps in industrial jobs, like those at Office Supplies, typically are the least likely to be offered formal training by their agency. Indeed, higher percentages of temps are offered training at HealthTech and We Deliver, largely because their agencies' training is geared to office and technical skills. Instead, employees in industrial jobs, whether temporary or permanent, have long learned skills on the job, either informally or formally through apprenticeships.

One other aspect of the client's organization is especially important for temps' employment outcomes: the presence or absence of internal labor markets. At We Deliver an internal ladder offers temps not only skill mobility and a sense of advancement but also wage growth and, ultimately, opportunities for permanent jobs elsewhere. In contrast, no internal job ladders are available for temps at Office Supplies. At HealthTech job ladders exist for only a small group of long-term temps; the rest have no chance for advancement unless they are able to obtain permanent jobs relatively quickly.

Teamwork, while often regarded as a form of work organization that benefits employees (Mohrman, Cohen, and Mohrman 1995), appears to be less important in explaining variation across the sites.

Temps work in teams at all three sites, but to varying degrees: temps at Office Supplies are almost always in teams, but teamwork is very informal at We Deliver. The only exception may be at Office Supplies, where job rotation across team positions to alleviate stress and boredom sometimes offers informal on-the-job skill development.

The fourth source of variation in mobility in our three cases arises from local labor market conditions. At the time of our data collection (2000 and 2001), U.S. unemployment rates were the lowest in decades, and all three firms in our case studies had relatively tight labor markets. Yet their labor markets differed in important ways. Office Supplies, for example, is located in a rural area where few good jobs with large employers are available. As a result, people are willing to travel up to sixty miles to take temp jobs at Office Supplies and to work for low wages. As one temp observed, "It's better than no job at all."

HealthTech, on the other hand, is located near a major city where unemployment is under 4 percent. The agency recruits temps within a thirty- to fifty-mile radius, but the typical commute is only ten miles. HealthTech successfully attracts and retains temps by paying above-market wages, providing a good working environment, and having a compelling mission and excellent reputation as a family-friendly employer. Skill development and advancement, by contrast, are not used as drawing cards.

We Deliver's labor market is similar to HealthTech's in terms of size and level of unemployment. The most notable difference is its location on the outskirts of the city, which makes it attractive to workers from the surrounding impoverished rural areas. We Deliver's greatest challenge is keeping wages competitive with the local labor market. As wages begin to lag, its agency has to recruit in new ways, for example, by posting job ads at post offices, churches, and even fast-food restaurants. In addition, turnover and absenteeism rose slightly between 1999 and 2001. We Deliver's career development opportunities appear to be a strategy to compensate for below-market starting wages.

Finally, some of the observed differences may result from managerial discretion. HealthTech stands out in this regard, owing to its decentralized use of temps. HealthTech managers decide how and when to use temps, starting wages and raises, and growth opportunities, including whether to hire temps for open positions. Because the agency and We Deliver's management negotiate wage rates and career paths, pay and career mobility decisions are relatively standardized and administered by the agency. The initial skill development received by the temps has also been standardized. In theory, Office Supplies' management of temps is also highly centralized. But it is clear that individual managers have much room for maneuvering "under the radar" and playing favorites in growth opportunities.

COMPARING PERMANENT AND TEMPORARY WORKERS

The Office Supplies and HealthTech cases allowed us to examine temporary and permanent employees side by side doing similar work. In this section, we take a brief look at their relative levels of performance, the social relations between the two sets of workers, and how those relations were influenced by differences in opportunities for wage and career mobility at the two sites.

David Broshack and Alison Davis-Blake (1999) have observed that there are few studies on the relationship between permanent and temporary employees, and that the studies that have been done focus on attitudes to the detriment of research on behaviors (see, for example, Van Dyne and Ang 1998; Geary 1992; Feldman, Doerpinghaus, and Turnley 1994; Rogers 1995). Broshack and Davis-Blake's (1999, 16) research on temporary and permanent employees at two U.S. locations of a multinational financial services firm found that, contrary to their hypotheses, "temporary workers were more productive than regular workers and continued this pattern even after their conversion to permanent status." However, temporary workers reported engaging in fewer extra-role behaviors than regular employees. They attributed these results to three factors: temporary work acts as an effective mechanism for matching workers to jobs; temporary workers are motivated to exert greater effort owing to their desire to demonstrate their competence and qualifications; and workers gain valuable skills and knowledge during temporary work that serve them when converting to permanent status.

PERCEIVED DIFFERENCES IN PERFORMANCE

Although we were unable to quantify differences in performance between temps and permanent employees in the sites we studied, we were able to obtain the perspectives of these two groups of employees and their managers on their relative performance. At Office Supplies, managers reported no clear pattern in the performance of temps versus perms. However, perms strongly believed that temps do not work as hard, owing to differences in pay levels. On the other hand, temps felt that perms "ride on the backs of temps" and that temps are blamed unjustly for mistakes or problems with production.

Managers' views at HealthTech varied greatly from one department to another. In several cases, managers felt that temps are less productive and reliable and show less pride in their work. Other managers, however, reported that temps are often overqualified for their positions and outperform perms doing similar work. Yet others qualified their response, indicating that temps willing to work long-term are the most productive. On average, they tended to agree that temps are more productive once they convert to permanent status. Our focus groups with temporary and permanent employees at HealthTech, however, surfaced no strong opinions on their relative performance levels.

DIFFERENCES IN SOCIAL RELATIONS

Temporary and permanent workers at HealthTech clearly had much better relations than at Office Supplies. HealthTech temps were more likely to report being treated fairly and with respect by managers. They indicated that they are seen as being part of the same team and their suggestions are equally valued. They reported closer working relationships with their coworkers, and they were more likely to indicate getting along with their coworkers. They were also more likely to say they are called upon for consultation by their coworkers, though they were less likely to seek information from their coworkers.

The greater tension between permanent and temporary workers at Office Supplies was partly a reflection of the differences in labor market outcomes for low-skilled temps at the two sites. Temps at Office Supplies have fewer opportunities to obtain a permanent job with the company than at HealthTech. The size of the core workforce at Office Supplies is stable. HealthTech, in contrast, is growing relatively rapidly and frequently uses temps as a means of screening employees for new permanent positions. In essence, temps at Office

Supplies are competing with permanent employees for a fixed pool of jobs, while HealthTech perms did not feel that their jobs are threatened by temps. The short-term nature of many of the temp jobs at Office Supplies added a further sense of urgency to obtaining a permanent job because temps in those jobs could not see beyond the next day or week.

CONCLUSIONS

During the economic boom of the mid- to late 1990s, lower-skilled and less-educated individuals faced the best labor market in a generation. Despite this, a growing number took temporary jobs. This study used data from multiple sources—archival payroll data, a survey, case studies—to answer a number of questions that this phenomenon raises about temps' skills, employment objectives, work experiences, and labor market outcomes.

Why do low-skilled workers accept temp jobs? Is a temporary job a preferred route or a last resort? Finding a permanent job is clearly the dominant motivation. With more and more firms using temps to prescreen for permanent jobs, temping plays an increasingly important role in the hiring process. The downside is that the benefits (and often higher wages) that accompany full-time employment are delayed during the screening process. The upside is that lower-skilled workers are able to sample different jobs before settling on the one best suited to their needs, as well as gain skills through work experience and training.

Does temping enhance labor market outcomes through opportunities to upgrade skills, get promotions and wage increases, and/or move into a permanent job? Less-educated, lower-wage, and lower-skilled temps are slightly less likely to experience wage growth of 10 percent or more in a year. Although these temps are less likely to be offered training, when they do take training, it offsets this disadvantage. We suspect that the temp agencies' staff may not fully understand and actively promote training for low-skilled temps, the group who perhaps could benefit the most. Less than half of temps in our survey reported being offered the free training that the agencies in theory provide, and just over half of those offered training (or 23 percent of the whole sample) took any training during the previous year. The typical temp receives only 2.7 hours of training annually, a minuscule amount compared with the 24 hours of employer-provided training that the typical permanent employee receives in the United States (Van Buren and Erksine 2002). Less-educated, lower-wage industrial temps are also more likely to find permanent jobs, an outcome that is consistent with their stated motivations for temping. Yet the agency is less helpful to them in finding these jobs than it is for their higher-skilled peers. The finding that taking training is negatively associated with finding a permanent job most likely indicates the importance of time constraints: taking the time to train requires taking time away from job search and/or turning down job offers.

What factors explain which low-skilled temporary workers advance into higher-skill and higher-paying positions? How do the work settings in which they are placed affect their career outcomes? The extent of internal labor markets and individual managers' discretion to reward and train temps seem especially important. Local labor market conditions also play a key role, since firms often calibrate temps' wages to minimize both costs and turnover; the end result is wages that neither out- nor underperform the local market radically. The availability of alternative nontemp jobs in which people can use their temp experience and the skills they have acquired also plays an important role. Industrial firms seem willing to use limited wage progression and career growth strategies for the least-skilled and lowest-paid segments of the workforce. But the agencies' training is more geared to office and technical skills, leaving industrial temps to do disproportionately more skill development on the job.

How do the experiences of lower-skilled workers in temporary jobs compare with those of other workers? Relative to perms in similar positions, lower-skilled, less-educated temps typically have much less generous benefits—if they have any at all—and they often have lower hourly wage rates. Skill development opportunity differences seem to depend predominantly on the role that the temps play relative to the perms in producing the firm's output. They are definitely paid less than higher-skilled, more-educated temps, an indication of perennial wage-skill differentials in the nontemp labor market. The difference in benefits is much less stark; however, to the extent that eligibility is based on hours worked and/or earnings within a fixed time frame, lower-wage temps tend to lose out because they earn less and work fewer hours.

What strategies do firms use when employing low-skilled temps to remain competitive in their markets? What impact do these strategies have on low-skilled temps' outcomes? Greater use of contingent work has been associated with better financial results and stock market returns (Nayar and Willinger 2001). Our findings are consistent with this: the primary driving forces in firms' decisions to use temps appear to be reducing the labor cost of each worker hired and increasing the firm's ability to respond quickly to fluctuations in demand in specific labor markets. In general, this is part of the larger negative trend that has diminished labor market opportunities in the United States for less-educated, lower-skilled workers. A positive aspect of this trend, however, is that companies are more likely to hire additional workers when demand picks up instead of just increasing overtime among existing employees. This practice can spread the benefits of economic growth more evenly across the workforce than might happen otherwise. And the more temps are used to staff core tasks of the firm, the more firms seem willing to provide them with both training and skill development opportunities, as well as competitive wages.

Looking forward, temporary agencies could do significantly more to raise the awareness of free training and make it easier for individuals to participate by modularizing their courses and making them available online, innovations that are already under way in some agencies. Even if these innovations take hold, however, they are likely to be targeted at office and professional workers, who have greater computer and Internet access and for whom CBT courses are most relevant. In the near term, the most common source of skill enhancement for most temps—as is true for most permanent employees—probably will continue to be informal learning from coworkers or experience garnered through moving from one job to the next.

Our case studies suggest that temporary agencies could play a larger role in workforce development in the United States. But it is the preferences of each client, not the temp agency, that play the most critical role in determining the opportunities that temp work offers to lower-skilled workers. At We Deliver, the agency works closely with the firm to provide formal training and career development, with the result that lower-educated temps are more likely to receive formal training, which is structured, taken on company time, and supported with mentoring. There is a dark side to this case, however: jobs at We Deliver that previously offered full benefits and greater security have been shifted into ongoing, temporary positions with no prospect for individuals to move into permanent positions. In contrast, at Office Supplies temporary workers have little opportunity for training, wage growth, or career progression while temping, but the agency makes it possible for very low-skilled individuals to move from welfare into a work setting where many are then able to find a permanent job.

For a minority of lower-skilled workers, the growing role of temp agencies offers a clear benefit. This is the group for whom temping is the preferred employment option either because they like the variety of assignments and flexibility that temping offers or they are constrained from taking a regular job by family or school-related responsibilities. In addition, the free training offered by many agencies and the on-the-job learning provide development opportunities to lower-skilled workers who otherwise might have more constrained access or no access at all. These opportunities are available both to those who want ongoing work as temps and those seeking permanent jobs.

Taken together, these results suggest that the growing role of temp agencies as intermediaries in the economy has been a double-edged sword for low-skilled workers. On the one hand, temp agencies clearly have helped provide job opportunities to millions of unemployed people who otherwise might not have found jobs without an intervening spell of unemployment. Lawrence Katz and Alan Krueger's (1999) evidence suggests that the role of temp agencies may have lowered the natural rate of unemployment in the 1990s by improving the match between jobs and job-seekers. On the other hand, the better temp agencies get at playing the intermediary role, the easier it is for companies to delay or avoid altogether hiring permanent workers as they shift jobs that used to be part of their core workforce into temporary or contract positions. More research is needed to quantify the net social welfare impact of these effects.

APPENDIX: CASE-STUDY METHODS AND DESCRIPTIVE STATISTICS

In each case we conducted:

1. Telephone and face-to-face interviews with the temporary agency representative(s) with overall responsibility for managing the client's account, to determine how the agency meets the needs of both the client

and the temps and its motivations for entering the relationship with the client

2. A face-to-face interview with the manager responsible for decisions around use of temporary employees, to understand the client's staffing strategy

3. Face-to-face interviews with one or more managers at the client who regularly oversee and work with temporary employees, to obtain more detail on the employment setting, the design and structure of temporary work, and the skill, wage, and career opportunities of the temporary employees

4. Focus-group interviews with six to twelve temps employed by the client, to get their perspectives on the work and how that work meets their needs and expectations

5. Focus-group interviews with six to twelve permanent employees—in cases where temporary employees work side by side with permanent employees doing the same work—to understand their views of working with temps and compare their skill, wage, and career opportunities

Table 9.A1 Regression Variable Descriptions and Summary Statistics

Variable Name in Table	Variable Description	Mean (Standard Deviation)	Minimum-Maximum
Offered training	Respondents who were offered the opportunity to take training	0.4 (.49)	0–1
Training participation	Respondents who took training, conditional on being offered	0.5 (.50)	0–1
Hours of training	Number of training hours respondent received in past year	21.0 (37.02)	1–400
Permanent job	Respondent obtained a permanent job	0.3 (.46)	0–1
Fast wage growth	Respondent experienced fast wage growth in year of maximum hours (1999 or 2000)	0.2 (.42)	0–1
Low education	Respondent has some high school education or a high school diploma	0.2 (.43)	0–1
Computer experience	Respondent's level of prior computer experience (ranging from "no experience" to "advanced experience")	3.3 (1.25)	1–5
Age	Age of respondent	37.9 (13.14)	17–82
Female	Female respondents	0.6 (.50)	0–1
Also a student	Respondent was also a student while at agency	0.1 (.35)	0–1
Long-term temporary	Reason for joining temp agency was to find long-term temporary work	0.3 (.44)	0–1
Short-term permanent	Reason for joining temp agency was to find short-term permanent work	0.2 (.42)	0–1
Long-term permanent	Reason for joining temp agency was to find long-term permanent work	0.4 (.49)	0–1
Fast wage progressor oversample	Respondent is part of the oversample of fast wage progressors	0.2 (.41)	0–1
Wage at time of survey	Respondent makes $8.00 an hour or less versus more than $8.00 an hour	0.3 (.46)	0–1

Table 9.A1 *Continued*

Variable Name in Table	Variable Description	Mean (Standard Deviation)	Minimum- Maximum
Occupation (clerical versus others)	Respondent's occupation is in the clerical field	0.4 (.50)	0–1
Occupation (industrial versus others)	Respondent's occupation is in the industrial field	0.3 (.44)	0–1
Training taken	Respondents who took training (no missing values)	0.2 (.42)	0–1
Working another job while at agency	Respondent was in another paid job while at agency	0.2 (.36)	0–1
Contribution of temp income to family income	Amount of overall family income coming from temp work (ranging from "very little" to "nearly all")	3.4 (1.40)	1–5
Percentage time working in three years prior to joining agency	Percentage time respondent was in paid work in the three years prior to joining the agency	77.1 (29.21)	0–100
Laid off in three years prior to joining agency	Respondent was laid off in the three years prior to joining the agency	0.3 (.47)	0–1
Unemployed immediately prior to joining agency	Respondent was unemployed immediately prior to joining agency	0.4 (.49)	0–1
Own a computer	Respondent owns a computer	0.7 (.47)	0–1
Use the Internet	Respondent uses the Internet	0.7 (.45)	0–1

Source: Authors' compilation.

Table 9.A2 Descriptive Information on Case-Study Survey Respondents

	Office Supplies	HealthTech	We Deliver
Number of temps employed	450 to 800	140 to 230	220 to 260
Number of valid survey responses	111	93	138
Survey response rate	14.7%	40.6%	50.0%
Female	72.5	89.3	88.9
Mean age (years)	30.6	40.5	30.8
Mean number of dependents	1.4	1.0	1.2
Student	29.4%	21.3%	19.1%
High school or less education	37.3	15.2	22.8
College degree or higher	10.9	28.3	14.7
Own a computer	48.2	82.8	61.0
Use the Internet	45.0	87.1	72.1
Not in paid work but looking	65.1	19.8	29.4
Objectives			
Short-term temps	11.1	28.1	2.9
Long-term temps	23.2	36.0	8.8
Short-term perms	34.3	5.6	35.8
Selective perms	31.5	30.3	52.6

Source: Authors' compilation.

Table 9.A3 Wage, Skill, and Career Growth Preferences of Temporary Workers

Most Important Attributes of Temp Work	Office Supplies	HealthTech	We Deliver
Competitive pay	1.35	1.12	1.72
Good benefits	0.68	0.29	0.92
Opportunity to obtain a permanent job	0.66	0.44	0.86
Long-term assignments	0.68	0.32	0.33
Skill development	0.35	0.32	0.31
Rapid advancement	0.28	0.08	0.28
Control over when and where one works	0.05	0.63	0.03

Source: Authors' compilation.
[a] *Score*: 3 = most important; 2 = second most important; 1 = third most important; 0 = not listed; seventeen choices offered.

Table 9.A4 Wage, Skill, and Career Growth Outcomes for Temporary Workers

	Office Supplies	HealthTech	We Deliver
Training			
Offered training	36.4%	73.9%	77.4%
Taking training (of those offered)	66.7	60.9	93.4
Median hours of training (of those taking)	15.0	5.0	27.5
Skills obtained[a]	3.43	3.77	3.79
Skills that are very marketable	3.41	3.71	3.72
Skills that are very specific to the organization(s) where I worked	3.45	3.82	3.85
Development–job matching scale[a]	3.69	3.78	3.93
Opportunity to enhance my skills through training	3.36	3.14	3.72
Opportunity to learn from other people at the workplace	3.95	4.10	4.07
Opportunity to learn new things on the job	4.00	3.99	4.04
Work that is closely matched to my skills and abilities	3.45	3.78	3.84
Interesting work	3.67	3.91	3.98
Pay equity–advancement scale[a]	2.76	2.98	2.69
Pay and benefits that are fair relative to other temporary or contract workers doing similar work	2.94	3.47	2.97
Pay and benefits that are fair relative to the work that I have performed	2.82	3.37	2.74
Pay and benefits that are fair compared to permanent workers doing similar jobs	2.18	2.68	2.17
Chance to move into a higher-level position	2.84	2.46	2.72
Chance to progress into better assignments	3.00	2.86	2.83
Not scaled: chance to increase my pay and benefits	2.66	2.73	2.85
Permanent job			
Accepted permanent job and no longer temping (at time of survey; location of job not known)	15.7%	26.9%	27.9%

Table 9.A4 *Continued*

	Office Supplies	HealthTech	We Deliver
Of above, obtained permanent job through temp assignments (at time of survey)	7.5%	42.3%	82.6%

Source: Authors' compilation.
[a] *Scale*: 1 = not at all; 3 = some extent; 5 = very great extent.

NOTES

1. Segal and Sullivan's (1997b) calculations imply that a much smaller 4 percent of the labor force temp annually.
2. Unfortunately, we cannot report the precise percentage for confidentiality reasons.
3. The proportion of professional and technical temps versus industrial and clerical temps is not necessarily indicative of their proportions among the population of temps at these agencies. The 6,500 number for the technical and professional group was chosen to ensure a large enough set of returned surveys to facilitate statistical analysis.
4. For technical reasons, we could only construct the difference between the maximum and minimum wages. We included all those with at least a 5 percent difference in wages. This includes both those whose wages *fell* by at least 5 percent and those whose wages *rose* by at least 5 percent. (Table 8.5 suggests that the latter outnumber the former by at least three to one.) In the analyses we control for the respondents who came from this oversample.
5. First, a representative sample of 100 offices specializing in industrial and clerical assignments was selected. A random sample of 7,500 temps from within those offices was then drawn. The total number of temps sampled from these offices was 8,441 (national plus oversample). The response rate for the 2 samples was virtually identical.
6. The amount of the payment varied across agencies. The results from two different pilot tests of the survey at one agency suggested that the bonus alone probably increased the response rate by three to four percentage points.
7. We excluded 329 respondents whom we were unable to match with payroll records, dropping the number to 4,171.
8. These are all averages conditional on working (that is, hours greater than zero).

9.   We have no information to determine whether the permanent jobs had higher wages or other positive attributes.

10. The questionnaire's wording was: "I have accepted a permanent job and am no longer taking temporary assignments." Only those answering "yes" to this statement were coded as having found a permanent job.

11. Specifically, if they said "yes" when asked whether they had accepted a permanent job and were no longer temping, they were then asked whether the permanent job was obtained through an assignment with the agency.

12. Note that "working another job while temping" is also negatively correlated (column 3). These people probably used temping to supplement income from their main job. Thus, "finding a permanent job" for them probably meant a *different* permanent job than their current one. If so, then the negative result means they were less likely to leave their current main job than other temps were to find a permanent job in the first place.

13. However, this is an overadjustment: the fourth column considers *any* negative wage growth, but the second column requires positive wage growth of *at least 10 percent*. The fraction of temps with negative wage growth of at least 10 percent is undoubtedly much smaller than the figures in the fourth column, and vice versa.

14. At these sites everyone who had worked there within the previous year was surveyed, including those no longer on assignment.

15. Both of these preferences may be true, as a high percentage of temps move quickly into permanent jobs and those remaining in temp assignments are more likely to prefer that option.

16. The temp agency at each of the other two firms in our case studies provided dedicated staff to manage the account with the client. Their role was limited, however, to traditional HR functions, not production and work design issues.

17. We Deliver's representatives expressed no concern that the use of temps could have increased the risk that the conversion would fail because of lack of experience and knowledge about the company's processes and products.

REFERENCES

Abraham, Katharine G., and Susan K. Taylor. 1996. "Firms' Use of Outside Contractors: Theory and Evidence." *Journal of Labor Economics* 14(3): 394–424.

American Staffing Association. 2001. "Staffing FAQs: Answers to Frequently Asked Questions." Available at: *www.natss.org/staffstats/staffingfaqs.shtml.*

Autor, David H. 1999. "Why Do Temporary Help Firms Provide Free General Skills Training?" Working paper. Cambridge, Mass.: Massachusetts Institute of Technology.

———. 2000. "Outsourcing at Will: Unjust Dismissal Doctrine and the Growth of Temporary Help Employment." Working paper. Cambridge, Mass.: Massachusetts Institute of Technology.

Autor, David H., Frank Levy, and Richard J. Murnane. 1999. "Skills Training in the Temporary Help Sector: Employer Motivations and Worker Impacts." Report to the U.S. Department of Labor Employment and Training Administration. Cambridge, Mass.: Massachusetts Institute of Technology (September).

Becker, Gary S. 1964. *Human Capital.* Chicago: University of Chicago Press.

Bjurman, Jonas. 1995. "New Survey Reports on Wages and Benefits for Temporary Help Services Workers." U.S. Department of Labor press release (September 6).

Brogan, Timothy W. 2000. "Thriving in a Dwindling Pool of Available Workers: ASA's Annual Analysis of the Staffing Industry." *Staffing Success* (May–June).

Broshack, David, and Alison Davis-Blake. 1999. "Is Temporary Employment an Effective Selection Tool?: The Relationship Between Temporary Employment and Job Performance." Paper presented to the annual meeting of the Academy of Management, Chicago (August).

Economic Policy Institute. 1997. *Nonstandard Work, Substandard Jobs: Flexible Work Arrangement in the U.S.* Washington, D.C.: Economic Policy Institute.

Farber, Henry S. 2000. "Alternative Employment Arrangements as a Response to Job Loss." In *On the Job: Is Long-term Employment a Thing of the Past?*, edited by David Neumark. New York: Russell Sage Foundation.

Feldman, Daniel C., Helen I. Doerpinghaus, and William H. Turnley. 1994. "Managing Temporary Workers: A Permanent HRM Challenge." *Organizational Dynamics* 23: 49–63.

Geary, J. F. 1992. "Employment Flexibility and Human Resource Management: The Case of Three American Electronics Plants." *Work, Employment, and Society* 6: 251–70.

Houseman, Susan N. 2000. "Why Employers Use Flexible Staffing Arrangements: Evidence from an Establishment Survey." Staff working paper 01–67. Kalamazoo, Mich.: W. E. Upjohn Institute for Employment Research (October).

Houseman, Susan N., and Anne E. Polivka. 2000. "The Implication of Flexible Staffing Arrangements for Job Security." In *On the Job: Is Long-term Employment a Thing of the Past?*, edited by David Neumark. New York: Russell Sage Foundation.

Katz, Lawrence, and Alan Krueger. 1999. "The High-Pressure U.S. Labor Market of the 1990s." *Brookings Papers on Economic Activity* 1: 1–87.

Levenson, Alec. 2000. "Long-run Trends in Part-time and Temporary Employment: Toward an Understanding." In *On the Job: Is Long-term Employment a Thing of the Past?,* edited by David Neumark. New York: Russell Sage Foundation.

Levenson, Alec, and David Finegold. 2001. "The Employment Outcomes and Advancement of Temporary Workers." Working paper. Los Angeles: Center for Effective Organizations, Marshall School of Business, University of Southern California.

Lynch, Linda M., and Sandra E. Black. 1998. "Determinants of Employer-Provided Training." *Industrial and Labor Relations Review* 52: 1.

Mishel, Lawrence, Jared Bernstein, and John Schmitt. 2001. *The State of Working America 2000–2001.* Ithaca, N.Y.: Cornell University Press.

Mohrman, Susan, Susan Cohen, and Allan Mohrman. 1995. *Designing Team-Based Organization.* San Francisco: Jossey-Bass.

National Center for Education Statistics. 1995. *National Household Education Survey: Employment-Related Adult Education.* Washington: U.S. Department of Education.

Nayar, Nandkumar, and G. Lee Willinger. 2001. "Financial Implications of the Decision to Increase Reliance on Contingent Labor." *Decision Sciences* 32(4): 661–81.

Polivka, Anne E. 1996. "A Profile of Contingent Workers." *Monthly Labor Review* 119(10): 10–20.

Prencipe. 2001. "Review Temporary Workers Status." *Infoworld* (*www.infoworld.com*), January 5.

Rogers, Jackie K. 1995. "Just a Temp: Experience and Structure of Alienation in Temporary Clerical Employment." *Work and Occupations* 22: 137–66.

Segal, Louis M., and Daniel G. Sullivan. 1997a. "The Growth of Temporary Services Work." *Journal of Economic Perspectives* 11(2): 117–36.

———. 1997b. "Temporary Services Employment Durations: Evidence from State UI Data." Working paper WP-97-23. Chicago: Federal Reserve Bank of Chicago (December).

U.S. Department of Labor, Bureau of Labor Statistics. 1999. "Contingent and Alternative Employment Arrangements, February 1999." News release, USDL 99–362. Washington, D.C. (December 21).

Van Buren, Mark E., W. Erksine. 2002. *The 2002 ASTD State of the Industry Report.* Alexandria, Va.: American Society for Training and Development.

Van Dyne, Linn, and S. Ang. 1998. "Organizational Citizenship Behavior of Contingent Workers in Singapore." *Academy of Management Journal* 41: 692–703.

CHAPTER 10

The Effects of Temporary Services and Contracting Out on Low-Skilled Workers: Evidence from Auto Suppliers, Hospitals, and Public Schools

George A. Erickcek, Susan N. Houseman,
and Arne L. Kalleberg

Temporary help employment grew dramatically over the last decade, accounting for 10 percent of net employment growth in the United States during the 1990s. Although government statistics on contracting out are not maintained, evidence from case studies and business surveys suggests that there has been dramatic growth in the outsourcing of functions to outside companies as well (Abraham and Taylor 1996; Houseman 2001b; Kalleberg, Reynolds, and Marsden forthcoming). In both cases, the workers providing services to the client firm are not the client's employees but rather the legal employees of the temporary help agency or the contract company. Through intensive case studies in manufacturing (automotive supply), services (hospitals), and public-sector (primary and secondary public schools) industries, we endeavor to shed light on employers' increasing use of these nonstandard employment arrangements and their implications for wages, benefits, and working conditions for workers in low-skilled labor markets.

Because workers in these arrangements often receive lower compensation than they would if they were employees of the client organization, the growth of temporary help and contracting out generally is viewed as inimical to workers' interests. We find, however, that the story is not that simple. Our case-study evidence points to circumstances in which workers *are* likely to be adversely affected by the outsourcing of jobs to agencies or contractors. These cases entail the long-term substitution of agency temporary or contract company workers for regular employees and the loss of wages, benefits, or union status.

In other situations, however, the effects on low-skilled workers appear to be minimal or even beneficial. Often organizations only contract out the management function, with little direct effect on low-skilled workers. Agency temporaries typically do not substitute for regular workers on a long-term basis. Moreover, employers often use temporary agencies to screen workers for permanent positions. Because temporary agencies lower the cost to employers of using workers with poor work histories or other risky characteristics, agencies may benefit these workers by giving them opportunities to try out for positions they otherwise might not have had.

Throughout our discussion we point to the important impacts of employment and labor law, unions, and other institutional factors on employers' incentives to use temporary agencies or contract companies, on the constraints that employers face in using these employment forms, and on the implications of such outsourcing for low-skilled workers.

BACKGROUND ON ECONOMIC CONDITIONS

The primary data for these case studies were collected in 1999 and 2000. During this time period all three industries faced tight labor markets for low-skilled workers. Moreover, although the sources of the pressure differed across industries, automotive suppliers, hospitals, and public schools were all facing intense pressure to cut costs. Automotive suppliers made intensive use of temporary help services, public schools contracted out functions, and hospitals used a combination of temporary services and contracting out. We argue that the utilization of temporary services and contract companies was one strategy employers adopted to reduce recruitment costs, increase productivity, or lower compensation or other costs.

AUTOMOTIVE SUPPLIERS

During the latter half of the 1990s, automotive suppliers witnessed tremendous growth as car sales reached new highs. In 1999, after enjoying three "good" sales years of more than 15 million units, car and light truck sales climbed to 16.8 million units, an industry record. Industry economists argued that the industry had established a new sustainable annual level of output of 16 million units, an increase from their earlier estimate of 15.5 million units. In 2000 car and light truck sales soared even higher, reaching 17.3 million units. In 2001, despite recessionary conditions in the nation's business investment sector, car and light truck sales stayed at 17 million units.

These high sales volumes came at the expense of prices; prices on cars and light trucks had been stable or declining during the preceding five years. Facing lower prices, automakers turned to cost reduction strategies to increase profits. Automakers pressured their suppliers to take on more research and development responsibilities and risks, to respond quickly to new orders and design changes, to deliver their product in a just-in-time environment, and to do all of this for less money. In this environment, use of temporary help agencies became an important staffing strategy in four of the five auto supply plants we studied.

HOSPITALS

Cost pressures on hospitals began to grow in the late 1960s, when there was a decline in reimbursement owing to changes in programs such as Medicare. These cost pressures increased during the 1990s, primarily because of declining reimbursement from the federal government and insurance companies.[1] Adding to cost pressures on hospitals was the growth of managed care organizations, which increased competition within the market for health care and often forced hospitals to offload nonprofitable businesses (such as nursing homes or dialysis services) and to focus more on their core competencies. These cost pressures led hospitals to undergo consolidation and other forms of reorganization.

A substantial fraction of a hospital's expenses are in the form of labor costs. Typically, an estimated 60 percent of a hospital's expenses are labor costs, of which 40 percent are accounted for by nurses. For these reasons, the nursing pool has been a target for cuts by hospitals seeking to contain costs, and nurses have often been replaced with lower-skilled, low-wage workers (Egger 1999). Nursing aides, whose wage is just 60 percent of the median for all workers (U.S. Department of Labor 1998), is one of the fastest-growing occupational groups in the United States. In addition, many hospitals have outsourced support functions, such as food and environmental services, in an effort to increase efficiency and reduce costs.[2]

PUBLIC SCHOOLS

The public schools in our study are located in Michigan. Two measures enacted in the mid-1990s greatly altered the competitive and financial environment for public schools in this state. The first was the licensing and funding of charter schools, which were intended to increase school choice for parents and students, primarily in poor urban districts, and to stimulate innovative educational practices for at-risk children. The second was the passage of Proposal A, which shifted public school funding away from local property taxes and onto the state sales tax. The new tax base was intended to equalize the funding of public schools across wealthy and poor districts and stabilize funding for poor districts that had suffered declining property values. The vast majority of a public school's funding now comes from a per pupil allowance from the state, set at $6,971 in 2001 to 2002. The per pupil allowance represents an average cost of educating a child, and the marginal cost is lower. An unintended consequence of the new funding mechanism is to reward expanding school districts and penalize districts with declining enrollments. Declining enrollments, in large part due to competition from charter schools, placed many school districts, especially urban districts, in severe financial straits.

One response by school administrators in financially troubled districts has been to cut costs in non-instructional services, such as bus, custodial, and food services, in order to maintain the quality of instructional services. Workers in non-instructional services are commonly unionized in Michigan, particularly in the larger urban and suburban districts. A 1994 amendment to the State of Michigan's Public Employment Relations Act, which precluded collective bargaining over the outsourcing of non-instructional services, paved the way to the outsourcing of previously unionized, non-instructional services.

CASE-STUDY METHODOLOGY

We studied the use of temporary services and contracting out in connection with the low-skilled workforce in five automotive supply establishments, six hospitals, and seven public school districts.

The five automotive suppliers were located in the Midwest; three of the hospitals were located in Michigan and three in North Carolina; and all seven public school districts were located in Michigan. In selecting automotive suppliers and hospitals for case study, we had no prior knowledge of the organizations' use of flexible staffing arrangements. In public schools, however, we intentionally selected districts that contracted out at least one non-instructional function.

Although the sample was restricted geographically, we endeavored to select a variety of organizations within each industry. Among the automotive suppliers, the workforce ranged in size from 430 to 2,100. Two of the plants were foreign-owned subsidiaries, 1 was a branch plant of a large U.S. company, and 2 were locally owned plants. Production workers in 2 of the 5 plants were unionized. The hospitals varied in size from a small Michigan hospital with 450 employees to a large North Carolina hospital with 6,000 employees. Half of the hospitals were public and half were private, not-for-profit institutions. One hospital was unionized. In public schools we interviewed a wide range of districts. Three of the districts were urban, 1 was a large suburban district, and 2 were small rural districts. One of the case studies was an intermediate school district, organized at the county level primarily to provide services for children with disabilities. The bus drivers in all of the school districts were unionized, even bus drivers who were employees of a contractor. Of the 6 districts with food service and custodial employees, food service workers were unionized in 3 and custodial workers in 4.

In all three industries we conducted extensive interviews with the organizations' managers, temporary agency or contract company representatives, and workers in order to gain various perspectives on why organizations used these staffing arrangements and what impacts they had on workers. We developed a set of questionnaires for each type of person interviewed (manager, temporary help agency, contractor, worker representative) within each industry. A core set of questions was asked at each site within a particular industry. However, we asked follow-up questions to allow interviewees to expand upon or clarify certain points. All interviews were tape-recorded and subsequently transcribed.

In the auto supply industry we interviewed the human resources director of each of the companies, at least one of the first-line production supervisors, and the on-site temporary employment agency representatives at the two production facilities with such representatives. At one company we were able to conduct two focus-group sessions, one with permanent workers and another with temporary agency workers.

Within hospitals we interviewed the human resources director and managers in key functional areas: nursing, clerical and administrative support, laboratory, food services and housekeeping, and clinical specialties (for example, radiology or physical therapy). We also interviewed selected temporary help agencies that provide clinical staff to hospitals and the regional manager of a national contractor that supplies food and cleaning services to hospitals.[3]

In each school district we interviewed the person or people in charge of non-instructional personnel and contracting out. In one very small school district this was the superintendent. In larger districts these duties were performed by a business manager and human resources manager. We also conducted interviews with the food service and cleaning contractors that were used by these public school districts and with union representatives in occupations affected by contracting out.

In addition to collecting information through interviews, we collected basic data on employment, wages, and benefits by occupation of regular full-time, part-time, and on-call employees at each organization studied. Where possible, we also collected similar information for the contract and temporary agency employees assigned to the organization studied.

LOW-SKILLED JOBS IN AUTOMOTIVE SUPPLY FIRMS, HOSPITALS, AND PUBLIC SCHOOLS

In this study, we focus on workers in low-skilled jobs. "Low-skilled" primarily refers to positions that do not require postsecondary education and whose tasks can be learned on the job in a relatively short period of time. This would exclude, for example, skilled trades positions. We use the term "low-skilled" rather than "unskilled" to denote the fact that although the training time needed to learn these jobs is relatively short, the jobs often require nontrivial skills. We further distinguish between "low-skilled" and "low-paid" positions. Workers in low-skilled positions typically receive relatively low pay, but this is not always the case, particularly when workers are unionized. In that situation, employers may have strong incentives to outsource these positions to temporary agencies or contract companies.

Low-skilled jobs accounted for a large share of employment in all three of the industries studied. In auto supply, production positions accounted for 60 to 75 percent of employment in the case-study plants. The overwhelming majority of these production positions were low-skilled or semiskilled; entry-level positions were typically learned on the job in two days or less.

Although registered nurses (RNs) form the single largest occupation in hospitals, hospitals have shifted work away from high-skilled, high-paid RNs to low-skilled, low-paid nurse assistants. Moreover, hospitals utilize a large number of workers in clerical, food service, and housekeeping functions. The vast majority of workers in these support functions are low-skilled. Among the hospitals we studied, between 40 and 50 percent of the staff were in low-skilled positions. Between 13 and 20 percent of staff were in low-skilled clinical positions, 15 to 21 percent were in low-skilled clerical positions, and another 7 to 10 percent were in housekeeping positions.

Like RNs in hospitals, teachers represent the core occupations in public schools, but also as in hospitals, public schools utilize many low-skilled workers in areas such as food service, cleaning, and transportation. Among the schools in our study, typically 15 to 20 percent of a district's employment was in these three non-instructional support occupations.

Most of the entry-level positions offer some possibility for career advancement. For instance, production workers may learn additional skills or stations, for which they receive higher pay. Eventually the best workers may be promoted to team leaders or line supervisors. The typical entry-level position in food service entails assistance with simple food preparation and serving. A worker may advance to cook or cashier, and eventually to a supervisory position. Custodians in schools may advance to be the head custodian of a school. Some occupations, such as bus drivers and nurse's aides, have no job ladder.

The low-skilled jobs in our sample are not always associated with low compensation. This point is pertinent to our study because organizations' incentive to outsource jobs to a temporary help agency or contract company and the effects on workers of such outsourcing are likely to depend on workers' compensation. Organizations would be expected to have a greater incentive to outsource jobs the higher the wages of their low-skilled workforce relative to low-skilled workers in other competing organizations. In turn, relatively high-paid, low-skilled workers potentially have more to lose from outsourcing.

Information on starting wages, the availability of health insurance benefits, and the union status of workers in low-skilled occupations in automotive supply, hospitals, and public schools is reported in appendix table 10.A1.[4] The wages and benefits for entry-level production workers in automotive supply tended to be better than those for low-skilled occupations in the other two industries. Production workers always worked full-time and received basic health insurance and retirement benefits. Perhaps most notable was the large variation in starting wage across auto suppliers. Two of the plants in our sample were unionized, and these workers received relatively high wages. However, one of the non-union plants paid the second-highest wages. Historically, this employer intentionally pursued a "high-road" strategy, paying above-market compensation to its workers. Its managers believed that by so doing it would attract the best workers and thereby reduce quality control and turnover problems. This employer had a reputation for being one of the best in the area and had little trouble attracting workers, even during tight labor markets. A high compensation strategy was also motivated by a desire to remain non-union.

Wages for entry-level positions in food service, housekeeping, and nurse assistants and clerical positions in hospitals tended to be quite low. Hospitals offered health insurance and retirement benefits to all full-time workers. However, many low-skilled hospital workers worked part-time and received prorated benefits, with either high copayments on health insurance or no benefits. Interestingly, the one hospital in our study with unions representing low-skilled workers had a high fraction of part-time workers in its low-skilled positions.

The wages for low-skilled workers in public schools varied considerably. Entry-level food service positions in public schools were almost always part-time, and the wage levels were quite low, even in cases where these workers were unionized. None of the schools in our sample offered health insurance to their part-time food service employees. Under state law, all public school employees, including food service employees, are part of a state retirement plan. Payment into the retirement plan is made solely by the school and amounts to between 12 and 13 percent of the worker's earnings. Entry-level custodians, who were often unionized, typically worked full-time and earned substantially higher wages and benefits than did food service workers. Bus drivers bear considerable responsibility and require special training, particularly in the area of safety. All of the bus drivers in our sample were unionized, even when they were employees of a contract company. The hourly wage of bus drivers tended to be similar to that of custodians, but many school systems experienced great difficulty recruiting bus drivers. One reason is that most positions were part-time, with hours concentrated in the early morning and mid to late afternoon. In an effort to recruit bus drivers, some school systems offered these individuals full-time employment with full benefits by utilizing them in other jobs in the intervening hours.

TEMPORARY HELP USE

The use of temporary agency help was common in our auto supply and hospital case studies.[5] Usage was particularly high among some auto suppliers. Although no statistics exist on the use of temporary agency employment at a detailed industry level, our case-study evidence of high use in auto supply is consistent with findings that temporary help in manufacturing has grown rapidly since the 1980s (Segal 1996; Segal and Sullivan 1997).

Statistical studies have shown that, on average, agency temporaries earn lower wages than comparable workers in regular positions (Segal and Sullivan 1997, 1998). They also tend to receive fewer benefits (Houseman 1999; Kalleberg, Reskin, and Hudson 2000). Based on these facts, it is often assumed that temporary jobs are "bad" for workers. Yet, as our case-study evidence shows, the implications for workers are often more complicated. First, differences in compensation between agency temporaries and regular employees in statistical studies are only averages; sometimes agency temporaries earn more than their counterparts in regular jobs, and often their compensation is similar. Moreover, the effects of temporary employment on workers depend on the reasons organizations are utilizing temporaries and the alternatives available to the worker. For instance, if the organization is using temporary staff to screen workers for permanent positions, temporary employment may have no long-term adverse effects on these workers and may allow low-skilled workers to audition for jobs for which they would otherwise not be considered. Finally, an organization's utilization of temporary staff may have an impact not only on the temporary workers but also on the regular staff, and the effects on these two groups may be quite different.

USE OF TEMPORARY HELP AMONG AUTO SUPPLIERS

Four out of the five auto supply plants utilized temporary agency help during the period of our interviews (table 10.1). In two of the plants the utilization of temporary employment was very high, accounting for 20 percent or more of production employment. In one unionized plant the use of temporary agency workers was strictly prohibited by union contract.

As noted already, all of the plants were operating at or near full capacity during the period of study, and employers faced tight labor markets. Human resources directors reported that, while they received many applications, the average quality of the candidates was low. The fact that auto suppliers continued to have a large number of job applicants, albeit of low quality, despite the tight labor markets probably reflected the fact that the entry-level jobs offered relatively high pay and good benefits for low-skilled workers. For the most part, the auto suppliers in our study used temporary help agencies to staff increases in production and to screen workers for permanent positions. Across the cases in our study, however, there were subtle but important differences in employers' motivations for using temporary staff, the terms by which temporary staff were hired, and the implications for temporary and regular staff. We distinguish three cases.

The Use of Temporary Help in Unionized Plants   Auto suppliers are often faced with sudden and temporary increases in production levels and thus have an inherent, periodic need for temporary workers. Auto Supplier D, the unionized plant prohibited by contract from using agency temporaries, instead hired temporary workers directly when production volumes increased significantly. The short-term workers received entry-level wages and could stay no longer than 120 days. They gained no seniority for their work effort, nor

Table 10.1   Use of Temporary Help Among Auto Suppliers and Hospitals

	Temporary Help
Auto suppliers[a]	
Auto Supplier A	3–6%
Auto Supplier B	22
Auto Supplier C	22
Auto Supplier D	0
Auto Supplier E[b]	0–9
Hospitals[c]	
Food service	
Hospital A[d]	NA
Hospital E	11
Housekeeping	
Hospital A	NA
Hospital E	5
Nursing and medical assistants	
Hospital A	4
Hospital B	7
Hospital C	2
Hospital D	5
Hospital E	0
Clerical—unit administrative support	
Hospital A	8
Hospital B	0.4
Hospital C	0.3
Hospital D	7
Hospital E	11

Source: Authors' compilation.
[a] As a percentage of production employment.
[b] At the time of our interview Auto Supplier E had recently terminated all of its agency help.
[c] As a percentage of hours worked within occupation. Hospital F did not maintain any central records of temporary agency use and so is excluded from this table.
[d] The contract manager of food and environmental services of Hospital A reported using agency temporaries, but data on these hires were not available.

did they gain any advantage from working at the plant if they later sought a permanent position.

Auto Supplier E, the other union plant in our sample, was strictly limited in its use of agency temporaries. The labor contract stipulated that individual temporary agency workers could be used for no more than thirty days, and then only after the unionized workers had turned down the opportunity of greater overtime hours. At the end of the thirty days the employer could either hire the temporary worker on its payroll or terminate the temporary's contract. In addition, by collective agreement, the agency temporaries earned the same wage the employer offered new production workers. Thus, in practice, the treatment of direct-hire and agency temporary staff differed little between the two union plants. For the companies, the one using the agency temporaries paid overhead to the agency, while the other incurred higher internal costs in recruiting and screening its own temporary workers. Although temporary help agencies probably enjoy economies of scale in recruitment and screening, the union company using direct-hire temporaries paid higher wages than the union company using agency temporaries, and thus it is likely that it was easier for the former to recruit temporary workers on its own.

It is important to note that the human resources directors at both plants expressed a desire to use or to increase the use of agency temporaries. Even paying similar wages and agency overhead, human resources directors felt that they could save money by using agency temporaries because they incurred no benefits costs on the temporaries and because they reduced overtime paid to regular staff. Thus, the provisions in the union contracts constrained management staffing decisions.

The Use of Agency Temporaries by Non-Union "High-Road" Auto Suppliers The non-union Auto Supplier C offered higher wages than one of the union plants in the sample, and its wages were substantially higher than those at the other non-union auto suppliers. The company was regarded as one of the best area employers for low-skilled workers seeking manufacturing employment. In addition to good wages, the company had a no-layoff policy for its regular workers.

An integral complement to Auto Supplier C's high-wage, strong job security policies for regular workers, however, was the extensive use of agency temporaries, who earned substantially lower wages than entry-level regular workers and had no benefits or job security. The company's rationale for using agency temporaries was twofold. First, the company carefully screened all new hires through a temporary help agency, which had an on-site representative. The company wanted to ensure that workers were high performers before offering them job security at relatively high compensation. The company also wanted to remain non-union. According to the onsite temporary agency representative, the agency used this probationary period to screen out individuals it deemed likely to sympathize with union causes. Temporary agency workers had to complete a minimum of six months of work before becoming eligible to apply for a regular position. Sometimes workers remained as temporaries for a year or more before being offered a regular position or leaving. This probationary period as a temporary worker was considerably longer than at any other auto supplier we studied.

A second reason Auto Supplier C used the agency temporaries was to buffer regular workers in the event of a downturn in production. According to the human resources director, the company believed it had to maintain about 10 percent of its workforce as temporary to provide an adequate buffer for regular workers in the event of a downturn.

At the time of our interviews, however, the fraction of production workers who were agency temporaries had climbed to over 20 percent. The high fraction of temporaries resulted from the fact that production had been expanding, all new hiring was being done through the temporary agency, and temporaries had been converted to permanent hires at a slow rate.

Whether the fraction in temporary employment should be substantially lowered by offering more temporaries permanent positions at a faster pace was the subject of intense debate at the time of our interviews. On the one hand, the accounting department had calculated that a five-percentage-point drop in temporary employment cost the company $1 million a year because of the higher wages and benefits earned by permanent workers. On the other hand, the human resources department expressed concern that the temporaries were not as committed to the organization as regular staff. Moreover, many good temporaries reportedly tired of the long wait for permanent employment and quit, resulting in increased training costs and the quality problems associated with high turnover among temporaries, factors not taken into consideration in the accounting department's cost-savings calculations. The human resources department had feedback from other companies reporting that they had hired many well-trained workers who worked as temporaries at Auto Supplier C but had quit or been passed over for promotion. The plant's human resources director summarized the internal debate:

> As we were growing the business and . . . trying to get product out the door, it's like, "Get some more temporaries, get some more temporaries," and one morning we woke up and we were at like 25 percent. And . . . quality is starting to have problems . . . and now it's like, "We've got to get this temporary ratio back down."
>   . . . We'll start edging back down to 20, and . . . then the goal becomes 15 percent. We haven't hit it . . . and now there's always this discussion, "Well, it's more cost-effective to have the temporaries." So it doesn't seem to be an initiative with the executives to get that ratio down. So even though they talk about it, we are never going to get this high rate down. We run at around 20 percent. So what I'm trying to say is, is there a cost advantage? If there is . . . let's decide this and we're going to operate within 20 to 25 percent. . . . But . . . we are in this constant state of denial, yet that number still stays up there and . . . the vice president of human resources is . . . [saying], "We've got to get it down."

We conducted two focus groups with production workers at this plant—one with regular employees and the other with agency temporaries—to better understand the workers' perceptions of the costs and benefits of the company's use of temporaries. Interestingly, the regular workers, all of whom had been hired through the temporary agency, saw no problems with the system and perceived it as fair. In marked contrast, the temporaries viewed the system as unfair. They understood that the company would want to screen candidates through the temporary agency, but they believed that a two- or three-month time period—as was typical at the other non-union plants we studied—was more than adequate to assess a job candidate. They believed that temporaries were not treated as well as regular staff by supervisors, and they deeply resented the low wages they earned as temporaries. However, this resentment did not affect their productivity, for they knew that only the best temporaries would be offered permanent positions.

In sum, at the time of our interview company executives de facto had chosen to keep high levels of agency temporaries. The recent dramatic growth in the use of temporaries at this company could be viewed as a backing off from—or at least a qualification of—their human resource commitment to high wages and job security. Their original "high-road" philosophy was premised on the belief that high wages and strong commitments to job security would be paid back through high quality and low turnover. However, by having a very long probationary period at much lower wages, the company in essence was recapturing some of the rents that workers earned subsequently. At least the prevailing group of executives had come to believe that wage and benefits savings outweighed other costs associated with this strategy.

The Use of Temporary Help Among Other Non-Union Auto Suppliers
Auto Suppliers A and B were non-union plants whose compensation levels were considerably lower than those at the other three facilities studied. They each made extensive use of agency temporaries. At the time of our interviews agency temporaries accounted for over 20 percent of production employment at Auto Supplier B, which had substantially increased its use of temporaries because of a transitory increase in production. The human resources director at this relatively small plant felt that it would have been extremely difficult to recruit and screen large numbers of workers quickly for a large increase in production—especially in the tight labor market prevailing at the time of the interviews—without the assistance of a temporary agency.

Both plants also used temporary help agencies to screen workers for permanent positions. Temporary agency workers were typically screened over a two- to three-month period. If the company chose to offer them a position at the end of their temporary contract, they were then placed in a probationary status for another ninety days as a direct hire of the company.

As was the case in the other auto supply plants, human resources directors complained about the low quality of the applicants in the tight labor market. Many applicants had little or no experience in a manufacturing setting. Moreover, some applicants had criminal records, and many had spotty work histories. Managers emphasized that, in the tight labor market, they were hiring job applicants they would have never taken a second look at in the past.

Although the entry-level tasks that workers were expected to perform required little or no previous skills, the jobs required "soft" skills, like being punctual and being able to get along with coworkers. Production supervisors stressed the need to hire workers who "fit" into their production teams, and the use of temporary workers provided the opportunity to see whether the new workers would fit. As one supervisor said:

> I have the opportunity to observe this person over a period of time. I don't have just a half-an-hour snapshot to go by, as in an interview. I can get to know the person, get to know their background a little bit, get to know what their behaviors are, what motivates them, what possible problem areas I might have with the individual.

Historically, these auto suppliers would have hired new workers directly on probation. Temporary help agencies offered a couple of advantages to these companies. First, while the workers were with the temporary agency, they were less costly to the company than if they had been hired directly by the company. Although the wage differentials between temporaries and direct-hire production workers were not as great as at Auto Supplier C, temporary workers assigned to Auto Suppliers A and B earned lower wages than new hires at these companies. Moreover, the rate at which the temporary agency billed the workers was lower than the total compensation costs of new hires.[6] Second, it was easier for a manager to terminate and replace a worker hired through a temporary agency. The manager could simply inform the temporary agency that the assigned worker was not satisfactory and request a replacement.

By lowering the compensation and firing costs, temporary help agencies made it more attractive for companies to try out workers with criminal records, poor work histories, or otherwise "risky" characteristics. In the absence of temporary help agencies, companies might have hired these risky workers anyway. But they also might have instead chosen to offer higher wages and attract more qualified candidates, bidding them away from other companies. The human resources director at Auto Supplier B specifically discussed this alternative strategy, saying that his company had tried it but opted instead to use agency help.

The use of temporary help agencies as a mechanism for screening risky workers was even more transparent at Auto Supplier A. At that company job applicants were channeled into one of two tracks. Applicants with good qualifications were hired directly with a ninety-day probation. Applicants deemed more risky were referred to the temporary help agency, which, in turn, could place the candidate with the company on a temp-to-perm contract. At the end of the contract successful candidates were hired directly and began the company's ninety-day probationary period. According to the human resources director, the company treated its agency temporaries fairly:

> If you are out on the line, you would not be able to distinguish a contract employee from one of our own full-time employees. There is no differentiation on the training perspective, on the assignments they are given. . . . Our intention in bringing [temporary workers] in is to bring them on full-time. It's just that their backgrounds [make it uncertain whether they will be able] to meet our pretty rigorous hiring criteria. Yet, if we sense that there is an opportunity for a good match, we will bring them in through contract. So there is never an intent to just bring them in for a short-term blip in production and then let them go.

Approximately 70 percent of the company's new hires came through the temporary help agency.

A key element allowing these auto suppliers to try out more risky workers through temporary employment agencies was the use of small production teams. Instead of the assembly-line approach to production, work at these plants was organized in small production areas at which the more experienced workers were able to perform many, if not all, of the tasks required. This setting allowed the more experienced workers to monitor the performance of the temp workers, catch errors before the product left the assembly area, and adjust quickly to possible bottlenecks that arose as the new workers learned their tasks.

Although agency temporaries earned lower wages than those hired directly, many of these workers potentially benefited from the exposure to jobs that temporary help agencies offered. By lowering the cost to companies of hiring them, temporary help agencies gave workers with risky backgrounds opportunities—which they otherwise might not have had—to try out for higher-paid, full-time manufacturing jobs with good benefits. Another advantage to these workers was that if they did not succeed in the position or did not like the job, the assignment simply ended; it was not recorded as a dismissal or a quit, which would have tarnished their employment records.

For regular workers, any costs of using agency temporaries were indirect. By lowering the cost to companies of trying out riskier workers, temporary help agencies effectively expanded the supply of potential labor to a company. In this way companies could avoid or minimize the need to raise wages in order to attract more qualified candidates; because increases in wages for new workers are almost always accompanied by increase in wages for existing workers, existing regular workers would benefit from higher wage levels.[7]

USE OF TEMPORARY HELP AMONG HOSPITALS

The hospitals in our study made use of agency temporaries in a number of low-skilled occupations. In clinical areas the use of agency temporaries in such occupations as nurse assistants and patient sitters was often cited in interviews. Patient sitters watch extremely ill or confused patients and call for help when needed. Because the need for patient sitters is so variable, hospitals tend to staff this position exclusively with agency temporaries. In nonclinical areas all hospitals cited the use of agency temporaries for clerical functions, and three hospitals indicated that they used agency temporaries in food and environmental services, although only one maintained records of this use.

Table 10.1 reports the fraction of total hours worked in a particular occupational area that were accounted for by agency staff in hospitals with data that permitted such a calculation. Economy-wide, temporary agency workers represent between 2 and 3 percent of paid employment.[8] Thus, the figures suggest that agency use in low-skilled hospital functions is often moderately high.

One reason hospital managers commonly cited for using agency temporaries was to circumvent the human resources department, which took too long, managers complained, to process new hires, in part because new hires needed to be carefully screened to work in a hospital environment. Managers felt that they could not perform the work with existing staff if there were several vacancies, and so they would often bring workers in as agency temporaries while they waited to have their paperwork processed by the human resources department. Managers cited the ability to quickly dismiss a worker as another advantage of using temporary agencies for new hires. Human resources departments in hospitals, particularly the larger hospitals, tended to have elaborate and lengthy procedures that managers had to follow in order to dismiss a worker. Therefore, some managers preferred to screen new workers through tem-

porary help agencies. In these situations, workers were simply being screened for a few weeks with a temporary agency, and such use
of temporary agencies would appear to have had little effect on
these workers.

The second major reason managers cited for using temporary
help agencies was difficulty in recruiting new workers. Hospitals
had come under intense pressure to reduce costs. At the same time,
given tight labor markets, their wage levels for low-skilled clerical,
food, housekeeping, and clinical positions were becoming uncom-
petitive with wages for low-skilled workers in other sectors. In the
words of one manager, "We had a problem attracting recruits.
Frankly, McDonald's and Burger King were paying what we were,
and [workers there] don't have to go through the stress or the has-
sle or the hours or the customer service that they are required to
perform here." In contrast to the situation among auto suppliers,
where managers complained that the quality of the applicants had
declined, some hospital managers complained that they had almost
no applicants, good or bad, for low-skilled positions. When hospital
managers had difficulty recruiting and retaining staff in low-skilled
positions, they often turned to temporary help agencies, on the
grounds that the agencies were better at recruiting workers.

However, temporary agencies could not always recruit workers at
these low wages either. For instance, one hospital manager reported: "We wanted a housekeeper . . . and only wanted to pay the
person $7.00 an hour. . . . You can't get a housekeeper for $7.00
an hour, and so we've made calls to four agencies and they only
laugh." Similarly, one hospital reported difficulty retaining workers
in patient billing; these positions paid low wages but nevertheless
required extensive training. When the hospital was unable to staff
the positions on its own, the hospital brought in a temporary agency
to staff it. Yet the agency could not retain workers in the position
either. A more common complaint was that while temporary agencies might be able to staff positions at low wage levels, the average
quality of the workers in these positions was very low.

In several cases hospitals reported that workers hired through
the temporary help agency earned *more* than regular workers on
staff. In these situations it is not the agency temporaries who are
potentially harmed by the arrangement but the regular workers. By
hiring through a third party like a temporary agency, employers
may effectively raise the wages for new hires without raising wages
for existing staff.[9]

Such wage differentials could cause deep resentment and morale problems among regular staff, however, if they became aware of them. One temporary agency placing nursing assistants reported poor treatment of their assignees because regular staff resented the high pay they made. Perhaps because of such morale issues, managers more typically reported that agency temporaries received about the same hourly rate as regular entry-level staff, though in many instances temporaries made less in total compensation when differences in benefits were taken into account.

In general, hospitals had less financial incentive to use agency temporaries than auto suppliers. In auto supply, temporary workers earned less than entry-level regular workers, and the agency's bill rate to the company was lower than the total compensation costs of hiring a new regular worker or of paying overtime to an existing worker. Thus, even though managers in auto supply plants complained about the quality of temporary workers, most felt it was a cost-effective way of screening job candidates and staffing for temporary increases in production. In hospitals, however, temporary workers typically earned about the same wage as regular workers. Managers reported paying a 40 to 50 percent overhead rate to the temporary agency. In the absence of agency temporaries, hospital managers would typically pay regular workers overtime to cover understaffed positions. Therefore, with a 50 percent overtime premium, many managers reported that the marginal hourly cost of paying overtime was about the same as hiring a temporary.

Given that temporary workers were regarded as less reliable than regular staff, a couple of managers in the food and environmental services areas reported moving toward reducing the amount of temporary help and offering high-hours positions for regular staff. For instance, one hospital reported that it recently had advertised sixty-hour-a-week positions. The rationale was that since the low-wage workers who were likely to take these positions already had to work two or three jobs to make ends meet, these hours could be consolidated at the hospital. Factoring in overtime made them effectively higher-wage jobs, thus benefiting both workers and the hospital.

Except to the extent that the use of temporary help agencies enabled hospitals to postpone wage increases for low-skilled workers, this use appeared to have little adverse impact on hospital employees, and it potentially benefited agency workers. Although the hospitals generally paid low wages, full-time workers did receive benefits, and thus, as in auto supply, it was possible to give very risky workers the opportunity to try out through a temporary help agency for jobs with benefits that they would not have otherwise received. However, because of the low wage levels in hospitals, temporary help was relatively expensive for hospitals to use, and most managers expressed a desire to reduce, not increase, their reliance on it.

One interesting fact that emerged from the comparison of temporary workers assigned to hospitals and auto suppliers in the same labor markets was that there seemed to be a "going" wage for low-skilled entry-level workers in temporary services. Unless specified in a union contract, temporary workers assigned to entry-level production positions seemed to earn little more than workers assigned to low-skilled positions in hospitals. Thus, with the exception of the unionized firm, the wage differentials between temporary and regular workers were much greater in auto supply than in hospitals. Yet, provided a worker could tolerate a manufacturing working environment, the assignment to auto supply offered better future prospects in terms of training and wage advancement. This example underscores the problems of trying to draw conclusions about the effects of temporary employment through simple wage comparisons of workers in temporary and regular positions. The implications of temporary employment for workers depend on companies' reasons for using agency temporaries and the workers' job alternatives.

CONTRACTING IN LOW-SKILLED OCCUPATIONS IN HOSPITALS AND PUBLIC SCHOOLS

No systematic national data are collected by the government on the extent to which business and government organizations contract out services. However, some data—including data from surveys conducted by private associations—are available on outsourcing in selected industries. For hospitals, the best data on national trends come from the annual Contract Management Surveys reported in *Hospitals and Health Networks,* a publication of the American Hospital Association. In 1999, 32 percent of hospitals reported that they outsourced their food services, with another 6 percent reporting that they planned to do so in the next two years. In addition, 27 percent outsourced housekeeping, while 3 percent reported that they planned to do so in the next two years. The two most commonly outsourced functions were pest control and laundry services, with 86 percent and 62 percent of respondents, respectively, indicating they outsourced these functions (Sunseri 1999).

Limited government statistics are available on contracting out of transportation and food services in primary and secondary public schools. The Federal Highway Administration estimates that about 30 percent of school buses were privately or commercially owned in 2000 (U.S. Department of Transportation 2000). Although in some instances these statistics reflect the outsourcing of transportation services to private companies, in other instances they capture the fact that some school districts lease their buses from private companies but continue to manage and employ all transportation workers. Among school districts nationwide that participated in federally funded school lunch programs, about 8 percent used food service management companies in 1994 to 1995, up from about 4 percent in 1987 to 1988 (U.S. General Accounting Office 1996).

Table 10.2 shows the patterns of contracting out low-skilled occupations in the hospitals and public schools in our sample. Interestingly, the nationwide surveys cited earlier on contracting out in hospitals and public schools do not distinguish whether an organization contracts out the entire operation or just its management. As is evident from table 10.2, it is quite common for hospitals and public schools to contract out only management functions and to keep workers on their payroll. Whereas all of the hospitals we studied outsourced the management of food services and/or environmental services, none outsourced the entire operation. Among public schools, five of the six districts with a food services operation contracted it out, but only two contracted out the entire function. The one district in our sample that contracted out custodial services contracted out the entire function. Two of the districts in our study contracted out the entire student transportation function.

In situations where only management was outsourced, managers, who were employees of the contract company, directed the hospital's or school's employees. They also took on primary responsibility for hiring and firing workers, under the guidelines and with the approval of the client's human resources department. Pay and benefits were established, however, by the hospital or public school. As discussed in the next section, whether an organization outsources its management functions or its entire operation may have important implications for workers.

Table 10.2 Outsourcing in Hospitals and Public Schools

	Food Service	Custodial and Environmental Services	Transportation	Other
Hospital A	Management	Management	—	All of security Laboratory (some) Landscaping and grounds-keeping
Hospital B	Management	—	—	Laboratory (some)
Hospital C	—	Management	—	Landscaping
Hospital D	Management	—	—	—
Hospital E	Management	Management	—	All of security
Hospital F	Management	—	—	—
Public school A	Management	—	—	—
Public school B	Entire service	—	—	—
Public school C	—	—	Entire service	—
Public school D	Entire service	—	—	—
Public school E	Management	—	—	—
Public school F	—	—	Entire service	—
Public school G	Management	Entire service in half of build-ings	—	—

Source: Authors' compilation.

WHY ORGANIZATIONS OUTSOURCE MANAGEMENT FUNCTIONS AND THE IMPLICATIONS FOR WORKERS

Hospital and education administrators typically view areas such as food service, cleaning, and transportation as outside their areas of "core competency." The choice to contract out is made with a view to improving services and reducing costs in these areas, while freeing administrators' time to focus on the business of health care or education. One common reason hospital and public school administrators gave for outsourcing was difficulty recruiting good managers in noncore areas. Because contract companies specialize in a particular service and have many clients, they can offer managers an internal career ladder and therefore attract managers more easily than an individual hospital or school can.

In addition, contractors often are part of large national companies that offer well-tested systems of quality and cost control and can provide their on-site managers with technical support. For instance, in the area of food service, contract companies have systems to estimate food usage and reduce wastage. They have dietitians at their corporate headquarters who can consult with hospitals and public schools on specific issues. Because they purchase in bulk, they can often get better prices on food than hospitals or school systems operating on their own. In public schools a complex set of regulations govern federal government reimbursement of school lunches for children eligible for free and reduced-price lunches. Contract companies offer expertise in packaging and marketing meals to comply with government regulations, thereby maximizing federal reimbursement. Transportation companies often offer more systematic safety training for bus drivers than that provided by individual public school districts.

The ways listed thus far in which a contract company might improve quality and reduce costs would have few consequences for workers. Indeed, in our case studies, the outsourcing of food or custodial services management by itself often appeared to have little impact on the workers in these areas. When workers were significantly affected by the contracting out of management, the issues generally revolved around productivity, workloads, and staff reductions. The contractors with whom we spoke reported that when they took over the management of food or custodial services, they often had to reduce staff and discipline workers because these operations were overstaffed and the quality of the work was poor. For instance, the contract environmental services manager at Hospital C reported that productivity was greatly increased when it took over the operation from the hospital and fired workers who had been "goofing off."

Reducing staff and making efforts to increase productivity may cause deep resentment and backlash among workers. For example, upon taking over the management of food services in Public School A, the contractor completely reorganized the structure of jobs, increasing workloads and leading to many complaints and quits among workers. At the time of our interview over half of the approved slots for food service workers were unfilled, leaving those remaining to work harder and longer hours. These food service workers, who were unionized, felt they were in an awkward position, being school district employees with a supervisor who was not. The union complained that, in this situation, contract company management often ignored union contract provisions.

Contract managers emphasized that improvements in worker productivity did not always—or even routinely—lead to layoffs. When staff reductions were desirable, contract managers typically worked with the human resources department at the hospital or school to reduce employment through attrition. Additionally, in food services in public schools, managers usually tried to improve quality and hence sales, which could lead to a net increase in jobs in spite of any productivity improvements.

Contracting Out Entire Functions and the Implications for Workers

The contracting out of an entire function has larger potential impacts on affected workers. In our case studies, apart from any impacts on work structure and workloads, low-skilled workers in functions that had been entirely contracted out received lower compensation, most importantly in the form of lower benefits, and sometimes they lost union status.

Under the Employee Retirement Income and Security Act (ERISA) and IRS tax laws, it is difficult for an employer to discriminate in its offerings of retirement and health insurance benefits among its full-time employees. Organizations with high-skilled and low-skilled workers tend to offer the same benefits packages to workers across skill levels, and low-skilled workers thus benefit from generous benefits packages offered at organizations with high-skilled workers. However, contractors with predominantly low-skilled employees typically offer less generous benefits. Hospital E, which outsourced all of its security function, mentioned benefits savings as a major motivation for contracting out this function. Within public schools, food service workers primarily work part-time and receive no health insurance benefits. Under Michigan law, however, all school employees are part of a retirement system financed by a 12 to 13 percent levy paid by the school district on these workers' wages. Although wage and benefits cost savings did not appear to be a primary factor in the decisions of Public Schools B and D to outsource their entire food service operations, administrators acknowledged these savings.

Public Schools C and F recently outsourced their entire transportation functions. Although the workers remained unionized in both cases, the bus drivers received lower benefits with the contract company, primarily because of the loss of the public pension. One district went to great lengths to protect bus drivers during the transition. It hired bus drivers near retirement in other district jobs to protect their public pension and for young drivers it guaranteed jobs and wages (but not benefits) with the contract company. Nevertheless, the contract company was allowed to hire new workers at lower wages, and thus, over time, workers in general were likely to be worse off. According to the results of a national survey published in *School Bus Fleet,* the average wage for bus drivers hired by contractors was $10.76 an hour in 2000, compared to an average wage of $12.23 an hour among bus drivers who were public school employees.

Public School G was the clearest case of a school motivated to cut wage and benefits costs by contracting out. This urban district was losing students largely as a result of competition with charter schools and, under Michigan's new school financing laws, suffered large revenue losses. Its non-instructional support staff was all unionized, and with legal changes prohibiting bargaining over contracting out of non-instructional services, this district immediately moved to contract out grounds services. According to school administrators, these employees were receiving wages well above private-sector levels. Decisions to outsource custodial services were made by principals, and about half of the district's schools opted to contract out this function. These principals realized costs savings because the contract company, which was not unionized, paid lower wages and benefits.

According to union representatives and school administrators, another key factor in principals' decisions to contract out was quality. The quality of the cleaning service was low at many buildings, and administrators either failed to discipline poor performers or had difficulty disciplining them, in part because of union grievance procedures.

Although union employees still worked in half of the district's buildings, the internal competition with the contractor greatly reduced the union's bargaining power. The union did not sacrifice benefits, but it made large wage concessions to higher-paid custodians. Perhaps most interesting, the union dramatically altered its position on the disciplining of workers. The union believed that its members could retain schools and receive higher compensation than the non-union contractor employees only if their productivity was greater than that of contract employees. Therefore, union representatives met with school officials to encourage them to discipline or dismiss poor performers.

Why the Outsourcing of Low-Skilled Functions Is Limited

Although we came across examples in our case studies of hospitals and schools contracting out entire services, with adverse consequences for workers' wages and benefits, contracting out is more typically limited to management. There are several reasons for this. First, schools and hospitals are reluctant to lose control of the quality of their staff. Both service vulnerable populations—children and very ill patients—and so are particularly attentive to the type of individuals coming in contact with them. Several school officials mentioned the direct contact that custodians, food service workers, and bus drivers have with children as a reason for not contracting out a particular service or for contracting out only management.[10] One contractor mentioned the extensive contact that food service workers and housekeepers have with patients as a reason so few hospitals fully contract out these functions.

In addition, the hospitals and schools in our study were all either public or private nonprofit organizations, which historically have adopted a protective attitude toward employees.[11] Public school administrators expressed a particular reluctance to outsource jobs to save money at the expense of employees. Moreover, some administrators who chose not to outsource jobs expressed a fear of backlash from the community were they to do so. Those who chose to outsource jobs described these decisions as among the most controversial they had made.

The main potential benefit an organization would derive from contracting out an entire function rather than simply contracting out the management of the function was savings on wages and benefits. Yet, with a few notable exceptions, the wages of low-skilled workers in hospitals and public schools in our case studies were relatively low. Although low-skilled workers typically earned more as employees of hospitals and public schools than they did as employees of contractors (primarily because of better benefits), the cost savings that an organization could realize from contracting out its low-skilled workforce were often perceived as limited. Instead, the organizations in our study often felt that the primary benefit of contracting out was better management, which would realize cost savings through increased productivity and through reduced expenditures on nonlabor inputs. In these instances, the impact on affected workers was ambiguous. Workers might face increased workloads or job reductions, but they might also reap benefits from more knowledgeable management.

Although the contracting out of entire functions in hospitals and public schools is currently limited, it is likely to expand if these organizations continue to face financial pressures to cut costs. As they realize cost savings from outsourcing management functions, organizations may seek further savings in the form of wage and benefits reductions by contracting out low-skilled staff. In support of this notion, a representative from a major company supplying contract food and cleaning services to hospitals and schools noted that his company had initially focused on the provision of management services but in recent years had begun to offer "full service accounts"—which involves putting all workers in the function on its payroll—on a region-by-region basis.

Finally, it is important to note that growth in competition from contractors affects wage and benefits even at hospitals and schools that do not contract out low-skilled staff. As was illustrated in the case of Public School G, which utilized both in-house union and contract custodial staff, the option of switching to a contractor greatly circumscribes workers' bargaining power.

CONCLUSION

Evidence from our case studies suggests that the effects of temporary services and contracting out on low-skilled workers vary considerably. In some situations the use of temporary agencies or contract companies appeared to have clear adverse effects on workers' wages, benefits, or other employment conditions. In other situations, any effects on workers appeared minimal or even beneficial.

Adverse effects are clearest when agency temporaries or contract company workers are substituted for regular employees on a long-term basis and receive lower compensation than they would as regular employees.[12] This situation arises when low-skilled workers in an organization receive relatively high compensation, and when employers are not blocked from substituting these employees with agency temporaries or contract workers by employment and labor law or by workers and their unions.

With respect to the first factor, we observed several situations in our case studies in which low-skilled workers were earning compensation well above that prevailing for workers in their positions. In two of the auto supply companies, this higher compensation was associated with unionization and in a third, at least in part, with the company's perceived threat of unionization. In Michigan public school unions were able to raise the wages of workers in some non-instructional services. Moreover, state law mandated that all public school employees be covered by an expensive pension plan. We also observed differences in the benefits received by low-skilled employees in hospitals and auto supply, on the one hand, and their counterparts in temporary help agencies and contract companies, on the other. Federal regulations governing private-sector benefits are designed to ensure that these tax-free or tax-deferred forms of in-kind compensation do not primarily benefit highly compensated employees; consequently, companies generally offer the same benefits to low-wage and high-wage employees. A result of this regulation is that low-wage workers in organizations with high-wage workers tend to receive more generous benefits than do low-wage workers in companies, such as many temporary help agencies and contract companies, that predominantly employ low-wage workers. Thus, unions or federal and state benefits laws may raise compensation levels of certain workers above prevailing levels, giving employers an incentive to outsource these jobs.

With respect to the second factor, unions in the auto sector were able to block the use of low-wage temporaries through collective bargaining. In contrast, the high-wage, non-union auto supplier substantially lowered labor costs by utilizing agency temporaries for extended time periods. In Michigan public schools, a change in collective bargaining law greatly weakened union power and opened the way to the outsourcing of non-instructional services to lower-paid contract company workers.

These examples from our case studies underscore the important interaction between unions and employment and labor laws in enabling low-skilled workers to raise their compensation *and* maintaining these higher compensation levels by preventing outsourcing. Evolving labor and employment law will have a similar impact on employers' incentives to use temporary agency and contract labor and on the implications of these employment forms for workers. For instance, evolving labor law governing whether and how temporary help workers are covered by collective agreements at a client company and the rules governing conditions under which employees of a temporary agency may form a union could have important implications for the future impacts of temporary help employment in low-skilled labor markets. Benefits regulations, as noted earlier, provide an incentive to companies to outsource jobs, particularly low-skilled jobs. Congress passed a law in 1982 requiring that a client provide benefits to agency temporaries assigned to it on a long-term basis, and the IRS has cracked down on the misclassification of employees as independent contractors. But some have called for further action to curb the use of alternative forms of employment for the purposes of circumventing benefits and other employment regulations (see, for example, Commission on the Future of Worker-Management Relations 1996; for a discussion of benefits regulations, see Houseman 2001a).

Nevertheless, many, if not most, of the instances of outsourcing in our case studies did not entail the long-term substitution of low-paid agency temporaries or contract company workers for regular employees, and, we argue, the effects on workers were largely benign or beneficial in these situations. Most of the temporary agency help we found in our case studies was indeed short-term. Organizations typically used agency help to cover for employee absences, to have adequate staff for temporary increases in workloads, or to screen workers for permanent positions. What is perhaps most striking about our case-study evidence on the contracting out of low-skilled workers is the fact that it did not happen very much. More often than not, when hospitals and public schools contracted out food services and when hospitals contracted out housekeeping services, they contracted out only the management function. The employees in these occupations earned relatively low wages, and the labor cost savings that could have been realized from outsourcing the entire function—including savings on benefits costs—were small relative to other cost savings these organizations felt they could achieve from outsourcing management. In the few instances where low-skilled employees' wages had become much higher than those at a contractor, hospitals and public schools outsourced the entire function when they came under financial pressure to cut costs.

There is an important caveat to the conclusion that because much contracting out in low-skilled areas involves management only the impacts on workers are relatively minor. Even if the practice of contracting out low-skilled work is limited, the very existence of such contractors may have a powerful effect on wages and benefits in low-skilled labor markets. As illustrated by the example of unionized custodians in one of our public school case studies, it will be difficult for workers and their unions to increase the wages and benefits of low-skilled workers significantly if organizations have the option of outsourcing this work to low-cost contractors.

Finally, workers may even benefit from a temporary agency or contract arrangement. Some workers, of course, prefer temporary positions. Workers may benefit from the superior management skills provided by a contractor. Moreover, organizations often screen workers with poor work histories or otherwise risky characteristics through temporary help agencies. Particularly with auto suppliers, where the cost of hiring through a temporary agency was substantially lower than the cost of hiring a worker directly, our case-study evidence suggests that employers often would have been unwilling to try out the riskier job applicants in the absence of temporary agencies. Thus, temporary agencies may provide an important linkage for these workers to full-time jobs with benefits.

We thank Lillian Vesic-Petrovic and Peter Einaudi for their assistance with data analysis, and Claire Black for her transcription of all interviews and her assistance in preparing the manuscript.

APPENDIX

Table 10.A1 Wages and Benefits in Low-Skill Occupations in Auto Suppliers, Hospitals, and Public Schools

Occupation	Starting Hourly Wage	Health Plan Offered	Union
Auto suppliers			
Auto supplier A	$10.60	Yes	No
Auto supplier B	9.62	Yes	No
Auto supplier C	13.28	Yes	No
Auto supplier D	15.51	Yes	Yes
Auto supplier E	12.35	Yes	Yes
Public schools			
Food service workers			
Public school A	6.82	No	Yes
Public school C	7.13	No	No
Public school D[a]	6.00	No	No
Public school E	7.40	—	Yes
Public school G	7.22	No	Yes
Custodial workers			
Public school A	8.40	—	Yes
Public school C	9.57	Yes	No
Public school D	11.49	Yes	Yes
Public school E	12.83	—	Yes
Public school G	10.16	Yes	Yes
Bus drivers			
Public school A	11.31	No	Yes
Public school C[a]	—	—	—
Public school D	11.42	Yes	Yes
Public school E	7.42	No	Yes
Public school G	11.25	Yes	Yes
Hospitals			
Food service workers			
Hospital A	6.40	Part-time prorated, 14% part-time	No
Hospital B	7.00	16% with partial benefits; 26% without benefits	No
Hospital C	8.03	9% without benefits	No
Hospital D	7.05	20% with partial benefits; 22% without benefits	No

(Table continues on p. 400.)

Table 10.A1 *Continued*

Occupation	Starting Hourly Wage	Health Plan Offered	Union
Hospital E	$6.48	Part-time prorated, 22% part-time	No
Hospital F	6.60	Part-time prorated, 65% part-time	Yes
Housekeepers			
Hospital A	6.40	Part-time prorated, 8% part-time	No
Hospital B	7.00	14% with partial benefits; 1% without benefits	No
Hospital C	7.95	5% without benefits	No
Hospital D	7.05	10% with partial benefits; 5% without benefits	No
Hospital E	6.48	Part-time prorated, 18% part-time	No
Hospital F	6.60	Part-time prorated, 27% part-time	Yes
Nurse assistants			
Hospital A	7.20	Part-time prorated, 22% part-time	No
Hospital B	7.40	10% with partial benefits; 12% without benefits	No
Hospital C	7.90	27% without benefits	No
Hospital D	8.67	23% with partial benefits; 4% without benefits	No
Hospital E	6.74	Part-time prorated, 5% part-time	No
Hospital F	8.96	Part-time prorated, 46% part-time	Yes
Clerical workers			
Hospital A	7.35	Part-time prorated, 3% part-time	No
Hospital B	8.00	13% with partial benefits; 23% without benefits	No
Hospital C	8.98	17% without benefits	No
Hospital D	8.23	33% with partial benefits; 5% without benefits	No

Table 10.A1 *Continued*

Occupation	Starting Hourly Wage	Health Plan Offered	Union
Hospital E	7.29	Part-time prorated, 22% part-time	No
Hospital F	7.50	Part-time prorated, 48% part-time	No

Source: Authors' compilation.
Note: Data reported are for lowest-skill occupation within a functional area.
[a] Occupation outsourced.

NOTES

1. The Balanced Budget Act of 1997 created various diagnostic related groups, which specified maximum reimbursement rates for medical procedures; these reimbursements were lower than those previously in effect.
2. See, for example, the results of the tenth annual Contract Management Survey (2000), reported in Burmahl (2001).
3. We conducted focus groups with regular and temporary nurses at two hospitals. The use of temporary nurses was the most important and controversial use of temporary services in hospitals. However, because nursing is a high-skilled occupation, we do not cover it in this chapter.
4. For auto supply, we report data for entry-level production workers. For hospitals and public schools, we report data for workers in the most prevalent occupational title within a particular functional area that coincides with the lowest-paying occupation. The precise occupational titles and the number of occupational titles in a particular functional area varied across organizations within an industry.
5. Temporary help agencies were used only occasionally for clerical positions in public schools.
6. According to data supplied by the companies, the hourly wage earned by agency temporaries was 75 percent, 83 percent, and 56 percent of that earned by new hires at Auto Suppliers A, B, and C, respectively. The agency bill rate was 79 percent, 85 percent, and 60 percent of the total compensation of a new hire at Auto Suppliers A, B, and C, respectively.
7. We develop the argument that temporary help agencies may reduce pressure on companies to increase wages in Houseman, Kalleberg, and Erickcek (forthcoming).
8. Because agency temporaries are somewhat more likely than other

workers to work part-time hours, the fraction of hours worked by agency temporaries is probably lower than the fraction of employment accounted for by agency temporaries.

9. We discuss the theoretical framework of such wage discrimination and cite numerous examples in which temporary help workers earn more than regular staff in high-skilled clinical positions in Houseman, Kalleberg, and Erickcek (forthcoming).

10. This sensitivity to contact with children was also a reason offered by one public school official for the greater prevalence of contracting out in other government sectors than in public schools.

11. Institutional arguments (see, for example, Dobbin et al. 1988) hold that exposure to the public sphere places organizations under greater pressure to conform to evolving norms about legitimate employment practices.

12. The possibility that lower compensation may reduce unemployment is an important caveat to this conclusion.

REFERENCES

Abraham, Katharine G., and Susan K. Taylor. 1996. "Firms' Use of Outside Contractors: Theory and Evidence." *Journal of Labor Economics* 14(3): 394–424.

Burmahl, Beth. 2001. "Making the Choice: The Pros and Cons of Outsourcing." *Health Facilities Management* 14(6): 16–22.

Commission on the Future of Worker-Management Relations. 1996. "Report and Recommendations of the Commission on the Future of Worker-Management Relations, Issued January 9, 1995." Report DLR 6, special supplement. Washington: Bureau of National Affairs.

Dobbin, Frank, Lauren Edelman, John W. Meyer, W. Richard Scott, and Ann Swidler. 1988. "The Expansion of Due Process in Organizations." In *Institutional Patterns and Organizations: Culture and Environment*, edited by Lynne G. Zucker. Cambridge, Mass.: Ballinger.

Egger, Ed. 1999. "Old Ways of Planning, Thinking Won't Work in Today's Volatile Health Care Industry." *Health Care Strategic Management* (September): 18–19.

Houseman, Susan. 1999. "Flexible Staffing Arrangements: A Report on Temporary Help, On-Call, Direct-Hire, Temporary, Leased, Contract Company, and Independent Contractor Employment in the United States." Report prepared for the U.S. Department of Labor, Office of the Assistant Secretary for Policy (August).

———. 2001a. "The Benefits Implication of Recent Trends in Flexible Staffing Arrangements." Working paper 2001-19. Philadelphia: Pension Research Council, Wharton School, University of Pennsylvania.

————. 2001b. "Why Employers Use Flexible Staffing Arrangements: Evidence from an Employer Survey." *Industrial and Labor Relations Review* 55(1): 149–70.

Houseman, Susan N., Arne L. Kalleberg, and George A. Erickcek. Forthcoming. "The Role of Temporary Help Employment in Tight Labor Markets." *Industrial and Labor Relations Review*.

Kalleberg, Arne L., Barbara F. Reskin, and Ken Hudson. 2000. "Bad Jobs in America: Standard and Nonstandard Employment Relations and Job Quality in the United States." *American Sociological Review* 65: 256–78.

Kalleberg, Arne L., Jeremy Reynolds, and Peter V. Marsden. Forthcoming. "Externalizing Employment: Flexible Staffing Arrangements in U.S. Organizations." *Social Science Research*.

Segal, Louis M. 1996. "Flexible Employment: Composition and Trends." *Journal of Labor Research* 17(4): 525–42.

Segal, Louis M., and Daniel G. Sullivan. 1997. "The Growth of Temporary Services Work." *Journal of Economic Perspectives* 11(2): 117–36.

————. 1998. "Wage Differentials for Temporary Services Work: Evidence from Administrative Data." Working paper 98–23. Federal Reserve Bank of Chicago.

Sunseri, Reid. 1999. "Outsourcing on the Outs." *Hospitals and Health Networks* 73(10): 46, 48, 50–52.

U.S. Department of Labor. 1998. *Employment and Earnings.* Washington: U.S. Government Printing Office (January), table 39.

U.S. Department of Transportation, Federal Highway Administration. 2000. "Bus Registrations—2000." Available at: *www.fhwa.dot.gov/ohim/hs00/mv10.htm.*

U.S. General Accounting Office. 1996. *School Lunch Program: Role and Impacts of Private Food Service Companies.* GAO/RCED-96-217. Washington: U.S. Government Printing Office.

PART V

Globalization: Always a Job Killer?

CHAPTER 11

The Future of Jobs in the Hosiery Industry

Rachel A. Willis, Rachel Connelly,
and Deborah S. DeGraff

This case study examines the industry of circular knitting for legwear. The industry is generally classified as hosiery manufacturing but can include products ranging from expensive, FDA-regulated medical compression garments to six-packs of socks for children sold at wholesale prices of less than twenty-five cents per garment. With manufacturing generally located in the southeastern United States for the last century, the concentration of firms in North Carolina, Alabama, and Tennessee over the last twenty years has led to unusual industrial cooperation strategies among firms that have helped the industry to survive.

Perhaps the most central of these strategies has been the creation of the Hosiery Technology Center (HTC) at Catawba Valley Community College in partnership with individual firms within the industry, industry suppliers, and the regional industry trade association. The HTC serves as a training facility, a research and development lab, and an industry consortium coordinator for business services. Most critically, with this strategy the HTC has evolved into an industry testing center to allow producers to certify that they meet certain quality standards. The HTC runs classes for buyers and designers on sock production and classes for machine operators throughout the plant. In cooperation with the U.S. and North Carolina Departments of Commerce, the HTC also hosts business strategy seminars for owners, managers, and supervisors to increase efficiency or improve access to foreign markets. In close collaboration with the Manufacturing Extension Partnership and the Department of Labor, the HTC offers services designed specifically with hosiery needs in mind. As the HTC's longtime director, Dan St. Louis, is fond of saying, the HTC's mission is simply "to keep the machine cylinders running in the Carolinas." Keeping the cylinders running preserves production jobs in the United States. This chapter explores the characteristics of this industry that led to these cooperative strategies and the ways in which such strategies could be broadened to other industries.

Due to substantial decreases in consumer demand for one segment of the industry, sheer pantyhose, we focus our investigation primarily on the manufacturing of half-hose, or socks. Although some special production attributes make socks "odd" in terms of surviving the export of industry, the industry employs several strategies that can serve as examples to other industries. In this chapter, we address the following questions: What is different about the hosiery industry? What major changes have occurred in this industry over the last decade? How do these changes affect workers? Based on this history, what can we learn about the future of jobs in the hosiery industry specifically, and about industries employing less-educated workers more generally? Our answers are based on interviews with key personnel at twenty hosiery firms, meetings and interviews with many more hosiery executives and owners at various trade meetings and industry events, extensive interviews with hundreds of hosiery workers over a five-year period, and aggregate statistics on the hosiery industry from government and industry sources.

Our focus in this study is on the production workers within the hosiery industry. In contrast to some of the other low-wage industries studied in this volume, all jobs in hosiery production require some skill on the part of the workers. Some of the jobs, particularly seaming, boarding, shipping, and finishing, can be learned within a week, though it takes a couple of months to develop the skill to work at production speed. Knitting, dying, and material handling require more training, the length of which depends somewhat on the product line and the technology level of the machinery in use. The most highly skilled production workers are the knitting machine technicians, dye room supervisors, and other machine technicians throughout the plant. These jobs require long periods of on-the-job training, from two to five years at a minimum. In addition, as new machines are acquired, significant continuing training is needed.

Very few hosiery industry jobs have formal education requirements, and production workers in this industry rarely have more than a high school education. As Richard Murnane, John Willett, and Frank Levy (1995) show, however, changing technology, particularly the computerization of machinery and the tracking of the material throughout the production process, has made cognitive and problem-solving skills as important to success for a hosiery production worker as manual dexterity and physical stamina. As the level of technology used in both manufacturing and organizing the production process increases, workers throughout the plant require more training related to the computer interface, even though some jobs have been deskilled.[1]

Our main findings are that when we compare the hosiery industry today to its recent past, jobs are now better in many (though not all) respects—better benefits, more varied and safer work, less varied hours, and in some cases higher pay for added skills—but for fewer people. Most of the contraction of employment is attributable to declines in demand, although changes in technology have also led to a substantial increase in the number of pairs of socks a worker can produce in a given time period. There has been some movement of production offshore, but far less than one might have thought before making the distinction between knitted wear (socks) and textiles. Because the basic steps of sock-knitting remain largely unchanged, the jobs that many workers perform are essentially the same as they were in the past. Technological improvements have resulted in improved worker safety in the seaming, dying, and boarding processes and in increased efficiency in the tracking of goods, in marketing, and in the ability to make more rapid changes in the production line. Until now, U.S. firms have staved off the forces of foreign competition in production by adapting to changing demand, by finding niches in global markets, and by being willing to embrace immigrant workers. The competitive pressures have pushed domestic producers to become more productive, to adapt to new technology more quickly, and to think more seriously about how to increase worker retention. A variety of cooperative strategies among firms, governments, and educational institutions have facilitated these necessary changes. Although hosiery jobs may not remain in the United States forever, we expect them to persist for the near future.

The continued presence of the industry in the United States may seem to be an anomaly, but this is not the case, and there are lessons that other industries could learn from hosiery. For example, other manufacturing industries may be able to create similar niches by concentrating on small production lots and rapid response delivery. In addition, lessons about public-private partnerships and industry cooperation may be even more broadly transferable. As we argue in this chapter, this type of cooperation could be applied to service industries, especially location-specific service industries such as education, health care, and transportation, in addition to other manufacturing industries.

This chapter provides evidence to support these conclusions, looking first at the history of the economics of sock manufacturing and then at changes that have taken place in the industry during the last ten years. Following these background sections, we examine the impact of these changes on production workers and conclude with lessons from the hosiery industry that may be relevant for other U.S. industries that employ less-skilled workers.

THE ECONOMICS OF SOCK-MAKING: WHY ARE SOCKS DIFFERENT?

The making of a sock seems simple: the sock is knitted as a tube; the toe is seamed; the sock is either bleached or dyed and then perhaps ironed before being packaged and sold.[2] However, the process is not quite as simple as this initial description suggests. A knitting machine has numerous needles and yarn feeds that perform a complex pattern of movements at relatively high speeds to form a carefully sized tube of interconnected loops of yarn.[3] The success of the sock in fulfilling the requirements of consumer wear depends on virtually every needle and yarn segment being in precisely the right position with identical tension.

The manufacturing of hosiery is distinct from that of other textiles because the process moves directly from yarn to garment, whether it is handmade or machine-made. Until the invention of the first frame-work knitting machine in England by William Lee in 1589, hosiery, including both stockings and socks, had to be hand-knit in a very time-consuming, tedious, and labor-intensive process. Because of the time and dexterity required to hand-knit this garment, manufacturers typically used the most durable and costly fibers, such as silk, ensuring that the cost of a pair of stockings was extremely high.

The development of the first frame-work knitting machine changed the production process entirely. Queen Elizabeth I refused to grant a monopoly patent right for the machine because of its implications for the future employment prospects of hand-knitters throughout England. Ironically, the machine evolved quickly and was the basis for the enormous employment of English frame knitters. The export of this complex technology was specifically outlawed by England to maintain its trade advantage with the colonies in the New World. Thus, machine plans for hosiery manufacturing came to the United States from England in the eighteenth century "smuggled" in the minds of frame knitters (Grass 1955).

The early knitting machines stood about eight feet high, occupied about a square yard of floor space each, and were driven by a complex system of belts connecting the machine to centrally located motors (Archives of the National Association of Hosiery Manufacturers 1905–1999; Catawba Valley Hosiery Association Archives 1959–1999). The modern electronic machines are a bit more compact, contain their own motors, and connect directly to an electrical source. The manufacturing of hosiery has few economies of scale, so production can and does occur at virtually any scale of operation. Individual machines can easily be powered at home and produce virtually the same intermediate product—greige goods.[4] We learned from our interviews with hosiery workers that it was not unusual in the United States, once rural electrification became widespread in the 1940s, for a skilled employee to work in a factory with hundreds of machines and also run a single knitting machine at home, selling his relatively small, but identical, greige goods to his employer.

Originally located mainly in New England, hosiery manufacturing moved south at the turn of the twentieth century, along with many other manufacturing industries, in order to take advantage of lower labor costs (Glass 1992). For more than half a century the southeastern United States has dominated not just U.S. but international hosiery manufacturing. The low cost of energy and labor attracted many textile mills to locate in central North Carolina along rivers that could provide water power. Although the economies of scale in the production of greige goods are small, positive externalities are gained from the spatial clustering of the mills.[5] These externalities stem from savings in transportation costs of greige goods and supplies, particularly the yarn. These location-based externalities have resulted in a concentration of mills in three geographically limited bands in western and central North Carolina, especially along the Catawba River (Glass 1992).

The lack of economies of scale in the production of greige goods leads to small start-up costs, and in fact, as we learned from managers, a number of new firms were still forming when we first began to study the industry in the mid-1990s. The lack of economies of scale, however, does not mean that the industry is labor-intensive. Just the opposite is true. Knitting operations are relatively capital-intensive compared to other garment construction processes. The capital-intensive nature of production is one reason socks are still made in the United States, but it is not the only reason. The development of a self-perpetuating, skilled labor force of machine technicians in this region has been critical to the continued success of the industry in North Carolina. Known as "fixers," these men historically served as apprentices for periods that typically lasted up to ten years. By that time a skilled technician not only could reset the machines for a change of style or size but, what is far more important, could look at a knitted sock in production and determine precisely which needle in the small diameter cylinder needed replacement, an adjustment in yarn tension, or other repairs. This skill is critical to manufacturing profitability, because undetected problems in knitting result in an enormous waste of raw materials.

In our interviews with workers we learned that traditionally the training of machine technicians was handled in-house, with the apprentice usually being taught by a male relative. Frequently, the complex and long-term training associated with maintenance and repair of the machines was passed from father to son on the shop floor, and one family would cover all shifts on a particular set of knitting machines. A machine technician was thus willing to share his acquired knowledge of the complex pattern setting and a specific machine's idiosyncrasies with other technicians, making his own shift easier but also increasing firm profitability.

The skills necessary to keep the machines running and the mills profitable were extremely valuable, and machine technicians historically passed on this knowledge only to members of their own family, their extended family, or, in more recent times, to people of their same race and nationality whom they perceive to be less of a threat to their own future employment. Sharing valuable technical knowledge with a younger, unrelated employee or a "foreigner" who might be willing to work for lower wages has seemed shortsighted and a direct route to possible unemployment. Even the tools necessary to fix the machines, nearly always privately owned by each machine technician, were lent only to family members, we were told. Neither physical capital nor human capital—the tools and the training— were shared with those who were perceived as being direct competitors for their jobs.

This form of intergenerational capital transfer created a training pattern within the mills that was initially supported by the development of mill villages. This in turn stimulated extended family labor supply patterns within mills that were further augmented by the predominantly female and child labor force employed in most other parts of hosiery production. Although the skilled technician is key to the success of the production process, most of the other labor inputs in the production process are unskilled; only a couple of weeks of training are needed for nearly every other position in a hosiery mill. With the exception of the dye house and the transportation of materials and finished product, nearly all other areas of hosiery manufacturing have long been dominated by female employees. Paid a "production wage" (usually by the piece), virtually all of the knitters, seamers, and finishers have been female. While some men boarded socks, it was far more typical for women to fill all the unskilled and semiskilled jobs necessary to produce a finished sock.[6]

Labor unrest from 1915 through 1935 resulted in strikes, violence, and the eventual dispersion of mill village communities (Grass 1955). Simultaneously, child labor laws were passed and later enforced. These changes caused the family labor patterns to change, but they persisted in an altered form, supported by the development of extensive highway networks throughout North Carolina and the increased employment of married women. The pattern of related machine technicians and female production workers in a largely rural manufacturing labor force continues to some extent to this day. One difference, however, is that with the relative proximity of the mills and increased ease of transportation, workers are now able and willing to switch employers more readily for minor differences in wages, benefits packages, and employee policies, or because of disagreements with supervisors or fellow workers.

This increase in employee mobility, managers told us, coupled with increasing education in the area and, consequently, a declining supply of unskilled labor, resulted in annual turnover in many mills of as much as 120 percent by the 1960s. This high turnover rate is precisely what initiated the hiring of African Americans early in the 1970s into what had been a nearly entirely "white" industry. Coinciding with the decline of segregation, the troop buildup in Vietnam, and the constant need for additional workers to keep the mills in operation, the desegregation of the mills led to the first round of redefining "community" for the mill workers. Black men joined the hosiery mill workforce, typically in handling positions such as yarn, greige goods, or shipping, and worked side by side with white men in these positions. Women were still racially segregated by shift and job, although there has been a gradual transition toward integration within the mills since the 1970s. This transition was marked by little turmoil or comment relative to similar changes in other regions and industries. Desegregation did not occur at any measurable level within the ranks of the highly skilled technicians.

We alluded earlier, in the discussion of greige goods, to a final important attribute of the manufacturing of socks. The trading of greige goods is often cost-reducing because it allows for greater specialization and differing volumes of production within a firm for greige goods versus final products; a firm can thereby take advantage of differences in economies of scale.[7] The ability to trade intermediate products has led to a substantial amount of cooperation among companies that were otherwise competitors. Also contributing to this cooperation is the fact that the product is small and produced in high physical volume (as opposed to furniture, for example). This industrial strategy of cooperation is unusual and, we would argue, an essential component of the survival of the industry. This historic cooperation has undoubtedly also been a factor in the high concentration of this industry in a few local areas. The perennial need to cooperate with competitors over long periods of time has clearly been an important component of the strategy pursued in recent years to develop regional resources for success.

MAJOR CHANGES IN THE INDUSTRY DURING THE LAST TEN YEARS

One of the most important forces for change in the hosiery industry in the 1990s was the generally tight labor market faced by hosiery manufacturers throughout the decade. Table 11.1 shows trends in unemployment rates, comparing the United States as a whole, North Carolina, and the Hickory SMSA (standard metropolitan statistical area) of North Carolina, which is one of the most concentrated hosiery manufacturing areas in the state. Table 11.1 shows

Table 11.1 Unemployment Rates for the United States, North Carolina, and Hickory, North Carolina, 1990 to 2001

	1990	1991	1992	1993	1994	1995	1996	1997	1998	1999	2000	2001
United States	5.6%	6.8%	7.5%	6.9%	6.1%	5.6%	5.4%	4.9%	4.5%	4.2%	4.0%	4.8%
North Carolina	4.2	5.8	6.0	4.9	4.4	4.3	4.3	3.6	3.5	3.2	3.6	5.5
Hickory SMSA	4.1	6.6	5.5	4.0	3.3	4.2	4.0	3.6	2.7	2.1	2.5	6.2

Source: U.S. Bureau of Labor Statistics (2002).

that, not only did unemployment rates generally decline during the 1990s at all three geographic levels, but unemployment in North Carolina was at least one point below the national average in every year except for the last two years. In addition, unemployment in Hickory was always below the North Carolina average except in the recession years of 1991 and 2001. The gap between Hickory's and North Carolina's unemployment rates grew wider during the late 1990s, corresponding to the period in which we have conducted research on the industry.

The tight labor market of the late 1990s created challenges for hosiery manufacturers' human resources officers. Every firm we interviewed had job openings it could not fill. Every manager we talked to knew the current unemployment rate in the area down to the nearest decimal point. Repeatedly we heard supervisors and managers wondering how they could fill their open positions, and they often resorted to hiring people who they suspected would not last. The limited supply of unskilled labor affected every discussion in the factory, such as whether to buy a new machine, run a third shift, bid on a contract, or ask employees to work as many as forty or more Saturday shifts in a year. Although the economic recession of 2001 loosened labor market conditions to some extent, the slowdown has not yet been substantial enough to fundamentally alter these dynamics within the hosiery industry. We discuss the effect of the economic recession more fully at the end of the chapter.

During the 1990s the hosiery industry was also increasingly competing with other and sometimes better job opportunities for workers in the same labor market. In particular, the market for good workers was further tightened by an increase in electrical component manufacturing in the area. This industry was attracted to the region, ironically, because of the reliable and technically skilled workforce available due to the presence of hosiery manufacturing. Jobs in electrical components frequently offer better wages and benefits than hosiery jobs.[8]

Wages increased during this period for all manufacturing jobs in the United States, as can be seen in figure 11.1. The rate of wage growth increased in the mid-1990s both in the United States as a whole and in North Carolina. The average manufacturing wage in North Carolina has consistently been lower than the U.S. average for production workers, but the pattern of change appears completely parallel. Wages in the hosiery industry in the Hickory area

Figure 11.1 Real Wages of U.S. and North Carolina
            Production Workers

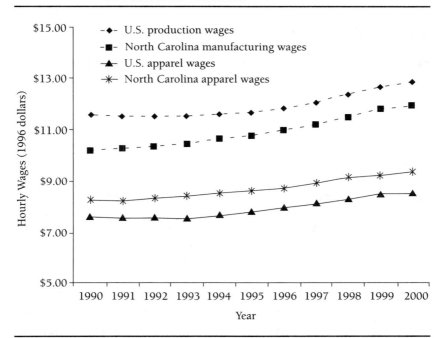

Source: U.S. Bureau of Labor Statistics (2002).
Note: For the North Carolina apparel series, the data represent production workers in the
hosiery industry rather than the broader apparel and textiles industries.

are higher than the average wage in North Carolina for apparel
workers, but lower than the average for all manufacturing workers.
The wage growth of hosiery workers follows fairly closely the wage
growth of all manufacturing workers, though the gap widened somewhat after 1996 as manufacturing wages in general increased faster
than wages in hosiery and apparel.

   In addition to increasing competition in less-skilled sectors of the
labor market in the area, the extremely low tuition rates for in-state
residents throughout the North Carolina public higher education
system have permitted far greater educational aspirations and access for recent generations of high school students.[9] This is readily
apparent in the hosiery mill, where parents routinely display pictures of their children in school or athletic settings, caps and
gowns, uniforms, and other visual forms of achievement. The pro-

duction workers speak of their children's accomplishments with particular pride. In our interviews these workers typically concluded with the comment: "They won't have to work in a hosiery mill like me." Discussions with parents in the mills suggested that they see the nonfactory jobs that are accessible through higher education as conferring higher social status as well as providing greater earnings potential, a lower likelihood of layoff, and a more favorable working environment. Many of the larger companies have employee newsletters that regularly report the increasing levels of educational achievement by the children of mill workers. The suggestion is that this may be the last generation of native-born Americans to fill the production jobs in the mills.

The strength of the economy and the growth of competing industries in the same labor market during this period represented enormous challenges to hosiery firms attempting to retain workers. Each firm has had to make difficult decisions about labor-saving capital in each part of the production process. The small profit margins and extraordinarily competitive day-to-day operations of the mills make the acquisition of unproven or problematic technology potentially catastrophic for a company. But missing the boat on technology can also be very costly. When companies do adopt new technology, they also must invest in developing the technical skills to repair and maintain the new machinery.

Although the macroeconomic climate of the 1990s affected hosiery manufacturers as demanders of labor, changes in the demand for their product also had a large impact on the hosiery industry during this period. Changing fashions, increasingly casual corporate dress, and the changing age distribution of the population have all led to a substantial decrease in the demand for sheer hose. Total employment in the industry has been reduced substantially as a result. In 1990, 71,200 people worked in the hosiery industry in the United States. Ten years later, 49,900 people worked in the hosiery industry (see table 11.2). Similarly, the share of hosiery employment as a percentage of total employment in the United States declined substantially during this period. These trends are also evident in North Carolina, which is home to a smaller percentage of hosiery workers than it was in the past.

The decline in the demand for sheers is not the only explanation for lower employment figures. During the same period that employment fell by 23.5 percent (1990 to 1998), the volume of hosiery

Table 11.2 Employment Statistics for the United States and North Carolina Hosiery Industry, 1980 to 2000

	1980	1985	1990	1991	1992	1993	1994	1995	1996	1997	1998	1999	2000
Number of employees in hosiery (thousands)													
United States	63.8	69.5	71.2	69.2	69.4	67.9	66.8	63.3	60.6	58.1	54.4	50.7	49.9
North Carolina	44.9	47.6	46.1	45.2	44.3	43.3	41.4	39.2	37.1	35.8	33.2	31.2	29.0
North Carolina share of hosiery employment (percentage)	70.4	68.5	64.7	65.3	63.8	63.8	62.0	61.9	61.2	61.6	61.0	61.5	58.1
Employment in hosiery as percentage of total employment[a]													
United States	.064	.065	.060	.059	.059	.056	.054	.051	.048	.045	.041	.038	.037
North Carolina[b]	1.89	1.80	1.48	1.47	1.42	1.33	1.23	1.13	1.05	0.98	0.88	0.81	0.73

Source: U.S. Bureau of Labor Statistics (2002).

[a] Total employment figures are based on civilian employment.

[b] Total employment figures for North Carolina exclude agricultural employment.

production in the United States increased by 41.5 percent (see table 11.3). Productivity increases have also reduced employment in the industry. Productivity changes are apparent throughout hosiery plants. For example, knitting patterns are now set by computer, meaning that styles can be changed more quickly and a single factory can offer a much more extensive line of products. This has in no way eliminated the need for machine technicians, but it changes somewhat the mix of tasks that machine technicians perform. In the past, machine technicians were responsible for changing the knitting pattern by manipulating a very complicated set of cylinders to achieve the desired pattern. Now the pattern is programmed into the machine by the designer, but the technician must interpret the diagnostic codes of the machine's computer display, respond to them, and then adjust or repair cylinders, needles or yarn feeds as necessary. Also, computer tracking is now used throughout the production process, reducing inventories and increasing the use of just-in-time manufacturing. In addition, the electronic data interfaces with retailers that have allowed manufacturers to produce in smaller runs help with input and output flows and reduce the need for unplanned overtime. Most recently, web software development within the industry (see the Hosiery Technology Center's website at *www.legsource.com*) has enabled firms to cooperate more easily on filling orders through the trading of greige goods or subcontracting with one another.

These changes in technology, when coupled with changes in the retailing of socks (discussed later in the chapter), have led to some economies of scale in sales (which is quite different from economies of scale in production). These changes also have created a greater need for workers throughout the factory to be able to work with the computer tracking system for raw materials, intermediate goods, and finished goods ready for shipment. With smaller lot sizes, workers must be able to interpret the bar codes rather than just respond according to a routine. We discuss the implications of these changes more fully later in the chapter.

In addition to changes in technology aimed at increasing the efficiency and flexibility of production, there have also been technological changes to improve worker safety. For example, seaming and boarding machines, the sources of most on-the-job injuries, have been modified substantially. The most dangerous and unpleasant part of hosiery production is boarding: pressing a sock against a hot

Table 11.3 U.S. Hosiery Production and Sales, 1990 to 1998

	1990	1991	1992	1993	1994	1995	1996	1997	1998
Volume of U.S. hosiery production (millions of pairs)	3,842	4,024	4,173	4,279	4,340	4,198	4,434	5,129	5,443
Retail dollar volume of hosiery sales (millions of dollars)	$6,000	$5,793	$6,118	$6,942	$7,097	$7,165	$7,633	$7,847	$7,477
Retail dollar volume of hosiery sales by distribution channel									
Department stores	11.9%	12.0%	10.9%	10.8%	10.2%	9.3%	9.9%	9.3%	9.9%
Specialty stores	8.7	9.7	10.4	9.9	9.2	9.2	9.5	9.7	9.8
Chains	12.6	13.1	13.1	11.5	11.0	12.0	11.9	11.9	11.8
Discount stores	37.9	39.8	40.8	40.8	44.6	46.1	46.4	49.0	48.1
Grocery or drugstore	17.6	13.4	12.7	13.8	12.6	11.3	10.2	8.7	7.5
Other	11.3	11.9	12.1	13.1	12.4	12.2	12.0	11.2	12.8

Source: U.S. Bureau of Labor Statistics (2002).
Note: The hosiery category is a combination of SIC codes 2514 and 2524.

metal form to set the dyes and retain the shape of the foot for more attractive packaging. Because of the burn hazard involved, boarding suffers from the highest turnover in the plant. As a result of cooperation between the Hosiery Technology Center at Catawba Valley Community College and North Carolina State University (NCSU) College of Textiles (COT), HTC and COT employees told us, a team of COT engineering students devised a number of prototypes for new boarding machines and then developed them for actual application to boarding and, in some cases, packaging processes. Other international machine manufacturers also responded to this challenge, and as a result, radically new combined boarding and packaging machines are now being used that dramatically reduce the risk of burns. Thus, by aggregating industry interest in this specific area, U.S. producers were able to facilitate development of technology to solve an important human resource problem.

Similarly, concern about injuries related to repeated motion has led to changes in the finishing part of the process. New work stations have been designed to reduce repeated motion injuries, and most finishers now do a variety of tasks instead of just one. Firms have also experimented with team production in the finishing phase of manufacturing.[10] In 1996 and 1997 "team finishing" was the buzzword of the industry as firms sought cost savings by moving away from an assembly-line approach. The switch to teams usually involved reorganizing the flow of work across the physical space of the shop floor and changing the compensation scheme from individual production to group production rates. Teams typically consist of three to four workers, who are selected by supervisors based on their skills and personality. Many workers were initially resistant to these changes, primarily because of concern that their own earnings could be adversely affected by a team member's performance. However, most workers seemed satisfied with the team approach by the time we interviewed them during this period, as long as supervisors took their input into account in establishing or adjusting team membership. Although newer management techniques—like "lean marketing" (minimizing inventory) and "supply chain management" (using computer technology to manage input flows)—have recently replaced the emphasis on team-based production within the industry, most firms are using a mix of team-based and individual-based finishing stations where appropriate.

The increased cost of the computerized knitting machines has created pressure to run the machines twenty-four hours a day, seven days a week (24/7). This pressure arises, in part, because the proportion of capital to labor costs is higher than it was in the past, and firms do not want to let expensive machines sit idle. Also pushing the industry in the same direction is the pressure from the large retail outlets to deliver orders quickly. In the past Sunday was fairly sacred as a day off in Hickory; this is no longer universally the case. Similarly, most factories in Hickory used to close for a week at Christmas and for a week around the Fourth of July. Pressure from the large retail chains has caused many firms to cancel the Fourth of July closing.

Another important change for the hosiery industry comes from changes in the retail industry. There has been a substantial increase in the importance of discount stores in the retailing of socks. In 1990, 38 percent of hosiery was sold in discount stores; by 1998, this percentage had increased to 48 percent. At the same time the percentage sold in grocery stores and drugstores declined from 18 to 8 percent, and in department stores from 12 to 10 percent (see table 11.3). Overall, these changes result in a greater concentration of hosiery retail in a smaller number of national discount chains. The power of several large retailers in this market has led to some consolidation of marketing units, but this does not necessarily lead to a consolidation of manufacturing.

The pressure from large retailers has resulted in the closing of some firms and the merging of others, but it has also led some firms to become wholesale producers only. Specifically, some firms have removed themselves further from the retail market and become subcontractors for other, usually larger firms that contract directly with the retail distributors. For example, Firm A gets a contract with a major catalog outlet or discount chain and then contracts with Firm B to supply the trouser sock part of that contract. Thus, economies of scale in marketing can (but do not necessarily) lead to increased firm size. Where they do not, they lead to interesting relationships between firms that may be competitors in some lines and have a supplier-buyer relationship in others. For example, one of the firms where we interviewed workers and managers was in the process of expanding its retail line to compete for contracts with the bigger retail outlets. They did this by buying socks from other firms to expand the type of socks they could offer to retailers. At the same time they specialized in the production of high-end tights and trouser socks and served as the supplier of these lines to another firm that retailed them under the other firm's name. Thus, both firms were buying and selling to each other as well as competing directly with each other for retail contracts. This strategy allows them to specialize in production but offer a wider variety of socks for sale.

Changes in the demand for women's sheer hosiery and the consolidation caused by retail economies of scale have led to a spate of firm closings in the industry over the last ten years (Catawba Valley Hosiery Association Archives 1959–1999). Owners told us that these financial failures have created a perception of instability for the entire industry that affects the finance opportunities even for stable firms. This "ripple effect" hinders a firm's ability to invest in machinery and creates uncertainty for employees. When skilled managers and administrative employees leave because of opportunities in more profitable industries, their departure creates a secondary impact that can be devastating for small- and medium-sized firms that maintain very few administrative positions.

In all, the technology changes outlined here, coupled with less waste as machine technicians become even more skilled, has allowed the domestic industry to maintain its competitive edge despite reduced international transportation costs and NAFTA pressures. This comes as somewhat of a surprise, because the radical development of deskilling technologies as well as the collapse of the U.S. capital industry in textile manufacturing led many to assume that all textile manufacturing jobs would be lost to offshore operations after the passage of NAFTA. This did in fact occur rather rapidly in the more highly mechanized sectors of textile production, such as the manufacture of fabrics, as well as in the labor-intensive cut-and-sew operations of garment construction. However, because of hosiery's unusual manufacturing characteristics, the wholesale export of hosiery manufacturing has not occurred—or at least it has not been possible in the same relatively short period that saw the rapid movement of machines to a number of Central American countries in other areas of textile production.

A large part of the explanation lies in the fact that consistent quality could not be guaranteed in offshore operations because of the crucial role of skilled machine technicians in the hosiery mills. Machine technicians have not been willing to train machine technicians in offshore operations, holding the line on the "family" knowledge. Instead, as we begin the twenty-first century, most socks continue to be made in the United States, and American companies are using a variety of strategies—increasing capitalization, investments in bilingual workplaces, community college–industry partnerships, unusual benefits packages—to maintain a sufficient supply of production workers. Thus far, these efforts, together with the concentration of experienced machine technicians, have kept most hosiery mills operating in North Carolina.[11] However, the patterns of employment in hosiery mills in North Carolina are radically different from what they were just ten years ago. The rapid influx of Hispanic workers and transplanted immigrants from Laos and Vietnam into the rural North Carolina labor force has transformed the production workers into an international workforce whose language, religious, and cultural differences must be accommodated.[12]

The influx of immigrant workers is the last major change in the industry in the last ten years, and it has been tremendously transformative. There has been a substantial in-migration of foreign-born workers, mainly Hispanic, Hmong, and Vietnamese, into the areas of the Southeast where most hosiery plants are located. These new groups have changed the face and the language of all manufacturing work in the Southeast. These workers have been welcomed by the firms because of the tight labor market and the related increase in job turnover. The immigrants have not always been welcomed by their fellow employees, but with most firms having trouble filling positions, the sense of displacement of native-born workers that is often a source of ethnic tension among workers has not arisen.

THE IMPACT OF CHANGES IN THE HOSIERY INDUSTRY ON PRODUCTION WORKERS' JOBS

The first thing to note when thinking about the effect of changes in the hosiery industry on workers is that the workers themselves have changed. The transformation of the hosiery manufacturing labor force over the past ten years, first with the introduction of Asian immigrants and then Hispanic immigrants, has changed the demographic characteristics of hosiery manufacturing workers forever.

The increase in immigrant labor has led to conflict both within factories and throughout the communities where the mill workers reside. The problems of assimilating immigrants in the workplace and the community are so pervasive and well known that they can be discussed in the broadest of terms for any situation, immigrant population, or time—conflict and misunderstanding about cultural differences, religious differences, values, and language abound. Add to these problems the pressures in housing, schools, and employment and resulting increase in crime associated with dramatic growth, and the possibility of permanently divided communities becomes very real. However, our sense after interviewing hosiery workers for the last five years is that ethnic tensions have declined over time, though it varies from community to community. Smaller communities in particular seem to be experiencing less ethnic tension as "groups" come to be perceived as individuals and neighbors more quickly than in larger cities.

Although the recent recession could reawaken some latent ethnic tension, as jobs become more scarce, the unemployment rates were so low in the 1990s, and the number of unfilled positions so substantial, that it would take a large increase in unemployment before hosiery employers could become more selective about who they hire. This point may have been reached, however, by late 2001; the Hispanic workers we interviewed at this time expressed some concern about differential layoffs by language group.

One reason for the overall decline in ethnic tension is the belief among many of the native-born workers with whom we spoke that the immigrant workers have saved the industry and that they are industrious, reliable, and available. In other words, the native-born workers today are more likely to view the immigrants, not as taking "American" jobs, but rather as solving a difficult labor shortage for the industry. Many native-born production workers expressed the view that without immigrant workers the industry would be unable to compete internationally and manufacturing would move offshore. This feeling, along with the changing pattern of education of children of manufacturing workers, has led to an amazing change in the transfer of knowledge about knitting machine repair.

After decades of jealously guarding the secrets of the trade, American machine technicians have gradually, but almost completely, become willing to train immigrants in the diagnosis and repair of the knitting machines. Today perhaps 20 percent of the machine technicians are Hmong men. Women have also joined these "privileged" ranks. We estimate that 10 to 15 percent of the machine technicians are now women. Training has changed, both in informal settings through the traditional apprenticeship-like training of machine technicians on the shop floor[13] and through a remarkable cooperative education program started by the Carolina Hosiery Association, whose membership includes many of the hosiery firms in North Carolina. Their 1990 decision to initiate, develop, and support the Hosiery Technology Center has been critical to the transfer of technological knowledge to new labor force entrants. The more recent dramatic increase in computer use in the technology of knitting has also fueled demands for more formal training for experienced and apprentice machine technicians alike. Knitting machine operators do not have to program the computer with new pattern settings, but they must be able to follow the computer instructions and interface with computer functions almost continuously. Thus, there have been changes in who is being trained, where the training takes place, and the nature of the training itself.

The (re)training program developed by the HTC for machine technicians is specifically designed to meet the needs of the industry given the workforce's relatively low levels of education. The training focuses on developing competency in entering the requisite information into a computer program and interpreting the information provided by the computer. Training materials developed by the HTC are designed to be easily read by workers with relatively low levels of textual literacy but higher levels of pictorial literacy (that is, they are more comfortable with machine schematics than with a paragraph of instructions). In addition, the training is generally not conducted on the factory floor because of the potential to disrupt production or to be disrupted by the everyday needs of production deadlines. Nonetheless, the training is very hands-on in nature, with the relevant equipment in place in the HTC labs. Furthermore, the timing of classes—two or three hours at a time, two days a week for four weeks—both takes into account workers' schedules and allows for iteration between intensive training and on-the-job practice. All of these features of the training make it possible for workers to use the new technology without achieving higher levels of traditional education.

The tight labor market, the willingness of the native-born machine technicians to train immigrant machine technicians, and the strong presence of the HTC have all led both immigrants and native-born workers to move up the skill ladder, particularly as machine technicians, but more broadly as well. As reported earlier, race and gender barriers have begun to come down. Though still a minority, women, along with Asian and Hispanic immigrants, have entered the ranks of the more highly paid supervisors as well as machine technicians.[14] Immigrants enter these ranks as increased tenure within a given company and improved language skills enable them to communicate more effectively with both management and the new immigrant population.

It is important to note that while the number of immigrant workers in the industry has increased dramatically, they are not evenly distributed across firms. For example, at one firm where we conducted interviews, 30 percent of the production workers were Hmong, but there were no Hispanics employed there. At another factory located less than fifteen miles away there were no Hmong employees and a sizable number of Hispanics. A third firm, located about twenty miles north of these two firms and across a river, had no immigrant workers at all during the same interview period. This relatively small distance within one area of rural North Carolina was enough to change the labor market from which this firm was drawing. It had only recently begun to suffer from the turnover problems faced by the more centrally located firms, so it is likely that its willingness to hire immigrant workers will change over time.

When firms hire non-English-speaking workers, they tend to specialize in one particular non-English-language group. This reduces the cost of employing non-English-speaking workers because company forms and employee procedures need to be translated into only one additional language. Sometimes firms hire from multiple non-English-speaking groups and keep workers segregated by language group in different work areas and shifts, using key workers as translators. This was the case with the Vietnamese in one factory we visited. They were all employed as boarders on the same shift, and one of the younger Vietnamese men who was attending community college while working part-time at the factory served as a translator between the other Vietnamese workers and their supervisor. An alternative explanation for the specialization in one non-English-speaking group and the segregation of language groups by job and shift is that these groupings are the result of family and friendship networks among employees that lead certain groups to apply to certain factories for certain jobs. We believe that both hypotheses are at work in the hosiery mills.

In addition to the changing demographic composition of the workforce and the loosening of family control over the machine technician jobs, there have been more widespread changes in training needs and practice. Increased training needs have affected all hosiery workers, not just machine technicians. As a result of high turnover, more experienced employees are often called upon to train new hires. The increased cost of training in terms of employee time has led some of the larger firms to set up separate training areas within the plant instead of simply assigning a new employee to learn from a more experienced one. Firms are also experimenting with different wage and training production levels to try to weed out sooner those who ultimately will not stay. Similarly, smaller firms are contracting with temporary employment services that supply workers who are not actually employees of the mill until after the probationary period. The training of more skilled workers has also changed. In the past all training took place on the job, with long periods of apprenticing. Today the HTC has greatly expanded its operation, running classes as needed by the employers and training workers for some of the more skilled jobs within the plant, including many of the female-dominated positions such as knitting, seaming, boarding, and packaging.

Changes in the industry have also affected workers' lives in the timing of the work, the pace of the year, the wages and benefits they receive, and the safety of the jobs. We discuss each of these in turn.

Approaches to 24/7 technology staffing have varied enormously across firms. Some firms have instituted rotating shifts, while others have completely separate weekend shifts. Virtually all of the firms have adapted their shifts to the specific equipment needs of production. Some firms have adopted variable work shift times as machine availability permits. However, most firms still close on Sunday.

While operating 24/7 increases the amount of person-hours of work during nontraditional work times (nights and weekends), it has also led to more regular hours as firms have adjusted production schedules to cover weekends and overtime capacity more routinely. In the past workers were often expected to work overtime, but it was unpredictable. Today employers think carefully about hours worked and try to provide their workers with steady hours. They understand that workers reward firms that provide regular hours and predictable income with lower turnover and a more ready supply of new recruits. Firms are as nervous about worker response to shift changes, given the extremely tight labor market, as they are about their retailers' demands. Other strategies for regularizing work hours without substantially altering the rate of in-house production—and thus work schedules—include the use of temporary workers and the purchase or sale of partially manufactured goods to supplement or reduce inventories of product.

The pace of the year for a hosiery production worker has changed over the past ten years, just as the variance in his or her hours of work per week may have changed. (Aggregate BLS statistics do not show a change in the average hours worked per week during the 1990s.) In the past mills simply shut down for two weeks of the year—the week of Christmas and the week of the Fourth of July. There was no paid vacation. While workers were not happy about going without pay for those two weeks, at least the breaks were reliable and their timing was predictable. Now, because of the demands of retailers for immediate shipping of orders (many orders arrive by fax or by electronic data interface and are expected to be filled in three days), the vacation schedule has been changed from traditional factory closing periods to employee-scheduled vacations. Thinking that workers would appreciate having more control over the timing of their vacations, we were surprised to hear many of them complaining about the changes. Interestingly, the Hmong workers were especially nostalgic about the Fourth of July week. It seems that they used that week to visit family in California, Minnesota, or Wisconsin.

When we reported to one of the human resources officers our finding that many workers missed the Fourth of July week closing, he reinstated it because of concern about keeping his workers happy in ways that did not increase costs. When we talked to him a year later, we heard the horror story of that closing. Their biggest retail client was so put out by the delays caused by that shutdown that the firm almost lost the account. For this mill, losing this account might have resulted in bankruptcy.

This story illustrates the double bind that all firms in this industry face: they are squeezed between strong oligopoly powers on the retail side and the tight labor market on the input side. The standard solution to tight labor of raising wages was used sparingly in the late 1990s (recall figure 11.1). If wages increase too much, a firm may choose to move offshore. The workers we talked to understood the fragility of the industry's position all too well, having seen many jobs in the area, particularly in textiles but also in sheer hosiery, end up lost to overseas competition.

The tight labor market has also affected hosiery workers' lives in that there is less of a penalty for absences than in the past. Most firms still do not have paid sick leave, but they are much more likely to hold a job for someone who is sick than they were when job applicants were plentiful. Of course, those firms with more than fifty employees are required to hold open a worker's job for twelve weeks under the Family and Medical Leave Act, but it is our sense that these firms' increased flexibility in dealing with absences is more a function of tight labor markets and increased investment in training per worker than a response to a legal requirement. In support of this, firms are also increasingly forgiving about absences on "mandatory" overtime days, and some plants have become substantially more flexible about work scheduling, both in allowing flextime for full-time workers and in allowing employees to work part-time to accommodate community college schedules, family needs, and so on.

Although worker benefits have generally increased in the hosiery industry in the last ten years—and they are better than for many of the other possible jobs in the area for less-skilled workers—they are still low compared to benefits for other manufacturing jobs across the country. The benefits package of most firms consists of a bare-bones health insurance plan, a 401k option for employees with a very small employer contribution, and some paid vacation days in those mills that have moved away from the Christmas and Fourth of July shutdowns. None of the firms we talked with offered paid sick days for production employees, although some partially subsidize short-term disability insurance for their employees. Employee demand for prescription drug cards has resulted in many firms providing them; however, the copayments are typically very high. On the negative side, the rapidly rising cost of health insurance and health care, as in many industries, has resulted in a reduction of real health benefits in some firms. Hardest hit is the cost of family coverage. The result is that fewer production workers are covering their families. This is especially difficult for older workers trying to

cover their spouse. Immigrant workers are less affected, not because they are choosing to cover their families but because their
families are younger and therefore on average healthier. Still, many
more workers are exposed to the financial risk of catastrophic ill-
ness because of the high cost of family coverage.

The chronic shortage of workers in the 1990s led some firms to
experiment with very different benefits mixes, including on-site
child care, fitness centers, and subsidized cafeterias, but most employers did not follow suit. The managers of the two firms we interviewed that offered on-site child care were quite committed to it
and convinced that it made good business sense for them. Although
one of the firms recently filed for bankruptcy, it kept the child care
center open for a period after closing the plant because it could
operate at a profit given that the facility already existed. At the
other firm, managers are so convinced of the rate of return to the
company from the child care center, they told us, that they did not
even consider cutting their subsidy to the center when they looked
for cost savings in 1999 after the entire industry had a bad year.
Instead, according to the owner, Christmas bonuses were eliminated and the factory shut down for two weeks. The firms that do
not have child care (the vast majority) seem equally convinced that
an on-site child care center is not appropriate for them, either because they are too small or their employees, they feel, would value
other benefits more highly.

We see the situation in this industry as an example of a potentially stable equilibrium in which some firms will continue to offer
the child care benefit and others will not. We have written extensively about on-site child care in this industry (Connelly, DeGraff,
and Willis 2002, 2003). In brief, the situation is one of "multiple
equilibria" in which different firms serving the same market have
different benefits packages, and these different benefits packages are
stable over a long period of time. Because child care directly benefits only a small percentage of the employee population, it may
make sense for only some firms to offer it. This should lead workers who value it most highly to move to that firm and workers who
value higher wages relative to benefits or some other benefit to
move to another firm. This is consistent with the Tiebout theory of
community amenities (Tiebout 1956) whereby people move among
communities with different levels of taxes and amenities.[15]

In terms of the more basic benefits that affect a larger proportion of employees, we believe that firms are moving toward a common level and mix of benefits as they compete for workers who are more mobile than in the past. While the firm twenty miles away had only recently begun to have turnover problems, all indications are that it will find itself increasingly competing in the same labor market with other firms. In other words, labor market areas are growing, and this will push firms toward similar benefits mixes of health insurance, retirement plans, vacation days, and disability insurance.

Positive change has also occurred in the area of worker safety. Jobs in hosiery manufacturing are generally safer than many other jobs available to workers with low education in this labor market. In addition, jobs throughout the plant are less dangerous today than they were ten years ago, and this certainly affects workers' lives. Changes have been made in dying, boarding, seaming, and finishing to increase safety and reduce health problems (Mock 2002). In the dye house, smaller dye lots and environmental concerns have reduced workers' contact with the harsh dyes. Changing sock fashions have reduced the need for boarding, and there have been efforts to reduce the risk of injury associated with boarding.[16] Seaming machines are also much safer than before. Finally, changes have been made in the physical layout of finishing tasks to reduce repetition-induced injuries.

Although there have been many improvements in hosiery workers' jobs during the 1990s, there have also been some changes for the worse. Most important, many small plants have shut down, especially in the more rural areas surrounding the bigger population centers. Many displaced workers, though able to find other jobs, lost substantial portions of their pensions in these shutdowns. They also travel farther to their new jobs than they did before. Some of the remaining workers told us that they feel more on-the-job stress related to the much faster turnaround time in production necessitated by the changing relationship between producers and retailers. Similarly, some workers experience stress owing to the expectation that they will learn new technology.

In addition, changes in the composition of the workforce and the timing of work have had negative consequences for workers. Because of the difficulty in filling positions, firms have recruited farther afield, leading to a significant increase in commuting time for many hosiery workers. Traveling more than an hour each way to the factory is no longer an unusual commute. Not only does this entail a time cost, but drawing from a geographically larger labor market contributes to a general lessening of the sense of community within the workplace, as far-flung workers are less familiar with one another. This sense is exacerbated by the greater diversity of the workforce among firms that employ immigrants and by higher rates of turnover more generally. Regarding the timing of work, some employees prefer the evening and weekend work shifts, but many of those currently assigned to those shifts would prefer to work a traditional schedule. Finally, as discussed earlier, the increased cost of health insurance has resulted in fewer family members of workers being covered than was the case in the past. While this trend is not at all specific to the hosiery industry, it is nonetheless a very real issue for hosiery workers.

DOES THE HOSIERY INDUSTRY MATTER TO THE FUTURE OF WORK FOR LESS-EDUCATED WORKERS IN THE UNITED STATES IN THE TWENTY-FIRST CENTURY?

Y2K has come and gone, and socks are still made in the United States. Fewer people are employed in the industry than ten years ago, and there are some new sources of tension in workers' lives, but their jobs are somewhat better compensated, safer, more varied, and more flexible. The demographic profile of workers in the industry has changed dramatically, and in many plants a substantial number of workers share a language other than English. Gender and racial segregation have been reduced.

What can we learn from our examination of the last ten years in the hosiery industry about the future of jobs in this industry specifically, and in industries employing less-educated workers more generally? Will socks still be made in the United States in the year 2010? Can any of the strategies this industry has used to survive the enormous economic impacts of globalization be applied to other industries that employ less-educated workers?

One always hesitates to commit to a prediction, but yes, we think a substantial proportion of socks sold in the United States will still be produced domestically in 2010 and beyond. Some of the production will certainly move offshore, particularly sheer hosiery and generic athletic socks. But a combination of factors has led to the industry's survival thus far, and some of these factors will play a role in the U.S. industry's continued survival. Other fortuitous factors, such as the simple advantage of being first in the industry, will erode over time. However, it is our sense that the combination of strategies used by the industry today could serve as a long-run solution. These strategies include: a high proportion of the costs coming from capital rather than labor; regional concentration; cooperative competition; successful identification of niche markets; influxes of new immigrant labor; the development of new voluntary quality standards and the testing equipment needed to implement them; and the demand emphasis on small lots and rapidly changing design. These are ingredients for the long-term sustainability of the industry in its current location.

Many of the lessons learned from our analysis of an unusual industry and community, we would argue, are much more widely applicable. It is essential to note that few manufacturers of goods and services operate in such a competitive daily environment at every level—in labor markets, in daily manufacturing, and in sales—as the hosiery industry. Squeezed between tight labor markets and powerful retailers, hosiery manufacturers must face daily competition from their regional collaborators and international competitors to a degree that few industries share. Errors in strategy at any number of levels can force a firm into bankruptcy in a matter of weeks or months. If hosiery manufacturers can continue to compete and survive in their industry, it is evident that other firms and industries can learn from their example. In particular, their model of an extremely dynamic and responsive regional cooperation strategy in partnership with educational and research institutions, policymakers, and the surrounding communities could be applied to many other industries.

Three conditions gave the hosiery industry the time it needed to implement changes in technology and organization and develop its regional cooperation model: unusual manufacturing characteristics that privileged the knowledge of a particular group of highly skilled technicians; the strong desire of Catawba Valley manufacturers and several key policymakers to continue manufacturing in their communities, and their resulting willingness to work cooperatively with competitors, state agencies, and a diverse set of educational institutions and formats to better enable them to do this; and the significant and successful absorption of a substantial number of immigrants into the hosiery labor force through a communitywide strategy that included far more than job training.

If the cost of labor were a larger part of the production costs, there would be a greater incentive for firms to look to foreign labor markets, as textiles has done. Eventually other countries would be able to develop a group of skilled machine technicians to keep their Italian-built knitting machines running, and they would be able to import or produce the yarn needed to make durable and comfortable socks. But labor is only 20 to 30 percent of production costs, managers and owners in North Carolina told us. With a pool of highly skilled, geographically concentrated technicians who were unwilling to move and a newly arrived immigrant labor force to fill in the other jobs in the manufacturing process, U.S. manufacturers have been shielded somewhat from the tremendous pressure to manufacture elsewhere.

Because they wanted to continue to produce locally, a group of key leaders in the hosiery manufacturing trade association for the region began in the late 1980s to investigate ways to retain their comparative advantage in the industry. Three interrelated strategies have emerged that seem to be working. The first is the creation of a partnership between state-funded educational institutions and the industry. The second is the development of voluntary quality standards. The third is the development of niche markets such as medical compression hosiery, high-tech athletic hosiery, and specialty products. These strategies are interrelated because the educational partnership has also played a role in the development of quality standards and niche markets by providing technical support to both projects. Add to these three strategies the high level of cooperation among firms through the buying and selling of greige goods and the specialization in manufacturing (but not in marketing), and it is possible that the U.S. industry will be able to maintain its comparative advantage for some time to come.

In adapting to meet the threat of global competition, the U.S. hosiery industry has in many ways improved jobs and maintained communities. Significant positive externalities have been created for native-born workers and their communities, as well as for immigrant workers and their families. These are among the most important lessons we can learn from the hosiery industry.

Before looking at the value of the partnership to the community (in other words, the justification of the expenditure of tax dollars to support private industry), first let us examine more closely the three strategies currently in use by the industry to stave off foreign competition. The strategy of the public-private education partnership can best be understood through the history of the Hosiery Technology Center and its diverse activities over time. Created in cooperation with the North Carolina community college system and a number of state agencies, it began as a community college–based training program. Initial problems to be addressed by the HTC were training for both highly skilled jobs, such as fixing in the knitting process and machine repair in other parts of the plant, and some of the less-skilled but essential jobs in the industry, such as knitting, seaming, and dying. The company owners were very aware that the technical knowledge of the machine technicians was key to their ability to produce high-quality goods and thus retain customers. They were concerned about the declining number of young men with mechanical ability and good work characteristics who were willing to consider a career in the hosiery industry. This concern led them to articulate a collective need for affordable, short-term training opportunities in the community. The additional need to train knitters and seamers—much lower-skilled jobs, but also jobs with substantial turnover—was handled at the same time.

Working with the Catawba Valley Community College, the manufacturers saw the proposal for a workforce training program take shape when they engaged the cooperation of the North Carolina Departments of Labor and Commerce, the Manufacturing Extension Partnerships, and the National Institute of Standards Testing in starting the program. It was quickly realized that the usual community college productivity measures of training (with program costs based on standard full-time equivalents [FTEs]) were counterproductive to effective training in hosiery, which requires a very low student-to-teacher ratio because of the need to work closely with extremely small parts of a relatively small machine. Up-to-date machinery was also essential. The industry worked with the community college by lending the school machines or asking its machine suppliers to donate machinery to the HTC. In return, the HTC created schedules tailored to the production needs of specific firms rather than an ordinary semester schedule, trained new workers both at the firm and at the center, and offered a regular schedule for retraining experienced technicians to meet the rapidly changing technology of computerized circular knitting machines. The integration of computer technology into circular knitting machines in the 1990s required teaching experienced machine technicians an entirely new set of skills related to the programming of pattern designs, the use of computer-based machine diagnostics, and repair and maintenance procedures for the computerized parts of the machines.[17] Once new workers began to enroll at the HTC, Dan St. Louis told us, immigrant workers were able to take classes in English as a second language (ESL) through the partnership with the community college.

From its beginnings as a training facility, the HTC has expanded to a set of other projects all aimed at aiding the survival of the hosiery industry. For example, the HTC regularly sponsors conferences for company management to keep them abreast of current business practices in other industries and to partner with economic development specialists to develop strategies for preserving hosiery manufacturing in North Carolina. They also regularly offer a one-day course called Hosiery 101, designed to introduce buyers, yarn makers, and new hosiery executives to the basics of hosiery manufacturing. As discussed earlier, the HTC was instrumental in defining and articulating the technological demands for a boarding machine to help the North Carolina State University consortium project build a safer boarding machine. The HTC maintains a website that formalizes the existing practice of buying and selling greige goods and subcontracting with smaller producers to meet a large contract. The website also provides information on one niche market—state and federal government purchasing—by providing procurement procedures and information on bidding opportunities. It also provides training to firms on Internet use and on an electronic data interface that permits retailers and suppliers to quickly track and replace purchases directly from manufacturers. The HTC now runs a state-of-the-art research lab that has been focusing on some of the environmental aspects of hosiery production, particularly in the dyeing phase, and on developing testing standards and related measuring equipment. Finally, and most recently, the HTC has offered education and assistance on export strategies, with the support of the federal and North Carolina Departments of Commerce.

In addition to its public-private educational partnership, the hosiery industry is also pursuing a strategy of creating voluntary quality standards. The idea is that if the U.S. industry can agree on standards and convince consumers that these standards are meaningful to the durability and attractiveness of socks, then standards may be a way to differentiate between domestically produced socks and imported socks in a market where name brands have meant almost nothing and price has until now been the primary criterion that consumers use in making purchases. This strategy, developed through the HTC, the North Carolina State University College of Textiles, the manufacturing firms, suppliers, customers, and manufacturers of testing equipment, has resulted in the careful development of the product testing standards methodologies that were agreed on in September 2000. The industry is close to introducing these standards and a certification process for quality testing. It remains to be seen whether the industry will be successful in "selling" the standards to consumers, but most of the major retailers seem interested in the development of this important consumer satisfaction method.

Finally, while not all manufacturers can survive by finding niche markets, some of the most successful firms have taken this path. The medical support hosiery industry is quite lucrative and has recently attracted a German firm to establish a plant in North Carolina to make compression hosiery. One firm where we interviewed makes high-end trouser socks and seamless tank tops. Another makes hiking socks with high-tech fiber blending for comfort, durability, and washability. These socks sell for more than fifteen dollars a pair at specialty stores. Another new firm makes multicolored socks that look hand-knitted and vary in pattern from one sock to the other in the pair. These socks are sold at college bookstores and other specialty shops.

Production for niche markets has contributed to a partial transition in the industry to producing in much smaller lots than in the past. This trend is reinforced by the evolving relationships between producers and retailers. For many firms, even those serving large retail accounts, their success hinges on being able to fill a small order for a single store immediately instead of guessing ahead of time which socks will be in demand and warehousing their output. In this context, a domestic location becomes an advantage instead of a disadvantage because it enables firms to save the retailers' warehousing costs and quickly respond to fashion changes. The resulting cost savings and the ability to respond quickly to retailer demands are important factors in keeping production from moving offshore. This is similar to the strategy used in the valve industry (see Bartel, Ichniowski, and Shaw, this volume).

The special circumstances of the hosiery industry gave it its unusual opportunity to develop an effective strategy, but the lessons learned are applicable to numerous other industries and communities. These include the value of finding niche markets, customized processing, cost savings through computerized tracking, inventory reduction, and training partnerships. The value of the hosiery example is evident when one considers the relatively small resources that were required to preserve manufacturing jobs and improve them simultaneously. The hosiery industry provides an excellent model of not only improving employment within an industry but also demonstrating that substantial community benefits accrue when the strategy is well integrated into the community.

There is a growing argument for the development of "hard industries" (as opposed to service industries) as an essential component of economic development (Fingleton 1999). When compared with the enormous amount of public resources paid out in the form of tax breaks for corporations by federal, state, and local government, training programs, and the other incentives used to recruit new manufacturing jobs into communities in recent years, it is clear that a cost-effective strategy of maintaining existing hard industries should be a policy priority as well. The current policy preference for competing with other states to attract new large-scale manufacturing facilities is an extraordinarily expensive strategy compared to the cost of assisting existing industries in becoming more competitive. Economic development resources could be far more effectively leveraged in communities if spent on improving the competitive position of existing industries that are characterized by attributes that have the potential for cost advantages. The hosiery industry example is important because it shows that the strategy of regional cooperation with institutional support can be very effective in meeting the economic development needs of communities for manufacturing employment.

Benefits accrue to communities beyond the employment of their members. Some of the most significant results for Catawba Valley are reflected in the positive impact of the sustained hosiery industry on home and business ownership, in the extraordinarily rapid entrance of second-generation immigrants into college, and in the establishment of immigrant churches and cultural centers. In addition, English-language acquisition has been accelerated and ethnic tension in the community reduced. The contrast in economic development between Catawba Valley communities, where the majority of sock manufacturers are located, and other southern communities with historical concentrations of textile manufacturers is readily apparent.

The lessons to be learned from the hosiery industry are not confined to manufacturing industries. Services that must be produced in the same location in which they are consumed—such as medical services, educational services, food and hospitality services, and transportation services—could also benefit from more industry cooperation and an increased public role in training. These industries cannot be physically aggregated off-site and continue to offer the same service to consumers. Community colleges have traditionally played a role in training skilled workers for these service industries by offering, for example, associate's degree programs for dental technicians, medical laboratory technicians, and teacher's aides, but more could be done in auxiliary areas such as billing, routing, and procurement. The model of short training programs tied closely to the workplace and on-site trouble-shooting by an industry-focused training center would work just as well in a hospital as in a hosiery mill. As in hosiery, where the main cost savings have come not from a fundamental change in the production process but in the way inputs, intermediate goods, and final products are tracked and managed throughout the production steps, there could be similar cost savings in heavily labor-intensive service industries. The need to develop strategies to train (or retrain) the labor force, to develop and adopt appropriate technological innovations, and to operate in efficient ways is essential to keeping costs down in these all-important service industries. In addition, continuous communication and complex systems of cooperation between private firms, educational and training institutions, and government, on a regional, state, and national basis, is critical to improving the jobs of those employed by these industries, increasing wages and other benefits, improving safety, and increasing the flexibility of workers' work lives.

EPILOGUE

Given that a substantial part of our story takes place during the tight labor markets of the 1990s, it is interesting and important to consider what changed as the recession of 2001 deepened. The hosiery industry experienced a weakening of demand in 2001, especially for the higher-end products. However, demand was less affected in the hosiery industry than in several of the other manufacturing industries in the same labor markets. Consequently, workers were less likely to voluntarily quit hosiery for these other industries. Hosiery manufacturing firms responded to lower demand by first cutting Saturday overtime. Some firms went a step further and cut the second shift, mainly through attrition. (The second shift is hard to staff and interferes with the flexibility to simply keep the first shift on for one more hour.) Where further staffing cuts were needed, they were mainly realized through reduced hours rather than layoffs. Companies were reluctant to reduce their workforce because of the investments made in the workers, the memory of their struggles in the tight labor market, and a sense that the downturn may be short-lived.

There has been no acceleration in the exodus of jobs offshore since the recession of 2001. In fact, just the opposite is the case. The recession and the public response to the terrorist acts of September 11, 2001, and the subsequent "war on terrorism" have increased the demand from retailers for "Made in the USA," both as a political statement and as a more dependable (less prone to transportation disruptions) source of product.

Current wage levels and benefits have not been affected very much, basically because they were minimal anyway and because firms are still interested in the retention of current employees. It is too soon to know what would happen to wages and benefits if the downturn continues for an extended period.

Finally, the economic situation facing some major hosiery retailers, especially the recent declaration of bankruptcy by Kmart, serves as an important reminder to hosiery manufacturers that their suppliers and retailers face the same uncertain economic future that they do. Globalization and technological change are having an impact on firms, their workforces, and their communities in more far-reaching and complex ways than could ever be imagined.

This study would not have been possible without the scores of interviewers, translators, and industry sources, educators, owners, managers, and workers who generously gave of their time and knowledge over the past seven years. The book manuscript "Knitting the Social Fabric: The Survival of Work Family Balance in the Global

Economy," by Rachel A. Willis, details the generous help of the individuals who were critical to the completion and quality of this study.

NOTES

1. For example, new boarding machines require less skill than old machines because safety improvements keep the operator farther from the hot form.
2. In the ironing process, called "boarding," the hose is pressed against a metal form of a foot and leg to acquire the shape while being dried out.
3. With anywhere from 70 to 480 needles around the narrow cylinder, a half-hose or "coarse good" machine is defined as having fewer than 300 needles. Tights or pantyhose—referred to as "sheer goods"—are produced on machines that have more than 300 needles in the cylinder.
4. From the French word *grège,* or raw, a greige good in hosiery manufacturing refers to a sock that has been knitted and seamed and is unfinished. Greige goods are frequently bought and sold from both competitors and employees manufacturing at home, as the intermediate goods for a given style and size are completely interchangeable within style, size, and yarn categories.
5. Average costs decline somewhat as knitting machines are added, but only up to the number of machines a given machine technician can handle (about forty). After that, average costs should be constant as additional knitters, machine technicians, and machines are added. See the more detailed discussion of the role of machine technicians later in the chapter.
6. Overall, the industry employed between 75 and 80 percent women as recently as 1995. The proportion of women has declined slightly as the number of immigrant employees, many of whom are male, has increased over the past few years.
7. For example, the economies of scale in dyeing are greater than the economies of scale in knitting and seaming.
8. Ironically, jobs in electrical component manufacturing did not fare well in the recession of 2001, and many of the production workers who left hosiery in the mid-1990s are returning in the early 2000s.
9. Ranked as the most affordable public schools in the nation, the University of North Carolina has an extensive system of sixteen campuses, and the separate community college system has more than thirty campuses. With the highest in-state tuition still less than $2,000 per year at the top campuses, and community college rates as low as

$15 per credit hour, education and training opportunities are widely available in the region and throughout the state.

10.   Finishing is the most labor-intensive phase of the production process. While some machines have been developed to mechanize the packaging of socks, these machines are only profitable to use with large lots and for products (such as tube socks) that require less quality control.

11.   The concentration of U.S. hosiery production in North Carolina has declined somewhat over this ten-year period, with the North Carolina share of domestic hosiery employment decreasing from 65 percent to 58 percent (see table 11.1). The areas in the United States that are gaining are Tennessee and Alabama. This change may be a foreshadowing of things to come, or it may simply reflect the tight labor market of the 1990s in North Carolina.

12.   Hosiery is by no means unique in this regard. From the poultry-processing plants in Arkansas and Missouri to the furniture-making plants down the street from the hosiery mills, the low-skilled workforce of southern manufacturing firms has been transformed. The 2000 census figures show that North Carolina ranked first among states in the rate of growth of the Hispanic population. All the other states in the top ten were southern except for Minnesota, which ranked ninth.

13.   No one is ever hired directly as a machine technician. A new machine technician usually begins as a knitter or a material handler. After showing strong mechanical ability and beginning to fix problems in his own set of machines, a more experienced machine technician may show the "candidate" a few new tricks and see how he responds. If the response is promising, the training is formally acknowledged. Today the aspiring machine technician might then be sent to the HTC for a training course or directed to a more formalized on-site training program.

14.   The continuing low percentage of women machine technicians is at least partly due to gender differences in mechanical background and to a preference among many women not to work the longer shifts sometimes required of machine technicians.

15.   It is impossible to test this hypothesis in our case given that only two firms have child care centers and there are large differences between these firms and others owing to many factors, only one of which is the presence of a child care center.

16.   With old boarding machines (still operating in many plants), the boarder must put the sock onto the hot, foot-shaped form. One slip and the worker's arm touches the form itself, causing a burn. The new boarding machines use vacuum pressure and a mechanical grab-

ber to put the sock on the hot form. The worker simply feeds the socks into the machine. The hot forms, which are now made of a new material that is less hot to the touch, are separated from the worker by Plexiglas.

17.   The mechanics of circular knitting is basically unchanged by the new machines, but where it used to take an experienced technician a day to change the knitting pattern on the old machines, the computer interface makes it easy to change patterns quickly. Interestingly, many firms continue to operate with both new and old machines. The old machines produce the standard socks, and the new machines produce the specialty socks.

REFERENCES

Archives of the National Association of Hosiery Manufacturers. 1905–1999. North Carolina Special Collection, University of North Carolina Library.

Catawba Valley Hosiery Association Archives. 1959–1999. North Carolina Special Collection, University of North Carolina Library.

Connelly, Rachel, Deborah S. DeGraff, and Rachel Willis. 2002. "If You Build It, They Will Come: Parental Use of On-site Child Care Centers." *Population Research and Policy Review* 21(3): 241–73.

———. 2003. "The Value of Employer-Sponsored Child Care to Employees." Unpublished paper, Bowdoin College.

Fingleton, Eamonn. 1999. *In Praise of Hard Industries: Why Manufacturing Not the Information Economy Is the Key to Future Prosperity.* Boston: Houghton Mifflin.

Glass, Brent. 1992. *The Textile Industry in North Carolina.* Raleigh: North Carolina Division of Archives and History.

Grass, Milton. 1955. *History of Hosiery.* New York: Fairchild Publications.

Mock, Gary. 2002. *The Century of Progress.* Raleigh: North Carolina State University Press.

Murnane, Richard J., John B. Willett, and Frank Levy. 1995. "The Growing Importance of Cognitive Skills in Wage Determination." *Review of Economics and Statistics* 77(2): 251–66.

Tiebout, C. M. 1956. "A Pure Theory of Local Expenditure." *Journal of Political Economy* 64: 416–24.

United States Bureau of Labor Statistics. 2002. "Employment and Unemployment." Available at: *www.bls.gov/data/sa.htm.*

CHAPTER 12

When Management Strategies Change: Employee Well-Being at an Auto Supplier

Susan Helper and Morris M. Kleiner

A s a result of increased international competition, over the last decade or two U.S. manufacturing firms have made major changes in both their product strategies and their human resource policies. Many firms have chosen one of two strategies: the "high road" of innovative products and skilled, highly paid workers, or the "low road" of commodity products and low-paid, unskilled workers (Appelbaum and Batt 1994). In this chapter, we examine the case of a firm that manages to combine elements of both "roads" in a profitable way: it makes innovative products with moderately skilled, low-paid workers. We think that this firm may well be a bellwether for overall trends in U.S. manufacturing, especially in auto parts.

Our firm, which we call SP (Small Parts), is a $600 million manufacturer of electrical and electronic products that it sells primarily to vehicle manufacturers (automakers and truck manufacturers).[1] Since the firm was founded in the 1960s, SP has undergone a number of changes in its markets and products over the years. In the next sections, we describe these changes, first in auto parts manufacturing in general and then at SP. These changes have had a significant impact on SP's human resource practices, including the nature of work, methods and levels of pay, and training.[2] We describe the impacts of these changes on worker satisfaction, based on surveys we conducted in four of SP's U.S. plants. In the conclusion, we discuss the rationale for the financial success of this firm and analyze outcomes for employees.

GENERAL TRENDS IN AUTO PARTS
PRODUCTS AND MARKETS

Auto parts manufacturing in the United States has changed a great deal in the last fifteen years. Between the 1930s and the 1980s, the "Big Three" U.S. automakers shared a tight oligopoly. A key goal of U.S. automakers was to protect their oligopolistic profits from suppliers by keeping barriers to entry in their input markets low. Suppliers did not need sophisticated product design, quality, or management capabilities; they were asked only to build simple products to the blueprints provided by automakers, who did not set high quality requirements. (Sometimes automakers asked suppliers to ship 10 percent extra parts to cover defects.) Automakers kept large stocks of components in part as a buffer against attempts by suppliers to hold them up for higher prices. Automakers also had several firms supplying the same part, and that made it easy for them to switch suppliers if necessary. This system contributed to automaker profits well above the manufacturing average. However, automakers' rent protection strategies led to a great deal of inefficiency. Quality was low and costs were high, owing to the costs of buffer stock, designs ill suited to supplier equipment, and supplier inability and unwillingness to make investments in new technology. In the late 1980s, in order to compete with the quality and low costs offered by Japanese manufacturers, U.S. automakers began to adopt many of their rivals' supplier relations practices (Helper 1991; Helper and Levine 1992).[3]

Automakers' expectations subsequently changed in several areas:

Product design: Suppliers are now expected to be capable of designing the components they produce rather than simply building to their customers' blueprints, as in the past. This system has led to improved quality and reduced costs, since suppliers now design products that fit their equipment (Wasti and Liker 1999).

Quality: Automakers in most cases no longer inspect parts upon receipt but send them straight to the assembly line. Defective parts thus impose huge costs (which are often charged back to the supplier), so acceptable quality levels are now measured in tens of parts per million.

Delivery: Where once a delivery was considered on time if an amount plus or minus 10 percent of the contracted-for number of parts arrived anytime during a three-day window, now suppliers are often expected to deliver an exact number of parts within a thirty-minute time frame. An early delivery is almost as bad as a late delivery, because automakers no longer have a lot of space to store additional parts.

Globalization: Automakers increasingly want suppliers that can supply them just-in-time in all of their plants around the globe. To meet this demand, suppliers must also have plants (or warehouses where final assembly is done) around the world.

Subassembly: Automakers no longer want to receive individual parts from suppliers; they want the suppliers to assemble several parts together. These subassemblies can have just a few parts (as when a stamping firm welds together several separate pieces), or they can be quite complex (as when a supplier delivers an entire seat or instrument panel to the assembly line). If the subassembly has only a few interfaces with other parts and can be tested as a unit (seats and instrument panels, for example), it is known as a "module" (Sako and Murray 1999).

Some of the reasons why automakers now want subassemblies from suppliers are efficiency-based. A plant producing a few parts can focus on quality more than is possible at an assembly plant, which may be overwhelmed with five thousand separate parts coming in the door. A supplier may also have expertise that the automaker cannot match. Another key reason is to save labor costs: assembly workers earn almost $20.00 an hour, with generous benefits, while supplier workers earn $8.00 to $14.00 an hour, with few or no benefits. Suppliers that combine lower labor costs with improved design have been quite successful in winning contracts for work that used to be done in assembly plants. Labor-cost savings alone have proven illusory, however, since they are offset by the increased size and fragility of modules.

Price pressure: Contracts from automakers now often contain promises that prices will fall 3 to 5 percent per year (Luria 2001). As a result, input prices in this industry have fallen.

To meet these new requirements, suppliers have developed new strategies:

Becoming a module supplier: Suppliers now supply geographically contiguous chunks of a car, such as an instrument panel.

Developing functional expertise: More suppliers are now specializing in areas such as stamping or plastic molding.

Becoming expert in a particular system: Systems expertise is especially good to develop if a product is relatively new (electronics, for example). Automakers are not experts in systems and do not want to invest in becoming experts.

Moving manufacturing to the rural or southern United States or to a foreign country: There has been no downward trend in total employment in auto parts (SICs 3714 and 3496); this figure has fluctuated with the business cycle around 100,000 since 1980. The location of these jobs has shifted dramatically, however, toward southern and rural areas, where wages are lower.

Consolidating the supplier sector: As a result of increased and different demands from automakers, there have been many acquisitions in the supplier sector. In addition, in the last three years both Ford and GM have spun off their component divisions as separate firms, each with multiple billions in annual sales.

These trends have been accompanied by changes in human resource policies, in particular a decline of unions, an increase in employee involvement programs, and stagnation in wages. All of these trends—devolution of responsibility for design and subassembly; increasingly strict requirements for quality and delivery; continued price pressure; deunionization; increase in employee involvement; and wage stagnation—are becoming characteristic of much of U.S. manufacturing, even outside the automotive sector. Suppliers in agricultural equipment have experienced all of these trends and refer to them as the "automatization" of their industry (Zeitlin and Whitford, forthcoming). Other examples are Dell computers (modules and delivery) and the apparel industry (fast response) (Abernathy, Dunlop, and Hammond 1999).

It is of considerable interest to students of human resource management to understand how firms in the auto parts supplier sector have changed their policies with respect to employees and the impact of these changes on wages, job satisfaction, and profits. In this chapter, we report on one company that let us survey its workers and spend time unaccompanied in its plants. The company exemplifies most of the trends discussed here.

METHODS

For this research, we combined qualitative and quantitative techniques. We made numerous visits to four of SP's plants. SP has two plants in Massachusetts, one in a suburban area and one in an urban area. We visited each Massachusetts plant five times—once in 1995, once in 1998, and three times in 2000—and visited the urban plant again in 2002. In 1995 and 1998 we took an extensive plant tour and heard presentations from most areas of management (including the group vice president who oversaw the plants and discussed strategy, the plant managers, quality managers, and human resources managers).[4] During these visits we had some very brief conversations with operators, asking them what they were doing.

In 2000 we returned to the plants to design and administer a worker satisfaction survey. First, we toured the plants again, and the plant manager and a product engineer gave us an overview of the products being produced. Then we conducted focus groups among hourly workers. (We also surveyed salaried workers but do not report these results here.) The focus groups consisted of two to three groups of blue-collar workers (assemblers and material handlers) per shift. We asked management to choose these workers and to include a mix of ethnic groups and both employees who seemed satisfied and some who seemed dissatisfied. Judging by our survey results, management did give us a sample that was representative on these variables. We also asked that supervisors not be present. This request was also granted, with one exception: one supervisor translated from Vietnamese to English in a group with Vietnamese-speaking workers. His presence had a noticeably chilling effect on the group.

Based on the comments received in the focus groups, we revised our survey and returned in the spring of 2000 to administer it. Workers were excused from their regular duties to answer our questions in groups of twenty to fifty. They appeared to do so quite carefully. About one-fifth of them took the time to write comments, a laborious undertaking for the many who were clearly not used to writing and not well educated. Some respondents also stayed later to discuss their experiences at the company.[5] Workers were informed that the survey responses would be kept anonymous, and no supervisors were in the room when the surveys were being filled out. We returned to each plant in the summer of 2000 to discuss our results with managers; at each plant the dozen or so top officials attended the meeting and offered comments. (We offered to present the results to workers as well, but management declined.)

We followed a more abbreviated process with the other two plants, one in rural Ohio, and one in Florida. In Ohio, we administered the survey in the spring of 2001; at the same time we took an extensive plant tour with an industrial engineer and had discussions with the controller and human resources managers. We had numerous informal discussions with workers about their reactions to the survey. We returned in the summer to present results at a meeting attended by managers and supervisors. Finally, we again toured the plant in the spring of 2002 and met with human resources managers, a supervisor, a team leader, an assembler, and an industrial engineer. We made two visits to Florida—the first time we administered the survey and toured the plant, and the second time we presented the results (again, only to management).

We also obtained extensive financial information from management at each of the four plants.

THE HISTORY OF SP

SP makes electrical and electronic components for vehicles, such as ignition switches and a product that indicates when a car door is ajar. Over the last decade the firm has become a functional specialist, building and acquiring capabilities in the design of electrical and electronic parts. A core competence at SP is design for manufacturing. The firm's original business, started in the 1960s, was assembling wire harnesses for farm equipment and for a division of General Motors. This was a relatively simple task. For the automotive product, all design was done by GM, and the plastic connectors and metal terminals that SP attached to the wires were also provided by GM. The key to success was keeping costs low and avoiding defects (since a loose connection was very difficult to find once installed in a car). The assembly jobs were simple but very monotonous. There was little training or effort to involve the workforce (Gillett 1992).

According to the firm's 10-K report, in 1987 the investors who owned SP changed their strategy. In that year SP began to move away from contract manufacturing to become a designer as well as a manufacturer. In 1989 it bought a small Massachusetts firm that made sensors and actuators for cars and boats. This firm was founded in 1909 and had a long history of toolmaking and design capability.

In 1997 SP went public in order to gain access to more capital and to allow the company's founders to take some of their money out of the firm. At the end of 1998 SP bought another firm that designed and manufactured sensors and had a plant in rural Ohio and one in suburban Florida. During the 1990s the firm also acquired some foreign operations (in Europe, Mexico, and Brazil). In 1999 the firm ended the contract manufacturing operation that had originally formed the core of its business to focus entirely on parts it designed itself.[6]

Thus, the firm exemplifies many of the trends discussed earlier: it has become an expert in the design and manufacture of electronic and electromechanical systems; it has become global; and it has grown dramatically, mostly through acquisition. It has also begun to introduce Japanese manufacturing methods, such as just-in-time inventory reduction techniques, manufacturing cells, and programs to promote manufacturing design and improve quality.

We surveyed workers in the two Massachusetts plants, the Ohio plant, and the Florida plant. Despite their origins in two different companies, the plants' production processes are remarkably similar. There are variations, however, in the workforce, turnover, pay, and training policies among the four plants. In table 12.1, we give the basic workforce characteristics of the four plants we surveyed. The two Massachusetts plants had the highest percentage of assemblers and the lowest turnover rates, but the largest percentage of temporary employees. The Florida and Ohio plants were similar, but the Florida plant had the lowest percentage of longtime employees (those with ten or more years of experience).

THE MASSACHUSETTS PLANTS

One of the Massachusetts plants was an older structure in an urban area. It was near the site of the firm's original building, which had supplied the auto industry since 1919, when it made dash lamp sockets for the Ford Model T. In the 1980s the plant was owned by a conglomerate, which "milked it" and did not invest in it. The plant also made a variety of other products, including trays for Life Savers candy, hair dryer switches, and blood pumps. In the 1960s half of its revenue came from selling military products. The workers were paid piece-rate, as was common in manufacturing in the area at the time. In 1985 a GE-trained manager (Mr. P) was brought in to run the plant. He and other top managers (including Mr. L and Ms. A) stayed with the plant when three years later it was sold to SP in a transaction that left the plant highly leveraged. (By 1998, however, the operation was debt-free.) In 1989 these managers built another plant in a nearby suburb that paid time rates and was more automated. This plant was closed in 1996, and its workers (and some from the urban facility) moved to a new plant, also in a nearby suburb.

In the 1990s the workforce at the Massachusetts plants was composed largely of first-generation immigrants. About one-third of the workforce was Vietnamese, and one-third was Cape Verdean. The rest of the workers were a mixture of immigrants from other countries, such as Poland, and U.S.-born workers. About 60 percent were female. The workforce was recruited by word of mouth rather than advertising, and many workers were related to each other. There were few blacks, though the plant was in a majority-black area. At the urban location most workers walked or took public transportation to work. Turnover was low; at the time of our survey two-thirds of the workforce had been at SP for at least four years (table 12.1).

At the time of our first visit in 1995 the plant was coming to the end of a transition begun in the mid-1980s. It had been a low-volume plant where quality requirements were not high and designs, generally dictated by the customer, did not change often. The new strategy was to become a "high-volume, precision operation," according to Mr. M, the plant manager in 1995. This transition involved changes in many areas.

Product Strategy   SP hired engineers to design products in-house and dramatically increased the rate at which new products were introduced (fifty in 1998) and retired. Under this new product

Table 12.1 Production Employee Characteristics at SP

	Number of Workers	Assemblers	Temporary	Less Than One Year	One to Four Years	Four to Six Years	Six to Ten Years	More than Ten Years
Massachusetts								
Urban	233	63%	17%	12%	27%	14%	12%	36%
Suburban	285	71	13	12	33	26	13	16
Ohio	634	54	0.6	4	35	17	20	25
Florida	482	46	1.1	17	37	18	22	7

Source: Authors' compilation.

strategy, products became increasingly sophisticated and many were patented. For example, a sensor based on the Hall Effect was written up in a technical journal.

Process Flow   The old process flow was individually paced. Sitting at a machine, a single worker added one or more pieces to a small assembly and then pressed a button or foot pedal to fasten the piece via welding or crimping. She then placed the partially completed product in a box; when the box was full, material handlers moved it to workers who did the next stage.

Management gradually brought in more automated assembly, eliminating individually paced jobs. Instead, six to eight workers sat around a circular work cell. Some stations were completely automated; at most stations a worker assisted the machine in assembling the part. When the part was finished, it was moved (automatically or manually) to the next station. At the last station, the operator packed the fully completed part into a box to be shipped directly to the customer. The cell was paced by the slowest worker. At many of the cells a lighted overhead sign kept track of the pieces made and compared that figure to the number of pieces that needed to be made to meet the day's quota. Since there was no buffer between operators, inventory in the cells was dramatically lower (and lead times faster).

By 2000 these assembly jobs employed the bulk of the workforce (see table 12.1). There was also a small plastic molding operation in which workers monitored machines and loaded and unloaded parts. In the suburban plant several cells were completely automated and monitored by technicians who had received three months of training and were paid more than the assemblers. Other blue-collar jobs included material handling and shipping and receiving.

Design for Manufacturing   The key to the success of the firm, according to Mr. P, was the tight integration of product and process. At the time of the survey the Massachusetts plants employed more than one hundred design engineers. They tried to design products that were not only sophisticated (many were patented) but easy to make and capable of automatic quality checks. (Manual inspection is less accurate, particularly when thousands of parts must be checked each day.) Examples of design for manufacturing included molding in small bumps on the piece whose only function was to help locate the part correctly in a machine (they had no function once the part was made), and simple setups that tested for the presence of certain parts and would not let the operator go to the next step unless all parts were there.

In the traditional approach, engineers were organized into functions, such as design engineering and manufacturing engineering; when a product left one stage, it was "thrown over the wall" to the next stage, with little communication between groups. To facilitate the new integrated approach, engineers were reorganized in 1995 into product teams that would follow a product all the way from concept to launch.

During our 1995 visit we saw several engineers working with operators to design "mistake-proofing" mechanisms. In several cases, the work seemed hampered by language barriers; we saw a lot of sign language being used as the operator and engineer struggled to communicate about quality problems. We saw fewer engineers on the shop floor in our later visits. One reason was that design-for-manufacturing principles had become codified (both by SP and others), so that more of the work could proceed without input from operators. These principles included ideas such as making sure that parts were either perfectly symmetric, so that orientation did not matter, or obviously asymmetric, so that a fixture could be built that would not allow work to proceed on an incorrectly oriented part. The move toward codification was given additional impetus by the fact that the design engineers in Massachusetts were increasingly called on to design parts for SP's other locations far away (including Europe and Mexico).

Method of Pay—Piece Rates Workers on the individually paced jobs were paid piece rate from the 1960s until 1996. Paying piece rates had been a common practice in the Massachusetts city in the 1950s and 1960s. Management recognized, however, that piece rates were not well suited to the new strategy. First, workers on piece rates wanted a large amount of inventory between stations so that they would not be constrained by someone working more slowly than they were. This practice had led not only to long lead times but to low quality, both because of the incentive to work as fast as possible and because many bad products could be made out of such large batches before they were caught by inspectors.

Another problem with piece rates was that new product introduction created big risks for both labor and management: workers were concerned that the rate would be set too stringently, and managers worried that the rate would turn out to be too easy. As Ms. A put it in 2000,[7] "New product development became a hurdle with the piecework system. Employees did not want to work on new product"; they would have to learn a new job, she noted, and they risked earning lower pay while they figured out shortcuts. "We had a lot of turnover in the plant at this time [late 1980s]. There were no good standards for new product, and there was no way to introduce new products unless we wanted to throw loose rates on them. This restricted us from doing new products."

Getting rid of the piece-rate system was not easy. "From 1985 to the early nineties," Ms. A told us, "we started to educate the employees in a series of roundtable meetings and business meetings that the security they felt they had in the incentive system was hurting the company and hurting them and hurting the quality of the business, and that we would have to make changes to the way they made their money." But some mistakes were made. "For our original steering committee, we selected [hourly] people who had trust in the plan—we didn't have the natural leaders. We had approached it as a control thing with employees," said Mr. P in 1995.

"The opportunity of expanding to a second plant in 1989 was the first chance of changing the pay system," according to Ms. A. Workers in this plant, located in a suburb, worked in cells and were paid an hourly wage. This wage was lower than in the urban plant, since the prevailing wage in the suburb was lower, and it was difficult to get people to help with the start-up. Thus, some were given promotions as an incentive. Piece rates were also gradually phased out at the urban plant between 1992 and 1996.

Some operators we interviewed in focus groups in 2000 remained upset about the change. Almost all operators had worked faster than the standard at which the piece rate was set. Management recognized this by setting the base time wage at 132 percent of the piece-rate base wage at the new plant. They also introduced a gain-sharing program, which they thought would pay an additional 10 to 15 percent. Managers said later that they did not intend to cut pay ("except that there were some people making 200 percent of the base rate, which is just unrealistic," according to Ms. A in 2002). Management was very worried, however, about setting the rates too high and locking the firm into a wage that was "too high."[8] (In one

Table 12.2 "Are You Making More Money Under the VAG
Plan?": Responses of SP Workers in the
Massachusetts Plants

Urban Massachusetts plant	
Strongly disagree	26.21%
Disagree	22.76
Neither agree nor disagree	25.52
Agree	14.48
Strongly agree	11.03
Suburban Massachusetts plant	
Strongly disagree	20.23
Disagree	21.97
Neither agree nor disagree	28.32
Agree	17.92
Strongly agree	11.56

Source: Authors' compilation.

case in 1995, Mr. P noted, "we underestimated the impact of automating the manual O-ring assembly—it almost killed the plan.")
The result was that management erred on the conservative side, and
45 percent of those who had worked under piece rates felt that they
had suffered a pay cut, according to our survey. Newer workers,
who had not yet figured out shortcuts on their job (or had been
assigned to a job with a "loose" rate) benefited; 27 percent of survey respondents who had worked under piece rates indicated that
they made more money now than before (see table 12.2). Workers
who had been on piece rates were kept at the same hourly pay for a
while. However, the fastest workers saw their hourly pay decline by
$4.00 to $5.00 an hour (40 to 50 percent) over several years. According to management, however, only about 10 percent of the
workers quit during this period.

Wages in 1999 for assemblers were $10.48 an hour in the subur-
ban plant, and $10.60 an hour in the urban plant. (There was no
seniority increment.) In the urban plant this wage was supplemented by a gain-sharing bonus (called the VAG) of about $1.00 an
hour. The VAG was much less (often zero) in the suburban plant,
owing mostly to quality problems and secondarily to difficulties in
accounting for the time of engineers who worked on products for
SP's other plants, according to Ms. A in 2002. This pay rate was far
below the U.S. manufacturing average in 1999 of $14.40 per hour—

and $15.03 for workers in industrial machinery (Jacobs 2000). Benefits (which included paid vacation and medical and dental insurance) were more generous than in the average U.S. factory but did not come close to offsetting the low pay. In addition, the Massachusetts plants were located in an area with a very high cost of living.

Method of Pay—Gain-Sharing   Under piece rates, individual operators had a strong incentive to figure out how to do their job as quickly as possible. This led to a sustained 2 to 3 percent annual productivity improvement over the decades, according to Mr. K, a semiretired manager now in his eighties who had worked at the plant since the 1950s. But piece rates did not promote the teamwork necessary to meet customers' new demands for just-in-time delivery of high-quality products that changed frequently. Increasingly, jobs were automated. Automation increased precision but frustrated the efforts of those workers who wanted to work fast.

Managers did not want to lose the incentive aspect of piece-rate pay, so they implemented a gain-sharing plan, beginning in 1992 with the help of a consultant. Gain-sharing was calculated on a plantwide basis: everyone (except the top three managers, who were in a corporate incentive plan) got the same percentage of their pay as a bonus. The bonus pool went up with productivity and down with the occurrence of defects or delivery problems.

When we visited the plants again in 1998, it was clear that gain-sharing was the centerpiece of management's strategy to make workers more aware of their impact on plant performance. Management put a lot of effort into figuring out what they considered to be a "fair" formula (one that would yield a 10 to 15 percent payout if things went well). If the payout was too small, workers would be demoralized; if it was too big, they would be getting too much money. Managers also felt that the formula needed to change if conditions changed, and so they spent a lot of time explaining the changes and justifying them. Initially the bonus pool was a function of the difference between current productivity and 1991 productivity, with deductions for defects and bad deliveries. The bonus could not exceed 15 percent. In 1998 Mr. P told us that they would soon need to revise the benchmark year ("raise the bar") so that the company could meet its commitment to Ford to reduce prices in exchange for a long-term contract. Materials and capital costs were not included in the formula, he said, because they were not under the control of most workers.

Several mechanisms gave workers the opportunity to increase the bonus pool for everyone and to receive recognition for doing so. Among them were "The Last Chance Club" for workers who had caught a defect just before it went out the door. In 1995, for example, a flood of volunteers sorted through eighty thousand parts, on their own time, to find the 5 percent that were defective in the ninety minutes before the customer's truck came. This action avoided an additional air freight cost of one dollar per part. Members of the Last Chance Club got their names on a plaque in the lunchroom; those so inscribed (including management) seemed genuinely pleased at the honor. (The culprit in this case turned out to be a vendor that had shipped defective parts. This firm was put in SP's continuous improvement program: someone from SP sat down weekly with the firm's president to monitor progress.) The gain-sharing also played an important role in changing engineers' incentives. "It used to be like pulling teeth to get engineers to leave their new products and solve problems on the floor. We need to leverage our 30 percent overhead as well as our 5 percent direct labor," said Mr. P in 1995. However, Mr. P observed in 1998 that gain-sharing seemed successful in getting on-time delivery, but not quality.

Among the mechanisms through which management communicated with employees were quarterly meetings with supervisors, monthly meetings with hourly workers (these were attended by one or two representatives from each department, chosen by management), and quarterly meetings to discuss the gain-sharing results. These meetings arose out of some management communication initiatives started in the 1980s. Union avoidance was the initial motivation for these initiatives, according to Mr. K, the older manager. There had been several organizing drives in the past, but none since about 1987, a development he attributed to Mr. P's quickness in addressing problems.

In 1998 management decided that materials and capital costs should be included in the gain-sharing formula to avoid the situation in which the company might owe a large bonus even though it made no profit because of large investments or materials price increases.[9] The program was renamed "Value-Added Gain-Sharing" at this time. (In contrast, Lincoln Electric, another firm with a large incentive pay component, borrowed money to pay the bonus in a year when high worker productivity was combined with materials price increases and losses on acquisitions.) The VAG formula became so complicated that "only three people in the company understand how it is calculated," said Ms. A. Nevertheless, almost all shop workers had a basic understanding that low productivity, defects, and delivery mistakes would cost them money. (Especially in the early months of the program, however, some of the workers' efforts seemed to far outweigh the individual monetary benefit they would receive; a defective part, for instance, would cost each worker about one dollar.)

In 1995, 10 to 15 percent of the workforce participated in continuous improvement teams. These were not in evidence in later visits. Instead, in 1998 the plants focused on obtaining ISO 9000 quality certification, and workers were somewhat involved in writing their own job descriptions. In 2000 the plants undertook a Six Sigma initiative, which was still going on in 2002. This program trains managers and supervisors to be "Six Sigma black belts" and "green belts," respectively; they learn techniques for reducing inventory and lead time and analyzing quality data. Operators join with supervisors and engineers to improve line layout, but according to one supervisor we talked with, they contribute very few useful ideas. Survey respondents corroborated the statement that workers contributed few ideas; the average worker made a suggestion only once a year or less. A majority of workers said they would like to participate more in decisionmaking at work.

We did not attempt an independent evaluation of the claim that few "useful" ideas were contributed by workers. The controller provided two examples of major improvements she thought had been provided by assemblers, but the ideas had actually come from engineers and supervisors, according to the supervisor. (As one reviewer pointed out, the supervisor's answer could have been motivated by a desire to show his continuing usefulness to the company.)

Overall, the improvement efforts have helped the urban plant to reduce costs by 3 percent every year since 1986. (Interestingly, this figure is similar to the 2 to 3 percent productivity improvement achieved by operators on piece rates, according to Mr. K.)

At the time of the survey the plants seemed to be placing less emphasis on suggestions to change the process and more on training to take over supervisory functions and avoid mistakes. This shift is one response to the quality problems that caused the VAG payout in the suburban plant to be zero in the year preceding the survey. (The urban plant continued to earn an average 7 to 10 percent VAG payout.)

Location Policies   Massachusetts management built a second plant in 1989 and then closed it in 1996 and moved to a larger factory nearby. There were long discussions with SP's board, which was based in Ohio, about the location of this operation. The board did not want a plant built in such a high-wage area far from the automakers in the Midwest. However, the local manager, Mr. P, prevailed; he refused to move, not even to New Hampshire, only an hour away. He argued that labor costs were only 6 to 7 percent of total costs, and he said that it was important to have the new plant close to the old one to ensure that most of the current workforce would stay. "I don't want to save 20 or 30 percent on labor costs by going somewhere else, and then lose it all due to carelessness on the part of an employee who doesn't care," he said in 1995.

Although management wanted to keep the same workforce, they also wanted to keep wages low by national standards. This dual desire seems to be responsible for much of the difficulty that management has had in implementing the new system.

THE OHIO PLANT

The Ohio plant was located in a rural part of the state, about thirty minutes from a medium-sized city where most of the managers lived. The company was started in the mid-1960s by a man, universally known as Jack, who had innovative ideas for electronics products and a paternalistic management style. Layoffs were done on a voluntary basis, and Jack was often seen on the shop floor until he semiretired and moved south (where he opened the Florida plant).

Both the Ohio and Florida plants were acquired in 2000 by SP for $370 million. According to Mr. P, the firm had excellent market positioning, but Jack had not invested in the business in recent years, and operational effectiveness was slipping. Both Mr. P and local managers felt that Jack had negotiated a very good deal for himself that left behind a financial burden for the Ohio plant to overcome. (They pointed out that SP's bid for the plant was 25 percent higher than competing bids.) There was growing tension between the Ohio managers and SP top management. In contrast to

Mr. P's perception, the Ohioans felt that their company was making a good profit but was dragged down by accounting charges made to reflect what SP felt were its managers' contribution to the business and financial problems caused by SP's other plants.

The Ohio workforce was very different from the workforce in the Massachusetts plants. Everyone seemed to be native-born, and all but a handful were white. The average age was forty-four, higher than in Massachusetts; about 20 percent appeared to be over sixty. (Management explained that many of them worked to supplement retirement benefits obtained from working on a previous job.) Although there was a core of experienced workers (see table 12.1), turnover was very high: 30 percent of those hired in 2000 had either quit or been fired by the end of the year. In 2001 the starting wage for an assembler was $6.85 an hour; after one year this increased to $7.80, and after three years to $8.27. After twelve years one assembler reported that she made about $9.00 an hour. This wage was supplemented by an annual check that was called "profit-sharing." The owner allocated a pool of money (based loosely on the past year's performance) that was divided among the workforce based on seniority and wages; the payment was typically equal to about two weeks' wages. In contrast to the VAG, management did not emphasize any effect on the payment of workers' productivity, and the size of the bonus pool was subjectively determined.

The Ohio plant's production process—semi-automated team assembly—was remarkably similar to those of the Massachusetts plants. (The Ohio plant also had some plastic molding.) The main improvement activity at the time of our visits was the War on Waste (WOW) program. This program, started in 1997, was led by Mr. S, an engineer who was truly an evangelist for lean production. In 1994 he had enrolled the plant in a program sponsored by the Toyota Supplier Support Program even though the plant had never had Toyota business. Several Toyota engineers had helped the plant with projects to improve the flow of product through the plant. Inventory turns (measured as inventory divided by factory cost) increased from five to fourteen between 1998 and 2002. According to Mr. S's calculations, WOW had saved the plant 2 to 3 percent of sales in the two years since its inception. Almost all of the ideas seemed to be generated by technicians and engineers, judging from the examples given on the plant tours we took and written up in the plant newsletters. "We don't involve operators enough. We do it

hardly at all—this is a failing," said Mr. S. We did not independently investigate how representative these examples were. The average worker contributes a suggestion about once a year, according
to our survey.

Mr. S did what he could to encourage participation, believing
that "people want recognition, not more pay. You could increase
pay and still have dissatisfied employees." Participation was rewarded in small ways: roughly 10 percent of the operators were
wearing a WOW T-shirt or using a WOW pencil on the day we
conducted the survey. And Mr. S believed that the VAG, implemented in Ohio in January 2002, did have an impact on participation, because it gave everyone a financial stake in eliminating waste.

Mr. S also believed that even though much progress had been
made with contributions from engineers and supervisors, worker
training would be key to continued improvement. For example, he
said that if inventory turns were to be increased still further, material handlers would need to follow prescribed routes for replenish-
ing work stations and bring only a set number of parts. He did not
believe they would (or could) do this unless they understood the
logic of the system: "You have to bring exactly two boxes [of parts
to be assembled] at a time, and then fifteen minutes later another
two boxes, and you'll mess up the flow if you bring one box sometimes and three boxes at other times."

THE FLORIDA PLANT

The Florida plant was very similar to the suburban Boston plant. It
was relatively new, about fifteen years old, and capital-intensive.
Unlike the Boston workforce, the workforce included a large number of retirees who had moved to Florida and found that their retirement income and savings were insufficient. Consequently, the
age of production employees was higher in Florida than at the
other plants.

The plant manager in Florida, Mr. Z, said that the plant was built
to serve as a semiretirement location for Jack, the founder of the
company. Consequently, the plant and the major offices for top
management were in separate buildings. The manufacturing plant
and its offices were plain with Spartan amenities. The main office
complex had carpeted offices that had windows and were generally

larger. The corporate meeting rooms and cafeteria were in the office complex rather than in the plant.

Although most of the jobs involved watching and adjusting controls on machines and checking for defects, there were many difficult and tedious jobs. These included packing parts and loading trucks; a particularly daunting job involved putting small round sensors into a hole the size of the eye of a needle for eight hours a day. Training was emphasized in the Florida plant: several rooms in the plant and office complex were devoted to training production workers and engineers. We attended a company meeting where the emphasis was on the costs to the company of defective parts. The key message was that small numbers of defects could lead to large costs that would harm the VAG bonus to production employees. The emphasis during the meeting was for employees to attempt to catch mistakes rather than to think of innovations.

CHANGING HUMAN RESOURCE PRACTICES

Using our understanding of the product market and the history of the company, we analyze in this section the impact of the change in pay policies on both the firm and its workers. The auto parts industry is highly competitive, so a key perceived element of survival is the ability to increase employee productivity.

We then examine the impact of changes in human resource practices on the overall satisfaction of employees in these production establishments. As noted earlier, the policies were different in SP's different plants. The urban Massachusetts plant changed from piecerate pay to value-added gain-sharing; the suburban plant changed from time rates to value-added gain-sharing. (Many of the workers at the suburban plant had also worked at the urban plant.) In addition, in both plants the work changed from individual and manual to group and automated, and formal training programs were instituted, especially in the suburban facility. SP's Florida facility changed from a time-rate method of pay to a value-added gain-sharing approach; the nature of the work did not change much, but some formal training was implemented. In the rural Ohio plant the method of pay was unchanged, and there was little change in the nature of work or training. In January 2000, however, the plant experienced its first involuntary layoff in its thirty years of operation.

PRODUCTIVITY EFFECTS OF
CHANGING METHODS OF PAY

The gain-sharing plan implemented by the company involved disproportionate weights for productivity, using a value-added approach, measures of customer satisfaction using returns or defective parts, and deductions for scrap. The initial estimates were established by a consulting firm that worked with the managers and engineers in the company to establish the VAG formula, which, as we have noted, was not widely understood. The gain-sharing payouts ranged from 0 to 15 percent during the period we examined, 1996 through 2001. For the Boston plant the average bonus averaged more than 10 percent from 1996 through 2001.

At the Florida facility the production employees were paid a time rate. On January 1, 2001, the plant shifted to a value-added gain-sharing method of pay. During the first few months of the program payouts were about 10 percent, but the recession that started in the early months of the gain-sharing program reduced the gain-sharing amounts to almost zero during the summer months of 2001. Payouts then rebounded during the fall, rising to almost 9 percent.

When we examined alternative specifications of the productivity equations for the various plants, we found them to be highly sensitive to the inclusion or exclusion of various plausible variables. Consequently, we have little confidence in these results and would suggest that the results on productivity are murky. We find little reason to think that the change in method of pay had much of an impact on plant-level productivity.

WHAT AFFECTS EMPLOYEE SATISFACTION?

The basic survey instrument we used to examine employee satisfaction was the Minnesota Multiphasic Satisfaction (MMS) Questionnaire, which has been used by industrial psychologists for almost fifty years to gauge employee satisfaction. We added questions to examine the impact of the pay systems in each plant. The baseline questions were scored on a Likert-type five-point scale. We also asked questions of the employees about their tenure with the company, types of jobs, and pay policies.

In our attempt to examine the determinants of satisfaction, we distinguish between a number of factors that go beyond the effect of the policies of the company. From the research literature in psychology, we know that there are individual differences that have an impact on job satisfaction (Arvey et al. 1989). Moreover, the specific question asked of respondents is also important. The central questions about job satisfaction measure different qualities, such as attachment to the job and quality of supervision. Consequently, these factors should be accounted for in any attempt to examine what is under the control of the firm versus other exogenous factors. Even though the firm adopted overarching policies at the plant level, group or team effects were also likely to influence satisfaction with work (Judge et al. 2001). Finally, the policies in force at the plant are also likely to have an impact on employee satisfaction.

In table 12.3, we show how much of the variation in total satisfaction can be explained by the more than two thousand SP employees who responded to the satisfaction survey. Not surprisingly, the greatest part of satisfaction can be explained by individual factors, or the person effect. This explains about 40 percent of overall job satisfaction. All the other factors are statistically significant but small in comparison to the individual differences. The smallest factor is the plant of employment, which can explain only about 1 percent of the total variation in overall satisfaction. Although plant-level policies may be statistically important, they would be considered small by any standard metric.

THE JOB SATISFACTION OF IMMIGRANTS

At the inner-city and suburban plants in Massachusetts we were able to gather more detailed information on the job satisfaction of employees. We were informed that a high percentage of the employees were immigrants from Vietnam and Cape Verde and could not speak or write in English. Consequently, we translated our questionnaire into Vietnamese and Portuguese; respondents chose the language in which they wanted to take the survey. Thus, we were able to differentiate individuals in the plant by their degree of fluency in English. In addition, we compared the degree of satisfaction with work for English-reading and -writing individuals with

Table 12.3 Productivity Effects of Changes in Human Resource Practices at SP's Plants in Three States

State	Method of Pay	Change in Productivity After Change in Human Resource Practice (Sales Per Employee)
Massachusetts	Piece-rate to VAG	−0.72% per employees
Florida	Time-rate to VAG	+0.2% per employee
Ohio	No change	—

Source: Authors' compilation.

that of persons whose main language was Vietnamese or Portuguese. Further, we compared their level of satisfaction with that of persons in the other plants whose main language was English.

The results of the mean answers to questions we posed in the questionnaire are presented in table 12.4, by language and plant. We also give a difference in means test results for persons in the four plants by language. The English-speakers in the Boston facilities were the least satisfied. In six of the eight categories, their responses are statistically significantly below the means of the other plants. In contrast, the mean values of the Vietnamese-speaking respondents are generally above the mean. The persons from Cape Verde, who took the questionnaire in Portuguese, are usually below the mean, but the results are not statistically significant.

By examining these results more closely, we find that Vietnamese-language speakers were less likely to perceive themselves as having many labor market opportunities relative to persons who were literate in English or Portuguese. For example, in agreeing or disagreeing with the statement, "It would be hard for me to find another job that provides the pay and benefits that this one does," the individuals who answered the question in Vietnamese indicated that they would have the most difficulty, with a mean value of 3.2. In contrast, persons who answered in English had a mean value of 2.7, and persons who answered in Portuguese had a mean value of 3.0. Among the three groups, persons who were fluent in English perceived their labor market opportunities as the best.

We also examined the level of self-reported "cooperation" or "getting along" among the three groups of individuals who took the survey in the different languages. The persons answering in Viet-

Table 12.4 Explaining Satisfaction By Assimilation Type for Massachusetts and Other Plants

	Number of Employees	Supervisors	Employment Security	Meaningful Jobs	Company Practice	Pay	Working Conditions	Coworkers	Overall Satisfaction
Ohio English	615	3.54 (1.35)	3.81 (1.12)	3.56 (1.25)	2.73 (1.15)	2.44 (1.25)	3.57 (1.21)	3.40 (1.28)	3.47 (1.19)
Florida English	463	3.41 (1.34)	3.99 (1.02)	3.65 (1.23)	2.95*** (1.18)	2.75*** (1.24)	3.37 (1.17)	3.43 (1.28)	3.60 (1.09)
Massachusetts English	160	3.36 (1.33)	3.62* (1.32)	3.16** (1.35)	2.89** (1.28)	2.47** (1.33)	3.04 (1.34)	3.21* (1.27)	3.13** (1.25)
Vietnamese	168	3.33 (1.27)	4.10 (0.95)	3.77 (1.17)	3.29 (1.16)	2.78 (1.34)	3.12 (1.21)	3.58 (1.20)	3.56 (1.05)
Cape Verde	164	3.65 (1.38)	3.42*** (1.43)	3.35 (1.32)	3.16 (1.28)	2.77 (1.43)	3.12 (1.32)	3.21* (1.40)	3.33 (1.40)

Source: Authors' compilation.
Note: Standard deviation in parentheses. Tests of means by groups are conducted.
* $p < 0.1$.
** $p < 0.05$.
*** $p < 0.001$.

namese reported a relatively high level of satisfaction in getting along with coworkers and in respect for coworkers. For example, the mean value for the 5-point scale was 3.6 and 3.7 for Vietnamese-speakers, 3.2 and 3.3 for English-speakers, and 3.2 and 3.6 for Portuguese-speakers. Similarly, Vietnamese- and Portuguese-speaking respondents had higher levels of pride in working for the company. The average level was 3.6 for English-speakers, 3.9 for Vietnamese-speakers, and 4.0 for Portuguese-speakers.

We also estimated a regression equation of the determinants of employee satisfaction with controls for type of job, shift worked, and time at the company. We found that English-speakers in the Boston facilities were significantly less satisfied than the other two groups even after the addition of these controls.[10]

DID THE CHANGE IN HUMAN RESOURCE PRACTICES AFFECT OVERALL SATISFACTION?

As part of the effort to examine the overall effects of the human resource practices on employee satisfaction, we examined the impact of change in the method of pay on employee satisfaction. Next, we examined the relative impacts of working harder and making more money on overall satisfaction.

In table 12.5, we show the impact of the change in human resource practices on the change in satisfaction. For the mean employee at SP, the impact was generally small. However, the satisfaction of employees who changed from time rates to VAG (mean values of 3.11 and 3.03) was higher than it was for employees who changed from piece rates to VAG (mean values of 3.04 and 2.88). This may be due to the cut in pay that persons who were under piece rates experienced after switching to the VAG formula.

In table 12.6, we show the coefficient estimates from a regression equation where the dependent variable is the change in satisfaction and the independent variable is the response to working harder under the new system and the increase in pay. In all cases the values for the independent variables are statistically significant. Not surprisingly, the values for increasing pay are about five times larger than for working harder. Working harder seems to be correlated with increased job satisfaction and perhaps is tied to the strong view about having pride in the company, but having more pay is of considerably greater importance.

Table 12.5 Impact of Change in Method of Pay on the Change in Satisfaction

	Means	Standard Deviation
Florida	3.00	1.06
Massachusetts suburban (LOC2)		
From piece-rate to VAG	3.04	1.29
From time-rate to VAG	3.11	1.21
Massachusetts urban (LOC1)		
From piece-rate to VAG	2.88	1.40
From time-rate to VAG	3.03	1.24

Source: Authors' compilation.
Notes: For Massachusetts it is variable, Q47a/b; for Florida, it is variable, Q37. All of these variables indicate the change of satisfaction after changing the plans. No such a question is asked for Ohio.

Although the changes to a VAG system of pay seem to have had small impacts on productivity and employee satisfaction, data from the firm suggest that profitability increased, especially when compared with overall industry productivity. SP's profitability increased in part because of the firm's ability to become a "full-service" supplier to auto firms, but also because the plants whose workers were paid by piece-rate methods were able to offer more diverse new products that had higher profit margins (Freeman and Kleiner 1998).

CONCLUSIONS

By most measures, SP has been a financially successful company. Although the second half of 2000 and 2001 were tough times and profits were relatively low, this was true for almost all firms in the auto industry. In other years the firm's return on equity was between 12 and 20 percent.

How does SP do this? It is not a particularly high-productivity operation; value added per shop worker at the Ohio plant is only $70,000, not far above the median for component producers, according to benchmarking data from the Industrial Technology Institute.

There seem to be several key elements to SP's success:

1. *The firm's organization:* SP combines a hands-on central office with a few small plants with some autonomy. This gives the firm the produc-

Table 12.6 Effect of Changes in Work Effort and Pay Levels on Changes in Satisfaction

	Change in Satisfaction		
Independent Variables	Massachusetts from Piece-Rate to VAG	Massachusetts from Time-Rate to VAG	Florida, from Time-Rate to VAG
Working harder	0.14	0.11	0.25
Making more money	0.55	0.55	0.40

Source: Authors' compilation.
Note: All variables are measured in Likert scale from 1 to 5.

tive aspects of a large firm (ability to invest in capabilities to develop sophisticated products and processes). However, SP does not lose the productive aspects of a small firm: for example, top managers who have a deep knowledge of the business and intuitive feel for the projects that make sense, and the ability to maintain some aspects of a paternalistic policy in plants. (Management knows workers by name.) The firm's plants are located in areas where engineers and management can find some amenities yet also have access to a workforce with few alternatives (immigrants in Massachusetts, rural workers in Ohio).

2. *Selective adoption of the principles of lean production:* SP has focused on inventory reduction and design for manufacturing. These efforts have allowed SP to use a relatively unskilled, low-paid workforce to produce at low cost. On the other hand, SP has not placed much emphasis (particularly recently) on encouraging broad-based participation from both line workers and engineers in generating ideas for continuous improvement. There are outlets for the ambitious other than union organizing or griping, such as team leader positions and participation in programs such as WOW or the Last Chance Club. But the "mistake-proofing" by engineers is sufficiently successful that a moderately motivated person can do the job successfully.

3. *Developing product and process expertise in a relatively unglamorous but growing niche:* In contrast to firms such as Johnson Controls and Magna, which have spent billions of dollars in developing or acquiring the capability to supply a large module (such as an automotive interior), SP is not overburdened with debt at present.

However, there are some tensions in the SP model, particularly with respect to the workforce. Management in each of the plants is concerned about both defect and cost levels. Efforts are either under way or being planned to exhort workers to avoid mistakes and train workers to take over some supervisory functions. These efforts are costly when turnover is high (as it is in Ohio). Recently it has seemed that the company is beginning to change its bargain with workers (consciously or not). This is particularly true in the acquired plants. In Ohio the work used to be moderately paced and allowed the worker to sit down, and jobs were secure. Now pay for knowledge is about to put pay at risk, and with the introduction of work cells workers now rotate jobs and work standing up—a drawback for the older workers who have formed a significant part of the plant's workforce.

To summarize, these plants are typical of a new breed of U.S. manufacturers in their product, process, and human resource strategies. They have succeeded in innovating, increasing quality, and maintaining productivity through the clever use of engineers without increasing pay for manufacturing workers. However, there are tensions in the model as firms integrate the workforces of acquired companies with different expectations and try to meet ever-rising cost and quality demands.

SP is unusual in several ways, especially in the clarity of its managers' thinking as they develop and carry out their strategy and in their attention to the fit between product, process, and human resource strategy. Many firms now have some form of incentive compensation for line workers, but few have emphasized it as much as SP has. Thus, we have a rare opportunity to watch an especially thoughtful and strategic firm explore the types of pay practices and supporting human resource policies that best complement its new marketing strategy as a full-service, global supplier.

The firm has been able to combine elements of both the "high" and "low" roads. In particular, it has been able to carry out a high-road product strategy of designing highly engineered products, introducing new products frequently, and delivering them on time and (usually) without defects. The firm has agreed to take on warranty responsibility for any field failures. This product strategy has not required SP to adopt all aspects of a high-road human resource strategy. Definitions of what this strategy entails vary (see Jones,

Kato, and Weinberg, this volume), but they usually include policies such as the use of self-managing work teams, efficiency wages, training, and worker participation in improvement activities. These are policies that SP has implemented either minimally or not at all. SP has done a masterful job, however, of implementing a contingent pay system and involving engineers in doing continuous improvement (in contrast to the belief expressed in the "high-performance" literature that employees themselves are the experts and the source of the best, or at least the cheapest, improvements).

Why does SP stay in a relatively high-wage nation and metropolitan area? This issue has been thoroughly analyzed by the firm. In the auto supplier industry, labor costs are a small percentage of total costs (about 7 percent), and defects are very costly financially and in reputation capital. SP has not had a positive experience with its Mexican plant, where there have been high defect rates and a loss of complementarity with engineering. The quality of its engineering workforce is difficult to replicate in Mexico, and SP believes that engineering is what gives it a competitive advantage. The opportunity of high-skilled engineers to observe the production process and adapt the manufacturing process all in one location has helped keep this complementary matching of high- and low-skilled labor effective.

What are the benefits of working at SP for its employees? According to one worker, one way to characterize them is that "workers at [SP] do fairly well compared to their alternatives." An optimist would emphasize the "do fairly well" part and point out that SP's wages are high by world standards, that SP's worker satisfaction levels are not much below national averages, and that many SP workers stay with the firm for a long time. There are several reasons why SP employees stay. First, the firm pays good benefits, including health care, pension, and paid vacation. The extra pay provided by the VAG is important. In the Massachusetts suburban plant applications for openings fell dramatically after the VAG payout fell from almost 7 percent to 0 percent. Second, the firm has found workforces that perceive themselves as having few labor market options. The firm hired many immigrants in Massachusetts, retirees and other rural workers in Ohio, and older workers and retirees in Florida. Third, in both Massachusetts plants, the sense of community provided by working with others of the same ethnic group—and sometimes the same family—in a plant that is perceived as well managed provides many first-generation Americans with a sense of economic and cultural security. In Ohio the no-layoff policy followed by the former owner created a secure atmosphere in which employees found stable employment and made friends, offsetting the low wages, according to a human resources manager there.

A pessimist would also agree that workers at SP "do fairly well compared to their alternatives," but would focus on how bad the alternatives are. In this view, the worker satisfaction measures capture mostly the feeling of workers that they cannot do much better.

Even with the VAG, SP pays below the "living wage" standard adopted by many American cities.[11] The VAG bonus pool is calculated very carefully by management, and many safeguards are put in to avoid too large a payout. However, the entire annual expenditure for the VAG incentive for the two hundred shop-floor workers in the urban plant is about $200,000—the salary of one top manager. From this point of view, the impact of the changes in product and human resource strategies is to give managers and stockholders more new products without paying a higher wage (and in the case of the urban plant, while actually paying a lower wage). Workers report that they work harder, and now that they work for a public company rather than a paternalistic owner, they are subject to layoffs. However, at least the firm survives, offering a fairly high probability of continued employment.

What general lessons can we learn from this case? First, over time firms can to some extent pick their product markets. This finding reduces the force of claims that some jobs are inherently low-productivity and hence must remain low-wage. Since 1987 SP has transformed itself from a low-tech producer of simple parts made to others' blueprints into a sophisticated producer of sub-assemblies designed (and in some cases patented) by the firm itself. Over this period SP increased its value-added per worker substantially and chose not to pass many of these gains on to workers. This finding also has implications for academics, in that it suggests that strict controls for product markets may take out some variation that is in fact due to managerial choice rather than unchangeable technical requirements.

Second, the transformation of human resource practices is fraught with tension. In particular, managers struggle with providing incentives to workers to remain at the company, while not paying more than a market wage. In the case of SP, a slightly higher wage might have actually increased profits in the long run by reducing turnover and dissatisfaction. In contrast, other firms studied in this volume seem to have been constrained by highly competitive product markets (see, for example, Willis, Connelly, and DeGraff, this volume).

A final insight is into the types of jobs that are likely to stay in the United States. The case of SP shows that even repetitive production work may stay here if it is complementary with product engineering and/or finding defects is difficult. Because direct labor costs are such a small part of total costs (about 7 percent), savings from finding a lower-wage labor force abroad are far outweighed by the advantages to SP of having a proven, flexible workforce that interacts easily with its product engineers.

We thank Eileen Applebaum for her helpful comments. We are grateful to the employees of the firm we call SP for their generosity with time and data, and to the Russell Sage Foundation and the National Bureau of Economic Research for financial support.

NOTES

1. We call the firm Small Parts under a confidentiality agreement with the company, which gave us proprietary information on the condition that we not use its name in our publications.
2. We find little evidence of causality running the other way, that is, from human resource practices to productivity or product markets.
3. There remain key differences. Japanese firms trust their customers more (Sako and Helper 1998) and are less likely to produce or design modules (Sako and Warburton 1999).
4. These visits were organized by Helper for economists affiliated with the National Bureau of Economic Research for the purpose of encouraging them to do field research.
5. As discussed later in the chapter, many of the workers were not native speakers of English. We were able to communicate with them in English and (somewhat) in Portuguese, but neither author speaks Vietnamese.
6. This information comes from SP's 2000 annual report, its Securities and Exchange Commission (SEC) 10-K filing (November 2001), and our interviews with managers.
7. This quote is from a very useful document, "Progression of Pay for Performance," which Ms. A wrote for us in February 2000.

8. It seemed that "too high" meant wages more than 15 percent above the average for unskilled manufacturing workers in the area. For example, Mr. P said in 1995 that if gain-sharing exceeded 15 percent, then it was time to cut prices to customers (rather than continue to increase compensation to workers). It is not clear how the 15 percent figure was arrived at.

9. The 15 percent cap on the payout was also lifted at this time. (It was never a binding constraint.)

10. About 10 percent of those who took the survey in English did so not because they were fluent in English but because we had not translated the survey into their language. (The largest such group was from Poland; they worked through the questionnaire diligently, with dictionaries and help from coworkers.) Thus, the differential labor market opportunities for fluent English-speakers are probably greater than our estimates.

11. It seems that most of SP's production employees would have trouble supporting a family of three (one parent, two young children) on their wages and benefits from the company. According to Jared Bernstein and his colleagues (2000, ch. 7), a wage of $13.00 an hour would be needed to support such a family in Baltimore, if health care were also provided (as SP does). This wage would provide for a "modest" two-bedroom apartment and a car but does not provide any funds for entertainment, restaurant meals, or savings. Housing costs in rural Ohio and Florida are less than the $628.00 per month budgeted in Baltimore; $400.00 would be a reasonable estimate for Ohio, cutting the necessary wage to perhaps $11.60. Still, this is significantly more than the $9.00 an hour made by long-term employees in Ohio. Workers in the urban Massachusetts plant would come close to earning the "living wage" defined by Bernstein. In this area a car would not be necessary, but high rents would offset this saving. A long-term employee would make more than $12.00 an hour in years in which the VAG payout was 10 percent.

REFERENCES

Abernathy, Frederick, John T. Dunlop, and Janice H. Hammond. 1999. *A Stitch in Time*. Oxford: Oxford University Press.

Appelbaum, Eileen, and Rosemary Batt. 1994. *The New American Workplace*. Ithaca, N.Y.: Cornell University Press.

Arvey, Richard, Thomas Bouchard, Nancy Degal, and Lauren Abraham. 1989. "Job Satisfaction: Environmental and Genetic Components." *Journal of Applied Psychology* 74(2): 187–92.

Bernstein, Jared, Chauna Brocht, and Maggie Spade-Aguilar. 2000. *How Much Is Enough?: Basic Family Budgets for Working Families*. Washington, D.C.: Economic Policy Institute.

Freeman, Richard B., and Morris M. Kleiner. 1998. "The Last American Shoe Manufacturers: Changing the Method of Pay to Survive Foreign Competition." Working paper 6750. Cambridge, Mass.: National Bureau of Economic Research (October).

Gillett, Frank E. 1992. "The Integrating Supplier: A Study of an Auto Industry Supplier's Relations Across Several Customers." Master's thesis, Massachusetts Institute of Technology.

Helper, Susan. 1991. "Strategy and Irreversibility in Supplier Relations: The Case of the U.S. Automobile Industry." *Business History Review* 65(4): 781–824.

Helper, Susan, and David I. Levine. 1992. "Long-term Supplier Relations and Product Market Structure." *Journal of Law, Economics, and Organization* 8(3): 561–81.

Jacobs, Eva. 2000. *The Handbook of U.S. Labor Statistics*. Lanham, Md.: Bernam Press.

Judge, Tom, C. Thorson, J. Bono, and G. K. Patton. 2001. "The Job Satisfaction–Job Performance Relationship: A Qualitative and Quantitative Review." *Psychological Bulletin* 127: 376–407.

Luria, Daniel D. 2001. "Price Squeeze in Auto Parts." Paper presented at the Michigan Manufacturing Technology Center, Plymouth, Mich. (November 15).

Sako, Mari, and Susan Helper. 1998. "Determinants of Trust in Supplier Relations: Evidence from the Automotive Industry in Japan and the United States." *Journal of Economic Behavior and Organization* 34(3): 387–417.

Sako, Mari, and Fiona Murray. 1999. "Modular Strategies in Cars and Computers." *Financial Times* (June).

Sako, Mari, and Max Warburton. 1999. "MIT International Motor Vehicle Program Modularization Project: Preliminary Report of European Research Team." Paper presented to IMVP Annual Forum, Boston (October).

Wasti, S. Nazli, and Jeffrey K. Liker. 1999. "Collaboration with Suppliers in Product Development: A U.S. and Japan Comparative Study." *IEEE Transactions in Engineering Management* 46: 444–61.

Zeitlin, Jonathan, and Joshua Whitford. Forthcoming. "Governing Decentralized Production: Institutions, Public Policy, and the Prospects for Inter-Firm Collaboration in U.S. Manufacturing." *Industry and Innovation* 10.

CHAPTER 13

Managerial Discretion, Business Strategy, and the Quality of Jobs: Evidence from Medium-Sized Manufacturing Establishments in Central New York

Derek C. Jones, Takao Kato, and Adam Weinberg

This chapter draws on ten case studies of manufacturing establishments in central New York to examine two key questions. First, are managers in medium-sized establishments that are located in an economically depressed geographic region and that employ workers with limited formal education able to exercise discretion with respect to the business strategy they adopt? And second, do the strategies that managers implement matter greatly for worker outcomes?

Some economic theorists argue that firms that operate in competitive labor and product markets, especially those subject to global competition, have very little discretion in setting wage, employment, and human resource management practices. Consequently, these practices are predicted to be broadly similar across firms in similar situations. However, we find clear and compelling evidence that medium-sized establishments in central New York offer and sustain practices that differ in important respects.

We reach three main conclusions. First, the establishments in our study vary widely in their workplace and labor relations practices. Second, plants are consistent in the practices they adopt. Thus, plants that make use of teams and incentive pay schemes are more likely to provide greater amounts of training as well. Indeed, differences among the establishments in our study in wage and employment practices, use of teams and incentive pay, and training and job content are sufficiently large that we discern three strategies, which we label high-road, low-road and middle-road. Finally, these varying management strategies matter for workers because they lead to differences in important worker outcomes such as empowerment, satisfaction, commitment, trust, communication, and work effort.

In the next section, we provide an overview of the case-study establishments and their environment. We then draw on our case-study data to explore how and why firms pursue different management strategies. That discussion is followed by an examination of the impacts of these strategies on workers. We focus in particular on high-performance work practices (HPWPs): incentive pay (profit-sharing, employee stock ownership), teams, quality circles, total quality management (TQM), and information-sharing. We conclude that HPWPs may provide important benefits to both employees and firms. In the final section, we summarize our findings and offer some concluding comments.

THE CASE-STUDY ESTABLISHMENTS

The establishments in this study operate in a depressed region of the country that has shared few of the national economic gains of the last ten years. They are located in central New York in Oneida, Onondaga, Herkimer, and Madison Counties. While the population of the average U.S. county grew by 35 percent during the period 1969 to 1999, these counties have either flat or falling populations, and in Oneida County population fell by more than 15 percent. These counties are more homogeneous (and white) than is the norm in the United States despite a decade or so of modest rates of immigration from countries including Bosnia, Russia, and Vietnam. Two of the four counties are more than 96 percent white, compared to a U.S. average of about 75 percent. While the proportion of high school graduates tends to slightly exceed the national average, the percentage of college graduates typically is below the national average.

With the exception of Madison County, employment growth over the last 3 decades has lagged behind the rest of the country. In the 4-county area in 1998 there were only 538 establishments that provided at least 100 jobs, and employment continues to depend heavily on manufacturing.[1] However, the postwar period has witnessed continuing capital flight and only limited success in maintaining highly paid manufacturing jobs in the region. Partly as a

Figure 13.1 Changes in Average Wage and Salary in
Oneida, Madison, Onondaga, and Herkimer
Counties, 1969 to 1998

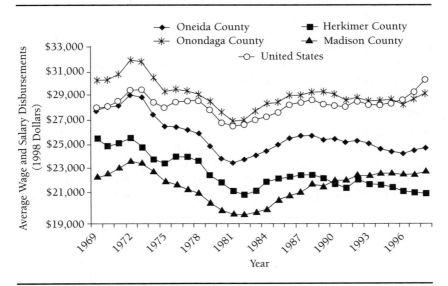

Source: U.S. Bureau of Economic Analysis.

consequence, average wage and salary disbursements in the counties (in 1998 dollars) were about the same or lower in 1998 than in
1969; in contrast, in U.S. counties in general these disbursements
rose over this period (see figure 13.1). The region is geographically
large and diverse. The challenges facing employers and employees
within the more isolated rural parts of the region are arguably different from those confronting their counterparts both in smaller
towns such as Utica and in the larger metropolitan area of Syracuse.

A total of 118 medium-sized manufacturing establishments operate in the 4-county region. A key concern in selecting establishments for this study was to find ones that primarily employ workers with limited education. The typical production worker in the
case-study establishments is a high school graduate.[2] A few employees have earned an associate's degree.[3] To highlight the effect of
differences in local labor markets, establishments in the study vary
in terms of location in a rural, urban, or metropolitan labor market.
The establishments also differ in terms of type of ownership, unionization, and the use of HPWPs. We are not always able to match

establishments in terms of the product lines they produce. However, all of the case-study establishments engage in light manufacturing operations, and employers are competing for workers with
broadly similar skills.[4]

Several types of data were gathered for this study. We conducted
lengthy interviews with diverse personnel, including managers and
union representatives where relevant. Questionnaires were completed using responses from human resources (HR) personnel. For
three of the plants, worker-shadowing exercises were done over periods of one to three months. Finally, for three establishments we
collected survey data from individual employees through more than
five hundred surveys returned to us. (Average response rate was
more than 80 percent.)[5] The worker survey data are used to investigate the impact of HPWPs on a broad range of worker outcomes.
We also examine less-studied practices and outcomes, such as peer
monitoring and absolute and relative worker effort.

Some of the key features of the ten establishments in this study
are summarized in table 13.1. Both publicly traded and private
firms are represented, as well as firms with and without local headquarters. For most firms, control is based in the United States and,
indeed, in central New York. Most establishments are part of larger
multiplant organizations. While some establishments have just over
one hundred employees, others are somewhat larger. Plants differ
widely in terms of age: some are quite new, and another has been in
existence at this site for two hundred years (making it one of the
oldest continuously operating plants in the United States).

There are also stark differences in the financial situations of the
plants and in managers' perceptions of the nature of the product
markets and competitive pressures they face. Some establishments
indicate that they have established a solid market niche, and sales
data for several plants show that they have recorded sustained
growth over the past few years. In the main, such plants tend to
face mainly domestic competition. More typically, managers perceive that they face rapidly changing markets, that sales tend to be
cyclical, and that profit margins are quite thin. These plants operate
in markets in which competitive pressures are growing, in some
cases from overseas competitors. The metropolitan plants face a
somewhat different situation. Two of them have aggressively entered emerging product markets, such as wireless and broadband.
Employment at these firms grew at an extraordinarily rapid clip

Table 13.1 Characteristics of Ten Central New York Manufacturing Establishments

Establishment	Strategy	Location	Age	Ownership	Part of Larger Organization	Employment	Competitors	Market
Materials	High-road	Rural	1980	Private, local headquarters	No	120	Few	Stable growth
Large Metal	High-road	Urban	1801	Private, local headquarters	Yes	505	Few	Cyclical
Machine Parts	High-road	Metropolitan	1949	Private, local headquarters	Yes	130	Many (domestic)	Highly cyclical
Electrical Parts	High-road	Metropolitan	1945	Public, headquarters overseas	Yes	450	Few	Very uneven; recent sharp contraction after rapid growth
IT Parts	High-road	Metropolitan	1970	Public, local headquarters	Yes	450	Few	Steady growth and rapid contraction
Small Fabrication	Low-road	Rural	1816	Private, headquarters elsewhere	Yes	490–505	Few	Cyclical
Small Machines	Low-road	Rural	1986	Private, headquarters elsewhere	Yes	120	Many	Stable growth
Medium Fabrication	Low-road	Urban	1989	Private, local headquarters	Yes	117	Few	Steady growth
Small Parts	Middle-road	Rural	1981	Private, headquarters overseas	Yes	275	Many and growing	Cyclical
Medium Machines	Middle-road	Urban	1988	Private, local headquarters	Yes	115	Few	Steady growth

Source: Authors' own interviews and survey.

between 1994 and 1999, and both firms have strong profit positions. However, some executives at these companies expressed uncertainty about whether these new markets would be sustainable over the long haul—a view that unfortunately proved to be far-sighted.

MANAGEMENT STRATEGIES

The latter half of the 1990s was a period in which fortunes reversed dramatically for many manufacturing establishments in central New York. As one human resources manager put it in early 2000: "If you said to me, what is the number-one issue your organization is facing, it is retention."

All the human resources managers we interviewed expressed similar sentiments, though labor market pressures were perhaps especially strong for the metropolitan plants. This heightened need to recruit and retain employees inevitably affected firm personnel policies, especially those concerning compensation and employment and workplace and labor relations practices.

Notwithstanding the fact that managers of medium-sized manufacturing in central New York face broadly similar market pressures, we find clear and compelling evidence that managers do have discretion in their employment practices and wage polices. Indeed, differences among our establishments are sufficiently great that we discern three sets of strategies, which we label high-road, low-road, and middle-road. In the rest of this section we present evidence on the existence of managerial discretion for our cases in three broad policy areas: wage and employment practices (and associated features of internal labor markets); the use of HPWPs; and skill, training, and job content.

THE HIGH-ROAD STRATEGY

There are broad differences among our cases concerning wage and employment practices. In general, we find indications that, in plants that adopt a high-road strategy, starting wages compare very favorably with those of other firms in the local labor market, and that more flexible wage and employment policies are evident, including job rotation and peer participation in performance evaluation. In addition, high-road establishments tend to have unusually low turnover rates compared to other plants in the area.

Important components of a high-road strategy include basic wage and employment policies that place the establishment in the top tier of plants in the relevant labor market. Thus, while starting wages for unskilled, inexperienced workers range from about $6.00 to $9.00 an hour in central New York, establishments pursuing a high-road strategy tend to pay above-average wages (table 13.2). Unsurprisingly, initial wage rates tend to be higher in metropolitan locations. For example, Machine Parts pays $9.00 an hour (and $10.00 to $12.00 an hour to those with 720 hours of local vocational high school, the Board of Cooperative Educational Services [BOCES]). At IT Parts a new entrant with no work experience or obvious skills ordinarily would start at $7.50 an hour. She would work in a semiskilled job such as utility operator or on the line assembling products in one of the feeder shops. Most likely these positions would be in the business unit that produces the least complicated final products. Starting pay at Materials and Large Metal is also well above average for comparable cases, although that is less surprising for Large Metal, since it is a unionized firm.[6]

Another potential pillar of a high-road strategy is a no-layoff policy. However, only one firm (Materials) advertises a no-layoff policy to its labor force. In all other cases, the informal reassurances concerning employment security that had been given when labor markets were tight tended to be downplayed or even forgotten following the rapid and largely unexpected onset of the current recession. Indeed, five firms were forced to introduce layoffs during 2001. However, no one appears to have been laid off at Materials.

The available evidence indicates that, in general, turnover rates are quite low in establishments that have adopted a high-road strategy. However, turnover is typically somewhat higher on average in metropolitan areas (where, until recently, alternative employment options were more readily available than in rural locations).

Information is available for all of the case-study establishments on the aspects of wage and employment policies described in table 13.2; additional evidence is available for some of the cases in related areas. For example, at IT Parts entry-level, inexperienced workers receive their first formal evaluation after a year. However, supervisors are authorized to increase wages (usually by twenty-five cents an hour) ahead of this schedule for workers judged to be

Table 13.2 Labor Force, Compensation, and Employment Practices

Establishment	Residence Labor Force	Turnover	Average Age	Minority	Female	Initial Hourly Wage	Pay Grades	Two-Tier Wages	Labor Union
Materials	Local	Low	34	5%	57%	$8.25	Few	No	No
Large Metal	Mainly in that town	Modest	48	<1	<1	$7.23 to $7.63	Many	Yes	Yes
Machine Parts	Some more than thirty miles away	6%	N/A	2	<1	$9.00 ($10.00 to $12.00 with 720 hours of BOCES)	Few	No	No
Electrical Parts	Some more than thirty miles away	13%	35	2	<1	$7.00	6	No	No
IT Parts	Some more than thirty miles away	10%	35	15	<1	$7.50	8	No	No
Small Fabrication	Local	Low	N/A	2	<1	$8.22 to $8.99	6	Yes	Yes
Small Machines	Local	Modest	28	1	18	$7.00	Few	Yes	No
Medium Fabrication	Mainly in that town	5%	38	<1	<1	$7.00	Few	No	Yes
Small Parts	Local	Stable core; rest high	38	2	56	$6.00	11	No	No
Medium Machines	Mainly in that town	10%	40	<1	20	$7.00	Few	No	No

Source: Authors' own interviews and survey.

superior performers. For jobs in that division, promotion to positions with higher grades is based mainly on the recommendations of supervisors in that business unit. But employees can bid on jobs elsewhere in the establishment. Arrangements at Electrical Parts are subtly different from those in place at IT Parts. The Electrical Parts system is essentially one of seniority wages within entry-level-grade jobs (and wages top out at $14.00 an hour in that grade, twice the starting wage). Also, the initial formal evaluation takes place earlier (after three months). Normally, workers are eligible to bid for a higher-grade job after one year. As at IT Parts, job ladders are based on merit rather than seniority. Traditional assessment arrangements prevail in most other firms—usually annual assessments conducted only by the immediate supervisor. For example, Machine Parts recently introduced a formal job evaluation program, though it is not used for pay determination. However, the system for performance evaluation differs quite a bit at Materials, which uses peer evaluations and provides opportunities for entry-level workers to receive rapid and sizable increases in pay as well as job reassignments.

There are also marked differences among firms in how they handle job rotation. Again, Materials is unusual in having a formal policy of job rotation, though Machine Parts also rotates production workers rather extensively to make them multiskilled. The human resources manager of Machine Parts stressed the benefit of having multiskilled workers, especially in reducing employee absenteeism. But not having such a policy in place, as at IT Parts, is more the norm. However, supervisors in different business units who see that encouraging this kind of cross-training is in the firm's interests have been encouraged to seek employees with matching interests.

A second important area of managerial discretion concerns the extent to which establishments adopt HPWPs. We find strong and clear support for our assertion that managers adopt multiple strategies concerning the adoption of HPWPs (see table 13.3). In establishments that pursue a high-road strategy, the incidence of HPWPs is typically well above average compared to other plants in comparable labor markets.

As is evident from table 13.3, five cases are classified as high-road, and each has adopted several HPWPs. The high-road category includes all of the establishments located in the metropolitan area. All three metropolitan cases have at least one mechanism, such as teams, by which employees can become involved in enterprise ac-

Table 13.3 High-Performance Work Practices

Establishment	Profit-Sharing	Employee Stock Ownership	Other Incentive Pay	Teams	Quality Control	TQM	Information-Sharing
Materials	Yes	No	Hybrid of profit-sharing and individual incentive pay	Yes	Combined with teams	No	All-employee monthly meeting
Large Metal	Yes	Yes	Individual incentive pay	Yes	Combined with teams	Yes	All-employee quarterly meeting
Machine Parts	Yes	Yes	None	Yes	No	Yes	All-employee quarterly meeting
Electrical Parts	No	Yes	None	Yes	Yes	Yes	All-production employee monthly meeting
IT Parts	Yes	No	None	Yes	No	Yes	All-employee monthly meeting
Small Fabrication	No	No	None	No	No	No	All-employee meetings twice a year
Small Machines	No	No	None	No	No	No	No
Medium Fabrication	No	No	None	No	No	No	All-employee monthly meeting
Small Parts	No	No	None	Yes	Combined with teams	No	All-employee monthly meeting
Medium Machines	No	No	Individual incentive pay	No	Yes	Yes	All-employee monthly meeting

Source: Authors' own interviews and survey.

tivities, as well as some provision for financial involvement. For example, Machine Parts has a comprehensive list of HPWPs. An employee stock ownership plan (ESOP) has been in place since the firm started in 1949. After working for thirty days, all employees become eligible for the ESOP. An amount equal to each employee's contribution to his or her 401K plan (up to 4 percent of pay) is contributed to the employee's ESOP account. Nearly all employees participate in the ESOP, and many take advantage of the full 4 percent contribution. Thus, employees with long tenure tend to have a substantial number of shares in the ESOP. The share price, which has been fluctuating in recent years, is evaluated annually by outside evaluators, who base their evaluation mostly on the share price of a comparable publicly traded firm. When an employee leaves the firm, the ESOP will buy back all shares at the most recently evaluated price. The human resources manager at Machine Parts stressed that the ESOP has been instrumental in keeping employee turnover relatively low in the past.

In 1994 the board of directors of Machine Parts decided to introduce a discretionary profit-sharing plan on top of the long-standing ESOP. The board sets a profitability target every year, and based on whether the target is realized and, if so, how much actual profitability exceeds the target, the board decides whether to give a profit-sharing bonus to each hourly employee. The bonus amount is the same for all hourly employees. In 1994 and 1995 each hourly employee received $100 as a profit-sharing bonus, whereas in 1999, because of weak firm performance, no bonus was given.

In addition, Machine Parts stresses the importance of the team approach, and most work is carried out in teams. However, teams are clearly led by line supervisors who often dictate, and thus they are not yet full-fledged self-directed teams. In addition, Machine Parts introduced TQM, largely at the request of its main customer. For information-sharing, Machine Parts has quarterly all-employee meetings for about half an hour over lunch. Since nearly all employees are shareholders through the ESOP, confidential information is shared during these meetings. In fact, recently a disgruntled Machine Parts employee leaked such information to a third party, and the firm had to engage in some damage control. During these meetings the company provides all employees with a casual lunch.

Among metropolitan establishments, perhaps the most developed set of HPWP policies is in place at Electrical Parts. The establishment provides incentives for employees at all levels to purchase company stock at subsidized rates. This kind of financial participation is part of a companywide scheme that was introduced primarily to link rewards to company performance. The scheme is complemented by an extensive set of programs that nurture and promote employee involvement. The establishment is organized into a series of mini-companies, each with separate financial accounts and governance structures. An important part of these arrangements (which exist at this plant but not throughout the company) is provision for each mini-company to have a network of teams that report to a salaried production manager. Although this manager determines basic decisions, such as production targets, teams have considerable discretion in other areas, such as scheduling tasks. During our visits to this case we became aware of quite a few examples of successful team initiatives. Many of these decisions, including simple tool changes and redesign of production layouts, helped to make the production process easier and lessen production error rates. The principal human resources professional glowingly described one example of a team success: "In a matter of three days a team redesigned their line."

Team members, and especially team leaders, receive extensive training. The teams hold frequent and regular discussions (at least weekly), and only modest rewards are provided (such as shopping vouchers or complimentary tickets to sporting events). Complementing these arrangements for teams are several mechanisms, including monthly meetings, at which information is shared with employees.

Comparable financial participation programs at IT Parts are much better developed. For about three years the establishment has had a profit-sharing scheme that provides production workers with an average payout of 3.5 percent of wages. Interestingly, the payout is distributed in cash at the end of a summer day during which all employees have participated in community service activities. During the period when we visited this plant an exciting innovation in the area of financial participation was about to be introduced—a plan to provide stock options to all employees. Although the details were still being worked out, the CEO was very excited about the potential for this plan and declared: "This is the last missing link in the overall compensation scheme."

Arrangements for employee involvement, however, are not nearly as advanced at IT Parts as they are, for example, at Electrical Parts. IT Parts has only elements of self-directed work teams. But it does have an interesting scheme whereby the CEO and the human resources director meet with small groups of workers (usually about twelve) over coffee for an hour or so each week. In less than a year all employees can expect to meet the CEO this way. These meetings are believed to be quite productive. For example, a proposal to introduce a broad-based employee stock option plan was first voiced at such a meeting by a production worker. IT Parts has other related practices in place, including monthly meetings at which real information appears to be shared. But for the most part, arrangements for employee involvement are much more informal and much less cohesive than at other high-road firms.

Two high-road establishments are not in the metropolitan area. Some of the HPWPs used at Large Metal do not work very well. Many workers do not perceive that teams are in fact self-directed, and neither the employee ownership nor the bonus schemes are highly evaluated. Also, because team meetings take place during regular hours, participants receive only their base wage for the time they spend at the meeting and have no opportunity to earn individual incentive bonuses (piece rates) during this period. Hence, in practice Large Metal might be more accurately assigned to the middle-road category.

Perhaps the best example of a high-road establishment is Materials, which has had self-directed teams for more than ten years. Team leadership rotates among team members on a monthly basis. Each team meets weekly, and meetings last for one hour during regular hours. Forty hours of training about teams annually is budgeted for each worker. Teams tackle a wide range of problems, including scheduling and task assignments, workplace reorganization, and tool innovation. This establishment also has had a profit-sharing scheme and a bonus plan in place for more than ten years. The profit-sharing plan is based on firm profitability. During the last decade this has averaged about 6 to 8 percent of average wages and is added to the employees' 401K plan. A bonus pool is first determined by firm profitability, and the employee's performance evaluation is then used to determine each employee's share of the bonus (which is paid in cash). The performance evaluation consists of: peer review by other team members (50 percent), evaluation by customers (25 percent), and evaluation by the supervisor (25 percent). A final HPWP used at Materials is information-sharing. This takes place primarily through an all-employee meeting each month. The human resources director reported that she believes that confidential information (for example, new products and new strategies) is sometimes shared with employees during these meetings. Although, as table 13.3 indicates, monthly meetings are a fairly common practice among our cases, we were unable to find another instance in which the provision of information is as frank and as commercially valuable as at Materials.

The third and final set of policies we examine for evidence of managerial discretion concerns skill requirements. Managers in plants gravitating to a high road tend to be more concerned than are managers of other establishments with enhancing employees' skills. For example, one of the least complex products was made by Materials. However, some positions in that plant involved more job content and required substantially higher standards for skills and more comprehensive training than was mandated at other establishments. Since skill standards and acquisition at Materials contrast sharply with these practices at other establishments that make more complex products (and whose concerns with employee skills are much more limited), there appears to be nothing inherent in products that explains these differences.

Worker-shadowing exercises, interviews, and worker surveys at Materials paint a rich picture of the ways in which these themes play out at this establishment. Most Materials employees, both managerial and nonmanagerial, are aware that work is simple. A human resources manager stated: "Operations consist of basically filling, which is actually putting the product pieces in pairs; production, which make the products; and the label department." She added: "There is just nothing really complicated about what we do. But we want it done well, and we want it done efficiently. That makes it more challenging."

However, Materials and other high-road firms, including Electrical Parts, view this as a problem to be overcome. At Materials, cross-training and teams are being used to increase the job content and skill level of jobs, and hence the level of training. Human resources personnel and managers talked about the need for employees to feel that the company is making a commitment to them and that they can develop by staying at the establishment. A human resources manager stated: "The company philosophy, the unwritten and unspoken, is that when we make a commitment to people, we want it to be a genuine commitment." She explained: "We want people to feel that they can continually grow as people and be rewarded for it."

High-road establishments are increasing the skills needed in simple production processes by giving workers more control over how the tasks are done, thereby increasing the soft skills content. A Materials manager stated: "People do, and are in charge of, their work." Another Materials manager said: "We don't want supervisors everywhere. We want people to be in charge. We want people to take the responsibility of being leaders, and we teach leadership skills here."

High-road establishments have developed elaborate training programs to help workers master the new soft skills content of their jobs. A manager at Materials put it this way: "We do leadership training that talks about team skills and all those things." She went on to explain that Materials has been aggressively working on a formalized, sequenced training program. Each month every worker receives some sort of formal training. It might start with hands-on skills and then move to more leadership training for longer-term employees. Even people who have been in the establishment for twenty years are getting new skills. She stated:

> So again, [training is] very important, and what we are trying to do this year which is a little different is . . . to do it at three levels. First is the corporate level: What are those skills that we need everybody to know organization-wise, whether it's leadership or whatever? And the next level would be: What do people within a given department need to know? . . . And the next level is the individual . . . what [do] you want to do, what are your career goals?

Materials pays for all of the training, with some classes offered by a local community college in the factory. When asked, one worker said: "That is how things are done around here." When asked about control, another worker stated: "The team constantly redesigns and reengineers parts of the production process. . . . Workers who use the machines every day can make any innovations in how the machines are used."

This awareness is clear in the way workers described their jobs and their relationship to the establishment. Our fieldworker who was shadowing workers at Materials noted that "they want a factory full of workers who make suggestions, help each other, and improve the overall process inside the company. The system of appraisal is carried out entirely by coworkers, not bosses. The review system requires that each worker fill out a review of his peers."

When we pushed the human resources manager to explain, we learned that the peer reviews are not overly helpful to the establishment. In other words, this system is not driven by the quality of peer review but rather provides "a chance to let our employees do something challenging. It's another way for us to make the work a little more demanding. . . . Then we provide them with some training to learn how to do it."

Evidence for other plants in this category is less rich and was derived mainly from interviews (rather than observation or employee interviews). Nevertheless, the picture that emerges for other high-road establishments on skills is broadly similar to that observed for Materials. Thus, at Electrical Parts training opportunities are given to interested employees to attain the skill level required in higher-skilled jobs such as testing. At IT Parts individual development plans are formulated by comparing individual skill sets with the evolving needs of the various departments. These plans are then implemented by working with BOCES to devise appropriate training programs.

The Low-Road Strategy

In contrast with policies at high-road establishments, starting wages in low-road plants (such as Small Machines) tend to be below average, job rotation is largely unknown, systems of performance evaluation and compensation (pay grades) are traditional and quite bureaucratic, and job ladders have few rungs. In low-road plants turnover tends to be above average.

A good example of an establishment paying lower starting wages than other plants in that labor market is Small Machines, where it appears that even informal job rotation is discouraged. At Small Fabrication most wage and employment policies seem dated and replete with unnecessary rigidities. However, starting rates compare favorably with those of other local establishments, and thus, in this respect, Small Fabrication seems to be an exception to the patterns at plants following a low-road strategy. However, its wage rates do not reflect managerial choice but rather its unionized status. (Unsurprisingly, starting rates tend to be higher in unionized firms.)

One consequence of collective bargaining is that a two-tier system of wages prevails in this plant. This practice dates back to a labor conflict that, in many workers' minds, still exerts a powerful and mainly adverse influence on attitudes.

At all of the low-road establishments there are workers who have worked at the plant for many years and/or are approaching normal retirement age. For these workers with high rates of seniority, wages sometimes exceed $25.00 an hour. However, there do not appear to be obvious differences between earnings for these workers who are approaching retirement in unionized and non-unionized firms.

There are sharp differences in the use of HPWPs between establishments following high- and low-road strategies. Some low-road plants rarely use such practices or, when they do, implement them quite poorly. For example, at both Small Fabrication, a long-established, unionized firm, and Small Machines, there is little evidence of either formal structures or informal practices that provide for employee involvement. Small Fabrication attempted to introduce quality control (QC) circles in 1994, yet they never took off. In addition, workers receive time rates of pay, and there are no mechanisms, such as gain- or profit-sharing, by which workers' rewards are linked with enterprise success. There has been some talk between Small Fabrication and its union over the introduction of profit-sharing or gain-sharing. However, the human resources manager at Small Fabrication was quite pessimistic about the prospect of such plans being introduced in the near future. Analogously, at Medium Fabrication there was no mechanism in place for financial participation. In addition, the only apparent device for employee involvement was a monthly information meeting.

There are also striking differences between low- and high-road establishments in their policy choices concerning skill and training. Low-road plants rely on structured work with narrow job content to minimize the level of skills needed and the amount of training they must provide. Our worker-shadowing exercises at Small Machines were very illuminating on this subject. As one human resources manager summarized it: "We have what you might refer to as a 'boot in the backside' approach to management. Our markets are getting very competitive. We need to cut costs and get more from our employees."

As noted earlier, workers in this plant tend to be men with only a high school education. Most workers grew up in the area and commute less than twenty minutes to work. They were recruited to the plant through a family member or friend and took the job because they needed work and this was the first opportunity that came along. They were hired because they had typical farm skills. One worker described his coworkers as follows:

> The reason many of the workers can settle for the sort of pay and work that they are given at [Small Machines] is they used to be farmworkers. They didn't own their own farms but worked on them. When farms in the area began to fail, these farm boys turned to factory work instead. Since they were only making about $200 a week on the farm—if they were lucky—the pay seems better than it is. They are also used to hard work, which translates into factory work.

Hence, workers at Small Machines have decent mechanical skills—they can fix an engine or machine and work with tools—and they have good basic soft skills (for example, a work ethic).

Most of the work is in assembly production. Of the 120 employees, 90 are in assembly production. Of those 90 workers, 20 work in fabrication, 20 work in welding, 40 work in assembly, and 10 work in finishing. Work is organized discretely by task, and tasks tend to be simple. The welding involved is a hard weld that does not require meticulous welding skills or sophisticated tools. The assembly is a process of putting finished pieces together with simple tools. What little training there is in this firm is "nothing formal," one worker said. "We just get a crash course introduction to where all of the parts are and pick up on things as we go along." Another worker stated: "If you need more skills for a job, you are expected to do that after work. [You] go to [the local junior college], but you have to do it on your time, and you have to be able to pay for it."

Given the aversion to training at Small Machines, there is also little cross-training. When asked, a manager explained:

> We don't do any cross-training for workers. It's too expensive. We don't really want to put that sort of investment in workers. We can't really. So we try to hire people with good skills who are used to working around machines. They fix things on the farm or they work

on cars. . . . We want them to be able to learn their job with a little training from a supervisor and get to work.

Similarly, work is organized so that workers do not need soft skills. Work is highly controlled, with lots of supervision. A worker described his shop floor manager: "He is extremely serious and doesn't really have much of a sense of humor. It makes it really nerve-racking to be around him because you're walking on egg shells. . . . [He] is very strict and has seemingly senseless rules."

Based on our interviews with the human resources director and the plant manager at Medium Fabrication, these features of limited skill requirements, limited job content, and limited training were also evident in that plant. For example, during the last three years only about 3 percent of production workers on average received formal training of any kind.

THE MIDDLE-ROAD STRATEGY

The remaining cases are classified as middle-road. These establishments have a mixed picture concerning the issues we are examining. For example, looking at general wage and employment policies, we noted that at Small Parts the initial wage rate tends to be especially low (close to $6.00 an hour). However, this plant has never laid off any workers. Indeed, in past downturns in demand for its product, it would occasionally dispatch workers, on a fixed-term basis (six months), to neighboring firms. Nevertheless, Small Parts has experienced a retention problem: only 30 percent of new hires are retained for more than one year. Medium Machines has a system of pay grades that is quite simple and comparable to similar-sized cases but also appears to have an above-average turnover rate.

Their use of HPWPs makes two establishments, Medium Machines and Small Parts, classifiable as middle-road. Both plants have introduced some HPWP innovations, but the formal set of practices is either not well balanced (Ben-Ner and Jones 1995) or not functioning well in some important respects. Medium Machines operates quality circles, has regular meetings to share information with employees, and operates an individual incentive pay plan, but it has not yet introduced teams in spite of having a production process that would facilitate teams. Moreover, Medium Machines practices neither profit-sharing nor employee ownership. Similarly, Small

Parts has very limited opportunities for the financial participation of employees; the main mechanism is a $500 discretionary bonus that is contributed to each employee's 401K plan each year it is awarded. However, Small Parts has introduced a system of teams consisting of A-teams, usually eight workers who constitute a cross-functional team, and B-teams, which comprise only managers and supervisors who may approve the suggestions coming from the A-teams. Teams meet weekly for thirty to forty-five minutes during regular hours. Although team members do not receive compensation for team participation, their participation is evaluated at annual performance evaluations. As explained later in more detail, however, Small Parts' teams are still in their infancy. The plant also has a system whereby information is shared with all employees each month, but the information shared tends to be briefer and less substantial than it is in high-road establishments, and many employees have trouble seeing the link between their bonus and firm performance.

It is also apparent that middle-road plants are making some efforts to upgrade their skill and training policies. Like other plants, they face increased competition. One Small Parts manager stated:

> We are driven by specific products and markets. We have been challenged because profit margins have become very thin. The industries that we serve are competitive. For example: [a large retail discount chain] is putting lots of pressure on [final product manufacturers] to lower prices. This pressure gets passed along to suppliers of parts like us.

He added that this pressure makes training hard but essential. Small Parts needs to keep costs low, and training is expensive. However, because quality control is also important to the firm's success, it needs good trained workers who will stay.

Generally, these firms are trying to use cross-training and teams to increase the content and skillfulness of the work. Consistent with the experience of high-road establishments, teamwork at middle-road plants requires more soft skills development. But these plants' attempts to provide this kind of training have typically been stunted, in two ways. First, only some workers are involved. For example, Small Parts introduced eight teams, and about one-third of all hourly employees are involved. While there are plans to expand the teams, the process is slow. Second, the teams often have limited control, which undercuts worker commitment to the training. For example, Small Parts that appears to be serious about soft skills development has a formal training program. It has hired a professional consultant to work full-time on the factory floor to train workers to work in teams, each of which goes through a minimum of fifteen hours of classroom training. The consultant uses a well-developed series of three modules that combine different styles of classroom work and are accompanied by a textbook. Watching these modules during a worker-shadowing exercise, our fieldworker described a class: "[A manager] lectured about flow, speed, quantity, and quality. He illustrated on the whiteboard and made flow charts, interacting with the workers. He said things like, 'Work is not productivity,' and, 'This is work. This is equal to making parts.'"

However, the plant's commitment to training is being undercut as workers realize the limited extent of their decisionmaking. In other words, they were asked to get more training so that the job content could be increased. By moving to teams, the workers will have more control and be able to develop new projects that enhance their work. It is clear to workers, however, that only a moderate amount of control is being ceded to them. Any decision must be approved by a B-team of managers before it actually gets to a level of decisionmakers. For example, in one meeting a plan was discussed to buy a bargain product tester. The team decided that this would be a good project. However, the facilitator informed them that the B-team had already decided that there were no funds available to purchase it. The team members felt as though their time had been wasted. They also felt powerless and frustrated and wanted to stop meeting.

The middle-road cases do seem to be trying to increase the content and skill level of jobs, but most of their attempts are meeting with only limited success and they are struggling. Hence, we might argue that they are stumbling forward.

WHY DO MANAGERS USE DIFFERENT STRATEGIES?

In accounting for managers' use of distinct strategies, one obvious factor is structural: the product line produced by a manager's plant could somehow shape the type of managerial choices available. However, our data do not substantiate that hypothesis. In both the worker-shadowing exercises and interviews, it became clear that the inherent nature of most plants' products places a ceiling on the hard skills content of the work. Even more complex products require only simple subassembly. Small Machines produces small machines for eventual sale to consumers, but the more complex parts (such as the engine) are produced elsewhere. Hence, little precision or use of sophisticated technology is required of its workers, and the necessary skill level has never moved beyond basic welding. Similar observations can be made of other establishments. For example, welders at Machine Parts appear to be more specialized than those at Small Machines, and yet they are still using rather traditional technology. The human resources manager at Machine Parts explained that "this is not a high-tech operation. We are welding and painting. It is hard to automate."

In other words, the basic hard skills content of jobs in each of the plants is low. Workers are mostly engaged in simple forms of assembly or subassembly production and use basic tools to engage in standard tasks that they mostly mastered as teenagers working on farm equipment and cars. As one worker put it: "We are farm kids. We knew how to do this stuff before we came to [Small Machines]. I grew up fixing tractors and racing cars." In our worker-shadowing exercises (for Small Parts, Materials, and Medium Fabrication), we noted an almost complete absence of computers or sophisticated tools for use in the production processes in these establishments, though observations for other plants paint a slightly different picture.

The key differences among establishments appear to be in how they are dealing with this skill ceiling. The high-road establishments use job rotation and teamwork to increase the content and skillfulness of particular jobs. They also have elaborate training programs. In addition, these differences in strategies sometimes reflect factors that have been stressed in the institutionalist literature, such as the ability of key actors to initiate change. This was clearly the case at Materials and IT Parts, whose CEOs apparently have played key roles in shaping a whole range of labor policies.

The establishments gravitating toward a lower road organize work into jobs with limited content and low skill levels. New workers have virtually no formal training, though sometimes they are expected to learn the more skilled aspects of a job through informal training from more senior workers. In other words, the low-road establishments use the low skill requirements as a cost-saving advantage and thus see no reason to enrich job content and skill levels through HPWPs and training. High-road plants, by contrast, see the limited skill needs and the simple nature of production as obstacles to overcome. High-road establishments make conscious and creative efforts to increase job content and develop skills. They offer comprehensive formal training programs, both in established needs and, in some plants, in newer areas required by the new information technologies. In addition, formal training programs are complemented by arrangements that enable newer workers to be informally trained by established workers. A variety of HPWPs are also used.

Middle-road establishments are struggling. They want to structure work to make it more skillful and meaningful, and they want to provide training. But they are apprehensive about how these practices would alter the flow of revenues and power within the establishment. As such, they are stumbling forward.

For us, these differences raise a vexing question about managerial choice. Why do different managers approach the "skill ceiling" problem differently? We believe that plant location does play a significant role in explaining this outcome. Employers and employees in the more isolated and rural parts of the region seem to face a set of problems and challenges that are arguably different from those that confront their counterparts in smaller towns (such as Utica) and in the larger metropolitan area of Syracuse (Salant and Marx 1995; Ramsay 1996; and Flora et al. 1997).

First, we believe that it is harder for managers in nonmetropolitan firms to innovate than it is for their metropolitan counterparts. One key difference we observed is that human resources personnel at establishments located in metropolitan labor markets (for example, Machine Parts and Electrical Parts) tend to be active members of professional organizations. This is much less common among human resources personnel in other kinds of establishments, especially those located in rural areas. Managers of plants in rural areas do not have easy access to local trade associations, active chambers of commerce, or even informal business associations. Since rural managers do not have these sorts of networks, they may have much more difficulty than do urban managers in learning new practices from other managers.

Second, this disadvantage is compounded by the lack of new managerial talent coming into the area. In our interviews, we were struck by the lack of new managers coming into these establishments from elsewhere. The rural establishments seldom (or never) get new professionals with MBAs or equivalent qualifications who come with "the latest ideas." Existing managers are thus less likely to even be aware of or thinking about new management practices.

Third, managers in isolated areas do not have easy access to universities and other institutions that can facilitate the discussion of new ideas—for example, by arranging for one-day seminars.

Fourth, rural establishments tend to develop long-term relationships with managers, who sometimes become complacent and lack incentives to be "up on the latest techniques." They are not being pushed by others or even expected to be innovative.

Fifth, ruralness also affects workers. Workers tend to have fewer employment options than their urban counterparts, and that situation in turn shapes labor relations. Thus, compared to Small Parts (which is at best a middle-road plant), workers at Materials spend less time commuting and are much more apt to continue to live and work in the area where they were born. It is important to remember that rural counties are geographically large, and transportation costs for low-income workers are a major expense. The effects of high transportation costs are compounded by the low education and skill levels of rural employees. Thus, we found substantial regional immobility of labor: most native-born workers remain close to the areas where they were born, and immigrants from overseas remain in the area where they initially arrived. Labor market experience is limited and usually restricted to one line of activity. These factors combine to create less incentive for establishments to use HPWPs. To be blunt, they can get away with not offering them. Workers perceive themselves as having no place else to go.

Of course, there are other possible reasons for the different strategies used by the establishments we studied. For example, establishments with strong market niches and less pressure on profit margins (such as Materials) can implement extensive employee participation and training and bear the costs of doing so. Despite this, we believe that our data raise two important issues: managerial choice does exist; and the rural location of some establishments seems to present additional challenges and obstacles to selecting a high-road strategy.

DO HPWPS MATTER
FOR WORKER OUTCOMES?

Our discussion thus far indicates that a key feature of a high-road strategy is more extensive use of HPWPs.[7] In this section, we use evidence derived from worker surveys to see whether the varying use of HPWPs has implications for worker outcomes. We conclude that the strategy chosen by management matters greatly for a variety of worker outcomes.[8] In turn, the use of HPWPs by high-road establishments may offer important points of hope for both workers and firms in economically depressed areas.

To develop these claims, we undertake three exercises (and present our findings in tables 13.4, 13.5, and 13.6). First, we compare worker outcomes in two of our rural manufacturing establishments. Both are quite comparable except that HPWPs are much more developed at Materials than at Small Parts.

By comparing these two cases, we hope to discern the possible gains from the use of HPWPs by medium-sized firms in the rural United States. Second, we compare worker outcomes at Materials and Large Metal, an urban manufacturing establishment with considerable experience of HPWPs. We show that the high-road rural plant compares well with the urban plant. Third, we compare worker outcomes for participants and nonparticipants in self-directed teams within case studies. This enables us to study the impact of teams on worker outcomes, having controlled for firm heterogeneity.

AN OVERVIEW OF THE THREE ESTABLISHMENTS

Before examining the evidence, we begin by recalling key features of Materials, a privately owned manufacturing firm with 120 employees, 75 of whom are hourly employees. Materials laid off no hourly workers during the 1990s, and the starting wage currently is $8.25 an hour. In the summer of 2000 we conducted face-to-face employee surveys on-site with 71 of 75 hourly workers who responded (a response rate of 95 percent).

Self-directed teams have been in place at this single-plant firm for more than ten years, and nearly all employees participate in them. Teams are quite active and participatory, with weekly one-hour meetings during regular hours. In addition, team leadership rotates among team members. Team activities are quite extensive, and every month each team works out scheduling and task assignments. Also, QC activities (including workplace reorganization, tool innovation, and new tool and equipment purchases) are often conducted in teams. A further indication that the firm seems to be quite serious about teams is that forty hours of training are budgeted for each team member each year.

Materials has an equally long history of financial participation. The firm contributes a certain percentage of each employee's pay, based on firm profitability, to his or her 401K plan. This percentage has varied between 6 and 8 percent during the last decade and is applied uniformly to all employees. In addition to this form of profit-sharing pay, the firm makes distributions each year from a bonus pool, whose size is determined, again, on the basis of firm profitability. These cash distributions to employees are based on their performance evaluations. The most important component in the interesting performance evaluation process is team members' peer reviews, which are given a weight of 50 percent in the overall assessment. Other input comes from customers and supervisors, whose views are each given a weight of 25 percent. Individual bonuses range from $200 to $1,800.

Materials tends to share information with all employees widely and openly. In particular, the firm holds all-employee meetings every third Thursday of each month. Typically these meetings last two hours and take place during regular hours. Examples of shared information include new products, new strategies, and financial statements. According to our interview with the firm's human resources director, confidential information is sometime shared during these all-employee meetings. In addition, employees occasionally suggest potential customers during the meetings.

Our second case, Small Parts, is also privately owned, though it is a subsidiary firm of a multinational. When we interviewed their marriages in the summer of 2000, the plant had 275 employees, including 200 hourly workers. We conducted on-site, face-to-face employee surveys, and 174 of the 200 hourly employees responded (a response rate of 87 percent). Hourly workers typically start at $6.00 an hour, though normally within a year they will be earning

$7.50. Like Materials, this firm had never laid off employees during the decade preceding our study, although occasionally the firm had dispatched workers on a fixed-term basis (6 months) to neighboring firms.

After the parent firm began using teams in its own organization (reflecting a newly discovered interest in employee empowerment), teams were introduced at Small Parts in 1999. There are two types of teams, A-teams and B-teams. A-teams are cross-functional, and each A-team has an average of eight team members, including one engineer. By contrast, B-teams consist of only managers and supervisors, and their main function is to decide whether to approve suggestions made by A-teams. Teams work on specific themes, such as workflow improvement, and meet for thirty to forty-five minutes weekly during regular hours. Participation in A-teams is in principle voluntary, yet management sometimes solicits workers to become team members. There is no compensation for team participation, although team participation is part of the annual performance evaluation process.

Like Materials, Small Parts holds a monthly all-employee meeting (on the second Thursday of every month, a payday). Unlike Materials, however, the meeting lasts only thirty minutes, there are rarely questions and answers, and confidential information is not shared. Finally, during the last four years the firm has been contributing $500 each year to each employee's 401K plan as a discretionary bonus. Employees seem to expect to get this unless the firm has a particularly bad year.

The third case, Large Metal, is a private, unionized firm with 505 employees, 365 of whom are hourly employees (Large Metal has a very small additional plant elsewhere). Again we conducted face-to-face, on-site employee surveys. In this case, surveys were team-based. In part because different workers worked multiple shifts at different times, this required that we make more than 30 visits to the firm at times ranging from 6:00 A.M. to 11:00 P.M. With 269 of 365 hourly employees responding, the response rate was 74 percent.

On paper, Large Metal is an impressive, high-road establishment that has been using "self-directed teams" for nearly a decade. Before introducing self-directed teams, the firm employed a full-time consultant for two years and invested a great deal of money in the new practice. To become trained to implement teams, all managers spent one full day a week for six months in training programs. During the subsequent six months, each hourly employee received training for one full day each week. All employees were then divided into more than forty teams, based mostly on their jobs, and each team elected its team leader from among its members.

These teams are combined at Large Metal with financial partici- pation, not only through profit-sharing (employees are give a cash bonus, of the same amount, based on company performance) and an ESOP (each hourly employee is given one thousand shares after working for the firm for five years). Also, the firm has quarterly all- employee meetings that last one to two hours and are a mechanism for sharing information.

Through our on-site, face-to-face surveys and meetings with team members we were able to meet the majority of them. We also often chatted with team members after administering the surveys. Based on these meetings and our interviews with human resources man- agers, it appears that many teams have been stagnating during the last few years. There are a number of possible reasons. Perhaps most important, during the last few years the overall relationship between management and union has deteriorated. Second, some team members have been discouraged because management has re- jected their suggestions. Third, unlike the original team members, workers who were hired after the introduction of their teams never received extensive team training. This falloff in the effectiveness of some teams has led many employees to suggest that the whole sys- tem of HPWPs has become less successful.

A Comparison of Materials and Small Parts

Since major differences in worker characteristics might be associ- ated with differences in worker outcomes, it is instructive to com- pare worker profiles before examining the evidence on worker out- comes. In table 13.4 we see that Materials' workers are more community-based than are Small Parts' workers. Seventy-five per- cent of Materials' workers grew up in the area and commute an average of only fifteen minutes, whereas only 57 percent of Small Parts workers grew up in the area, and they commute an average of twenty-six minutes. Also, Materials' workers are younger and less likely to be married. However, in terms of some key characteristics, such as general and firm-specific experience, education, gender,

Table 13.4 Basic Worker Characteristics

	Small Parts	Materials	Large Metal
Total labor market experience (mean years)	16.12	14.81	29.52***
Tenure (mean years)	4.47	4.30	21.77***
Mean age	37.96**	34.38	47.97***
Mean hourly wage	$10.36	$9.79	$13.07***
Commuting time (mean minutes)	25.51***	14.72	20.69***
Proportion male	43.68%	42.25%	97.74%***
Proportion with at least some college	47.31	47.14	43.56
Proportion white	97.70	95.77	94.23
Proportion with extra job	30.54	36.62	27.78
Proportion married	59.88***	39.44	72.62***
Proportion married with working spouse	77.98	90.00	64.25***
Proportion with a dependent child	44.58	53.52	30.74***
Proportion of workers who grew up in the area	57.32***	78.87	87.22*
Number of respondents	174	71	269

Source: Authors' own survey of employees at Small Parts, Materials, and Large Metal.
* The difference between Small Parts and Materials or between Large Metal and Materials statistically significant at the 10 percent level.
** The difference between Small Parts and Materials or between Large Metal and Materials statistically significant at the 5 percent level.
*** The difference between Small Parts and Materials or between Large Metal and Materials statistically significant at the 1 percent level.

and race, workers at Materials and Small Parts are quite similar. Also, both firms hire their workers mostly from their local rural labor market. Unsurprisingly in view of the relative homogeneity of workers in both firms and the nature of their local labor markets, average hourly wages are also comparable.

The relevant columns of table 13.5 compare various worker outcomes at the two firms. In the reported findings we focus on differences that are statistically significant at least at the 5 percent level.[9]

We find that Materials workers consider themselves more empowered than do workers at Small Parts. Compared to Small Parts workers, Materials workers sense that more information is shared by management. Also, they communicate more often with workers outside of their work groups or other teams within the firm, and

(Text continues on p. 511.)

Table 13.5 Worker Outcomes: Interfirm Comparisons

	Small Parts	Materials	Large Metal
Empowerment			
"I have a lot to say about what happens on my job."	2.52***	2.04	2.51***
"My job allows me to take part in making decisions that affect my work."	2.40***	1.86	2.47***
Communication			
"Management is usually open about sharing company information with employees at this company."	2.16***	1.89	2.91***
How often do you personally communicate about work issues with managers or supervisors in your work group or work team? (proportion of employees who replied "at least weekly")	85.09%	88.73%	73.51%***
How often do you personally communicate about work issues with managers or supervisors outside of your work group or work team within the firm? (proportion of employees who replied "at least weekly")	49.11	39.44	36.60
How often do you personally communicate about work issues with workers outside of your work group or work team within the firm? (proportion of employees who replied "at least weekly")	57.52**	71.83	40.38***
How often do you personally communicate about work issues with technical experts outside of your work group or work team, such as engineers, technicians, accountants, or consultants within the firm? (proportion of employees who replied "at least weekly")	47.32***	25.35	20.45

Table 13.5 *Continued*

	Small Parts	Materials	Large Metal
Effort			
How much effort do you put into your work beyond what your job requires? (1 = none, 4 = a lot)	3.49	3.55	3.28***
Relative effort defined as the effort put into a typical hour of work versus the effort put into a typical hour of watching TV (0 = hardly any at all, 10 = all your energy)	5.09***	6.51	4.13***
Days missed in the last year	10.90	11.56	18.32***
Hours worked per week	40.24	41.01	41.72
"My effort at work affects my pay."	2.09***	1.69	2.28***
Teamwork and peer monitoring			
"I help my coworkers when they need it."	1.54***	1.35	1.74***
To what extent have other employees at this company taught you job skills, shortcuts, problem-solving, or other ways to improve how you work? (1 = to a great extent, 4 = not at all)	2.02	1.87	2.10**
"My effort at work is affected by the effort of my coworkers."	2.19	2.21	2.30
"The work of my coworkers affects my pay."	2.79	2.89	2.37***
"If I saw a coworker slacking off, I would say something to that worker."	2.44	2.30	2.92***
Proportion of workers who have ever said anything to a coworker when they saw that worker slack off	57.23%	68.57%	41.51%***
Commitment			
"I am willing to work harder than I have to in order to help this company succeed."	1.90***	1.50	2.14***
"I would take almost any job to keep working for this company."	2.74**	2.48	2.90***

(*Table continues on p. 510.*)

Table 13.5 *Continued*

	Small Parts	Materials	Large Metal
"I would turn down another job for more pay in order to stay with this company."	2.96***	2.55	3.22***
Trust			
"I am treated fairly by the company."	2.17**	1.88	2.43***
"To what extent do you trust management at this company?" (1 = to a great extent, 4 = not at all)	2.25	2.41	3.07***
"In general, how would you describe relations in your workplace between management and employees?" (1 = very good, 5 = very bad)	2.46	2.66	3.19***
Job satisfaction			
"All in all, how satisfied would you say you are with your job?" (1 = very satisfied, 4 = very dissatisfied)	2.13*	1.99	2.26***
Intrinsic rewards			
"My job makes good use of my knowledge and skills."	2.45***	2.09	2.38***
"What I do at work is more important to me than the money I earn."	2.90	2.76	3.21***
Job stress			
"My job is stressful."	2.14	2.22	2.25
Number of respondents	174	71	269

Source: Authors' own survey of employees at Small Parts, Materials, and Large Metal.
Note: Unless otherwise indicated, each respondent is given four choices: 1 = strongly agree; 2 = agree; 3 = disagree; and 4 = strongly disagree.
* The difference between Small Parts and Materials or between Large Metal and Materials statistically significant at the 10 percent level.
** The difference between Small Parts and Materials or between Large Metal and Materials statistically significant at the 5 percent level.
*** The difference between Small Parts and Materials or between Large Metal and Materials statistically significant at the 1 percent level.

they communicate less often than do Small Parts workers with technical experts outside of their work groups or other teams within the firm. We found that workers at Materials put more relative effort into their work and are more aware that their effort affects their pay. Our findings also indicate that Materials workers are more likely to help their fellow workers and to engage in peer monitoring. Furthermore, for all three areas we examine, Materials workers display stronger organizational commitment and also are more likely to consider themselves to be treated fairly by their firm. Finally, Materials workers are more satisfied with their jobs and more positive about the use and contributions of their knowledge and skills.

A COMPARISON OF MATERIALS AND LARGE METAL

From table 13.4 it is clear that there are important differences between Materials and Large Metal workers. Compared to Materials workers, Large Metal workers have much longer general work experience and tenure with the firm. Also, they are much older and better paid. Since Large Metal is a long-established, unionized firm that hires workers from its urban labor market, some of these differences are unsurprising. By contrast, Materials is a relatively new, non-unionized firm that hires workers from its very rural labor market. Also, Large Metal workers are more apt to be male and married and less likely to have a dependent child or a working spouse.

Worker outcomes at the two firms are compared in table 13.5. Materials workers clearly consider themselves to be more empowered than do workers at Large Metal. Materials workers sense that management shares more information. These workers also communicate more often with managers within their work groups, as well as with workers outside of their work groups but within their firm. We found that Materials employees work harder at their jobs and are more aware of a link between their effort and their pay. They also miss fewer days than do Large Metal workers. In addition, Materials workers are more likely to help their fellow workers and more likely to engage in peer monitoring.

Materials workers display stronger organizational commitment. Not only are they more likely to consider themselves to be treated fairly by the firm, but they also trust management more and consider labor-management relations to be better. Importantly, Materials workers are more satisfied with their jobs. In addition, they are more positive about the use and contributions of their knowledge and skills, while they are no more stressed on the job than Large Metal workers.

Comparisons Within Firms

Finally, we compare outcomes within a given firm for participants and nonparticipants in self-directed teams. Such a comparison helps to separate the effects on worker outcomes of participation in self-directed teams from other unobserved firm characteristics that may affect worker outcomes. We begin with an analysis of Small Parts. Since only about one-third of its labor force participated in a team, in principle this presents the ideal case for an intrafirm comparison.

First, when we compare the basic characteristics of participants and nonparticipants, we find that they are similar in most key respects (including age, tenure, and education). This absence of key differences in the characteristics of team participants and nonparticipants is important; it means that differences in outcomes between the two groups can be more persuasively attributed to "teamness" than to differences across workers.

In table 13.6, selected outcomes between participants and nonparticipants are compared. One clear finding is that, as expected, participants consider themselves more empowered than do nonparticipants. Consistent with our expectations, we also find that, compared to nonparticipants, participants sense that managers share more information with them. In addition, we find that participants communicate more often with managers and supervisors within their work groups or other teams, and they communicate more often with workers outside of their work groups or teams. Participants are also found to put more effort into their work and, on average, to work more than two hours longer per week than do nonparticipants.

When we investigate organizational commitment, we find some evidence that participants display stronger loyalty to their company as well as more trust in management. In addition, participants are more satisfied with their work, and insofar as they are more positive about the use and contributions of their knowledge and skills at their workplace, participants appear to have more intrinsic rewards.

Next we undertake a similar analysis using data from Large Metal. However, this analysis is more complicated, since for high-road firms (Materials and Large Metal) nearly all employees *formally* participate in teams, and thus it does not appear to be feasible to compare outcomes for participants and nonparticipants within these firms. Nevertheless, we believe it is worthwhile to determine whether employees in these firms actually perceive that they participate in a *self-directed* team—that is, a team in which employees supervise their own work and make their own decisions about pace, flow, and, occasionally, the best way to get work done. Interestingly, when this question was asked, only 54 percent of Large Metal workers responded that they did participate in a self-directed team.[10] Hence, for high-road firms we choose to compare worker characteristics and worker outcomes for workers who do and do not consider themselves to be participating in self-directed teams. The observed differences in worker outcomes between the two groups are interpreted as the effects of belonging to a *well-functioning* self-directed team.[11]

When we compare the basic characteristics of Large Metal workers who believe that they do and do not participate in well-functioning self-directed teams, some interesting differences are revealed. Participants have shorter tenure, own more ESOP shares, and are more likely to have a working spouse than are nonparticipants. But for all other basic characteristics, participants and nonparticipants are similar. In particular, we observe that there is no difference in wages between participants and nonparticipants. Considering the shorter job tenure of participants, this means that participants are paid more than nonparticipants with comparable tenure.

Table 13.6 contrasts worker outcomes for participants and nonparticipants. As expected, we find that participants consider themselves to be more empowered than do nonparticipants. Also, the evidence indicates that participants communicate more often with managers within their work groups as well as with managers, workers, and technical experts outside of their work groups or teams. However, no statistically significant difference was found for the sense of open communication with management. Participants were found to put more absolute and relative effort into their work and to work longer hours. Consistent with the greater effort levels exerted by participants, participants were found to be much more aware

(Text continues on p. 518.)

Table 13.6 Worker Outcomes: Intrafirm Comparisons Between Participants and Nonparticipants

	Small Parts		Large Metal	
	Participants	Nonparticipants	Participants	Nonparticipants
Empowerment				
"I have a lot to say about what happens on my job."	2.26***	2.68	2.34***	2.69
"My job allows me to take part in making decisions that affect my work."	2.14***	2.54	2.29***	2.68
Communication				
"Management is usually open about sharing company information with employees at this company."	1.93***	2.29	2.87	2.94
How often do you personally communicate about work issues with managers or supervisors in your work group or work team? (proportion of employees who replied "at least weekly")	91.07%*	78.57%	78.01%*	68.60%
How often do you personally communicate about work issues with managers or supervisors outside of your work group or work team within the firm? (proportion of employees who replied "at least weekly")	53.57	43.64	42.14**	29.41
How often do you personally communicate about work issues with workers outside of your work group or work team within the firm? (proportion of employees who replied "at least weekly")	65.45*	48.21	46.43**	32.77

How often do you personally communicate about work issues with technical experts outside of your work group or work team, such as engineers, technicians, accountants, or consultants within the firm? (proportion of employees who replied "at least weekly")	49.09	43.64	26.09**	15.00
Effort				
How much effort do you put into your work beyond what your job requires? (1 = none, 4 = a lot)	3.66***	3.38	3.39***	3.15
Relative effort, defined as effort put into a typical hour of work versus the effort put into a typical hour of watching TV (0 = hardly any at all, 10 = all your energy)	5.32	5.00	4.70***	3.42
Days missed in the last year	10.48	9.79	18.18	18.54
Hours worked per week	41.95***	39.38	42.41*	40.91
"My effort at work affects my pay."	1.98	2.15	2.10***	2.50
Teamwork and peer monitoring				
"I help my coworkers when they need it."	1.49	1.54	1.67	1.81
To what extent have other employees at this company taught you job skills, shortcuts, problem-solving, or other ways to improve how you work? (1 = to a great extent, 4 = not at all)	1.93	2.05	1.92***	2.28
"My effort at work is affected by the effort of my coworkers."	2.18	2.21	2.18**	2.40
"The work of my coworkers affects my pay."	2.93	2.75	2.21***	2.56
"If I saw a coworker slacking off, I would say something to that worker."	2.40	2.46	2.78***	3.05
Proportion of workers who have ever said anything to a coworker when they saw that worker slack off	57.89%	56.36%	43.17%	41.18%

(Table continues on p. 516.)

Table 13.6 *Continued*

	Small Parts		Large Metal	
	Participants	Nonparticipants	Participants	Nonparticipants
Commitment				
"I am willing to work harder than I have to in order to help this company succeed."	1.82	1.95	2.00***	2.25
"I would take almost any job to keep working for this company."	2.61*	2.84	2.75***	3.06
"I would turn down another job for more pay in order to stay with this company."	2.89	3.03	2.08***	3.38
Relative knowledge, defined as knowledge of the job and the firm knowledge of favorite TV show (0 = hardly any knowledge, 10 = complete knowledge)	—	—	1.95	1.50
Relative interest, defined as interest in the quality of the job and the firm versus interest in favorite TV show (0 = hardly any interest, 10 = total interest)	—	—	2.91	2.26
Trust				
"I am treated fairly by the company." (1 = strongly agree, 4 = strongly disagree)	1.96***	2.31	2.33**	2.56
To what extent do you trust management at this company? (1 = to a great extent, 4 = not at all)	2.07**	2.36	2.96**	3.18
In general, how would you describe relations in your workplace between management and employees? (1 = very good, 5 = very bad)	2.37	2.54	3.08**	3.33

Job satisfaction				
All in all, how satisfied would you say you are with your job? (1 = very satisfied, 4 = very dissatisfied)	2.00**	2.22	2.15***	2.39
Intrinsic rewards				
"My job makes good use of my knowledge and skills."	2.23**	2.59	2.27**	2.52
"What I do at work is more important to me than the money I earn."	2.81	2.98	3.07***	3.37
Job stress				
"My job is stressful."	2.13	2.10	2.23	2.28
Number of respondents	57	111	141	121

Source: Authors' own survey of employees at Small Parts and Large Metal.

Note: Unless otherwise indicated, each respondent is given four choices: 1 = strongly agree; 2 = agree; 3 = disagree; and 4 = strongly disagree.

* The difference between Small Parts and Materials or between Large Metal and Materials statistically significant at the 10 percent level.

** The difference between Small Parts and Materials or between Large Metal and Materials statistically significant at the 5 percent level.

*** The difference between Small Parts and Materials or between Large Metal and Materials statistically significant at the 1 percent level.

of the possible link between their level of exertion and their monetary rewards.

Table 13.6 also reveals that participants are more aware of the team nature of their work and the benefits of teamwork. In tandem with this finding, we establish that participants are more willing to engage in peer monitoring. Also, participants are found to have stronger organizational commitment and to display more trust in management. In addition, participants are happier with their jobs and more optimistic about the use and contributions of their knowledge and skills. There is no evidence that stress levels differ for the two groups.

We also asked a series of questions concerning how the two groups assess the major features of the HPWP system at this firm. In all respects we found strong and persuasive evidence that participants evaluate HPWPs—such as teams, bonuses, profit-sharing plans, ESOPs, quarterly meetings, and monthly letters—much more positively than do others.[12]

In sum, the evidence presented in this section provides strong additional support for the general hypotheses that HPWPs are associated with better worker outcomes. All of our analyses indicate that when workers participate in HPWPs, they develop a stronger sense of empowerment, reap more intrinsic rewards from their jobs, and achieve higher levels of job satisfaction. In turn, these empowered and more satisfied workers tend to trust management more and develop stronger commitment to the firm. These attitudinal changes are accompanied by behavioral changes. When workers participate in HPWPs, they tend to have more open and frequent communication with management (as well as with their coworkers), to exert more effort (shirk less), and to engage in more peer monitoring (or horizontal monitoring). Finally, HPWPs are not associated with increased stress. As such, HPWPs appear to offer a strong point of hope for labor, management, and policymakers who are interested in better outcomes for firms and workers, even in firms located within a depressed region.

We also find some evidence in support of our hypotheses concerning the importance of location. Compared to their metropolitan (and even their urban) neighbors, firms located in rural regions are at a disadvantage in introducing and sustaining high-road HPWP policies. This is clearly shown in the experiences of Small Fabrication and Small Machines. At the same time, the extraordinary achievements of Materials indicate that the disadvantages posed by a rural location need not be binding. In appropriate circumstances, these disadvantages can be overcome.

CONCLUSIONS

Based on our ten case studies of manufacturing plants in central New York and multiple data sources for these establishments, we are able to draw some firm conclusions. First, we find that industrial and labor relations practices vary widely in our cases. In particular, there are sharp differences in the broad areas on which we focus, including skill, training, and the use of HPWPs. These differences exist not only across our cases but also between establishments in different labor markets, whether they are urban, rural, or metropolitan.

Second, establishments are consistent in the sets of practices that they adopt. Establishments that tend to encourage skill formation among workers with low levels of formal education are also more likely to adopt group-based incentive pay schemes. In contrast to these plants that pursue a high-road strategy, some low-road plants pay minimal attention to employee training and are not open to implementing practices that provide for employee involvement or incentive compensation.

The third clear and compelling finding is that in medium sized-establishments HPWPs can yield favorable worker outcomes: workers are more empowered, satisfied, committed, trusting, communicative, and hardworking. Based primarily on evidence derived from worker surveys, this finding is strongly established for workers in both rural and urban locations. A related finding is that worker outcomes seem to be greater when more workers participate in employee involvement arrangements and when HPWPs have been in place for a long time.[13]

In important respects, these findings largely complement those emerging from other studies. Many previous researchers have provided evidence of diversity in employment outcomes (see, for example, Doeringer and Piore 1971). The changing nature of "work in America," as well as the uneven character of these developments, has been spotlighted by many.[14] There is now a large body of evidence suggesting that, when properly introduced, HPWPs have beneficial effects.[15] But it is important to recall that the firms and workers we investigate tend to be different from those covered in most of the existing literature. Thus, our study is one of the first to report findings on these diverse issues among workers with low levels of formal education and at medium-sized plants located in labor markets in a depressed area.[16] It is reassuring to find that the hypotheses in the received literature, which were largely based on firms and workers with other characteristics, also carry over to our cases. Moreover, our findings provide some support for our hypotheses about the importance of local labor market conditions—for example, the role of geographical isolation in accounting for differences in the use of HPWPs. Finally, in investigating relationships between HPWPs and particular worker outcomes—notably absolute and relative work effort and peer monitoring—our approach arguably includes measures that improve over those used in most previous studies.

We believe that our findings have several implications not only for central New York but also for firms and workers located in similar communities. The evidence suggests that a range of managerial choice is possible. For light-manufacturing firms to survive and flourish in central New York, the evidence does *not* suggest that only a single policy configuration—a low-road strategy—can meet the pressures arising from the need to compete in increasingly globalized world markets. Indeed, the evidence suggests that even if choosing a low-road strategy is understandable in the short term, over the long haul this choice may lead a firm into a low-equilibrium trap.

By contrast, our findings on the beneficial effects of HPWPs have potentially important implications for rural community development and rural revitalization.[17] The real question for community development is *jobs*. Communities tend to do better when they increase the stock of jobs both quantitatively and qualitatively. An economic development strategy for rural and depressed communities such as those in central New York should consider the important role that HPWPs might play in rural revivals. Bringing more HPWPs into rural and depressed communities like those in central New York could also bring more "good jobs" (ones that are meaningful and stable, offer better pay and benefits, and provide opportunities for skill enhancement) to central New Yorkers. It is also important to introduce strategies that enable HPWPs to be nurtured even as the business environment facing firms becomes more difficult. Given the ability of employers to adopt diverse employment strategies, it is important that firms and employees be made aware of the beneficial effects of high-road policies, including HPWPs. Arguably, consideration should be given both to public policy that promotes the dissemination of information about best-business practices, such as HPWPs, and to fiscal policy, such as tax incentives for the adoption of particular HPWPs. In this process, as some have argued (for example, Weinberg 1999, 2000), universities based in rural areas could play important roles.

The research reported in this chapter was supported by a grant from the Russell Sage and Rockefeller Foundations' Future of Work Program. We have benefited greatly from comments made by the editors on previous drafts. We are also grateful to our home institutions (Colgate University and Hamilton College) and the establishments in central New York that granted us the opportunities to study them.

NOTES

1. Data on size and industrial distribution of establishments in central New York for 1998 are obtained from the U.S. Bureau of the Census (1998).

2. High school graduation was required for employment in some firms (for example, Electric Parts), though not in others (for example IT Parts).

3. However, in three establishments almost half of the production workers had some college experience (though very few had even an associate's degree).

4. Our confidentiality agreements with the establishments prohibit us from identifying the specific products produced by each establishment.

5. The research is part of a broader research project in which we are investigating diverse hypotheses concerning the *nature and determinants* as well as the *outcomes* of employment practices in central New York. In the larger project we are making use of two other kinds of data as well. First, we are surveying all for-profit establishments in local counties in central New York as well as a sample of establishments in other counties in central New York. These surveys stress human resource matters and seek some financial information for several years. The other key data source is four waves of the first random sample telephone survey of adult residents in the upstate region of New York. These surveys provided an opportunity to ask respon-

dents several questions on workplace practices. For findings based on the first waves of this survey, see Jones, Kato, and Weinberg (2001).

6. Small Fabrication pays higher wages in spite of its low-road strategy, possibly because it is unionized.

7. We also have other kinds of evidence besides worker surveys for cases other than the three examined in detail in this section. For example, IT Parts' introduction of a broad-based employee stock option plan was clearly welcomed by production workers. In addition, we have other kinds of evidence for the three cases examined in this section. For example, interviews with managers at Large Metal broadly corroborated the findings reported for this establishment that are derived from worker surveys.

8. We consider diverse worker outcomes, including not only outcomes directly in the interests of the workers (such as job satisfaction, intrinsic rewards, and stress) but also outcomes directly in the interests of the organization (such as organizational commitment, trust, effort, and peer monitoring). See, for example, Appelbaum, Bailey, and Berg (2000).

9. Our list of measures includes not only the standard gauges used in prior work but also measures used for the first time in the literature on HPWPs—notably assessments of absolute and relative work effort and peer monitoring.

10. There are two possible interpretations of this apparent anomaly. First, within a particular high-road firm it may be that some teams are functioning as self-directed teams whereas others do not function as such. Second, it may be that all teams are in fact functioning as self-directed teams but some employees do not perceive their team in this way. Interviews with human resources managers and workers, as well as worker-shadowing, tend to support the first interpretation. For example, the human resources manager at Large Metal admitted that the firm's forty teams fall into several categories, including eight "star" teams and ten "okay" teams. Of the remainder, ten are "more or less functioning" teams, and twelve are "nonperforming" teams.

11. At Materials, 66 percent of the workers answered that they participated in a self-directed team. We also conducted a similar analysis at this firm and found only a few statistically significant differences between participants and nonparticipants. This finding may well be due to the weak power of statistical tests, since Materials had a relatively small sample size to begin with and thus ends up with a very small number of nonparticipants. The results for Materials are available upon request from the authors.

12. For all questions, differences between the views of the two groups are statistically significant at the 1 percent level.

13. These findings tend to complement those reported in Jones, Kato, and Weinberg (2001). Those surveys of individuals provided strong evidence that HPWPs tend to occur in clusters. Also, the finding that financial participation HPWPs are less prevalent in rural locations supports the hypothesis of the role of geographical isolation. In addition, we found that all forms of HPWPs are associated with employees receiving higher pay.
14. This includes Appelbaum and Batt (1994), Blair and Kochan (2000), Cappelli et al. (1997), Kochan and Osterman (1994), Levine (1995), and Osterman (1988).
15. For the United States, studies include Appelbaum, Bailey, and Berg (2000), Black and Lynch (2001), Freeman, Kleiner, and Ostroff (2000), Bartel (2000), Helper (1998), Ichniowski, Shaw, and Prennushi (1997), Levine and Tyson (1990), MacDuffie (1995), and Neumark and Cappelli (1999). For the interesting case of Japan, see Jones and Kato (1995) and Kato and Morishima (2002).
16. However, there is an important and emerging literature concerned with employment policies for workers with low levels of education; see, for example, Freeman and Gottschalk (1998) and Holzer (1996).
17. For broader discussions of rural revitalization issues, see, for example, Audirac (1997).

REFERENCES

Appelbaum, Eileen, Thomas Bailey, and Peter Berg. 2000. *Manufacturing Advantage: Why High-Performance Work Systems Pay Off*. Ithaca, N.Y.: ILR Press.

Appelbaum, Eileen, and Rosemary Batt. 1994. *The New American Workplace: Transforming Work Systems in the United States*. Ithaca, N.Y.: ILR Press.

Audirac, Ivonne. 1997. *Rural Sustainable Development in America*. New York: John Wiley and Sons.

Bartel, Ann P. 2000. "Human Resource Management and Performance in the Service Sector: The Case of Bank Branches." Working paper 7467. Cambridge, Mass.: National Bureau of Economic Research.

Ben-Ner, Avner, and Derek C. Jones. 1995. "Employee Participation, Ownership, and Productivity: A Theoretical Framework." *Industrial Relations* 34(4): 532–54.

Black, Sandra E., and Lisa M. Lynch. 2001. "How to Compete: The Impact of Workplace Practices and Information Technology on Productivity." *Review of Economics and Statistics* 83(3): 434–45.

Blair, Margaret, and Thomas Kochan. 2000. *Human Capital: The New Relationship*. Washington, D.C.: Brookings Institution.

Cappelli, Peter, Laurie Bassi, Harry Katz, David Knoke, Paul Osterman, and Michael Useem. 1997. *Change at Work*. New York: Oxford University Press.

Doeringer, Peter, and Michael Piore. 1971. *Internal Labor Markets and Manpower Analysis*. Armonk, N.Y.: M. E. Sharpe.

Flora, Jan L., Jeff Sharp, Cornelia Flora, and Bonnie Newlon. 1997. "Entrepreneurial Social Infrastructure and Locally Initiated Economic Development in the Nonmetropolitan United States." *Sociological Quarterly* 38: 623–45.

Freeman, Richard B., and Peter Gottschalk. 1998. *Generating Jobs: How to Increase Demand for Less-Skilled Workers*. New York: Russell Sage Foundation.

Freeman, Richard, Morris Kleiner, and Cheri Ostroff. 2000. "The Anatomy of Employee Involvement and Its Effects on Firms and Workers." Working paper 8050. Cambridge, Mass.: National Bureau of Economic Research.

Helper, Susan. 1998. "Complementarity and Cost Reduction: Evidence from the Auto Supply Industry." Working paper 6033. Cambridge, Mass.: National Bureau of Economic Research.

Holzer, Harry. 1996. *What Employers Want: Job Prospects for Less-Educated Workers*. New York: Russell Sage Foundation.

Ichniowski, Casey, Kathryn Shaw, and Giovanna Prennushi. 1997. "The Effects of Human Resource Management Practices on Productivity: A Study of Steel Finishing Lines." *American Economic Review* 87(3): 291–313.

Jones, Derek C., and Takao Kato. 1995. "The Productivity Effects of Employee Stock Ownership Plans and Bonuses: Evidence from Japanese Panel Data." *American Economic Review* 85(3): 391–414.

Jones, Derek C., Takao Kato, and Adam Weinberg. 2001. "Changing Employment Practices and Job Quality in Central New York: Evidence from Case Studies and Individual Survey Data." Proceedings of 53d Annual Meeting of the Industrial Relations Research Association Series, New Orleans (January 5–7).

Kato, Takao, and Motohiro Morishima. 2002. "The Productivity Effects of Participatory Employment Practices: Evidence from New Japanese Panel Data." *Industrial Relations* 41(4): 487–520.

Kochan, Thomas, and Paul Osterman. 1994. *The Mutual Gains Enterprise*. Boston: Harvard Business School Press.

Levine, David I. 1995. *Reinventing the Workplace: How Business and Employees Can Both Win*. Washington, D.C.: Brookings Institution.

Levine, David I., and Laura D'Andrea Tyson. 1990. "Participation, Productivity, and the Firm's Environment." In *Paying for Productivity*, edited by Alan S. Blinder. Washington, D.C.: Brookings Institution.

MacDuffie, John Paul. 1995. "Human Resource Bundles and Manufacturing Performance: Organizational Logic and Flexible Production Systems in the World Auto Industry." *Industrial and Labor Relations Review* 48: 197–221.

Neumark, David, and Peter Cappelli. 1999. "Do 'High-Performance' Work Practices Improve Establishment-Level Outcomes?" Working paper 7374. Cambridge, Mass.: National Bureau of Economic Research.

Osterman, Paul. 1988. *Employment Futures: Reorganization, Dislocation, and Public Policy.* New York: Oxford University Press.

Ramsay, Meredith. 1996. *Community, Culture, and Economic Development.* Albany: State University of New York Press.

Salant, Priscilla, and Julie Marx. 1995. *Small Towns, Big Picture: Rural Development in a Changing Economy.* Washington, D.C.: Aspen Institute.

U.S. Bureau of the Census, Department of Commerce. 1998. "County Business Patterns." Accessed December 30, 2000, at: *www.census.gov/epcd.view/cbpview.html.*

U.S. Department of Commerce. Various years. "Regional Accounts Data." Accessed April 23 and 24, 2001, at: *www.bea.gov/bea/regional/data.htm.*

Weinberg, Adam. 1999. "The University and the Hamlets: Revitalizing Low-Income Communities Through University Outreach and Community Visioning Exercises." *American Behavioral Scientist* 42(5): 794–807.

———. 2000. "Sustainable Economic Development in Rural America." *Annals of the American Academy of Political and Social Sciences* 570: 173–85.

Index

Boldface numbers refer to figures and tables.